Advancing Civil Justice Reform and Conflict Resolution in Africa and Asia:

Comparative Analyses and Case Studies

Elijah Tukwariba Yin
University of Cape Coast, Ghana

Nelson F. Kofie
Northern Virginia Community College, USA

IGI Global
PUBLISHER of TIMELY KNOWLEDGE

A volume in the Advances in Public Policy and Administration (APPA) Book Series

Published in the United States of America by
IGI Global
Information Science Reference (an imprint of IGI Global)
701 E. Chocolate Avenue
Hershey PA, USA 17033
Tel: 717-533-8845
Fax: 717-533-8661
E-mail: cust@igi-global.com
Web site: http://www.igi-global.com

Library of Congress Cataloging-in-Publication Data

Names: Yin, Elijah Tukwariba, editor. | Kofie, Nelson F., editor. |
Title: Advancing civil justice reform and conflict resolution in Africa and Asia: Comparative analyses and case studies/ Elijah Tukwariba Yin, Nelson F. Kofie, editors.
Description: Hershey, PA : Information Science Reference, 2021. | Includes bibliographical references and index. | Summary: "This book delves into issued of 'Civil justice' which refers to that part of a legal system that is concerned with the legal relations between people (including 'legal persons') as distinct from 'criminal justice' i.e. that part of the legal system concerned with actions by the state against people and looks at contracts, personal injury, property and the breakdown of family relations as familiar examples of civil disputes"-- Provided by publisher.
Identifiers: LCCN 2021019422 (print) | LCCN 2021019423 (ebook) | ISBN 9781799878988 (hardcover) | ISBN 9781799878995 (ebook)
Subjects: LCSH: Justice, Administration of--Social aspects. | Dispute resolution (Law)
Classification: LCC K2100 .H353 2021 (print) | LCC K2100 (ebook) | DDC 347--dc23
LC record available at https://lccn.loc.gov/2021019422
LC ebook record available at https://lccn.loc.gov/2021019423

This book is published in the IGI Global book series Advances in Public Policy and Administration (APPA) (ISSN: 2475-6644; eISSN: 2475-6652)

British Cataloguing in Publication Data
A Cataloguing in Publication record for this book is available from the British Library.

For electronic access to this publication, please contact: eresources@igi-global.com.

Advances in Public Policy and Administration (APPA) Book Series

ISSN:2475-6644
EISSN:2475-6652

Mission

Proper management of the public sphere is necessary in order to maintain order in modern society. Research developments in the field of public policy and administration can assist in uncovering the latest tools, practices, and methodologies for governing societies around the world.

The **Advances in Public Policy and Administration (APPA) Book Series** aims to publish scholarly publications focused on topics pertaining to the governance of the public domain. APPA's focus on timely topics relating to government, public funding, politics, public safety, policy, and law enforcement is particularly relevant to academicians, government officials, and upper-level students seeking the most up-to-date research in their field.

Coverage

- Government
- Law Enforcement
- Political Economy
- Politics
- Public Administration
- Public Funding
- Public Policy
- Resource Allocation
- Urban Planning

IGI Global is currently accepting manuscripts for publication within this series. To submit a proposal for a volume in this series, please contact our Acquisition Editors at Acquisitions@igi-global.com or visit: http://www.igi-global.com/publish/.

The Advances in Public Policy and Administration (APPA) Book Series (ISSN 2475-6644) is published by IGI Global, 701 E. Chocolate Avenue, Hershey, PA 17033-1240, USA, www.igi-global.com. This series is composed of titles available for purchase individually; each title is edited to be contextually exclusive from any other title within the series. For pricing and ordering information please visit http://www.igi-global.com/book-series/advances-public-policy-administration/97862. Postmaster: Send all address changes to above address.

Titles in this Series

For a list of additional titles in this series, please visit: www.igi-global.com/book-series

Handbook of Research on Policies, Protocols, and Practices for Social Work in the Digital World
Fahri Özsungur (Mersin University, Turkey)
Information Science Reference • ©2021 • 679pp • H/C (ISBN: 9781799877721) • US $245.00

Global Issues Surrounding Outer Space Law and Policy
Doo Hwan Kim (Korea Society of Air and Space Law and Policy, South Korea)
Information Science Reference • ©2021 • 231pp • H/C (ISBN: 9781799874072) • US $175.00

Global Politics, Political Participation, and the Rise of Nationalism Emerging Research and Opportunities
Emily Stacey (Rose State College, USA)
Information Science Reference • ©2021 • 213pp • H/C (ISBN: 9781799873433) • US $175.00

Redefining Theory and Practice to Guide Social Transformation Emerging Research and Opportunities
Beth Fisher-Yoshida (Columbia University, USA) and Joan Camilo Lopez (Columbia University, USA)
Information Science Reference • ©2021 • 200pp • H/C (ISBN: 9781799866275) • US $195.00

Africa's Platforms and the Evolving Sharing Economy
Immanuel Ovemeso Umukoro (Pan-Atlantic University, Nigeria) and Raymond Okwudiri Onuoha (Pan-Atlantic University, Nigeria)
Information Science Reference • ©2021 • 288pp • H/C (ISBN: 9781799832348) • US $195.00

Processual Perspectives on the Co-Production Turn in Public Sector Organizations
Anja Overgaard Thomassen (Aalborg University, Denmark) and Julie Borup Jensen (Aalborg University, Denmark)
Information Science Reference • ©2021 • 340pp • H/C (ISBN: 9781799849759) • US $195.00

Handbook of Research on Global Challenges for Improving Public Services and Government Operations
Cenay BABAOĞLU (Selçuk University, Turkey) Elvettin AKMAN (Süleyman Demirel University, Turkey) and Onur KULAÇ (Pamukkale University, Turkey)
Information Science Reference • ©2021 • 622pp • H/C (ISBN: 9781799849780) • US $295.00

Behavioral-Based Interventions for Improving Public Policies
Viorel Mihaila (University of Bucharest, Romania)
Information Science Reference • ©2021 • 318pp • H/C (ISBN: 9781799827313) • US $195.00

IGI Global
PUBLISHER of TIMELY KNOWLEDGE

701 East Chocolate Avenue, Hershey, PA 17033, USA
Tel: 717-533-8845 x100 • Fax: 717-533-8661
E-Mail: cust@igi-global.com • www.igi-global.com

Table of Contents

Detailed Table of Contents

The chapter takes an integrative look at a largely neglected field of conflict resolution mechanism in Ghana: the extent to which belief in traditional deities both enhance and undercut justice delivery systems in society. It contends that through duabɔ (imprecation) there is an enduring influence of traditional deities as part of legal regulatory frameworks in society. The chapter, thus, uncovers the hidden resources of traditional deities as useful channels of conflict resolution. The chapter draws on proceedings from the Akan customary conflict resolution mechanism to demonstrate both the usefulness and challenges of traditional justice delivery method in contemporary Ghana and encourages the need for its modification to suit the needs of legal modernity. The chapter is the product of a qualitative analysis of empirical ethnographic material gathered from the everyday facts of Ghanaian religious communities and public domain.

Since the Vedic period, India is known for its commitment to justice, democratic values, the rule of law, and the welfare of individuals. The thrust of the chapter is an examination of tools of civil justice in ancient as well as modern texts underlining the bond of 'social contract'. The analysis aims to identify similarities and gaps in the traditional and contemporary aspects of civil justice in India. These findings would enable legal scholars and practitioners to draw from, and to connect, the history of accumulated legal guidance and reasoning to the modern mechanism of justice. The examination of those concepts in the context of contemporary relevance accompanied with the principles of interpretation can maximise the utility of these principles. The discussion may offer important clues for policymakers, community organisations, law-making agencies, and citizens to strengthen their faith in the judicial system, being a blend of aboriginal and modern.

"Justice delayed is justice denied" and "justice hurried is justice buried" are oft quoted proverbs in legal studies. While the latter is rarely prevalent in India, the former has maligned the image of the Indian legal system considerably. Delay in disposal of cases, pendency of cases, especially those of civil and commercial nature, and inducing unnecessary procedural complexities in litigation process are hindrances that come in the way of access to justice. Several reports of the Law Commission of India have pointed out that the present situation is very grim with escalating number of pending cases in the courts in India. To add to this compelling situation, the COVID-19 pandemic has further disrupted the court proceedings by increasing burden, moving the hearings from physical to virtual courtrooms. The endeavour of the authors in this chapter has been to search for convincing reasons that have led to inordinate delays in disposal of civil cases and to find out possible solutions to this problem plaguing the Indian legal system.

This chapter aims to examine the costs and delays in accessing justice in Ghana and Sierra Leone. It is argued that despite the promising and legal history of Ghana and Sierra Leone, with existing court structures and legal procedures on civil and criminal matters, the legal spaces of both countries are fraught with costs and delays in accessing justice. The authors used secondary data from the World Bank, Afrobarometer Report, statutes, court documents, website articles, etc. to underpin the write-up. It was found that citizens in both countries were confronted with delays and costs in accessing justice. It is recommended that in an era of cell phones and various apps, the justice sector should endeavour to go hi-tech by sending alerts to litigants, lawyers, and witnesses warranting their presence at an appointed date and time.

In 2009, the Fundamental Rights Enforcement Procedure (FREP) Rules of 1979 was revised to ease the cumbersome process encountered by applicants/lawyers in advocating for the enforcement of fundamental human rights in court. Despite this, human rights lawyers still encounter several challenges when representing applicants for the enforcement of fundamental human rights in court. This chapter examines these challenges and adopts primary research method. Data were gathered from human rights lawyers via video conferencing platforms: Skype and Zoom. Findings reveal that issues of procedural rules of court and disrespect for court orders are some of the challenges encountered by human rights lawyers. The chapter recommends that judges should avoid placing unnecessary emphasis on the procedural rules of court. In addition, human rights lawyers and non-governmental organizations (NGOs) should maintain continuous advocacy for the enforcement of fundamental human rights towards holding government and its agencies more accountable for disrespect of court orders.

Adjudication of issues in the Ghanaian jurisdiction can be traced back to the pre-colonial era where powers were vested in chiefs, elders, and representatives of all the major tribes. Chiefs and elders adjudicated on most issues with the family heads serving as lawyers. During the colonial era, judicial powers were vested in the Privy Council, which took away the powers of the chiefs and elders. At times parties to a dispute may want to resolve the dispute in a form other than the normal court system, hence the alternative dispute resolution (ADR). However, ADR lacks stare decisis since it set no precedent to guide similar disputes in the future. Also, there is no right of appeal when parties opt for ADR. The purpose of this chapter is to assess the use of ADR in Ghana, the challenges, and the way forward.

The chapter explores the dilemma of alternative dispute resolution (ADR) and access to justice for women in Ghana. It argues that introduction and use of ADR has contributed to improving access to justice with regards to reducing delays in formal court procedures, cost reduction, time saving, opening spaces for less-resourced individuals and groups, particularly women, to have access to justice. Above all, ADR does bring access to justice systems close to remote areas, serving the needs of disadvantaged individuals including women and others who are most vulnerable. However, the weaknesses and challenges in the formal legal system, coupled with the historical and cultural dynamics of the Ghanaian society, which is patriarchal in nature, have prevented mostly women from reaping the maximum benefits of ADR. Revisiting the challenges of the justice system and the historical and cultural norms of Ghana would help increase and enhance women's access to justice through ADR.

In 2012-2016, the number of cases referred to CCADR for mediation was 14,900. And out of these cases, 5,789 were successfully resolved to represent 38%. The total number of mediated cases pending were 9,111, representing 62%. Though there seems to be an improvement in terms of a decrease in pending cases, the number of pending cases leaves much to be desired. Premising on the above statistics, it has been noted that 9,111 ADR cases were pending in CCADR. Meanwhile, mediation under the CCADR program is known to be faster, affordable, and to reduce the overloaded courts' dockets. This has boosted the interest, trust, and confidence people had in mediation, and this has resulted in the increasing number

Preface

The idea for this book is largely owed to my former PhD student, and now a colleague, Dr. Elijah Tukwariba Yin. At the time he conceived the idea of this book, I had some reservations, however, I agreed to collaborate. My reservation stems largely from tackling a specialized subject matter while hoping that the call-for-proposal would generate ample and varied responses.

The initial responses to the call for proposal fell short. To boot, several potential authors dropped out of the project for a host of various reasons. The main reason being COVID-19 and related adverse impacts. I took the approach of searching online and sending direct invitations to academic experts in the field in various universities in various countries to consider submitting chapters. Dr. Yin pursued his network of faculty in West African universities. All our efforts combined, the second round of solicitations yielded additional chapters needed to form this book.

The outcome of the chapter submissions is a surprise. The chapters are predominantly focused on civil justice issues in Africa and Asian countries. On the surface it is disappointing that there are no chapters on industrial democratic countries. But then, the disappointment is unnecessary; books and academic journals on civil justice in industrial democracies predominate academia. Another consolation is that the colonial histories of these industrial democracies continue to cast long shadows. There are hardly any books and articles on civil justice in India and any African country which is devoid of the historical impacts of colonial legal jurisprudence. To this end, this explains how and why this book came to be.

This is hardly a comprehensive compilation of civil justice. Rather, it is a mélange of topics tackling variants of issues related to civil justice as it is known and practiced in some traditional cultures, understood by academicians, practiced by lawyers in court, and drawn on by mediators and arbitrators in dispute resolutions.

Contextually, the chapters range from the pre-colonial indigenous practice of what could be considered rudimentary forms or pre-cursors to formal civil justice - rooted in religious beliefs and practices as they were in India, Ghana and various African countries - to the colonial heritage of rational-legal practices, and the resultant legal pluralism in post-colonial societies. The chapters also follow the ways post-colonial societies have inherited, modified, and built upon their current courts and justice systems, and the predicaments they confront in sustaining and practicing civil justice in their emerging democracies. Each chapter is unique and makes a good contribution to the literature.

The advent of Western colonization along with its introduction of a layered rational-legal system altered the trajectory of many societies and their traditional legal practices especially in the Global South. The exception, however, was the literate society of India. It had a well develop and documented legal jurisprudence that predated the arrival of British rule in the 1800s. The dominant tendency of any colonial power was to subjugate indigenous selected practices of justice by prohibiting, subverting, and coopting it where necessary to suit its administrative goals in "civilizing" the natives. It is a widely shared experience in almost all colonized societies that in all instances, the colonizers fell back on indigenous civil justice wherein to reinforce indigenous leadership positions to further its practice of indirect rule. This strategy enabled the colonial regime to carve out legal spheres of control, namely the Criminal Justice (such as murder, defilement, violations against colonial rule) while relegating local ones to indigenous traditional courts (such as theft, dishonor, imprecators, marital interpersonal disputes, and conflicts). The historical outcome is the legacy of legal pluralism that endures today.

It is appropriate then to attempt a definition of civil justice while contrasting it with criminal justice. In many emerging democratic societies, the judicial branch lacks the luxury of designating judges as civil court judges or criminal court judges. Notwithstanding, there is a clear understanding of the differences between civil and criminal laws.

To take an illustrative approach towards definitions and differentiation: When one calls the police to report a crime such as burglary, car theft, bank holdup, these fall into the sphere of criminal justice. However, when one files a case directly at the courthouse about a breach of contract or defamation, it constitutes civil justice.

In contrast to the rigidly structured rational-legal justice system, the indigenous courts (variously known as native, traditional, chiefly, raj) are found in most towns. For persons who are largely unschooled in the state society, the government and its agencies are a distant and incomprehensible phenomenon.

The traditional courts do offer a sense of comfort to the illiterate and poor. Formal courts are alien, and the legal maneuverings of lawyers, judges and court proceedings all present confusion, and anxiety to many citizens. In the traditional courts, the assembled elders draw on a body of knowledge/wisdom common to the ordinary native. The chapter contributors offered compelling insights into the issues they studied.

Below are some glimpses into the various chapters.

Chapter 1

The chapter takes an integrative look at a largely neglected field of conflict resolution mechanism in Ghana: the extent to which belief in traditional deities both enhance and undercut the justice delivery system in society. It contends that despite the colonial authoritarian attempts to privilege state-instituted approaches to justice delivery, the practice of *duabɔ* (imprecation) endures as an entrenched part of legal regulatory frameworks in society. Drawing on proceedings from the Akan customary conflict resolution mechanism and ethnographic materials gathered from the everyday facts of Ghanaian religious and public domain, the chapter uncovers the hidden resources of traditional deities as useful channels of conflict resolution, and argues for the need for its modification to suit the needs of legal modernity.

Chapter 2

Since the Vedic period, India is known for its commitment to justice, democratic values, the rule of law, and the welfare of individuals. Examining the tools of civil justice in ancient and modern texts underlining the bond of 'social contract', the analysis aims to identify similarities and gaps in the traditional and contemporary aspects of civil justice in India, and to connect the accumulated legal guidance and reasoning to the modern mechanism of justice. The discussion may offer important clues for policymakers, community organisations, law-making agencies, and citizens to strengthen their faith in the judicial system, being a blend of aboriginal and modernity.

Chapter 3

Civil justice comprises the entire system of the administration of justice in civil matters. Over the last three decades, the discourse on civil justice reforms has pervaded the academic debates. Missing, however, are the African approaches to civil justice jurisprudence encompassing a variety of theoretical and normative elements that shape the way Africans conceive justice delivery. The chapter argues that the African position to civil justice in the current reforms debate must not be pinned to just the doctrinal option imbedded in statutes, but also be based on methods and procedures nurtured on the soil of Africa that align with the practical needs of the people encompassing social, political, cultural, and religious values. The chapter concludes that the African system of justice delivery is largely mirrored in the Ghanaian experience of the justice system in civil jurisprudence.

Chapter 4

Whilst there are various mechanisms to curb incidents of police abuse of power, legal control provides one of the most effective ways of enhancing police accountability. Though enforcement of the legal instruments may be a challenge, the mere presence of the legal instruments may provide a fertile ground for other accountability measures. This paper, which is largely based on literature and documentary survey, explores the legal instruments of accountability in the Republic of Zimbabwe. Couched in the Constitution and the Criminal Procedure and Evidence Act, the paper gives an overview of the international and regional legal framework, and the extent to which they inform the national legal framework for police accountability.

Chapter 5

The Indian Subordinate judiciary of a nation plays an important role in administering and dispensing justice, and yet it has been marginalized by the various ruling regimes over decades. A judicial officer in the subordinate courts performs a "pious duty" in the service of justice. Majority of the members of the society come in contact with the trial court judges rather than with the appellate or higher court judges. No law, court, precedent or custom can provide guidelines for better administration of justice, because there is no fixed formula to find the solution to the problem. To this end, it is the exhibited training, integrity, and the professional experience of the trial judge of the subordinate judiciary that the true picture of the Judiciary as a whole presents itself to the nation. The mind of the Judiciary can be known to the public only through the pronouncements of the subordinate or trial court judges. Notwithstanding, the subordinate courts and judges are at their breaking point. This chapter draws on investigative reports, qualitative and empirical data to expose the decaying and declining state of the Subordinate Judiciary in India, and offers practical recommendations for capacity building.

Chapter 6

"Justice delayed is justice denied" and "Justice hurried is justice buried" are oft quoted proverbs in legal studies. While the latter is rarely prevalent in India, the former has maligned the image of the Indian Legal System considerably. Delay in disposal and pendency of cases, especially those of civil and commercial nature, the purposive misuse and abuse of procedural technicalities, and corruption have undermined the effective administration of justice. The recent COVID-19 pandemic has intensified an already grave situation. Drawing on empirical data and various government reports, the authors uncover the behavioral, and structural problems underlying the seemingly normalized delays in the disposal of civil cases, and provide salient recommendations in restoring the Indian Legal System.

Chapter 7

This chapter aims to examine the costs and delays in accessing justice in Ghana and Sierra Leone. It is argued that despite the promising and legal history of Ghana and Sierra Leone, with existing court structures and legal procedures on civil and criminal matters, the legal spaces of both countries are fraught with costs and delays in accessing justice. We used secondary data from the World Bank, Afrobarometer report, statutes, court documents, website articles, etc. to underpin our analysis. It was found that citizens in both countries were confronted with delays and costs in accessing justice. It is recommended that in an era of cell phones and various Apps, the justice sector should endeavour to go hi-tech by sending alerts to litigants, lawyers, and witnesses warranting their presence at an appointed date and time.

Chapter 8

In 2009, the Fundamental Rights Enforcement Procedure (FREP) Rules of 1979 was revised to ease the cumbersome process encountered by Applicants/lawyers in advocating for the enforcement of fundamental human rights in court. Despite this, human rights lawyers still encounter several challenges when representing Applicants for the enforcement of fundamental human rights in court. Utilizing video conferencing platforms such as Skype and Zoom, the authors interviewed willing human rights lawyers about their perceptions and experiences in accessing justice for, and representing especially, the poor and illiterate in the court of law. The findings reveal that issues of procedural rules of court and disrespect for court orders are some of the obstructions encountered by human rights lawyers. The chapter recommends that judges should avoid placing unnecessary emphasis on the procedural rules of court. In addition, human rights lawyers and Non-Governmental Organizations (NGOs) should maintain continuous advocacy for the enforcement of fundamental human rights towards holding government and its agencies more accountable for disrespect of court orders.

Chapter 9

Adjudication of issues in Ghanaian jurisdictions can be traced back to the pre-colonial era where powers were vested in chiefs, elders, and representatives of all the major tribes. Chiefs and elders adjudicated on most issues with the family heads serving as lawyers. During the British colonial era, judicial powers were vested in the Privy Council which took away the powers of the chiefs and elders. At times parties to a dispute may want to resolve the dispute in a form other than the normal court system, hence the Alternative Dispute Resolution (ADR). However, ADR lacks *stare decisis* since it sets no precedent to guide similar disputes in the future. Also, there is no right of appeal when parties opt for ADR. The purpose of this chapter is to assess the use of ADR in Ghana, the obstacles, and the way forward.

Chapter 10

The chapter explores the dilemma of alternative dispute resolution (ADR) and access to justice for women in Ghana. It argues that the introduction and use of ADR have contributed to improving access to justice with regards to reducing delays in formal court procedures, cost reduction, time-saving, opening spaces for less-resourced individuals and groups, particularly women, to have access to justice. Above all, ADR does bring access to the justice systems close to remote areas, serving the needs of disadvantaged individuals including women and others who are most vulnerable. However, the weaknesses and challenges in the formal legal system, coupled with the historical and cultural dynamics of the Ghanaian society--which is patriarchal in nature--have prevented mostly women from reaping the maximum benefits of ADR. A critical interrogation of the justice system and the historical and cultural norms of Ghana would help increase and enhance women's access to justice through ADR.

Chapter 11

In most dispute situations, there are varied attempts for resolution. Mediation comes as an important component in this regard. Over the years, the court system is over-burdened with cases. The most recent report showed 382,220 cases pending in courts from 2012 to 2016 in Ghana (Judicial Service Report, 2012-16). Of the 14,900 referred by the courts to the Court-Connected Alternative Dispute Resolution (CCADR), 5,789 cases, representing 38 percent, were successfully resolved. That is not to say that mediation as a form of CCADR has not made any success; it has. But unfortunately, the system that was instituted to deal with the challenges of the orthodox system has been overwhelmed by the same problems. Drawing on data trends and interviews, the authors examine underlying sources of backlog of CCADR cases, the impediments characterising the service, and deducing findings and recommendations to inform policy making. Being relatively new in Africa, the study will add to the literature in this academic area as well as broaden our understanding of issues associated with CCADR.

Chapter 12

Immunities, though part of the law of the land, is to a certain extent an exemption from the general law. Certain rights and immunities such as freedom of speech belong primarily to individual members of parliament and exist because the House cannot perform its functions without unimpeded use of the services of its members. Ostensibly, the degree to which Members of Parliament are immune from legal inquiry may presumably accord them a greater probability to abuse their mandate. In general, a court summons is the beginning of a legal case. It signals the issue that needs to be adjudicated. However, the introduction of immunity invalidates some tenets of modern democracy such as a court summon. The authors seek to examine some of the uncertainties and ambiguities that might have arisen out of the Court decision in the case *Republic v. Mahama Ayariga* (2019) with much consideration of other cases. The chapter provides a thorough picture of the systems of parliamentary immunity and recommends ways of curbing observed challenges with the practice.

Chapter 13

The concept of Civil Justice has existed from time immemorial. The reform of Civil and Criminal Justice systems is a contentious issue that has become the top priority for the international community in re-establishing the rule of law. The justice systems in many common law jurisdictions are perceived to be 'in crisis' deformed by exorbitant delay, cost and complexity in proceedings. The level of resources engulfed in the judicial system has very little or no impact on judicial performance and effectiveness. Comparative and comprehensive analysis of the law not only leads to a better realization of the foreign laws but also aids with law unification. This research paper will attempt to highlight the issues in the civil and criminal justice system and comparatively analyze the scenario in England, Singapore and India. In furtherance, the authors will interrogate the possible methods to curb the delay in the various justice systems, and to advance the modern trends in civil and criminal justice policies.

This book has undoubtedly added to the literature. It is useful for legal and non-legal scholars as well as practitioners.

Elijah Tukwariba Yin
University of Cape Coast, Ghana

Nelson F. Kofie
Northern Virginia Community College, USA

Acknowledgment

We want to thank all chapter contributors. Without them, this project would not have materialized. We also want to express our gratitude to all our reviewers for taking the time to read the various chapters. To the staff of IGI Global, we appreciate your patience throughout the phases of the project. It was your encouragement that brought the project to fruition.

Chapter 1
Akan Deities as Agents of Conflict Resolution Mechanism in Ghana:
Promises and Pitfalls

Seth Tweneboah
University of Education, Winneba, Ghana

ABSTRACT

The chapter takes an integrative look at a largely neglected field of conflict resolution mechanism in Ghana: the extent to which belief in traditional deities both enhance and undercut justice delivery systems in society. It contends that through duabɔ (imprecation) there is an enduring influence of traditional deities as part of legal regulatory frameworks in society. The chapter, thus, uncovers the hidden resources of traditional deities as useful channels of conflict resolution. The chapter draws on proceedings from the Akan customary conflict resolution mechanism to demonstrate both the usefulness and challenges of traditional justice delivery method in contemporary Ghana and encourages the need for its modification to suit the needs of legal modernity. The chapter is the product of a qualitative analysis of empirical ethnographic material gathered from the everyday facts of Ghanaian religious communities and public domain.

INTRODUCTION

The topic of duabɔ (imprecation) is an underexplored field and remains at the margin of the justice delivery system. Evolving from various "sacred traditional states" (Meyerowitz, 1951, pp. 27—29), the post-independence Ghanaian state exhibits both continuity and disjuncture when it comes to matters of religion, law and politics (Tweneboah, 2020). In its public sphere, there is an increasing demand for the application of secular tenets in ways that conform to legal universalism. At the same time, there is an overwhelming influence of religion and customary resources on the daily activities of the people (Crook et al., 2011a, 2011b; Yin 2018). Accordingly, the question of the best mode of providing effec-

DOI: 10.4018/978-1-7998-7898-8.ch001

tive, trusted and accessible justice to the citizenry in ways that consider the people's understanding of justice — underpinned by their religious and customary worldviews — begs for answers. As a secular state whose populations are attached to religiosity, questions bothering on how the spiritual forces promote or undercut, and how people tap into the religious realm to correct political and legal wrongs continue to demand further enquiry. In particular, the transition from the previous sacred traditional states to the modern nation-state has led to a significant legal and justice delivery disjuncture. This is particularly true when it comes to the decisive role of the spiritual forces in matters of conflict resolution mechanism.

Throughout its long history, particularly in post-encounter periods with Western religious and legal norms, traditional African deities have demonstrated their capacity to adapt to the changing realities of society. Crucially, European colonialists and missionaries' attempts to supplant traditional modes of justice delivery and norm conformity made very little effort in the day-to-day activities of the people (Gray, 2000, 2001; Tweneboah, 2020). Precisely because traditional deities have demonstrated their vitality in diverse areas of conflict resolution and peace building in society, in recent times, there have been appreciable tendencies for high-profile political actors resorting to duabɔ (imprecation) instead of appealing to civil court trials to seek redress (Tweneboah 2014; 2021). Intriguingly, while the society undergoes secularisation and democratisation, access to political office almost invariably continues to appeal to the spiritual forces. Political actors and other wilders of power continue to tap into the spiritual realm which they believe would help them not only galvanise votes and support but also to correct any wrongs wrought by their opponents (Dovlo, 2004, p. 213; Max-Wirth, 2016).

In Ghana and elsewhere, traditional deities, thus, have proven themselves to be an immensely useful mode of justice delivery (Agyekum, 1999; Oba, 2008; Tweneboah, 2014, 2021). The supposed power of the deities makes a binding commitment on its adherents. Yet, there have also been reported cases of concern especially when it comes to fairness, enforcement and human rights (Crook et al., 2011a; Tweneboah, 2014). To be sure, such concerns challenge theories and praxes of legal modernity. A vital relevance of the public manifestation of the influence of traditional African deities is that it suggests the contemporary significance and the resiliency of the traditional spiritual mode of justice delivery.

Consequently, this chapter will contend that in spite of the attempts to privilege state-sponsored approaches to justice delivery, through *duabɔ*, we see the enduring influence of traditional deities as part of legal regulatory frameworks in society. The resilience of *duabɔ* in the Ghanaian public domain, the chapter demonstrates, reflects the religious and legal plurality of the Ghanaian society. This chapter, thus, uncovers the hidden resources of traditional deities as useful means of conflict resolution. It does not seek to serve as an apologetic defence of *duabɔ*. Rather, it considers *duabɔ's* valence to imprecators. Consistent with the famous Thomas theorem, the chapter notes that the ways in which situations are framed define the "true" definition of the situation. Drawing on the Akan customary arbitration mechanism as a reference point, the chapter demonstrates both the promises and pitfalls of the Akan traditional conflict resolution method in contemporary Ghana and encourages the need for its modification to suit the needs of legal modernity.

Methodologically, this chapter is the product of a qualitative analysis of empirical ethnographic material gathered from the everyday facts of Ghanaian religious communities and the public domain. The crux of the chapter is to provide a detailed understanding of the links between religion, law and justice delivery. The chapter employs an interdisciplinary approach rooted in sociological, anthropological, political, economic and cultural perspectives. The method used in compiling the material for this chapter includes participant observation and open-ended interviews which took place in some selected shrines and villages in the Techiman and Nkoranza Traditional Areas of the Bono East region of Ghana.

Participation in the proceedings at shrine courts and piacular rituals for reversing cases of *duabɔ* was an opportunity to problematise the prestige and influence of Akan traditional deities when it comes justice delivery system.

TRADITIONAL DEITIES AND THE LEGACY OF COLONIALISM

This section demonstrates the ways in which traditional deities and their actors have historically become essential components of Ghana's legal and political modernity. It pays attention to the depth to which traditional religious resources became an essential constituent of the nationalist struggle against colonial domination.

Much of the early studies on customary laws suggest that religious customary laws were deemed unimportant, a liability to the needs of legal modernity. The dominant narrative has been that the traditional justice delivery system that appeals to the spiritual forces is an unreliable ally to legal modernity. It is significant that throughout most of Africa, British colonial expansion undercut traditional forms of legal system (Daniels, 1991; Mazrui, 1986). Traditional jurisprudence especially its conflict resolution treasure which invoked the power of the deities came under attack from the colonialists. Even more significant is the fact that the colonial order made no attempt to differentiate between customary and religious norms of the people (Tweneboah, 2020). In a rather stereotypical manner, these were lumped together. The people and their practices were described in more offensive manner. A.B. Ellis, a noted colonial administrator, derogatively reported of his observation of the relationship between the people and their deities thus: "In short, the people of Gold Coast, being low in the stage of civilisation, have imagined gods with equally low mental characteristics" (Ellis, 1887, p. 11).

British jurisprudence sought to provide a model par excellence of civil justice delivery. Traditional shrines which served as a forum for mediating between litigating parties were held as an unswerving limiter to British interest. Indeed, the shrines played a major function in resisting colonial rule. Sensing that their interest was challenged, the colonial regime used several legal aggressions to suppress the traditional religious activities and operations. In 1883, for example, through the promulgation of the Native Jurisdiction Ordinance, chiefly powers that previously extended to matters of life and even death were curtailed from traditional authorities; only matters bothering on misdemeanour were left in the hands of the chiefs. Yet chiefly actors who were naturally in constant touch with their people continued to handle felonious cases such as rape, torture, murder, and other such crimes. The domiciliary management of crimes despite prohibitive laws implied that albeit the legal maneuver of modern legal system and social change on traditional institutions of control, traditional modes of crime prevention continued to be invoked and patronised. As I detail later, this situation persists even in contemporary Ghanaian society (Akpabli-Honu, 2009). In a mass survey conducted by Crook et al (2011), it was observed that contrary to popular perception, for majority of the population, the state civil dispute resolution mechanism, represented by the magistrate courts, for example, was a preferred choice. They noted that the magistrate courts which are the first instance courts, were basically privileged by the majority of the people owing to the general belief that these courts represent justice, fairness, certainty and enforceability of remedies (Crook et al., 2011a, 2011b).

Intriguingly, the survey also noted that despite the people's powerful attraction for civil approaches to the justice system, over 70 percent of the respondents indicated their trust in traditional forms of settling disputes led by chiefly, family and religious leaders (Crook et al., 2011b).

A striking evidence of how the colonialists curtailed traditional religious powers is the execution of the Dante Bosomfo (the chief priest of the Dante shrine), Kwasi Gyantrubi. In November 1894, he was executed by the Germans for his passionate and vehement local economic policies "which precluded complete German control over the area" (Maier, 1981, p. 242). The Germans sensing that they could not tolerate such competition, ordered the priest shot before a firing squad. As Meir has noted, "the Dante Bosomfo had to be removed for much the same reason that ultimately Asantehene Agyeman Prempeh (who was exiled in 1896) was removed by the British: for pursuing too successfully both traditional and innovative solutions to the changing conditions of the nineteenth century" (Maier, 1981, p. 242). Such political and legal disturbances also sought to alter traditional modes of conflict resolution that appeal to the power of the deities.

By the beginning of the twentieth century, anti-witchcraft shrines which specialised in spiritual offences had, in theory, been effectively criminalised (Gray, 2000, 2001). A ban was also placed on the activities and operations of these shrines under the 1923 Native Ordinance. The usurping law made it an offence to consult or supplicate (Gray, 2000, 2001; Quashigah, 1999; Tweneboah, 2014, 2021). The law imposed stiffer penalties for violators and also empowered colonial District Administrators to institute harsher punishments on anyone found to have violated it. Yet this did not go unopposed by influential traditional priestly and chiefly authorities. Several tensions ensued in most parts of southern Ghana. The remarkable flourishing of anti-witchcraft shrines during the 1920s provides excellent evidence of this view.

Interestingly, Ghana's post-independence civil justice system gives an ambivalent picture of traditional customary conflict resolution. As a matter of fact, traditional customary practices are well acknowledged. Under the current (1992) Constitution, customary practices are guaranteed. The plain words of Article 11(3) define customary law as "the rules of law, which by custom are applicable to particular communities in Ghana." Sections 54 and 55 of the Courts Act, 1993 (Act 459) affirms the plural legal nature of the Ghanaian society suggesting the tacit acknowledgment of the application of religious laws in settling disputes. At the same time, state civil laws have openly and tacitly continued to weaken the legal role of the chiefs on matters of traditional justice delivery mechanism. Despite the existence of state-sanctioned chieftaincy alternative dispute resolution (ADR), as already noted, chiefly powers are limited to interpersonal disputes or misdemeanours. Certainly, the chiefly institution has demonstrated its capacity to resolve hard-to-manage political grievances. Chiefly actors have, in several ways, handled political disputations, calling political parties and their actors to order. The challenge, however, is that the institution is legally limited to causes and matters affecting chieftaincy as is spelt out in Chapter 22 of the 1992 Constitution.

The state also acknowledges faith-based fora for settling disputes, whereby religious actors employ the diverse religious norms of society as mediators and conciliators in the settlement of grievances in society. In spite of this, misconceptions continue to hover around the traditional deities and through the lens of European colonial and missionary legacies, reliance on traditional deities is continually held as a product of some ridiculous delusion. As Justice Acquah has noted:

Today society is fast expanding and changing in line with rapid scientific and enlightened ideas. Science has made it possible to explain what was inexplicable in the olden days. Bareness in women, infant mortality, drought, and sudden death arising from heart-failures and so on, are now known not to be the work of any juju or witches. And customary offences based on such obsolete ideas cannot be permitted to exist in modern days. To tolerate a community that still brooks such primitive ideas and resort to punishing innocent subjects accused of such practices, is to condone primitive brutality (Acquah, 1991, p. 56).

It is also interesting to notice that the overarching effect of these is that traditional modes of justice delivery which rely on the power of the deities are still seen as a preserve of uncultivated peoples and cultures as alluded to by colonial actors (Ellis 1887; Hawkins, 2002, p. 165; see also RAT ADM 430). Empirical studies have pointed to a large section of respondents (87.8 percent) indicating a very low level of trust for traditional priestly actors when it comes to issues of justice delivery in society. Alongside the impact of European colonial and missionary legacies, the increasing sense of Pentecostal moral revulsion about the traditional religious resources has also contributed greatly to the low levels of trust in and the reification of traditional justice delivery. Pentecostalism admonishes its adherents to cut ties with the ancestral religion which is cast as purveys of demonic influences and failures of life (Meyer, 1998).

The irony, however, is that there is an observable problem of confusion over which type of legal avenues to employ in times of human rights violations or claims. While modern state preference in matters of justice delivery is clearly evident in society, some Ghanaians still prefer non-court legal procedures. Prominently, non-state agents and legal options persist because many Ghanaians still live in close proximity to each other and relationship undergirded by tradition remains a norm. Besides, dispute settlements and amends making are largely led by familiar elders, ensuring instant easing of what could be otherwise a protracted antagonism. Certainly, even in urban areas where social life is more formal, many people appeal to traditional conflict resolution mechanisms as they avoid the courts.

TRADITIONAL CONFLICT RESOLUTION MECHANISM

On 9 February 2020, the author and a team of researchers visited the Tom Kramo shrine, a dreaded deity at Tom, a small town in the Nkoranza Traditional Area. The visit was part of a research project: the intercessory role of African traditional religious shrines in sustaining youth migration to Libya and across the Mediterranean to Europe. The visit, however, became an occasion to gain diverse insights from traditional conflict management mechanisms. Significantly, the visit coincided with one of the three days (Tuesday, Friday and Sunday) dedicated to ritual reversal of imprecations loosely referred to as curses. The elders and attendants of the shrine, procurers from different parts of the country and parties in several litigations had, therefore, gathered. In many measures, it was, therefore, a period to witness first-hand three of such mediatory proceedings, two of which were followed by the piacular sacrifice and the ritual for reversing curses.

The main proceeding of interest for the current purpose was a case between two parties pseudonymously labelled as Akwasi, the imprecator, and Yaw, the imprecatee. The dispute leading to the imprecation arose out of Akwasi's inability to control himself due to intoxication from large volumes of alcoholic contents he had consumed. Yaw called him to order by assaulting him. Sensing that his life was in danger from the assault, Akwasi thereupon appealed to the dreaded Tom Kramo deity calling its wrath upon the head of his assaulter. The case was therefore reported to the elders of the shrine who called the parties for mediation which was followed by the piacular reversal of the imprecation. The entire proceeding which followed the general Akan traditional processes of settling disputes (see Agyekum, 2008; Obeng, 1999), was carried out in less than an hour. It began with the shrine panel inviting the parties to narrate their versions of events starting from Akwasi, the assaulted party. His narration was succinct and insightful, relevant portions of which are quoted below:

I summoned him [Yaw] to nananom [the deities] because he had unlawfully assaulted me. A few days ago, after the hustle of the day, I went out to take a few drinks. I became intoxicated and decided to go home and find a place to lay my head. While lying there, I experienced some pains resulting from an assault melted out to me by Yaw. I had not done anything to deserve it. I asked him why he was assaulting me and he said I was rowdy. In the course of assaulting me, I realised I needed something to save my head [life]. As the elders say, sebe, when in distress, the sheep also bites. I then said that if I am in my own house and in my own room and without any provocation you can assault me like this, then nananom should intervene for me. So, I called upon the Tom Kramo deity to rescue me from my attacker.

After his narration, as the procedural practice demands, the shrine panel asked Yaw to cross-examine his accuser. He began by explaining why he acted that way but the elders brought in on track demanding to know if he had any questions for the accuser. Yaw responded in the negative. He was then given the opportunity to bring his own defence. In his defence, Yaw also recounted his story thus:

I did not assault him with any ill intention. Nananom [Elders] have a saying that when the tree holds your cloth, it is your face it yearns to see. On that fateful night, at about 8pm, I received a desperate call for help from Akwasi's sister that he was misbehaving, insulting and making life uncomfortable for tenants. Upon reaching the house, I found my colleague in an uncontrollable state of mess and decided to calm him down. He rather became unrulier. I therefore used a tiny belt belonging to a school boy to whip him just for him to stop what he was doing.

Yaw narrated that he afterwards left the scene but was later informed that Akwasi had imprecated him for arbitrary intrusion and intolerable assault.

This case presents a belief in the power of the deities as a convenient mode of settling disputes. Like the two previous cases handled before this particular one, this case was fast-tracked by the shrine elders. The Tom Kramo court did not find it necessary to call any witness. It reasoned that in their narration, both parties had offered reasonable evidence sufficient enough to pronounce their judgement. This is consistent with the Akan legal maxim that where there are no witnesses, the panel uses part of the case. Unlike Yaw, Akwasi was not given any opportunity to cross-examine his accuser. The court found Yaw's own evidence to be self-implicatory enough to warrant a decision. They reasoned that an intoxicated person did not have the full use of his faculty and therefore was not expected to be as sober and reasonable as the assaulter expected. The assault was therefore warrantless and perverse. As an elder inquired from Yaw: "Do you throw stones to where the eggs are gathered?" In its judgement, the court affirmed that Akwasi had been needlessly assaulted and recommended that he should be compensated for an amount of GH₵ 200. This is a remarkable feature of the Akan customary legal system which shares a component with the common law tradition, at least in relation to the application of the M'Naghten rule which provides a standard test or grounds for exemption for (criminal) responsibility.

The Tom Kramo's courts proceeding, accordingly, had implications for societal notions of responsibility, culpability, and liability (Diwan, 2004). In truth, it accords well with existing accounts of the general patterns of African traditional modes of protecting the innocent in society. Kofi Agyekum has noted the fixed formula for ruling a case in Akan traditional arbitration proceeding thus: "If X had not reported this case for the elders to have listened with attention (good ears); and if you had taken a club to hit him, and killed him you would have killed him like a beast" (Agyekum, 2008, p. 366). The Kenyan political historian, Ali Mazrui, records the crucial mode of protecting the innocent in traditional society:

In indigenous terms, the protection of the innocent was precisely the main focus of law enforcement, rather than the punishment of the guilty per se. Arising out of this came the victim-focus law enforcement rather than the villain-focus. When a crime was committed it was more fundamental to have the victim's family compensated, than to have the villain or culprit punished (1986, p. 205).

It is convenient, in the main, to say that African traditional or customary law tilts more towards civil justice and less so to criminal justice. Mazrui (1986) also implicates the arrival of the Western system of law enforcement as playing havoc with African systems of compensation, especially in the field of criminal law.

The Tom Kramo shrine proceeding is not an out-of-the-ordinary episode in many African traditional settings. To ensure harmony in the household or the community, elders attend to disputes, violations and infractions over household management, child maintenance, parental irresponsibility, divorce and land disputes, among others. These cases were frequently nipped in the bud before they escalate into full-blown conflict. Below I detail this.

Apart from the amount of convenience involved in this case, there was also an element of restorative justice, a good display of amiableness. Interestingly, the Tom shrine case highlights one of the prospects of making amends in traditional society. Although unhappy about the assault which led to the imprecation, Akwasi pleaded that his assaulter's punishment be mitigated. This is worthy of attention. In pleading for clemency for his assaulter, Akwasi argued thus:

Nananom, pardon me to say that Yaw's punishment is mitigated for I cannot accept this compensation. Yaw and I have been friends since our infancy days. We have never harboured any ill-feelings between us. We drink and share ideas. What happened on that day was an accident. I imprecated him out of the pain I was enduring and I needed something to save my head. Tomorrow if I am lying motionless, he will still be the one who will first come to my aid, perhaps he will even mash kenkey and push it into my throat. I cannot roast my tongue and eat and still feel the taste. Nananom I beg to reject the compensation.

Akwasi's plea for clemency for his assaulter strikes proudly when it comes to matters of preservation of relationships in society. Among the criticisms of the state-sanctioned approaches to justice delivery is the fact that many citizens are unhappy with the adversarial system of justice delivery, which often is confrontational and produces outright victors and losers. The concern is that, under this system, the parties bear the burden of proof, which very often occurs in an antagonistic manner, "with the court playing the role of an umpire" (Atuguba et al., 2006, p. 13). This situation provides avenues for the justice system to be weighted in favour of rich and influential parties, a condition that prepares the stage for the parties to carry the litigation from the court to the domestic setting. In rejecting this compensation, Akwasi paid attention to the circumstances that diminish the culpability of his assaulter. A trustworthy friend of Akwasi, Yaw had argued that he acted from a motive of congeniality. He arrived at the scene seeing his friend hopelessly intoxicated and immersed in chaotic situation which needed to be remedied.

Ironically, while *duabɔ* has the intention of seeking death or something terrible to the intended target, there is a general antipathy in Ghanaian society regarding seeking legal redress in the civil court. Taking someone to court is thought of as a sign of vindictiveness and a sense of punishment (Atuguba et al., 2006). In this sense, in Ghanaian society, a resort to the state-sponsored courts is considered as punishment to the offender. Accordingly, in trying to understand why Akwasi prefers not to accept the compensation but rather decided to imprecate his friend, I find Abamfo Atiemo's work on interpersonal relationships revealing. Writing on the plight of abused women in domestic circle, Atiemo observes that when it comes to domestic affairs, most women in Africa would normally wish to be protected from abusive relationships but through mechanisms that are not adversarial or confrontational. Indeed, some may even prefer that some minimum sanctions be applied as a deterrence to their husbands from being abusive but in ways that would not lead to marital dissolution. Unless in situations where severe harm occurs, when an abuse is reported to the police, the idea of complaining about abuses is not to get the abusive husbands jailed (Atiemo, 2012).

A key concept in the Akan traditional justice delivery system is the manner in which the guilty party is presented with the opportunity to plead for clemency.

THE DEITIES AND JUSTICE DELIVERY

Akan traditional religious and legal rule requires everyone's deeds are known to and judged by the spiritual forces. Giving evidence of the function that the spiritual forces play in the justice delivery system of the Akan society, K.A. Busia recounted that:

In 1946 the Akwamuhene [a divisional chief] of Ankaase, a village near Kumasi, died. Forty days before, he had given evidence at court in a case in which another man had been accused of murdering the Akwamuhene's own father. The accused person was acquitted chiefly on the evidence of the Akwamuhene, who a few days later fell ill. On the twenty-eighth day of his illness he confessed to a friend he believed that his father's ghost was punishing him because he had given false evidence at the trial. He did not recover from his illness, and died. No other explanation was required, for it was the general belief that his father had punished him for his conduct (Busia, 1968, p. 24).

As already indicated in the introductory section, *duabɔ* largely operates based on people's beliefs, for as the famous Thomas theorem says, "If men define situations as real, they are real in consequence (Thomas and Thomas 1928)." In traditional Akan cosmology, no one's actions will escape from the ancestor's examination. This evinces the intercessory function of the spiritual forces in seeking justice in society. Busia recounts that the conduct of the Ashanti is continuously regulated by the thought that the ancestors are ever-watchful of the activities of their forbearers, and one day the individual will join the ancestors to give account of their deeds, especially of his conduct towards his kinsmen. This thought, according to Busia, is a supremely potent sanction of morality (Busia, 1968, p. 25).

To be sure, notwithstanding the attempts by the post-independence state to decouple the traditional justice delivery system and the deep moral revulsion associated with the traditional field, *duabɔ* is still an effective instrument of justice for many. The 2020 presidential and parliamentary elections provided the most blatant episodes of political actors resorting to *duabɔ* to settle political disagreements. For example, on June 5, 2020 the Ghanaian media reported stories of how some displeased members of the New Patriotic Party in the Offinso South and Juaben constituencies invoked curses on party executives believed to have masterminded the disqualification of their favourite candidates (ModernGhana, 2020; Tawiah, 2020; Zurek, 2020).

While a very common practice, not very much is documented about *duabɔ*. Its exact meaning, therefore, excites lively alternative interpretations (Agyekum, 1999; Tweneboah, 2021). Despite the unclear scholarly account on the genealogy of *duabɔ*, the shared assumption, however, is that it is a vital traditional decision-making and problem-solving mechanism. From the cases presented so far, one can say that the power of the deity is invoked as an expression of indignation resulting from broken relations. According to Agyekum, *duabɔ* is a practice of "invoking supernatural powers in defence and the execution of certain forms of justice. This has given rise to the origin of imprecation based on the desire of the imprecator to harm the target." (Agyekum, 1999, p. 358). *Duabɔ*, thus, provides a conceptual model of justice delivery. It tells the story of how justice is achieved, maintained and understood at the popular level. It occurs as a function of betrayal of trust in society. Some have labelled *duabɔ* as "grievance imprecation." Agyekum (1999) opines that the practice is related to supernatural powers which believers hold as valuable and powerful. It, hence, emerges from situations where there is a grievance between the imprecator and the imprecatee.

There are several reasons for duabɔ's persistence as a spiritual justice delivery despite the negativity associated with it. In the first place, its invocation largely stems from unequal access to and control over the limited legal resources of society. Some reports on access to justice have acknowledged that a properly functioning democratic society affords its citizenry with easy, inexpensive, speedy, efficient, effective and user-friendly access to quality justice (Atuguba et al., 2006). Access to justice, then, becomes a central tenet of good governance. The challenge, however, is that traditional customary justice delivery that appeals to the power of the deities is largely neglected when it comes to discussions on the justice delivery system in Ghana and most of Africa. But the public manifestation of *duabɔ* further suggests that legal positivism which projects state civil law structures over the ancestral mode of justice delivery is not the only means of accounting for what law and order are and how they operate; instead, the spiritual forces of nature continue to play a role despite the secularisation of society. Essentially, *duabɔ's* presence in the public domain highlights the idea that traditional normative legal norms are not merely a means of legal control but also exhibit a dynamic ability of the spiritual forces to adapt to the changing society than is often assumed.

The second way to look at this is to consider one of the debilitating challenges confronting state approaches to justice delivery - the problem of legal cost. The high cost of legal services or even the cost of filing a case, to begin with, is identified as well beyond the means of ordinary and vulnerable citizens. These categories of citizens, thus, barely present their case in court; when they appear in court, they do so as defendants in civil suits and criminal prosecutions. It is for this reason that some have seen the civil court system as "a business, an industry, a club" (Atuguba et al., 2006, p. 14).

Despite the religion-state separation, in the Ghanaian public sphere, there continues to be a vital trust in the deities for their fairmindedness. In an important survey conducted in 2011, participants who undoubtedly believed in state-sponsored approaches to justice delivery named "God-fearing" as an important quality required of a judge (Crook et al., 2011b). Thus, community expectation undergirded by religious understanding of the people serves as a crucial mode of administering justice. It is often said that a people's sense of the human determines the way rights must be "given." Consequently, the religious nature of the people constitutes a very potent means of administering justice and settling disputes.

The spiritual forces are believed to deliver their decisions fairly. Through the ritual of imprecation, the belief in the adjudicatory power of the deities is acted out. For example, following Ghana's Supreme Court ruling on the 2012 presidential election, a leading member of the New Patriotic Party, unhappy with the court's decision, noted that the next time the party got such a case, they would send it to Antoa, a much-feared deity in the Ashanti region (Ghanaweb, 2013). The fear of the wrath of the spiritual forces inculcates in the people traditional models of moral and social justice best accessed by those who remain faithful to their demands. There is the sense that traditional deities are swift and impartial in their judgements. Unlike the monotheistic God who pushes judgement till the end of the world, traditional deities are held as those who fast-track their judgements. As a result, in various ways, some have negatively labelled the deities as "jealous gods, jealous of their dignity, jealous of the adulation and offerings paid to them; and there is nothing they resent so much as any slight, whether intentional or accidental, which may be offered them" (Ellis, 1887, p. 11).

PITFALLS

I now turn my attention to demonstrate how traditional modes of settling disputes sometimes challenge certain ideals of legal modernity. The discussion has shown that traditional justice delivery systems are largely in consonance with the desires and values of local communities. Yet, these cases also present several challenges, three of which I have chosen to discuss below.

Composition of panels: In employing the services of the shrine courts, there is the problem of the composition of panels that are unreflective of or unrepresentative of the diverse nature of the changing society. Except on very rare occasions, the composition of the shrine panel has completely been all males. The concern here is that such uneven representation of elder males leads to open and shrewd politicisation of justice delivery especially in situations where a woman makes claims against an elderly man.

In the previous sacred traditional states, the societies were mainly homogenous. Members conformed to the same sets of rules and beliefs. Today's society, however, is heterogenous. As such, the application of customary norms that do not reflect the needs of majority of the population in a society that has become so diverse religiously and ethnically constitutes a fundamental pitfall. It is against this backdrop that to stand the test of time, the ongoing revitalisation of traditional religious spaces (Nzrenzah, 2015) must consider the heterogenous nature of the society in which the tradition now finds itself. Already some chiefly actors have undertaken consistent effort to bring their traditions and customs at par with contemporary realities. For example, at a town in the Wenchi Traditional Area of Bono region, a chief noted that the growing homogeneity of his territory has given rise to the need to embrace key actors of identifiable imported religious and migrant cultural groups in his council of elders (Personal interview, 6 December 2014).

Incorporation of more fairness: We have already seen how in traditional modes of administering justice fairmindedness becomes a major sociolegal capital and a source of attraction for many. Even so, there have been times when the panel at the traditional court resorts to authority instead of law, a situation leading to further tensions and conflicts in society. In Akan arbitration, the chiefly panel is said to have institutional and linguistic monopoly to bring about peace and harmony in society. "They may use the power-laden and derogatory linguistic forms and attention-seeking devices" (Agyekum, 2008, p. 368; Obeng, 1999, p. 216) To explicate this further, I present an interesting case that occurred at a town in the Techiman Traditional Area some years ago. This case betrays further how in traditional society, it is not every time that the council talks of law; sometimes they talk of authority.

In this particular case, a young man, Kofi picked up an argument with an elderly woman, Akosua who was a local restaurant (chop bar) operator over the unsatisfactory performance of Akosua. The case, to be sure, was a civil one. Akosua, the complaining party alleged that the responding party had verbally abused her. Kofi, however, argued that a contract between him and Akosua had been unjustifiably broken. He averred that the fufu he bought was not up to expectation; the soup was tasteless and watery, liking it to a local stream. Akosua became offended and summoned Kofi before the *odikro's* (local chief's) court. The chiefly court systematically reasoned with the complainant and awarded some damages to the her in the form of a sheep and bottles of schnapps since the insult to the elderly woman was also against the good sense of the ancestors of the town (Rattray, 1929, p. 310). Kofi justified his conduct and questioned the damages as unlawful. He even questioned the locus standi of the *odikro's* court, describing the chiefly panel as less intelligent in comparison with his father. His disinclination to have his case tried at the *odikro's* court infuriated the chiefly actors a situation which led them to order the palace youth to mercilessly assault him.

This case raises a number of alarms in light of state laws that seek to project the rights of the individual member of the community. Firstly, the idea that the young mans actions constitute contempt of the *odikro's* court calls attention for a review of some portions of traditional modes of justice delivery. Contempt of court here implies that there has been a disrespect or an affront to the authority of the *odikro* and his elders as well as the dignity of their court; that their court was unimportant and merits no respect as the young man said. As Brobbey (2008) explains, under the laws of Ghana, contempt of court implies that the contemnor also seems to give the impression that he or she is capable of challenging the authority of the court and the 1992 Constitution itself (Brobbey, 2008, p. 460). For Brobbey, until such time that a customary arbitration will be raised to the level of a court or judicial tribunal, the rules on contempt of court or contempt of tribunals cannot apply to customary arbitration proceedings. This implies that disobedience of an order of customary arbitration cannot give rise to contempt of court (Brobbey, 2008, p. 449). This presumes that the *odikro's* court had no recognition and the order to assault the young man was unlawful and warrantless. However, such is not usually the case especially in places that are distant from the reach of the central government. The leaders of these societies assert their authority and will in matters that come to their courts.

Secondly, an argument can be made that the young man's actions clearly go against the spirit and letter of section 6(c) of the Chieftaincy Act, 2008, (Act 759). The said section mandates that anyone who "knowingly uses disrespectful or insulting language or insults a chief by word or conduct, commits an offence and shall be liable to a fine or imprisonment or both." The difficulty here has to do with the mode of sanction imposed. The challenge with traditional justice delivery is that the members of the panel, in exercising their powers, exceed their authority of adjudication by instituting certain sanctions that are a violation of natural justice and equity. As Agyekum (2008, p.368) notes, during proceedings and cross-examinations, the *ɔkyeame* (spokesperson) have control over the use of expressions that ordinarily are deemed as impolite and taboo if spoken outside the court. Akan conflict resolution practice provides that if such words are verbalised outside the court, the *ɔkyeame* can be held liable for this, which becomes a basis for litigation in society.

Regard for Human Rights and Dignity: Albeit the praises for traditional justice delivery system that deploys the power of the deities in decision making and problem-solving, there are some obverse sides to their activities over matters of rights and dignity of their clienteles. As noted in the just narrated case, sometimes traditional actors of justice engage in certain actions that constitute a fundamental human rights breach in society. In fact, as just noted above, cases of abuse and disregard for human rights in the application of traditional religious sanctions have led to various criticisms of traditional justice as being at odds with legal modernity or universalism. In July 2020, the story of a 90-year-old woman who was subjected to undignified death in the name of witchcraft exorcism gained national and international news attention (BBC, 2020; Duodu, 2020). The woman was said to have been subjected to trial by ordeal, a usual practice associated with most past and some present traditional spiritual justice delivery systems. In truth, concerns about the correct and proper mode of enhancing the dignity of suspected or accused persons who submit themselves to this system have historically presented some of the main difficulties of justice delivery.

As already noted, under the colonial regime, this became the basis for the promulgation of some ordinances including the Native Ordinance, 1923. The accusations, past and present, are that under the shrine court system, underprivileged, vulnerable and socially marginalised categories of people often receive different levels of respect, dignity and rights owing to their status. Justice, in this sense, is "given" to the influential and privileged in society. This situation is at variance with modern conception of rights which points toward equality among all members of society regardless of their social standing. Thus, age, sex, creed, etc do not constitute a barrier to the full realisation of one's potential and demand for justice in society. It is for this reason that the state under the general legal instruments has enacted laws that make it unacceptable to subject anyone to any form of torture in the name of the detects of one's deities. The Criminal Code, (Amendment) Act, 2003 (Act 646), for instance, makes it clear under sections 314 and 315 the unlawfulness of subjecting anyone to trial by ordeal. Belief in the power of the deities to adjudicate in matters will continue to have purchase. As such, regulating the operations of these shrines through training on modern conceptions of rights and dignity is ideal as it will curb the arbitrary imposition of the will of people deities.

CONCLUSION

Postcolonial African society's transition from religion-based societies to constitutionally secular states led to a form of religious, legal and political continuity and disjuncture. This situation is variously discussed in the literature in terms of tradition and modernity, universalism and particularism, the rational and irrational domain, the secular and the religious spheres. Alongside state civil law structures, traditional customary beliefs and usages which are largely underpinned by religion continue to influence the public domain. In spite of the growing influence of secularisation and modernisation in post-independence Ghana, religion continues to be strong in the public sphere. National political actors continue to tap into the power of traditional religious resources to augment their political prospects. *Duabɔ*, a traditional religious mode of justice delivery is a politically powerful channel to deflect accusations and counter-accusations in Ghanaian politics. Again, the political deployment of *duabɔ* provides sufficient explanation for the ways in which religion, politics and justice delivery are complexly interconnected.

The daily realities of the power of the deities in matters of justice delivery lead to the tempting conclusion that religious customary norms are indispensable not as a matter of conviction, but rather necessity. This is particularly so when we take into consideration the fact that the majority of the people are unable to assess the benefits of the state civil justice delivery system.

This chapter, therefore, has paid attention to the scholarly neglect of the role of the spiritual forces in local conflict resolution. Using the Akan traditional society as a reference point, the chapter has shown that in most societies of contemporary Ghana, when it comes to justice delivery, people depend on the political and legal authority of their traditional and religious leaderships whose positions have historically overlapped and competed with the office of national leaders. The chapter has given account of how postcolonial Constitutions and other legislations — themselves a British colonial legacy — while entrenching the traditional modes of justice delivery, have undermined and reified the religious bases of these mechanisms. It has demonstrated that notwithstanding these efforts, among other reasons, the weaknesses inherent in post-independence nation-states of Africa have made traditional justice delivery system which is largely underpinned by the spiritual forces, indispensable legal forum; this is especially the case in areas far removed from the reach of the central government. In demonstrating this, the chapter has presented *duabɔ* as a delicate religious, legal and political phenomenon of interest in contemporary Ghana.

From all that has been said, it is clear that even with the deep moral revulsions and the state legal manipulation to subordinate it, people including high-profile political actors appeal to it (Tweneboah 2014; 2021). Even so, like the state's own civil justice system, the many weaknesses associated with the proceedings and sanctions of the traditional justice delivery system make it a test to legal modernity. Just as the state constantly attempts to better its justice system, the Akan traditional justice delivery system which has demonstrated its dynamism historically must look toward the future and adopt to the changing times.

We have also seen that cultural specificity and tradition cannot be invoked as a justification for abuse. Actors of traditional mode of justice delivery particularly those that appeal to the power of the deities must reach out to state and non-state agents on ways of modifying the system to suit the heterogeneity of the new society and its diverse populations. In a legally plural society such as Ghana, attending to this will project the traditional justice delivery system not as mere supplementary justice delivery but as an equally competitive and standalone option.

It is worth nothing that though a significant tool of dispute mechanism and social control, to the extent that state civil law structures recognize *duabɔ* as relic of the past society, it will remain on the margins of the mainstream legal framework. Again, *duabɔ* in its present form is without any legal documentation or records of the proceedings and outcomes. It is purely verbally expressed in process, informal in deliberations and a collective experience for community members. Even so, its consequence that has become a public issue, of course, cannot be overlooked. They offer an opportunity for debate on issues of religion and law and the crucial function religion plays in justice delivery in the Ghanaian public domain. The chapter notes that state regulation of justice delivery becomes a better option as it helps to side-step acting according to the arbitrary pleasure of one's deity. In this sense, human reason is held as adequate enough to direct human conduct.

REFERENCES

Acquah, G. (1991). Customary Offences and the Courts. *Review of Ghana Law*, *18*, 36–67.

Agyekum, K. (1999). The Pragmatics of Duabɔ "Grievance Imprecation" Taboo among the Akan. *Pragmatics*, *9*(3), 357–382. doi:10.1075/prag.9.3.03agy

Agyekum, K. (2008). Akan Traditional Arbitration: Its Structure and Language. *Journal of Multilingual and Multicultural Development*, *27*(5), 359–374. doi:10.2167/jmmd428.1

Akpabli-Honu, K. (2009). The Legal versus Domestic Treatment of Child Sexual Defilement Cases in Ghana. In S. Tonah (Ed.), Contemporary Social Problems in Ghana (pp. 229-240). Legon: Research and Publication Unit.

Atiemo, A. O. (2012). Punish My Husband but not so Hard: Religion, Customary Values and Conventional Approaches to Human Rights in Ghana. *Religion and Human Rights*, *7*(2), 71–93. doi:10.1163/187103212X650059

Atuguba, R. A., Agyebeng, K., & Dedey, E. (2006). *Access to Justice in Ghana: The Real Issues.* Final Report: Desk Review for Civic Foundation.

BBC. (2020, July 27). *Nanabaa: Ghana community for Kafaba lynch 90-year-old woman who dem accuse of witchcraft.* Retrieved April 11, 2021, from https://www.bbc.com/pidgin/tori-53554465

Brobbey, S. A. (2008). *The Laws of Chieftaincy in Ghana.* Advanced Legal Publications.

Busia, K. A. (1968). *The Position of the Chief in the Modern Political System of Ashanti: A Study of the Influence of Contemporary Social Changes of Ashanti Political Institution.* Frank Cass & Co. Ltd.

Crook, R. C., Asante, K., & Brobbey, V. (2011a). Popular Concepts of Justice and Fairness in Ghana: Testing the Legitimacy of New or Hybrid Forms of State Justice. In P. Albrecht, H. M. Kyed, D. Isser, & E. Harper (Eds.), *Perspectives on Involving Non-State and Customary Actors in Justice and Security Reform.* International Development Law Organization.

Crook, R. C., Asante, K. P., & Brobbey, V. K. (2011b). Popular Concepts of Justice and Hybrid Judicial Institutions in Ghana. *IDS Bulletin, 42*(4), 64–75. doi:10.1111/j.1759-5436.2011.00212.x

Daniels, W. E. (1991). The Development of Customary Law. *Review of Ghana Law, 18*, 68–94.

Diwan, M. A. (2004). Conflict between State Legal Norms and Norms underlying Popular Beliefs: Witchcraft in Africa as a Case Study. *Duke Journal of Comparative & International Law, 14*, 351–387.

Dovlo, E. (2004). Religion and Politics in Africa: The Ghanaian Case. In S. E. Quainoo (Ed.), *Africa Through Ghanaian Lense.* Vesta International Press.

Duodu, S. (2020, July 24). 90-year-old woman accused of witchcraft lynched at Kafaba near Salaga. *Daily Graphic.* Retrieved from https://www.graphic.com.gh/news/general-news/90-year-old-woman-accused-of-witchcraft-lynched-at-kafaba-near-salaga.html

Ellis, A. B. (1887). The Tshi-Speaking Peoples of Gold Coast of West Africa: their Religion, Manners, Customs, Laws, Language, Etc. Anthropological Publications.

Ghanaweb. (2013, September 20). *NPP should have gone to antoa instead of court — Kofi Jumah.* Retrieved April 10, 2021, from https://www.ghanaweb.com/GhanaHomePage/NewsArchive/NPP-should-have-gone-to-antoa-instead-of-court-Kofi-Jumah-286392

Gray, N. (2000). *The Legal History of Witchcraft in Colonial Ghana: Akyem Abuakwa, 1913-1943* (Unpublished doctoral dissertation). Columbia University.

Gray, N. (2001). Witches, Oracles, and Colonial Law: Evolving Anti-Witchcraft Practices in Ghana, 1927-1932. *The International Journal of African Historical Studies, 34*(2), 339–363. doi:10.2307/3097485 PMID:18198526

Hawkins, S. (2002). *Writing and Colonialism in Northern Ghana: The Encounter Between the LoDagaa and "The Wold on Paper," 1892-1991.* University of Toronto Press Inc. doi:10.3138/9781442657564

Maier, D. J. E. (1981). The Dente Oracle, the Bron Confederation, and Asante: Religion and the Politics of Secession. *Journal of African History, 22*(2), 229–243. doi:10.1017/S0021853700019423

Max-Wirth, C. (2016). *Juju and Statecraft: Occult Rumors and Politics in Ghana* (PhD dissertation). Victoria University of Wellington.

Mazrui, A. A. (1986). *The African: A Triple Heritage*. Little, Brown and Company.

Meyer, B. (1998). "Make a Complete Break With the Past": Memory and Post-Colonial Modernity in Ghanaian Pentecostalist Discourse. *Journal of Religion in Africa. Religion en Afrique*, *28*(3), 316–348.

Meyerowitz, E. L. R. (1951). *The Sacred State of the Akan*. Faber and Faber Ltd.

ModernGhana. (2020, June 5). *Offinso South NPP Youth Invoke Curses On Any Executive Who Tries To Disqualify Any Of The Two Aspirants From Contesting The MP*. Retrieved from https://www.modernghana.com/news/1007195/offinso-south-npp-youth-invoke-curses-on-any-execu.html

Nzrenzah, G. (2015). *Modernizing Indigenous Priesthood and Revitalizing Old Shrines: Current Developments on Ghanas Religious Landscape* (Unpublished PhD dissertation). University of Bayreuth.

Oba, A. A. (2008). Juju Oaths in Customary Law Arbitration and their Legal Validity in Nigerian Courts. *Journal of African Law*, *52*(1), 139–158. doi:10.1017/S0021855308000065

Obeng, S. G. (1999). Grammatical Pragmatics: Power in Akan Judicial Discourse. *Pragmatics*, *9*(2), 199–229. doi:10.1075/prag.9.2.01obe

Quashigah, E.K. (1999). Legislating Religious Liberty: The Ghanaian Experience. BYU Law Review, 1999(2), 598-607.

Rattray, R. S. (1929). *Ashanti Law and Constitution*. Clarendon Press.

Tawiah, O. (2020, June 5). *Juaben NPP supporters invoke curses on party executives*. Retrieved from https://www.adomonline.com/juaben-npp-supporters-invoke-curses-on-party-executives-video/

Tweneboah, S. (2014). The Culture of Duabɔ (imprecation), Legal Dysfunction and the Challenge of Human Rights in Ghana. *Human Rights Research Journal*, *9*, 1–10.

Tweneboah, S. (2020). *Religion, Law, Politics and the State in Africa: Applying Legal Pluralism in Ghana*. Routledge.

Tweneboah, S. (2021). *Religion, Law, and Politics in Ghana: Duabɔ (Imprecation) as Spiritual Justice in the Public Sphere*. African Journal of Legal Studies., doi:10.1163/17087384-12340081

Yin, E. T. (2018). *Religion as an Organising Principle in Ankaful Maximum Security Prison, Ghana* (PhD Thesis). University of Cape Coast.

Zurek, K. (2020, June 8). NPP directs suspension of members who invoked curses on leadership. *Daily Graphic*. Retrieved from https://www.graphic.com.gh/news/politics/npp-directs-suspension-of-members-who-invoked-curses-on-leadership.html

KEY TERMS AND DEFINITIONS

Akan Justice Delivery System: A mode of seeking justice in Akan traditional societies that deploys the power of the deities or the spiritual forces. The term is used here to refer to the arbitration that occurs in the traditional setting especially at the chief's or the shrine's courts as, traditionally, these courts call on the spiritual forces as witnesses to their final decisions.

Anti-Witchcraft Shrines: Shrines that flourished in the southern parts of the Gold Coast (independent Ghana) during the 1920s and 1930s. These shrines specialised in cases of witchcraft, promising to offer protection to clientele and also reversing the harmful effects of those already believed to have been bewitched.

Duabɔ: An Akan term for imprecation. It is a traditional justice delivery practice that invokes or appeals to the power of the supernatural forces in settling disputes.

Nananom: This term has a very generic meaning in the Akan Twi language. It is simply used here to refer to both the chiefly actors (Elders) and the deities. When uncapitalised, it is used in reference to the deities.

Piacular Rituals: The rituals performed as part of the mechanism for reversing a curse (imprecation).

Sacred Traditional State: The belief that the old Akan states were marked by sacrality based on the links between the founders of the states who are held as the sacred ancestors and the living members of the state.

Tom Kramo: The name Tom Kramo is a combination of Tom (a small town in the Nkoranza north district of the Bono East region of Ghana) and Kramo (an Akan term for a Muslim). While a traditional deity, the shrine combines elements of both Islamic and the Akan traditional religious rituals and practices.

Chapter 2
Administration of Civil Justice in India:
Ancient and Modern Perspectives

Tarun Arora
Central University of Punjab, Bathinda, India

Neelu Mehra
Guru Gobind Singh Indraprastha University, India

ABSTRACT

Since the Vedic period, India is known for its commitment to justice, democratic values, the rule of law, and the welfare of individuals. The thrust of the chapter is an examination of tools of civil justice in ancient as well as modern texts underlining the bond of 'social contract'. The analysis aims to identify similarities and gaps in the traditional and contemporary aspects of civil justice in India. These findings would enable legal scholars and practitioners to draw from, and to connect, the history of accumulated legal guidance and reasoning to the modern mechanism of justice. The examination of those concepts in the context of contemporary relevance accompanied with the principles of interpretation can maximise the utility of these principles. The discussion may offer important clues for policymakers, community organisations, law-making agencies, and citizens to strengthen their faith in the judicial system, being a blend of aboriginal and modern.

INTRODUCTION

.......in determining a nation's rank in political civilization, no test is more decisive than the degree in which, justice, as defined by the law, is actually realized in its judicial administration (Henry Sidgwick, 1907).

Search for an order is a continuum. It is beyond one's imagination to visualize peace and order in a society without justice (*Shantiparva,* 67). Administration of justice in society is *prima facie* evidence of the

DOI: 10.4018/978-1-7998-7898-8.ch002

quality of governance. Accessibility of justice in political society is indeed the execution of the social contract between the government and the people. An effective and efficient administration of justice guarantees the transformation of society without bloodshed. Fine-tuning legal texts, their interpretation, and redress of grievances of 'the electorate' is a great leveler. Since the Vedic period, India is known for its commitment to justice, democratic values, the rule of law, and the dignity of individuals. Maxmuller pointed out the rich glory of ancient Indian heritage as such:

...If I were asked under what sky the human mind has fully developed some of its choicest gifts, has most deeply pondered on the utmost significant problems of life, and has found solutions of some of them which well deserve the attention even of those who have studied Plato and Kant- I should point to India.

The chapter offers an overview of the basic tenets of civil justice, covering substantive, procedural, and interpretative aspects. It critically evaluates the strengths and values of the traditional Indian judicial system. Inspired by the respect accorded to the principles of natural justice, fairness, and the rule of law on the Indian landscape, the chapter draws an analogy between the sources of law prevailing in two periods- ancient India and modern India. During ancient times, *Shrutis, Smritis,* and *Dharmasutras* were considered significant sources of law and driving the process of justice. In contrast, modern times witnessed the sources of precedents and legislations based on *Volksgeist* (common consciousness) across the world. The significance of principles of international human rights laws and the governments' obligation to ensure access to justice to their respective citizens in post 2nd world war era cannot be undermined.

Nonetheless, the assertion or claim of having designed the Indian judicial system exclusively on the principles of international law warrants a revisit. India has its unparalleled and aboriginal rich legacy on polity, governance, and justice. It is true that in the 21st century, when the whole world has turned itself into a global village, the absolute alienation of international law and municipal law is impractical. Indeed, municipal laws have to be consistent with the ultimate goals and standards set out by international law like peace, prosperity, and progress (as spelt out in the United Nations Charter). Ontological inquiries in history reveal that peace does not mean the absence of war. As observed by Baruch Spinoza, 'it is a virtue of the mind, a disposition for benevolence, confidence, justice' (Bennett, 1984). Thus, the goals of peace, prosperity, and progress can be realized only if the basic human rights of the people (as spelt out in the Universal Declaration of Human Rights) are recognized and enforced effectively to ensure harmonious living. Indian lifestyle has always been supporting the welfare of all as a duty. India is a duty-based society. The similarity between the Universal Declaration of Human Rights and *Vedas* has been eloquently put in words by Justice Rama Jois as under:

Article 1 of UDHR provides - All human beings are born free and equal in dignity and rights. They are endowed with reason and conscience and should act towards one another in a spirit of brotherhood.

RIGVEDA10.191.4 states - Let there be oneness in your resolutions, hearts and minds. Let the strength to live with mutual cooperation be firm in you.

ATHARVAVEDA (Samjnan Sukta) - All have equal rights to articles of food and water. The yoke of the chariot of life is placed equal on the shoulders of all. All should live together in harmony supporting one another like the spokes of a wheel of the chariot connecting its rim and the hub.

It is more a duty-based society where *the right given to an individual is the right to perform the duty.* Ancient Indian literature emphasized more on the concept of duties, as it is evident from *Vishnupuran.* Among the various countries, *Bharat* is regarded as great because this is the land of duty in contradistinction to others, which are lands of enjoyment, i.e. based on rights. *Bhagvad Gita* in Chapter II says, your right is to perform your duty. Let all be happy, let all be free from diseases, let all see auspicious things and let nobody suffer from grief (*Brihadaranyaka Upanishad* 1.4.14). A similar analogy can be drawn from the work of Western jurist Duguit (1859-1928) wherein he propounded that for the peace and happiness of human beings, it is necessary to establish a duty-based society. To quote:

The core of the law lies in duty, which is the means of securing that each one fulfills his part in the furtherance of social solidarity. The only right, which any man can possess, is the right to always do his duty. What are commonly called rights are only incidental to the relations with other people, which arise in the course of performing one's social duty. The reality is thus not the right but the duty.

The forthcoming discussion elaborates the resourcefulness of the ancient judicial system and its synchronization with the current framework of justice and its relevance in modern times.

Driven by a proverb, '*Backward Pull and Forward Push*' of Bodenheimer (1974) in his instrumental work '*Power, Law and Society*', the chapter provides insights into the richness of the past and utilizing its classical contents for the future endeavor in the administration of justice. One of the thrust areas of this chapter is to underline that the aboriginal civil justice mechanism in India pre-dates western colonialism. The forthcoming discussion reveals that the Indian legal system has its deep roots in history. It had a well-established mechanism of substantive law, procedural laws, and principles of interpretation. Sir Henry Maine underscored the significance of the ancient Indian legal system. To quote, '...study of comparative jurisprudence cannot be brought into existence unless the legal lore of ancient India is properly studied'. Accordingly, the objectives of the chapter are:

1. Revisiting the ancient texts defining substantive rights, procedural aspects, and interpretive techniques concerning a few specific aspects of civil justice such as contractual and matrimonial matters.
2. Identification of similarities and analysis of gap in traditional and modern aspects of civil justice in India.
3. Underlining the bond of 'social contract' in ancient as well as modern texts.
4. Contextualizing the contemporary relevance of information in social, cultural, legal, and constitutional contexts.

BACKGROUND

Justice has always been accorded a vital place in Indian polity. According to the *Manu Smriti* (The Laws of Manu):

Dharma (Law) protects those who protect it. Those who destroy Dharma (Law) get destroyed. Therefore, Dharma (Law) should not be destroyed so that we may not be destroyed as a consequence thereof (Manu 8.15).

Justice-social, economic, and political is enshrined as a yardstick of good governance through its Preamble to the Constitution and in ancient Indian scriptures such as *Vedas, Vedangas, Upanishads, Dharmasutras, and Smritis*. The sources of law prevailing in the form of codes, traditions, customs, and usages carried great value in the life of individuals. The traditional framework was quite comprehensive. It covered the concepts of ownership, title, possession, easements, weights and measures, trade and commerce, partnership, crimes, breach of contract, partnership, gift, pledge, sale, mortgage, payment, and recovery of debts, surety under civil laws (*Vyavaharadharma).*

Dharma (Law) constitutes the foundation of all affairs in the world. People respect one who adheres to Dharma (Law). It insulates man against sinful thoughts and actions. Everything in this world is founded on Dharma (Law). It, therefore, is considered the same (Taittiriya Samhita).

The above verse highlights the importance of law as an instrument of social order stipulating the code of conduct. The present work aims to elaborate on historical and contemporary perspectives on civil justice in India. Various *Smritis* such as *Narada, Manu, Yajnavalykya, Vashistha, Prasara, Katyayana, Brishaspati* contain numerous legal principles applied in India. According to *Badarayana*, '*Dharma* which is infallible regarding all that is imperceptible'. It is a valid means of knowing as it is independent ……'. (Ravi Illa, 1998). This is a well-developed framework of interpretation in the form of *Mimansa-Purva Mimamsa* by *Jaimini* was available in ancient times. Later on, *the* works of *Kumarila Bhatta, Sabar, Prabhaka*r indicate the rich literature on *Mimamsa.*

In the context of the above landmark instruments of knowledge, the authors have reviewed various books and articles. We refer to a few here:

M. Rama Jois, (2012) *Legal and Constitutional History of India- Ancient Legal, Judicial and Constitutional System* is a comprehensive treaty for studies in Indology, political science, sociology, law, and public administration. According to Justice Krishna Iyer, this work is the journey into our legal past and constitutional roots. It is most fascinating, rewarding, and eruditely informative. The work is a testament to an ancient yet captivating legal order governed by the highest law of the State (*Rajadharma*). The functions of the state, the composition and role of the judiciary, substantive civil laws (*Vyavaharadharma*), and rules of interpretation (*Mimamsa*) have been elaborated in detail with the support of verses from various sources of law.

F. Max Muller's work (1879), *The Sacred Books of the East,* highlights the ancestral treasures of ancient Indian wisdom. He pointed out that the laws of India in ancient times were so comprehensive and developed that they cover every single activity in a concrete way. Maxmuller has made the best efforts to retain the spirit of Sanskrit texts in simple English. Various verses in *Khandogya Upanishad, Talavakara Upanishad, Aitareya Aranyaka, Kaushitaki Brahmana Upanishad, Vagasaneyi Samhita* Upanishad have been translated to introduce the English speaking world with ancient Indian wisdom.

Manu's Code of Law- A Critical Edition and Translation of the Manava Dharmasastra by Patrick Olivelle (2006) explains the sources, framework, socio-politic circumstances contributing to the emergence of Indian classical literature. It affords valuable insights into Indian jurisprudence for scholars from different backgrounds. The author has translated each chapter of *Manu Smriti* in a simple language and presented notes to the translation.

K. L. Bhatia's (2010) *Concept of Dharma Corpus Juris of Law and Morality- A Comparative Study of Legal Cosmology* discusses the relationship between law and morality with the help of religious texts.

He has tried to explain the relationship between law and morality with the help of indigenous texts and their relevance in contemporary times.

Justice Markandey Katju's (1993) article on *Mimamsa Principles of Interpretation* is an eye-opener in his early days as a judge in Allahabad High Court. It laid the foundation of his championship for the cause of the revival of *Mimamsa* principles of interpretation. The article refers to the various judgments depicting the use of *Anusanga* principle, *Laghava* principle, *Samjansya* principle, *Atidesh* principle, *Vakya* principle. The author expressed his concern over the undue reliance of Indian legal fraternity on Maxwell and Craies's work on Interpretation of Statutes and ignoring *Mimamsa* principles.

In addition to the above, the original as well as translated texts of Manu, *Katyayana, Yajnavalkya, Narada, Parashra, Brihaspati, Dharmasutras* such as *Apastamba, Harita, Gautama, Baudhayana, Vasista* and *Vishnu, Kautilya's Arthashastra, Neetishaktam* have been analyzed as these sources of law introduce the stakeholders with Indian approach to jurisprudence. It exhibits the outstanding contribution of the Hindu jurists in the development of law.

ANCIENT PERSPECTIVES ON CIVIL JUSTICE

According to Indology, the oldest idea of law owes its existence to *Rta* (order or arrangement) in *Rig Veda*. It implies supreme transcendental law or cosmic order that governs the universe and to which everyone, even the creators, owes allegiance. Later, *Dharma* substituted *rta*. *Dharma* signifies a law, and its source was in *Smritis* and other literature. The teachings of *Shantiparva (Mahabharata)* indicate that *Dharma* discloses that even before the existence of the State, in the hoary past, there existed an ideal stateless society where the human rights of every individual were protected by others conforming to *Dharma* (*Shantiparva*, 59-14). This state of affairs appeared like Lockean theory of 'social contract' where the people at first protected themselves by means of ethics (*Dharma*) alone without a king or coercion. But later when they deluded and lost their knowledge of morality, society became a mess (Ram Sharan Sharma, 1987). *Dharma* was further defined as the number of duties under the heads of *Rajadharma* (duties of the King), the *Prajadharma* (duties of the subjects), *Vyavaharadharma* (duties in day-to-day life). Brihaspati distinguished civil law (*Vyavaharadharma*) from criminal law and clarified that civil law deals with the matters arising out of wealth (*arthsamuthani*) and duties towards fellow living beings and state (P.C.Roy, 1890). Indian jurisprudence was very rich in the context of criminal as well as civil laws. However, the state of administration of civil justice in ancient India with special reference to contractual and matrimonial obligations can be discussed under the following heads:

Substantive Law

Civil justice in ancient Indian culture was addressed as *Vyavaharadharma*. It covered different aspects concerning the civil rights of individuals. The etymological meaning of *Vyavaharadharma* implied removing doubt concerning the rights and obligations of parties. This branch of law dealt with the rights and liabilities of parties in legal proceedings (Rama Jois, 2017).

The duty to administer justice in matters concerning *Vyavaharadharma* was imposed on the King:

Daily the King should decide one after another all disputes which fall under the eighteen titles of law according to the principles drawn from local usages and the institutes of sacred law (Manu, 8.3)

Further, the King should decide the suits of men who contend on any of the above 18 titles as per the eternal law (*Manu,* 8.6). The King was authorized to delegate his adjudicatory power to a learned *Brahamana* (*Manu,* 8.9). The judges (*Sabhasads)* should be impartial in performance of their duties and ensure justice (*Manu,* 8.12). It says where justice, wounded by injustice, approaches, and the judges do not extract the dart, adverse effects of failure in performance of their duty would also damage them (Rama Jois, 2012). *Bhishma* cautioned the King in context of protection of the interests of the subjects and administer justice, to quote:

If the king did not exercise the duty of protection, the strong would forcibly appropriate the possessions of the weak......[nobody] would be able to say 'this is mine'... the very idea of property would disappear... all restrictions about marriage and intercourse would cease... agriculture and trade should fall into confusion..... the three Vedas would disappear. Sacrifices would no longer be performed... society itself would cease to exist (Shantiparva, 67).

Here the caution of Bhishma reminds one of the 'state of nature' as visualized by Hobbes (Black, 2016). In lieu of the performance of *Rajadharma,* the king was entitled to raise taxes to enable him to fulfill his responsibility of protecting the people against violence, both from one another and external attack (*Shantiparva* 67; *Neetishaktam* 37). The duty of judges (*Sabhasads)* to provide justice has been considered as the foundation of order in the society in verses 8.14-8.15 as under:

Justice is destroyed by injustice or truth by falsehood; while the judges look on, they shall also be destroyed (Manu, 8.14).

Justice, being violated destroys; Justice, being preserved, preserves: therefore justice must not be violated, lest violated justice destroy us (Manu, 8.15).

Fulfillment of obligation of protection of those who need safety by the King brings him honor. Such a king receives 1/6 of the spiritual earning of the parties as a reward by nature. In case he does not protect his subjects, he gets 1/6 of part of the demerit of deeds of subjects also (*Manu* 8.303- 305). The social order was divided into four *Castes- Brahamin, Kshtriya, Vaishya* and *Sudras.* The concept of Twice Born *(Dvija)* in the Hindu social system was strictly applicable. It implied that the upper three castes were eligible for initiation ceremony *(Upanayana Samskar)* and study, listening or reciting *Vedas*. The people from *Sudras* category were not allowed to read *Vedas*. *Manu Smriti* prohibited even recitation of religious texts in the presence of *Sudras* (4.99). If they were willing to gain merit and they should perform their duty and imitate the practice of virtuous men but without reciting the sacred texts (10.127). If any *Sudra* assumes the distinctive mark of twice-born, he would be corporally punished (9.224). Any upper caste *Brahmin*, if obtain wealth from *Sudras*, he would be censured among others who recite Vedas. Apart from these discriminatory provisions under civil laws, there were several provisions under penal laws providing different sentences to different castes. According to *Brihaspati*, the goal of polity is the fulfillment of *Dharma*, *Artha* and *Kama* (*Brihaspati* 2.43). It was further endorsed by *Kautilya* in his *Arthsastra,* 'The *Trivarga* (*Dharma, Artha and Kama*) should be obeyed together (L.N. Rangarajan, 1987).

Likewise, the duties of the subjects, as referred below in eighteen titles, have been elaborated comprehensively in *Manu Smriti*. These are as under*:*

1. *Rundaana* (Payment of debts) *(Manu,* 8.4*)*
2. *Nikeshepa* (Deposits) *(Manu,* 8.4*)*
3. *Aswamy Vikraya* (Sale without ownership) *(Manu,* 8.4*)*
4. *Sambhuya Samuthana* (Joint undertakings) *(Manu,* 8.4*)*
5. *Dattasyanapakarma* (Resumption of gift) *(Manu,* 8.4*)*
6. *Vetanadana* (Payment of wages) *(Manu,* 8.5*)*
7. *Samvidvyatikrama* (Violation of convention of guilds and corporations) *(Manu,* 8.5*)*
8. *Krayavikrayaanusaya* (Sale and purchase) *(Manu,* 8.5*)*
9. *Swamipala Vivada* (Dispute between master and servant) *(Manu,* 8.5*)*
10. *Simavivada* (Boundary Dispute) *(Manu,* 8.6*)*
11. *Vakparushya* (Defamation) *(Manu,* 8.6*)*
12. *Dandaparushya* (Assault) *(Manu,* 8.6*)*
13. *Steya* (Theft) *(Manu,* 8.6*)*
14. *Sahasa* (Offence by violence) *(Manu,* 8.6*)*
15. *Strisangahana* (Adultery) *(Manu,* 8.6*)*
16. *Stripurndharma* (Duties of husband and wife) *(Manu,* 8.7*)*
17. *Vibhaga* (Partition) *(Manu,* 8.7*)*
18. *Dyutasamahvaya* (Betting and gambling) *(Manu,* 8.7*)*

The enumeration of the above topics in Chapter eight of *Manu Smriti* reveals that most of the civil suits in those days were concerning these eighteen topics. However the discussion in this chapter has been confined only to contractual and matrimonial obligations.

Contractual Obligations

1. **Competence to Enter into a Contract-** An insane or intoxicated person, a cripple, a dependent, an infant, or a very old person or by an unauthorized person cannot enter into a contract (*Manu*, 8.163).
2. **Agreement Contrary to Law-** In no case, an agreement that has been entered into contrary to law or the settled usage has no legal force (*Manu*, 8.164).
3. **Contract without Free Consent is Invalid-** A fraudulent mortgage or sale, a fraudulent gift or acceptance, and any transaction where the fraud is detected shall be null and void (*Manu*, 8.165 & 168). These provisions cover coercion, fraud, mistake, and undue influence.
4. **Debt Incurred by a Wife, Slave, Mother, or Son for Family Necessity-** A debt incurred by wife, slave, mother, or son for family necessity even without the consent of the head of the family is valid and binding on the head even if it was incurred in his absence (*Katyayana,* 545 & 568, *Yajnavalkya, 2-48, Vishnu p.* 45- 37).
5. **Contract against Public Interest** - Any transaction entered into by an enemy of, or opposed to the interest of the nation is invalid (*Mit. On Yajnavalkya,* 2-32).
6. **Liability for Breach of Contract and Forfeiture of Earnest Money**- Where there is a failure to perform a contract even though earnest money has been given by one party, then the king should make the other party (who is in default) pay double (of earnest). The purpose of taking earnest money is to make the party suffer the loss of it when he does not abide by the agreement (*Katyayana,* 541).

7. **Disqualification of Convict to Enter into Contract-** *Kautilya's Arthashastra* provides an additional disqualification, i.e. a convict cannot enter into a contract (L.N. Rangarajan, 1987).

Manu, through verses 47- 125 of Chapter 8, dealt thoroughly with debt, repayment of the debt, duties of the debtors and kinds of witnesses, the procedure to examine the witnesses, the method to extract the truth of witnesses, caste wise oath administration of witnesses, fine and punishment for false statement, disqualification of witnesses, etc. Reminding any dereliction in the performance of the obligation to administer justice, verse 8.127 mentions, 'unjust punishment destroys reputation among men, and fame after death, and causes even in the next world the loss of heaven; let, him therefore, beware of inflicting it'. Further, 8.128 states that a king who punishes those who do not deserve it punishes not those who deserve it brings great infamy on himself and invites nature's wrath.

In the context of property, verse 8.148 of *Manu* recognizes the doctrine of adverse possession in the case where the owner is of sound mind and still does not mind the enjoyment of his property by another, he will be divested of the right to own the property, and the possessor shall retain the property. The civil matters concerning the rate of interest, liabilities of surety, and debtor have been explained (8.150 to 8.162 of *Manu, Yajnavalkya* II-52-53, 56, *Narada* 71,121, *Brihaspati* p. 328-44, *Katyayana* 531-532, 538, 539 and 540)(Rama Jois, 2012).

Law of *Adhi,* meaning thereby law of pledges and mortgages, was very comprehensive. *Adhi* implied the security furnished by a debtor to the creditor by depositing a moveable property or hypothecating or transferring the possession of any immovable property to the creditor for the repayment of the loan. These texts did not make any specific difference between pledges and mortgages. (Rama Jois, 2012) It merely treated the handing over the property- moveable or immovable in possession of the creditor as spelt out in *Narada*, p. 77-139. One important thing worth highlighting here is that there were two kinds of *Adhi* based on the duration of *Kritakala* and *Akritakala*. *Kritkala* meant a pledge for a specified period, and it had to be redeemed within that period. *Akritakala* meant pledge without a time limit, and the property will remain the possession of the creditor till repayment of the loan is made. (*Narada,* 27.124:125*)*. The usufructuary pledge was called *bhogyavadhi* to meet the interest. It was further divided into two categories (i) *sapratyaya bhogyavadhi* and (ii) *apratyaya bhogyavadhi*. The former implied 'the enjoyment of the pledged property not only in lieu of interest but also in lieu of a portion of the principal amount as agreed to. It implied, the entire repayment of the amount with time, and ultimately the creditor had to return the property to the debtor'. *Apratyaya Bhogyavadhi* meant 'the enjoyment of the pledged property only in view of interest, and the property could be returned only after discharge of debt'. *(Katyayana,* 516). The rights and liabilities of the pledger and pledgee, liability for unintentional, negligent, or wrongful use of the property, the duty of the pledgee to use due care and caution, etc., have been comprehensively elaborated. *(Manu, Gautama, Katyayana, Narada, Brihaspati)*

Matrimonial Obligations

1. **Dependence of Male and Female** - This verse places the women in dependence on the males and also imposes an obligation on them to keep themselves under control against sensual enjoyments. (*Manu,* 9.2)
2. **Marriage as a Sacrament**- It was the most critical *rite* to complete the sacrament of marriage. It was considered that the relationship became irrevocable with the performance of the *rite* of seven steps. It started while the bridegroom commencing his clockwise seven circles around the sacred

fire. These seven circles in Hindu tradition were assumed following seven promises by the husband towards wife- first for food, second for strength, third for wealth and prosperity, fourth for comfort, fifth for progeny, sixth for the enjoyment of seasons, seven for being a friend and united. By completing the seventh circle of *Sapatpadi*, the patrilineage of the wife gets transferred to her husband's gotra *(Manu,* 227, *Aswalayana Grihya Sutra,* 1-7-19, *Parasara Grihya Sutra,* 1-8-1*).*

3. **The Obligation of Guarding Females in the Family**- In childhood- father, in youth-husband and old age- sons shall bear the obligation to protect the woman. She has never been considered fit for independence (*Manu,* 9.3). The father, the husband, and the sons have been declared reprehensible if they do not perform their obligations to protect the females (*Manu,* 9.4). Considering the females as sensitive and vulnerable, the *Manu Smriti* provided that they must be guarded against evil inclinations. Abdication of the guardian responsibility will bring sorrow on two families (*Manu,* 9.5- 9.6). Furthermore, the duties of the husband to take due care of the wife during pregnancy, fulfilling her basic needs, preserving the purity of offspring, virtuous conduct have been spelt out (*Manu,* 9.7-9.9).
4. **Prohibition on Use of Force and Obligation to Provide Necessities**- To preserve the woman's dignity, it provided that no man can completely guard women by force. Still, they can be guarded by the employment of collection and expenditure of his wealth, keeping everything clean in religious duties, preparing food, and looking after the household utensils (*Manu* 9.10-9.11).
5. **Duties of the Women**- Certain duties of women towards their family have also been referred such as avoiding drinking liquor, association with wicked people, separation from husband, rambling abroad, sleeping at unseasonable hours, and dwelling in other men's houses, etc. Women must be guarded against such deviant acts. Besides, *Manu Smriti* mentions that the women had a passion for men, through their mutable temper, through their natural heartlessness, they become disloyal towards their husbands, however carefully they may be guarded in this world. Therefore, the man has been given the responsibility to guard the women strenuously in view of the disposition of women. It asserted that women had been allotted their love for bed at the time of creation, their seat, and ornament, impure desires, wrath, dishonesty, malice, and bad conduct. On account of this inherent trait, the women have been absolved of sacramental rites in sacred texts. Law of *Manu* declared them destitute of strength and destitute of the knowledge of Vedic texts, impure- falsehood. Since they are unknown to the sacred texts, they should be made to hear the texts to expiate their sins (*Manu* 9.12-9.19). In the family, the male had more power even being worshipped. Women were generally given a lower position. Although some women theologians took part in philosophic discussions and some queens participated in coronation rituals, ordinarily women were thought to be inferior and subordinate to men (Ram Sharan Sharma, 1982).
6. **Adultery**- A prudent man who knows the Veda and its Angas and desires for long life will never cohabit with another's wife (*Manu,* 9.41).
7. **Prohibitions on the Marriage of Widows**- Sacred texts are silent on the remarriage of widows (*Manu*, 9.65).
8. **Desertion**- A barren wife may be superseded in the eighth year, she whose children die in the tenth, she who bears daughters in the eleventh, but she who is quarrelsome without delay (*Manu*, 9.81).

Judicial Proceedings

Yajnavalykya, Brihaspati, Katayayana, if read together, provide the detailed sequence of judicial proceedings in civil matters. These instruments refer filing of suit or complaint (*Yajnavalakya,* II-5; *Brihaspati,* 290-506), contents and drafting of plaint (*Katayana,* 124-128), acceptance of plaint (*Katayana,*130-131), grounds for rejection of plaint of complaint in *limine* (*Katayana,*136-141, *Kautilya's Arthashastra,* 3.1.21), summoning of defendant to reply (*Katayana* 143, *Kautilya's Arthashastra* 3.1.17,18), amendment of pleadings (*Brihaspati* 292-15, *Kautilya's Arthashastra* 3.1.27-31), grounds of defense available to defendant such as admission (*satyam*), denial (*mithyam*), special plea or counter claim or set off (*pratyavakanadanam*) (*Kautilya's Arthashastra,* 3.1.26), *res judicata* (*purva nyaya*) (*Katayana* 165, *Kautilya's Arthashastra,* 3.1.26), contents of written statement (*Brihaspati,* 290-6), Interim injunction (*Katayana,* 104-105; *Narada,* 1-47; *Narada,* 18.15-54; *Katayana,* 111.1), penalty for misuse or disobedience of restraint (*Narada,* 18.49-51), appearance of defendant (*Katayana,* 100-101), burden of proof (*Narada,* 30.27-31, *Brihaspati* 294.3, *Yajnavalakya,* II.17) grounds for defeat without hearing (*Narada,* 31-33), adjournments (*Brihaspati* 293.5-1), consequence of undue delay by a litigant (*Katayana,* 201), *ex parte* (*Katayana,* 208), furnishing of security (*Yajnavalakya* 2.10), appointment and fee of lawyer (*Niyogi- Sukra,* 2.5, 224-231), free legal aid (*Kautilya's Arthashastra,* 3.20.22), penalty for misconduct by a lawyer (*Sukra,* 4-5, 231), execution of decree (*Manu,* 8.139, *Yajnavalakya,* 2.42, *Kautilya's Arthashastra,* 3.11.39-42).

Principles of Interpretation

All of the above treaties were in cryptic and complicated language. To ensure uniformity and correctness of meaning to be drawn from the texts, principles of interpretation (*Mimamsa*) were developed. The literal meaning of this *Sanskrit* term *Mimamsa* is **hermeneutical inquiry.** It was first used in *Aitareya Aranyaka* in the sense of *'Vicharayanti'*. Later, it was used in *Taittiriya Samhita* to derive the correct meaning of something and draw a certain conclusion from it. In *Chandogyopanishad,* this term was referred to as knowing the truth after considering the pros and cons of the issue about which there is doubt. The scholars of language and grammar developed these principles to apply the law in proper perspectives (Anirvan, 1970). Maharshi *Jaimini* is considered an exponent of *Mimamsasutras,* who complied *with Mimamsasutras*. He introduced other *Acharyas* who preached the skill of drawing out the sense of the text. *Maharishi Vyasa* believed that it would be difficult for future generations to read and understand this knowledge repository. Therefore, he instructed his disciple to compile the principles of interpretation, and *Jaimini* complied with *Mimamsasutras, also* known as *Purva Mimamsa.* According to V.A. Parasurama Sastri, Prof. Jacobi, and Dr. Damodar Visnu, the *Mimamsasutras* were compiled around 500 BC. After that, the schools of *Purva Mimamsa* were developed with *Sabara, Kumarila Bhatta and Prabhakar*. These three are the foremost authorities on *Mimamsa*, and they continue to be the most referred to sources by Judges of the Supreme Court as well as High Courts in India for logical interpretation (explained later). Knowledge of *Shrutis, Smritis* and the principles of *Mimamsa* was considered pre-requisites for the appointment of a judge (*Sabhasad*). Besides, *Mimamsa* scholars were usually inducted into the legislative assembly (Ravi Illa, 1998).

Elementary Principles of Interpretation

1. **The *Sarthakya* Principle**: Every word and sentence must have some meaning and purpose.
2. ***Laghava* Principle**: Where one rule or proposition would suffice, more must not be assumed.
3. **The *Arthaikatva* Principle**: To a word or sentence occurring at the same place, double meaning should not be given. Uniformity in the sense to be given to a word used repeatedly in the same context and same statute.
4. ***Gunapradhan:*** Where a word or sentence which, on the face of it, purports to express a subordinate idea which clashes with the principle idea, the former must be adjusted to the latter or altogether disregarded.
5. ***Samanjasya***: Contradiction between words and sentences is not to be presumed where it is possible to reconcile them.
6. ***Vikalpa:*** Where there is a fundamental contradiction, one of the contradictory matters may be adopted at one's option (A. Beeriedale Keith, 1921).
7. **Rules of Construction**: These rules of construction were as under:
    a. ***Shruti* or Direct Assertion**: When a sentence is complete and explicit in sense and grammar, no attempt should be made to strain or twist its meaning.
    b. ***Linga* or Indicative Power:** Where a word or expression in a provision carries more than one meaning, its meaning has to be ascertained by the context in which it has been used. Indicative power is the power or capacity of a word to denote a certain thing. Not only the text but the context also should be a guide for determining the real meaning of a provision of law. Maxwell in his landmark treaty on Interpretation titled *On the Interpretation of Statutes* (1875) explains that individual words are not considered in isolation but may have their meaning determined by other words in the section in which they occur.
    c. **Syntactical Connection:** *Vakya* or syntactical connection means that where words and sentences are not connected in an explicit or clear manner, these words should be joined grammatically to make a sensible proposition. Presently it is known as the 'rule of purposive construction'. A well-recognized rule of construction that the meaning of words used in a text should be purpose-oriented. According to *Jaimini,* 'So long as single-purpose is served by several words, which on being separated are found to be wanting, they must be treated as one sentence.' All words, phrases, and clauses should be put together to serve a single purpose and should be read conjointly as forming a single sentence.
    d. **Context or *Prakarana:*** It implies that when a sentence or clause makes no complete sense by itself, however clear its meaning and grammatical composition may be, the meaning of such a sentence or clause should be ascertained by reading it with some other passage with which it correlates, having due regard to the context in which such a clause or sentence is used. *Sabara* observed that what is meant by *prakarna* (context). *Prakarna* is the declaration of what is to be accomplished and which needs a procedure.
8. **Order of Preference for Rules of Construction**: As spelt out in *Mimamsa Darshan*, 'Among the several means of ascertaining the true meaning of provisions namely, *Shruti, Linga, Vakya, Prakarna, Sthana and Samkhya*, the one that precedes is more authoritative than the one that follows'.

The order of preference implies that where the *Shruti* rule of construction is not helpful, or the meaning is ambiguous, then the interpreter should have recourse to the rule of *Linga or Lakshanarth.* Suppose the meaning of a provision cannot be ascertained from the first two methods. In such a case, only *the Vakya* principle should be resorted to, i.e., rearranging the sentence to give effect to the real purpose of the rule, without which it would be unworkable. *Prakarna* should be followed only as a last resort.

9. **The Rule for Ascertaining Meaning of Words**: It is like using the word 'shall' and its inference in modern times. It says that if the scriptures indicate the meaning of a word used in a text, then that meaning alone should be given.
10. **The Conflict between Primary Rules and Rules of Procedure**: It implied as whenever there is a conflict between substantive and procedural rules, the former are to be regarded and prevailed.
11. ***Paryudasa* (Proviso or Exception)**: *Paryudasa* is like a proviso or an exception incorporated into a rule in modern statutes. Where the leading clause of a passage contains a general direction for the performance of a certain act, and there is a prohibition of it under certain circumstances, the prohibition is to be taken as a legitimate exception or proviso (Rama Jois, 2012).
12. **Classification of Provisions**: *Jaimini* classified the Vedic texts as under:
    a. Obligatory or mandatory rules:
        i. *Vidhis*- positive commands;
        ii. *Nishedhas*- negative commands.
    b. Non-obligatory:
        i. *Arthaveda*s- non-obligatory rules connected with Vidhis;
        ii. *Namedheyas*- non-obligatory rules which are not connected with any *Vidhis.*
13. **Maxims of Interpretation**:
    a. ***Pathakramanayayaha*:** It implies the order of sequence of various acts required to be performed in the same order in which they are mentioned in the verbal text.
    b. ***Satranyayaha**:* At a *Satra,* if there is some disqualification in one of the masters, there may be a substitute for him.
    c. This principle was equivalent to the modern-day requirement of quorum. There were total 17 numbers of masters. If anyone of the masters became disqualified, the vacancy had to be filled up by a qualified person, as the performance of the function by any number less than the prescribed number was invalid.
    d. ***Dvayo-pranayatinyayaha***: This principle is equal to the present-day doctrine of estoppel under the law of evidence. *Nyayalaya* would not allow a party to take an inconsistent stand. According to *Jaimini* 7.3.19:
    e. The exact text should not be taken as a case of *Paryudasa* and again as *Pratishedha.* According to K.L. Sarkar, an authority on the *Mimansa* Rules of Interpretation applied to Hindu Law, and great importance is attached to this principle by Hindu jurists. However, it lays down a very elementary principle that one should not blow hot and cold at the same time (Markandey Katju, 1993). The maxim is that "a positive and a negative text may be either in conflict with each other or not. If there be reasons to hold that they are in conflict, you must stick to that view and vice-versa. You cannot shift your position at your whims".
    f. ***Darshapurnamasanyanyayaha**:* It is concerned with a performance of a single act by several persons. The acts though separate, should be regarded as 'one act' because they are related to a single purpose and because they are named by a single term.

g. ***Kalanjanyayaha:*** It implies that negative implications for the prohibitory act should be construed accordingly. This rule is applied to interpret *Nishedha Vidhi or Aparadhik Vidhis,* like strict construction of penal statutes in contemporary times.
h. ***Madhyadipikanyayaha:*** Its literal meaning is 'lamp in the centre.' This principle was applied in the interpretation of statutes. It implies that a word could be shown to throw light on the preceding as well as the succeeding clause, just as a light placed on a half partition wall throws light over both the apartments.
i. ***Mandukaplutinyayaha:*** It is meant as 'frog's leap' to convey that sometimes a clause lying between two clauses is skipped over to make a reasonable interpretation of the statute.
j. ***Gobaleevardanyayaha:*** It is meant as 'cattle and bull' maxim to convey that when two adjoining words having an almost similar meaning, are used in a provision out of which one is general, the other is more specific; the subsequent words qualify the former.
k. This rule is analogous to the contemporary maxim of *Ejusdum Generis.*
l. The King should take care of barren women, who have no sons, who have no family, wives who are faithful to their respective husbands, widows, who are afflicted and have none to look after.
m. ***Samanyavisheshanyayaha:*** *Apavadaihi utsarga bodhyante.* General rules are set aside by special ones like in present times, *Generalia specialibus non-derogant-* special provisions exclude general provision.
n. ***Apavadaihi Utsarga Bodhynate:*** General rules are set aside by special ones. Where there are two laws, special will prevail.
o. ***Sandhigdhe Nyayaha Parvartate' iti Nyayaha*:** In case of a doubt arising out of the interpretation, the reason shall come into play.
p. ***Sandhigdhe Vaky Asehsannirnayaha***: It implies that the meaning of an ambiguous expression is to be determined from the context. The whole scheme of legislation must be adhered to reach the right sense.

14. ***Nibandas* or Commentaries and Digests**: The codified form of the *Smritis* and the development of *Mimamsa* afforded scope to jurists to contribute to the development of laws to make these compatible with the needs of a dynamic society. As stated earlier, most of the *Smritis* were in the form of verses and were difficult to understand. Thus, the Smritis laws became accessible, practical, and understandable largely due to accumulated commentaries over centuries of legal reasoning. The main *Nibandhas* known are *Mitakshra* by Vijnaneswara, *Dayabhaga* by Jimutavahana, *Smritichandrika* by Devanna Bhatta, *Vivada Ratnakara* by Chandewara, *Prashara Madhaviya* by Madhavacharya, *Vivada Chintamani* by Vachaspati Mishra, *Vivad Chandra* by Laxmidevi, *Saraswati Vilasa* by Pratapa Rudradeva, *Dayatatve* by Raghunandana, *Vyavahara Nirnaya* by Varadaraja, *Vyavahara Mayukha* by Milakantabhatta, *Viramitordaya* by Mitramisra, *Nirnaya Sindhu* by Makalakara, *Yajnavalakya Dharamsastra* by Apararka, *Dattaka Mimamsa* by Nandapandita, *Dattaka Chandirka* by Kubera and *Dayakarma Sangraha* by Srikrishana Tarkalankar. These landmarks depict that Hindu jurisprudence was well developed, several of the principles propounded remain relevant, and they are still being adopted by the modern legislature.

MODERN PERSPECTIVES ON CIVIL JUSTICE

The administration of civil justice in contemporary India, as compared to ancient India, is completely transformed. For the purpose of better understanding, its framework can be classified into the following three categories-

1. Structural, legal regime – substantive laws and procedural laws;
2. Operational mechanism - principles of statutory interpretation;
3. Institutional mechanism

1. Structural Legal Regime in Modern Times

The civil justice system in India is based on different statutes. There are several statutes conveying the essence of law in codified form. With the advent of codification and progress of democratic functioning, governments worldwide have developed laws in codes, Acts, Ordinances, and Bye-laws for regulating different aspects of individuals' lives. Laws on each aspect of individual life, personal, family, health, occupational, social or public, relation with fellow human beings, nature, animals, use of technology, mobility, etc., have been introduced in the last three centuries in almost all the nations across the globe. India is not an exemption from the tendency of introducing laws in the form of codes. Another landmark feature of governance in modern times is the relationship between international law and domestic laws. The fraternity of nations makes and adopts various laws and resolutions respectively under the aegis of the United Nations. These laws and resolutions set the parameters on which nations have to shape their domestic or national laws. Under the theory of social contract, the individual is the focal point of governance, and the governments have to guarantee their life, liberty, and property. It is expected from civilized nations to integrate the principles of international laws into their national laws and accord respect to universal human rights. So far as the response of the Indian legislature in the post-independence scenario is concerned, it has responded to the call of international fraternity by ingraining the basic principles of human rights jurisprudence laid down in various Conventions and other declarations from time to time. However, a few statutes are sustaining the essence of the ancient laws and legal principles, such as codifying statutes and consolidating statutes dealing with contractual obligations of the parties, i.e., guarantee, agency, bailment, sale of goods and partnership; marriage and related issues concerning divorce, maintenance, adoption, inheritance, pledge, mortgage, debts; property issues like actionable claim, lease, gift, sale, exchange, mortgage, etc. It is important to mention here that these statutes depict progressing trends by extending the ambit of dignity of individuals to all and bringing caste system to end in the eyes of law.

The forthcoming discussion deals with the framework of substantive civil laws:

Law of Contract

The Law of Contract is an expression of broader amplitude. In fact, it consists of two kinds of statutes-Framework Contractual law and Sectoral Contractual Laws. The Indian Contract Act, 1872 is a framework contractual law that provides fundamental principles of contractual obligations and commercial transactions. Sectoral laws represent fragmented and sector-specific activities of individual life- such as consumer protection, bank transactions, employment, immigration, intellectual property, taxation, agency, partnership, company etc. Though the web of these sectoral laws is scattered extensively yet, it is based on a single foundation, i.e. Indian Contract Act, 1872. A precise discussion on distinct features of framework law and cursory reference of the prominent sectoral laws can be made as under:

Indian Contract Act, 1872

It is a framework contractual law applicable in the whole of federal republic of India. By its origin, it is a colonial law. But it's important to highlight that most of the provisions given under this Act are similar as given in *Smritis*. In 2022, it would complete its 150th anniversary. Though it's law of 19th century yet it is satisfying the needs of contemporary generations. The courts have construed the text of the statute by invoking progressive interpretation. It lays down legal norms concerning the capacity to enter into contract, communication of proposal and acceptance, free consent, factors vitiating free consent, void agreements, voidable agreements, agreements without consideration, contingent contracts, performance of obligations, discharge or execution of contract, renovation of contract, validity of agreements in context of public policy, damages in case of breach of obligations, indemnity, guarantee, bailment and agency.

Sectoral Contractual Laws in India

The scope of sectoral contractual laws is quite comprehensive. It covers variety of legislations wherein the direct or indirect instances of application of fundamental principles of the Indian Contract Act, 1872 are available. These Acts are as under:

- The Arbitration and Conciliation Act, 1996 (amended in 2016)
- The Biological Diversity Act, 2002
- The Building and Other Construction Workers Act, 1996
- The Central Goods and Services Tax Act, 2017
- The Companies Act, 2013
- The Competition Act, 2002
- The Consumer Protect Act, 2019
- The Contract Labour (Regulation and Abolition) Act, 1970
- The Copyright Act, 1957
- The Customs Act, 1962
- The General Financial Rules, 2017 (applicable in public procurement laws)
- The Indian Partnership Act, 1932
- The Industrial Disputes Act, 1947
- The Industrial Employment Act, 1946
- The Information Technology Act, 2000
- The Insolvency and Bankruptcy Code, 2016
- The Insurance Regulatory and Development Authority Act, 1999
- The Integrated Goods and Services Tax Act, 2017
- The Legal Services Authority Act, 1987
- The Maintenance and Welfare of Parents and Senior Citizens Act, 2007
- The Patent Act, 1970
- The Payment of Bonus Act, 1964

- The Payment of Gratuity Act, 1972
- The Payment of Wages Act, 1936
- The Sale of Goods Act, 1930
- The Securitization and Reconstruction of Financial Assets and Enforcement of Security Interest Act, 2002
- The Transfer of Property Act, 1882
- The Weight and Measures Act, 1956
- The Workmen Compensation Act, 1923 (amended in 2000)

In relation to matters of civil nature, the above list is not exhaustive. It is just for reference that major laws operative in India has been enumerated. The above Acts are substantive in nature. These specify the rights and duties of the stakeholders. To implement these rights, the procedure has been prescribed in the Code of Civil Procedure, 1908. There are few concepts such as parties to a suit, pleadings- plaint, written statement, amendment of pleadings, *ex parte* proceedings, pauper suit, suit by indigent person, interest, injunction, decree, and free legal aid, etc. which have been dealt with under Code of Civil Procedure, 1908. To administer justice in civil matters, the Code of Civil Procedure equips the courts with discretionary power to render justice in accordance with the law. Further, additional remedies in matters concerning infringement of civil rights are stated in Section 34 of the Specific Relief Act, 1963. The Supreme Court and the High Courts have also been equipped with inherent powers to do justice under the Constitution.

Matrimonial Laws of India

India today is altogether different from India B.C. It has turned into a cosmopolitan nation accommodating people from different ethnic, cultural, religious backgrounds. The establishment of the United Nations after the 2nd world war and the adoption of the Universal Declaration of Human Rights imposed numerous obligations on the member states to guarantee human rights to all humans across the globe. Dignity, equality, and liberty of individuals need to be protected by each state without discrimination based on race, religion, caste or creed, sex, place of birth, etc. India is a sovereign, socialistic, secular, democratic, and republic nation. The Constitution of India envisions a secular state treating all religions equally. Through its Article 44, it lays down that the state shall endeavor to secure a Uniform Civil Code for the citizens throughout the territory of India. Though the purpose of Article 44 is to address the discrimination against vulnerable groups and harmonize diverse cultural groups across the country yet rare efforts have been made in this direction. Only Goa, has the Portuguese Civil Code, 1867 but that does not serve the real purpose of the Uniform Civil Code. It is rather inclining towards legal pluralism and permits different practices for different communities. However, it has not been enacted by the State legislature. It is age-old legislation introduced by the colonial government of Portugal in 1869. At present, marriage laws in India are scattered, and discussion thereon can be made as under:

Hindu Marriage Act, 1955

This Act was enacted in 1955 to amend and codify the law relating to marriage among Hindus. It is applicable to any Hindu person by religion in any form or development, including a *Virashaiva, a Lingayat,* or a Brahmo, *Prarthana,* or *Arya Samaj* follower. According to Section 2(b) of the Act, Hindu includes a person who is Buddhist, Jaina, or Sikh by religion and to any other person domiciled in the territories to which this Act extends who is not a Muslim, Christian, Parsi, or Jew by religion unless it is proved that any such person would not have been governed by the Hindu law or by any custom or usage as part of that law in respect of any of the matters dealt with herein.

In the context of conditions for a valid Hindu marriage, the Act carries forward the concept of prohibition of marriage in a certain relationship as prescribed in Manu and Other *Smritis* like *Sapinda* relation and Prohibited degree of relations. Essential conditions mention that none of the parties to the marriage should have a spouse living at the time of marriage, and they must have attained the age of 21 years for the bridegroom and 18 years for the bride. The parties to the marriage should be capable of giving valid consent (Section 5).

The rite and ceremonies, including *Saptapadi,* have been recognized under Section 7, and registration of Hindu marriage has been made compulsory under Section 8. In view of the change in the social structure and placing individuals at the centre of governance and bearer of rights, the dissolution of marriage has been introduced. Husband and wife, both have been permitted to file a petition for dissolving the marriage by a decree of divorce on the grounds of other party's adultery, cruelty, desertion, conversion or turning incurable of unsound mind or mental disorder, suffering from venereal disease in a communicable form or renouncing the world or not been heard of as being alive for a period of seven years (Section 13). The divorced persons have been allowed to remarry. The District Judge usually decides the petition of divorce. Regarding the place of suing, Section 19 prescribes that the court having jurisdiction over either of the place of marriage, place of stay of the respondent or where the parties to the marriage last resided together or if the wife is petitioner, place of her residence on the date of filing of the petition. The Act itself provides maintenance allowance during and after the proceedings, custody of children, disposal of property, and provisions of appeal.

Law Governing Muslim Marriage in India

Discussion on Muslim marriage law can be made under the following heads:

1. Recognition of Marriage

Under Islam, marriage is considered a civil contract (*Nikahnaama*) between a Muslim man and a woman. There is no special statute on Muslim marriages. The Muslims of India are governed by the Muslim Personal Law (*Shariat*) Application Act, 1937. It covers different aspects concerning marriage, succession, inheritance, and charities among Muslims. The registration of marriage has been made compulsory under the Muslim Marriages Registration Act, 1981. Marriage by a follower of Islam outside religion is void. However, marriage by a Muslim man with a non-Muslim woman is not void but irregular and can be validated by conversion of the woman to Islam or other Abrahamic religions.

2. Dissolution of Marriage

In this regard, there is an Act namely The Dissolution of Muslim Marriages Act, 1939, aimed to consolidate and clarify the provisions of Muslim law relating to suits for dissolution of the marriage by women married under Muslim law and to remove doubts as to the effect of the renunciation of Islam by a married Muslim woman on her marriage tie. It recognizes the right of the woman married under Muslim law to obtain a decree for the dissolution of her marriage on grounds referred under section 2 of the Act.

So far as the custom of giving divorce by pronouncing *Talaq* three times, it has been criminalized recently by passing a law. The Muslim Women (Protection of Rights on Marriage) Act, 2019 declares triple *talaq* a crime. Since it is a matter beyond the purview of civil law, so just cursory reference is supplied.

Laws Concerning Christian Marriages in India

The law relating to marriage and divorce of a person who professes Christian religion in India is available under different legislations. (1) The Indian Christian Marriage Act, 1872, (2) The Indian Divorce Act, 1869 (3) The Special Marriage Act, 1954, (4) The Indian Succession Act.

The Indian Christian Marriage Act, 1872

The Act is applicable to the solemnization of marriage of a person who professes Christianity. Previously this Act applied throughout India except for Cochin, Manipur and Jammu, and Kashmir. However, the 15th Report of Law Commission of India on *Law Relating to Marriage and Divorce Amongst Christians in India* recommended extending the scope of the territorial extent to Cochin and Manipur, etc., as these provinces were merged in the Union of India in 1960. Recently, after the passing of the Jammu and Kashmir Reorganization Act, 2019, the territorial application of this law has been extended to Jammu and Kashmir as well.

The Act laid down certain conditions for a valid marriage. Along with fulfilling the rituals of Christianity concerning marriage, the marriage must be solemnized by the person duly authorized by the state government to perform it. The authorized person issues a marriage certificate, which is recorded with the Registrar of Marriage. The Act provides detailed provisions regarding the solemnization of marriage as to time and place of marriage, eligible age consequences of violation of conditions, issuance of the certificate by the Minister of Religion, a notice of the intended marriage, and its publication before the actual marriage ceremony, registration of marriage, penalties related to false declarations, etc.

The Indian Divorce Act, 1869

The Act provides the framework for the dissolution of marriage solemnized under the Indian Christian Marriage Act, 1872. There are mainly three conditions mentioned under this Act to dissolve the marriage, (1) by mutual divorce, (2) unsoundness of mind or incurability of spouse, (3) availability of three exclusive grounds of rape, sodomy, and bestiality for a wife.

The Indian Succession Act, 1925

The rules of distribution of a person's property die intestate are codified under the Succession Laws in India. The Indian Succession Act, 1925 provides the provisions related to the inheritance laws for all other religions, including Christians. Therefore, the rules for Succession among Christians have been codified under the Indian Succession Act. However, the court also considers certain customary practices that influence the principles of Christian inheritance.

Sikhs Marriage Law

Followers of the Sikh religion are living across the nations and constitute a substantial part of the cultural heritage of modern India. The marriage between the Sikhs is solemnized by the ritual of *Anand Karaj*. The literal meaning of *Anand Karaj* is a 'blissful event' consisting of *Lavans* by the groom, followed by the bride, around the holy *Sri Guru Granth Sahib* in the presence of chanting of the hymns composed by the fourth Guru of Sikhism Shri Guru Ram Das as an essential practice.

Regarding legal recognition of marriages performed through *Anand Karaj*, the British government enacted the legislation titled *Anand* Marriage Act, 1909. The purpose of this was to remove doubts about the validity of the marriage ceremony common among the Sikhs, called *Anand*. Before 2019, it was applicable to the whole of India except the State of Jammu and Kashmir. At present, it is also applicable in the Union Territory of Jammu and Kashmir and the Union Territory of Ladakh. Before 2013, only five sections were validating the *Anand* marriages. An amendment was inserted to add section 6, making registration of *Anand* Marriages compulsory in 2013. This provision empowered the State Governments to make rules for the registration of *Anand* marriages without prejudice to anything contained in the Hindu Marriage Act, 1955. In pursuance of the mandate of Section 6, Haryana was the first state to have framed Haryana *Anand* Marriages Registration Rules, 2014, followed by Punjab *Anand* Marriage Registration Rules, 2016. Since most of the Sikh community has their roots in Punjab, the Punjab Government has passed legislation titled The Punjab Sikh *Anand Karaj* Marriage Act, 2018. It appears as a progressive legislation as apart from validating and registering *Anand* marriages by the Registrar also provides a dispute resolution mechanism in the form of Arbitration Council to entertain matters concerning the dissolution of marriages (Section 6).

The Special Marriage Act, 1954- A Secular Matrimonial Law

The distinct feature of this Act is to recognized inter-caste and inter-religious marriages, unlike other community-based laws. The above-discussed Acts are applicable to the respective communities of Hindu, Muslims, Sikhs, Christian, Parsi, etc. The purpose of the Special Marriage Act, 1954 infuses legitimacy in the solemnization of marriage between two consenting adults irrespective of their faiths, community, or religious background. It is also applicable to all Indian nationals in foreign countries.

Live-in Relationships and LGBTs

With the consistent and vigours approach of the Indian judiciary, the rights of individuals to live in relationships as well as the rights of LGBTs have been recognized. The Supreme Court has stretched the wheel of justice to its wider extent through its liberal judicial approach. (*Payal Sharma* v. *Nari Niketan* 2001, *Ramdev Food Products (P) Ltd.* v. *Arvindbhai Rambhai Patel* 2006; *Madan Mohan Singh* v. *Rajni Kant* 2010; *S. Khushboo* v. *Kanniammal* 2010; *Alok Kumar* v. *State*, 2009. The rights of LGBT have been also recognized under the umbrella of the right to privacy. (*Navtej Singh Johar* v. *Union of India* 2018)

2. Operational Framework: Principles of Statutory Interpretation

For interpretation of statutes, there is nothing as such a code or statute. However, the rules of interpretation of statutes to find out the intention of the legislature applicable in other countries are applicable in India as well. The primary rule of interpretation is known as the Literal rule of interpretation, Mischief rule of construction, Golden rule of interpretation, Rule of beneficial construction, Harmonious construction, Liberal interpretation, Purposive construction, Strict interpretation, and Latin maxims of interpretation are the part of the normal functioning of judicial functioning.

There have been several instances wherein the Indian courts have relied on *Mimamsa* principles of interpretation in the pre-independence and post-independence scenarios to address the difficulties in interpretation. In this regard, the views of Sir John Edge underscored the importance of *Mimamsa* principles of interpretation for the construction of the texts of the sacred books of the Hindu law. He expressed his concern in 1892 on overlooking rules for constructing the sacred texts and law of the Hindus by Judges and English text writers. Referring to the Tagore Law Lectures, 1888, he observed that the *Mimamsa* principles are the rules of the highest authority. Sir John Edge appreciated the pleas raised by Mr. Colebrooke referring *Mimamsa* of *Jaimini*. According to Colebrook, the logic of *Mimamsa* is the logic of the law and the rule of interpretation of civil and religious ordinances. Each case is examined and determined upon general principles, and from the cases decided, the principles may be collected. A well-ordered arrangement of them would constitute the philosophy of law; and this is, in truth, what has been attempted in the *Mimamsa*……Instances of the application of reasoning, as taught in the Mimamsa to the discussion and determination of juridical questions (*Beni Prasad* v. *Hardai Bibi* 1892).

The *Mimamsa* principles of interpretation, as laid down by *Jaimini* in his sutras and as explained by Sabar, Kumarila Bhatta, Prabhakar, Madan Mishra, etc. were regularly used by the renowned Indian jurists like Vijnaneshwar (author of *Mitakshara)*, Jimutvahan (author of *Dayabhag*), Nand Pandit (author of *Dattak Mimansa*) etc. Whenever there was any conflict between two *Smritis*, e.g., *Manu Smriti* and *Yajnavalkya Smriti,* or ambiguity or obscurity in any *Smriti,* these principles were utilized. There are several instances of addressing the inconsistencies and issues concerning the construction of matrimonial laws in the pre-independence era (*Nachiappa Gounden, Minor by his Guardian Nallammal* v. *Rangasami Gounden and Others* 1914; *Meenakshi* v. *Muniandi Pannikkan* 1915; *Subramania Ayyar* v. *Rathnavelu Chetty* 1918*; Yellavajhula Surayya* v. *Yellavajhula Subbamma and Others* 1919*; Muthusami Gurukkal* v. *Meenammal and Others* 1920*; Prdda Rami Reddi* v. *Gangi* 1924*; Narayan Pundlik Valanju* v. *Laxman Daji Sirsekar* 1927*; Madhvarao Raghavendrarao Purandare* v. *Raghavendrarao Sadashiv Rao* 1945). These judgments depict the use of *Mimansa* principles for the construction and interpretation of sacred legal texts.

In post-independence era, the scope of application of *Mimamsa* principles of interpretation have been extended by the Supreme Court and the High Courts from matters of family laws to commercial, contractual issues, land transaction matters (*Sadu Ganaji* v. *Shankerrao Deoraoji* 1955*; Moti* v. *Lachhman* 1959*; R.Muthammal and Another* v. *Sri Subramaniswami Devasthanam, Tiruchendur and Others* 1960*; Bhoodan Yagna Samiti, UP* v. *Braj Kishore* 1988; *Tribhuwannath* v. *DIOS* 1992; *Mahabir Prasad Dwivedi* v. *State of UP and Others* 1992*; Sardar Mohammad Ansar Khan* v. *State of UP* 1993*; Vinay Khare* v. *State of UP* 1992*; Keshavji Ravji and Co.* v. *CI* 1990*; Rajbir Singh Dalal* v. *Chaudhari Devi Lal University & others* 2008*; Gujarat Urja Vikash Nigam Ltd.* v. *Essar Power Ltd.* 2008*; Ganpatrao v. State of Maharashtra* 2017*; Ispat Industries Ltd.* v. *Commissioner of Custom, Mumbai* 2006*; Vijay Narayan Thatte & Others* v. *State of Maharasthra and Others* 2009*; UP State Agro Industrial Corporation Limited* v. *Kisan Upbhokta Parishad and Others* 2007*; M/S Harvel Agua India Private Ltd.* v. *State of HP and Others* 2014*; M/a Malaysian Airlines* v. *Union of India* 2010*; Krishna Kumar* v. *District Collector* 2009*)* Even in taxing matters, the Customs Excise and Service Tax Appellate Tribunal (CESTAT) invoked the *Mimamsa* principles of interpretation in the new millennium (*Mangalore Refinery* *and Petrochemicals Ltd.* v. *Commissioner of Central Excise, Mangalore* 2006; *Jaipur Golden Transport Co. Pvt. Ltd.* v. *Commissioner of C.EX.* 2007*)*.

The recent examples of expanding the scope of *Mimamsa* principles of interpretation are concerning Municipality Building Laws and the distinction between private property and public property (*Ranjana* v. *Corporation of Thrissur* 2019; *Dr. B. Vijayakumar* v. *Dr. B. Vijayakumar* 2020). It would not be an exaggeration to state that Justice Markandey Katju has championed the cause of the revival of *Mimamsa* principles of interpretation through his judgments. During his tenure at the High Court of Allahabad and the Supreme Court of India, most of his judgments underscored the importance of *Mimamsa* principles of interpretation.

3. Institutional Mechanism

India has a well-established and progressive institutional framework to administer justice. It has a three-tier mechanism to administer civil justice, namely the Supreme Court- as a final interpreter and the highest appellate authority, the High Courts and the Civil Courts at the district level. In order to provide speedy justice and expedite legal proceedings, there are various other kinds of Tribunals or Forums exercising judicial and quasi-judicial authority in the adjudication of civil cases such as family courts, labour courts, labour tribunal, three-tier Consumer Disputes Redressal Commissions, election tribunal and so on. Alternative Disputes Resolution through arbitration, conciliation, mediation, negotiation, *Lok Adalats*, etc., is also in existence by virtue of the Arbitration and Conciliation Act, 1996 and the Legal Services Authority Act, 1987.

Furthermore, to ensure access to justice, as spelt out in the preamble to the Constitution of India, different provisions recognize the right to free legal aid. It has been made available under different statutes such as Article 39-A read with Article 21 of the Constitution, Order 33 & Order 34 of the Code of Civil Procedure, 1908 and the Legal Services Authority Act, 1987, etc.

CONCLUSION

On the basis of Bodenheimer's dictum 'backward pull and forward push', the major findings to increase the quality of administrative justice can be presented as under:

1. **Contractual obligations -** Ancient laws of contract were comprehensive and based on unification of moral, ethical, religious and legal principles as expounded by Kautilya in *Trivarga* doctrine. Provisions concerning capacity to enter into a contract, pledge, mortgage, guarantee, repayment of the loan, and interests can be placed in the basket to 'push forward'.

Current Relevance - These provisions have relevance in modern times and can be of great help in improving the quality of justice by adding the constituent of ethical-religious consideration in law. As opined by Fredrick Carl Von Savigny, custom having its roots in the common consciousness is superior to legislation, which is usually considered as imposed by external authority. In the longer run, illumination of stakeholders based on their own culture and consciousness instead of imposed norms by sovereign powers may result in better performance of obligations. *Kautilya* in his *Arthshastra* also expounded the doctrine of *Trivarga*- an ensuring system of values holding good in the social, political, domestic and international planes of human business (Rama Jois, 2017). It may lessen the burden on the courts by bringing about transformation in the conduct of subjects.

2. **Matrimonial Obligations-** The laws in ancient India were more comprehensive and developed than other legal systems. However, the application of the filter of basic tenets of social contract theory reveals that there were many provisions in texts, which marginalize women and push them in sense of fear, oppression and subjugation. Such provisions cannot sustain their normative validity in the present age of human rights jurisprudence. The dignity of the individual is the foremost value to be preserved in governance in the aftermath of the 2nd World War. In the present age, several international conventions are recognizing the rights of women, children, and trans-genders. The major areas of concern in ancient texts are:
    a. Silence on widow's remarriage;
    b. Permanence of bond of marriage;
    c. Principles of heavenly blessings in choosing a partner;
    d. Prohibition on taking the matrimonial matter as a plaint;
    e. Unequal treatment to girl child and advantage to a male child;
    f. Non-release of a wife by husband either by sale or by repudiation;
    g. Being subject to cohabit with brother in law or other *Spinda* of husband in case husband is failed to cohabit for offspring;
    h. Right of husband to remarry in case woman drinks spirituous liquor or is of bad conduct, rebellious, deceased, mischievous, or wasteful;
    i. Non-availability of grounds of separation or divorce to the wife;
    j. Supersession of a barren wife in the 8th year, whose children die in the 10th, who bears only daughters in the 11th, but she who is quarrelsome without delay.

The above provisions portray a very dismal picture from the modern perspective of equality, liberty, and dignity. The women were in subjugation because of their dependence on males for their basic needs. Marriage in those days was considered a sacrament, and the absence of disassociation of marriage depicts oppressing conditions of women. Analysis of the various verses of *Manu, Narada, Vashsitha, Dharmakosha* reveals that the sanctity of the marriage was considered supreme. Narada provided, 'husband and wife should not lodge a plaint against one another, with their relations or with the King, when a quarrel has arisen through jealousy or scorn. *Satripumdharma,* also known as the Code of Conduct (*Achara Samhita*), mentioned that in case of any dispute between husband and wife, it used to be settled by the assembly of either relative or elderly members of the caste. However, Justice *Rama Jois,* while comparing the spirit underlying the provisions concerning matrimonial issues, observed that the difference between legal provisions of *Vashishta* and *Narada* regarding remarriage of widows indicates the progressive nature of laws. If Manu conveyed silence on re-marriage of the widow, *Vashishta* permitted it if no consummation took place and *Narada* allowed in all situations. However, Kautilya Arthashastra 3.15.11-13 mentions that in higher *varnas,* a marriage agreement was allowed to be revoked till *Panigrahana* in ordinary circumstances. But in case of sexual defect such as loss of virginity or impotency discovered after marriage, the marriage could be revoked. In case of *Sudra*s, a marriage agreement could be revoked until consummation. Under no circumstances, marriage could be revoked if the girl has conceived a child by the man (L.N. Rangrajan, *1987*).

Comparing Hindu Marriage Act, 1955 with *Manu Smriti* reveals a few progressive features of this Act endorsing a forward push approach. It provides an alternate relief in divorce proceedings in the form of judicial separation by the court or divorce by mutual consent. Some of the progressive features are:

- Equal right to the women to file a petition for divorce;
- Breaking the barrier of not to approach any forum for any dispute in marriage;
- Recognition of grounds for women to seek a divorce;
- Maintenance pendant lite and permanent alimony;
- Facilitating women to file the petition at the place of her present stay;
- Right to remarry.

Current Relevance- Except *Saptapadi. Spinda* and degree of Prohibited relations and few other features, the ancient Indian laws of matrimonial obligations can be put on the shelves of history as women nowadays are financially independent and bearers of equal rights. Treating them like an object or commodity in a family would deprive them of their equal right to dignity, self-respect, and pursuit of happiness.

3. ***Mimamsa Sutras-*** The discussion with the help of catena of judgments and contribution of legendary judges makes it crystal clear that *Mimamsa* principles of interpretation are basically classical and still carry their 24 caret gold value in resolving difficulties in the interpretation of texts. The application of maxims of *Gunapradhana, Sarthakya, Laghava, Arthaikatva, Samanjasya, Vikalpa, Linga, Vakya, Prakarna, Kalanjanyayaha, Nishedha, Samanyavisheshanyayaha, Apavadaihi Utsarga Bodhynate, Gobaleevardanyayaha* in different cases to derive the correct sense of words used in the statutory language reveals their utility even after 2500 years. In Maxwell's, *Interpretation of statutes*, these maxims have been discussed as Harmonious Construction, Golden Rule of Interpretation, Context should be read as a whole, *Contemporanea Expositio, Generalia Specilibus non-Derogant*, etc. Justice Markandey Katju has consistently expressed his concern on ignorance of the present generation and budding lawyers towards *Mimamsa* principles of interpretation (Markandey Katju, 1993). To quote:

It is deeply regrettable that in our courts of law, lawyers quote Maxwell and Craies, but nobody refers to the Mimansa principles of interpretation. Most lawyers would not have even heard of their existence. Today our so-called educated people are largely ignorant about the great intellectual achievements of our ancestors and the intellectual treasury they have bequeathed us. The Mimansa principles of interpretation are part of that tremendous intellectual treasury. Still, it is distressing to note that apart from the reference to these principles in the judgment of Sir John Edge to these principles in the judgment of Sir John Edge, the then Chief Justice of Allahabad High Court (Beni Prasad v. Hardoi Bibi, 1892) a hundred years ago, there has been almost no utilization of these principles even in our own country. Many of the Mimamsa principles are rational and scientific and can be utilized in the legal field.

Current Relevance- Application of the *Mimamsa* principles of interpretation in pre-independence times even by the English Judges presiding over the Benches in the High Court, in the Privy Council and in post-independence era till 2020 leaves not even an iota of doubt regarding their significance and relevance. An integrated approach based on the amalgamation of *Mimamsa* principles of interpretation and modern tools of statutory interpretation will equip the judges as well as lawyers to draw their analogies and observations more objectively and substantively.

Institutional Framework- The modern mechanism of justice is better than the ancient one. Few issues like understaffing, the pendency of millions of matters in the courts, dilatory tactics, inherent defects in the adversarial system are destructive forces and may dent the people's faith in judiciary. However, the judiciary is equipped with advanced technology and it could sustain the blows of Coronavirus 2019 (COVID-19). Nonetheless, it warrants consistent up-gradation of infrastructural resources and capacity building of judicial officers. The capacity building programmes should also carry out an orientation of judges in which transmutation of *Mimamsa* principles of interpretation in alignment with modern tools of statutory interpretation can produce positive results. Such an exercise, if implemented properly, can groom judicial officers to draw quick analogies.

Recommendations

The upshot of aforesaid discussion is that it is wrong to infer that the modern Indian legal system is based on borrowings exclusively from England. The indigenous legal system of India was spectacular and meticulous in context of the inner morality of law whether civil or criminal and its premise was based on *Trivarga* and harmonious living. The classic nature of *Mimamsa* principles of interpretation is evident through their application even after 2500 years. The discussion reveals the gap only in area of women empowerment, caste-based discriminatory practices, which can be addressed by substituting modern principles of human rights jurisprudence at respective places. Therefore, to optimize the benefit of the rich heritage of the Indological approach to law and justice, it is recommended to synchronize the principles of ancient laws and modern laws for the effective administration of justice. The contribution of legal academics and regulatory agencies such as National Judicial Academies (NJAs), University Grants Commission (UGC), Bar Council of India (BCI), Bar Council of States (SBCs) and statutory bodies of the Higher Educational Institutions (HEIs) can be improved by connecting the legal fraternity to its roots and build their capacity to restore the forgotten treasure of rich heritage. It can be realized by revisiting structure of legal education, orientation of human resources and upgrading the infrastructural support. Here, it will be apt to quote the words of wisdom of Justice S.S. Dhavan (former judge of Allahabad High Court) in *Why Study Indian Jurisprudence at all* (1966):

I consider that the teaching of Indian jurisprudence in our law faculties is essential for the health development of our judicial process...Today a law student in India is virtually ignorant of Indian jurisprudence. He does not know as I did not know- that the Indian juridical system and the Indian judiciary have the oldest pedigree of any existing judicial system in the world, that the 'dharamasthiyam' part of Kautilya's Arthsastra is, in the words of present Chief Justice of India, 'one of the earliest secular codes of law in the world', and the high level at which legal and judicial principles were discussed, the precisions with which statements of law are made and the absolutely secular atmosphere which it breathes throughout give it a place of pride in the history of legal literature. (Rama Jois, 2017)

Taking inspiration from the above words, the authors recommend that the knowledge of *Mimamsa* principles and other aspects of Indological jurisprudence should be revived and disseminated. Especially in the context of the *Mimamsa* principle of interpretation, multipronged efforts at a multi-level with the help of multi-media on a multi-durational basis are required to globalize these principles in the interest of those- in quest of justice.

FUTURE RESEARCH DIRECTION

Efforts have been made only by the judges so far to revive the Indian legal knowledge system through their judgments as well as limited academic endeavors. Hitherto, the majority of the books and reference material in this area has been produced by Sanskrit Scholars. The instances of contribution or discussion on the indigenous legal system by legal academics are rare. Though discussion on *Mitakshara* and *Day-abhagha* by the academic fraternity takes place in curriculum yet there are many other aspects where the legal fraternity can carry out research such as judgments in the ancient times; application of *Mimamsa* principles of interpretation in matters concerning Succession; Adoption; Maintenance; Pious liability; Interest; Taxation; Constitutional Law (*Rajadharma*); Criminal Law; Investigation, Trials and so on. There is adequate scope for legal research in the context of the indigenous legal system or Indological Jurisprudence to connect vestiges of contemporary practices to their historical roots.

Therefore, the research assignments can be undertaken in three-tier phases- short-duration project, mid duration and long duration project at Bachelor, Master and Doctorate level respectively. The findings of such projects may enable the policy makers and law-makers to filter and ingrain the constructive and progressive resources in modern legislations and policy to make justice available.

ACKNOWLEDGMENT

Basically, this work is a tribute to legendary Justice M. Ram A Jois for his illustrious contribution in connecting legal fraternity to Indian Jurisprudence. We express our gratitude towards Prof. Jagbir Singh, Chancellor, Central University of Punjab (IND) for designing the roadmap to explore in the area of Indological perspectives on Jurisprudence. A special mention of Prof. Kuldeep Chand Agnihotri, Advisor, Ministry of Cultural Affairs, Government of India and Prof. Raghavendra Prasad Tiwari, Vice-Chancellor, Central University of Punjab, Bathinda (IND) for encouraging us to contribute to the revival of the ancient Indian legal system.

REFERENCES

Anirvan. (1970). *Veda Mimamsa* (Vol. 3). Sanskrit College.

Basu, B. D. (Ed.). (1923). *The Sacred Books of the Hindus*. Panini Office.

Bennett, J. (1984). *A Study of Spinoza's Ethics*. Hackett Publishing.

Black, A. (2016). *A World History of Ancient Political Thought*. Oxford University Press. doi:10.1093/acprof:oso/9780198790686.001.0001

Bodenheimer, E. (1974) Power, Law and Society: A Study of the Will to Power and the Will to Law. *WASH. U.L.Q.*, 375.

Court for Use of Mimamsa Principles of Interpretation. (2009, Aug. 21). *The Hindu.*

Illa, R. (1998). *The foundation of Indian Ethics: A special reference to Manu Smriti, Jaimini Sutras and Bhagavad Gita* [Unpublished doctoral dissertation]. University of Hyderabad. http://hdl.handle.net/10603/25297

Jois, M. R. (2012). *Legal and Constitutional History of India- Ancient Legal, Judicial and Constitutional System*. Universal Law Publishing Co.

Jois, M. R. (2017). *Uniform Law regulating the Constitution and Organization - Durga Das Basu Memorial Lecture*. WBNUJS.

Katju, M. (1993). The Mimamsa Principles of Interpretation. *Supreme Court Cases, 1*(16).

Keith, A. B. (1921). *The Karma Mimamsa*. Association Press.

Olivelle, P. (2006). *Manu's Code of Law- A Critical Edition and Translation of the Manava Dharamasastra*. Oxford University Press.

Patel, R. (2009). Indian Muslim Women, Politics of Muslim Personal Law and Struggle for Life with Dignity and Justice. *Economic and Political Weekly*, 44.

Rangarajan, L. N. (Ed.). (1987). *KAUTILYA- The Arthashastra*. Penguin Book.

Roy, P. C. (1890). The Mahabarharta of Krishna – Dwaipayana Vyasa, Vol. 2: Translated into English Prose from the Original Sanskrit Text, Sabha Parva and Vana Parva (Part 1). Oriental Publishing Co.

Sarkar, K. L. (1905). *Mimamsa Principles of Interpretation: Tagore Law lectures* (J. M. Katju, Ed.). Modern Law Publications.

Sastri, G. A. (1903). A Collection of Sanskrit Works: Tantarvaritka- A Gloss on Sabara Svami's Commentary on the Mimamsa Sutras by Bhatta Kumarila. Benares Sanskrit Series.

Sharma, R. S. (1983). *Ancient India*. NCERT.

Sidgwick, H. (1907). *The Methods of Ethics*. Macmillan.

Srikrishna, B. N. (2004). Maxwell v. Mimamsa. *Supreme Court Cases*, *6*(49).

Vidyarnava, S. C. (1918). Yajnavalkya Smriti- With The Commentary of Vijanesvara Called THE MITAKSARA and Notes from the Gloss of Balambhata (Book 1). The Panini Office.

Vijayaraghavan, B. (Ed.). (2005). *Taittiriya Samhita*. Sanksritweb.net/ index.html

Yatinder, S. J. (2012). *Farewell speech*. gov.in/artical/FarewellJudgesclubAllahabad.pdf

APPENDIX: ADDITIONAL RESOURCES

Ancient Indian Epics

- Atharvaveda
- Brihadaranyaka Upanishad
- Brihaspati Smriti
- Katyayana Smriti
- Manu Smriti
- Narada Smriti
- Prasara Smriti
- Rigveda
- Taittiriya Samhita
- Vashishta Smriti
- Yajnavalkya Smriti

Acts, Rules and Regulations

- The Arbitration and Conciliation Act, 1996 (amended in 2016)
- The Biological Diversity Act, 2002
- The Building and Other Construction Workers Act, 1996
- The Central Goods and Services Tax Act, 2017
- The Companies Act, 2013
- The Competition Act, 2002
- The Consumer Protection Act, 2019
- The Contract Labour (Regulation and Abolition) Act, 1970
- The Copyright Act, 1957
- The Customs Act, 1962
- The Delhi Anand Marriages Registration Rules, 2018
- The General Financial Rules, 2017 (applicable in public procurement laws)
- The Haryana Anand Marriage Registration Rules, 2014
- The Indian Partnership Act, 1932
- The Industrial Disputes Act, 1947
- The Industrial Employment Act, 1946
- The Information Technology Act, 2000
- The Insolvency and Bankruptcy Code, 2016
- The Insurance Regulatory and Development Authority Act, 1999
- The Integrated Goods and Services Tax Act, 2017
- The Jammu and Kashmir Reorganization Act, 2019 [There are total 106 Central laws listed under Schedule V, which have been made applicable by this Act in the Union Territory of Jammu and Kashmir and the Union Territory of Ladakh.]
- The Legal Services Authority Act, 1987
- The Maintenance and Welfare of Parents and Senior Citizens Act, 2007

- The Patent Act, 1970
- The Payment of Bonus Act, 1964
- The Payment of Gratuity Act, 1972
- The Payment of Wages Act, 1936
- The Punjab Anand Marriages Registration Rules, 2016
- The Punjab Sikh Anand Karaj Marriage Act, 2018.
- The Sale of Goods Act, 1930
- The Securitization and Reconstruction of Financial Assets and Enforcement of Security Interest Act, 2002
- The Transfer of Property Act, 1882
- The Weight and Measures Act, 1956
- The Workmen Compensation Act, 1923 (amended in 2000)

Reports and Declarations

- Law Commission of India (1960), 15th Report, *Law Relating to Marriage and Divorce Amongst Christians in India.* New Delhi
- Universal Declaration of Human Rights, 1948

Cases

- Alok Kumar v. State (2009) 12 SCC 331.
- Badri Prasad v. Director of Consolidation AIR 1978 SC 1557.
- Beni Prasad v. Hardai Bibi (1892) 14 All. 67 FB.
- Bhoodan Yagna Samiti, U.P. v. Braj Kishore (1988) SCC 274.
- Dr. B. Vijayakumar v. Dr. B. Vijayakumar WA No. 478 of 2020, 21 May 2020.
- Ganpatrao v. State of Maharashtra 21 December 2017 (Mah. High Court).
- Gujarat Urja Vikash Nigam Ltd. V. Essar Power Ltd. AIR 2008 SC 1921.
- Ispat Industries Ltd. v. Commissioner of Custom, Mumbai (2006) 12 SCC 583.
- Jaipur Golden Transport Co. Pvt. Ltd. v. Commisioner of C.EX., Surat 3.8.2007 Misc. Order No. M/951-959/2007- CESTAT.
- Keshavji Ravji and Co. v. C.I. (1990) 2 SCC 231.
- M/S Harvel Agua India Private Ltd. v. State of H.P. and Others CWP No. 776/2013 9.7.2014 (H.P. High Court).
- M/s Malaysian Airlines v. Union of India CWP 3269/2004. 9.8.2010 (Bombay High Court) 1.
- Madan Mohan Singh v. Rajni Kant (2010) 9 SCC 209.
- Madhvarao Raghavendrarao Purandare v. Raghavendrarao Sadashiv Rao 31 July 1945.
- Mahabir Prasad Dwivedi v. State of U.P. and Others AIR 1992 All 351.
- Meenakshi v. Muniandi Pannikkan AIR 1915 Mad 63.
- Mohabaat Ali Khan v. Md. Ibrahim Khan AIR 1929 PC 135.
- Moti v. Lachhman 21 October 1959, 167/1954 (Rajasthan High Court).
- Mr. Krishna Kumar v. District Collector 5 June 2009 W.P.(c) No. 8771/09.

- MRP Ltd. v. Commissioner of Central Excise, Mangalore 17 November 2006 Misc. Order No. 623/2006 CESTAT.
- Muthusami Gurukkal v. Meenammal and Others (1920) 38 MLJ 291.
- Nachiappa Gounden, Minor by his Guardian Nallammal v. Rangasami Gounden and Others (1915) 28 MLJ 1.
- Narayan Pundlik Valanju v. Laxman Daji Sirsekar ILR (1927) 51 Bom 784.
- Navtej Singh Johar v. Union of India, 2019.
- Payal Sharma v. Nari Niketan, 2001 SCC Online All 332.
- Prdda Rami Reddi v. Gangi 15 December 1924.
- R.Muthammal and Another v. Sri Subramaniswami Devasthanam, Tiruchendur and Others 14. January 1960.
- Rajbir Singh Dalal v. Chaudhari Devi Lal University & others 6 Aug. 2008. 2008 (9) SCC 284.
- Ramdev Food Products (P.) Ltd. v. Arvindbhai Rambhai Patel, (2006) 8 SCC 726.
- Ranjana v. Corporation of Thrissur, Kerala High Court, 7 August 2019.
- Ratan Chand v. Askar Nawaz Jung 1991 (3) SCC 87.
- S. Khushboo v. Kanniammal (2010) 5 SCC 600.
- Sadu Ganaji v. Shankerrao Deoraoji, ILR (1955) Nag 467.
- Sardar Mohammad Ansar Khan v. State of U.P. CWP No. 3807/1993.
- Subramania Ayyar v. Rathnavelu Chetty ILR (1918) 41 Mad 44 (FB). U.P.
- Tribhuwannath v. D.I.O.S. (Writ Petition 17544/1990 decided on 30.3.1992).
- U.P. State Agro Industrial Corporation Limited v. Kisan Upbhokta Parishad and Others (7 December 2007) 2008 (1) AWC 1 (SC) (207 13 SCC 246.
- Vijay Narayan Thatte & Others v. State of Maharasthra and Others 2009 (3) GLH 221, SC.
- Vinay Khare v. State of U.P. AIR 1992 All 351.
- Yellavajhula Surayya v. Yellavajhula Subbamma and Others 11 April 1919

Chapter 3
The Civil Justice Reform Debate:
An African Perspective

Francis Kofi Korankye-Sakyi
University of Cape Coast, Ghana

ABSTRACT

Civil justice comprises the entire system of the administration of justice in civil matters. One significant discourse concerning the civil justice system in the last three decades is reform. This is due to various controversies around the subject resulting in crises. African approaches to civil justice jurisprudence encompass a variety of theoretical and normative elements that shape the way Africans conceive justice delivery. Over the years of the reform debate, not enough light has been shed on this to explain the existence of such perspective. It is argued that the African position to civil justice in the current reforms debate must not be pinned to just the doctrinal option imbedded in statutes but also be based on methods and procedures nurtured on the soil of Africa that align with the practical needs of the people encompassing social, political, cultural, and religious values. The chapter concludes that the African system of justice delivery is largely mirrored in the Ghanaian experience to justice system in civil jurisprudence.

INTRODUCTION

"Law is not to be regarded simply as the product of lawmakers' decisions and intentions but as embodying fundamental values which gain normative force independently of what is decided, written or intended by lawmakers." Atudiwe P. Atupare (2021)

In the last few decades, civil justice jurisprudence has seen fundamental changes in the world (Genn, 2009). One significant discourse concerning the civil justice system is reforms. According to Kourlis (2016), '[C]ivil justice reform is [finally] a hot topic.' He further describes the situation as a movement (Kourlis, 2016). There is always the thought of different forms of controversy, call it a crisis, surrounding how civil justice is administered in nations around the world (Zuckerman, 1999). The subject of civil justice is embedded with inherent controversy even with its scope and composition. According to Sir Jacobs (1987), the phrase "civil justice" is often used in place of "civil procedure" under the common

DOI: 10.4018/978-1-7998-7898-8.ch003

law of the United Kingdom (UK). Civil justice thus means 'the entire system of the administration of justice in civil matters' (Jacobs, 1987). This gives civil justice a wider scope than it is generally perceived with far-reaching coverage, thus comprising civil procedure law which has not been widely considered (Jacob, ibid). In the wider sense, the expression "civil justice" has three components that include; first, the institutional component; second, the professional component and third, the procedural component (Jacob, ibid). This is supported by the juristic position that considers the attempt to distinguish between substantive and procedural law as artificial and illusory (Gerdy, 2000). In essence those for this theory consider that there is no difference. Admittedly, it is very difficult to distinguish between substantive and procedural law (Gerdy, ibid). This broad dichotomy and coverage of civil law in itself serves as a source of controversy in terms of definition and categorisation. This is so, especially, when procedural law[1] Under most legal juristic jurisprudence is also distinguished from substantive law (Procedural Law vs. Substantive Law, n.d.).[2] In fact, procedural law and substantive law are seen as two separate branches of law (Loggerenberg, 2016).

These controversies reinforce the movement for reforms and the whole debate theory is grounded on this so-called crisis. Aside from the general reasons assigned for the crises including but not limited to the lack of concise definition and scope, cost, delays and predictability of cases of civil nature (Zuckerman, ibid; Yin & Seiwoh, 2021), another constructive ground can be in the jurisdictional values such as cultural, religious and social norms that characterise most African countries affect the administration of justice. On this basis, the appreciation of the civil justice system from the African perspective enriches the reforms discourse on the whole.

One cannot think of any civilised society without structured systems to offer the fora for its citizens to seek redress against abuses, infringements and curtailments of their personal liberties and entitlements. The justification for the civilised redress of disputes is to build peaceful societies and ensure respect for legal and civil rights irrespective of status in society. The forum for seeking civil justice is the court which is structured and clothed with the legal impetus to dispense justice at all times fairly and dispassionately. Every citizen has the right to seek constitutional enforcement of their rights (Lord Diplock, 1981, p. 976). This constitutional access to the enforcements of rights and remedies is the duty of every democratic government to ensure and provide the amenities for it. The jurisprudence on civil justice is a terrain well discovered and discussed by legal jurists and academics such as Sir Jack Jacob, J.A. Jolowicz, Adrian Zuckerman and Jeremy Bentham (Jacobs, 1987; Jolowicz, 2000; Zuckerman, 1999; Callaghan, 1992). I do not intend to do any appreciation of the theories and expositions of these scholars. African approaches to civil justice jurisprudence encompass a variety of theoretical and normative elements that shape the way Africans conceive justice delivery. Over the years of the reform debate, not enough light has been thrown on this to explain the existence of such a perspective. The chapter's objective is to bring to the debate a perspective from Africa that is not characteristic of the centuries' discussions. The discourse in this paper intends to undertake a doctrinal, other than empirical discussion of the effects of social, cultural and religious considerations on the civil justice system and justice delivery in general in Africa, especially in common law traditions such as Ghana. This chapter, therefore examines both the theoretical and experiential issues on civil justice from an African perspective and how that affects efficient justice delivery. In this circumstance, Ghana will be used as a case study for the analysis throughout. I will review primary and secondary literature on the subject matter to make a case for further empirical studies to advance the course of the African perspective to civil justice in the reform debate with a formidable position.

LEGAL TRADITIONS AND THE GHANA LEGAL SYSTEM

Legal tradition is a common concept often used in legal history and comparative law (Duve, 2018). According to Palmer (n.d.), in conceptualising legal traditions, "[T]he treatment of the history of English law has not been handled by distinguishing between the legal tradition and successive legal systems, but rather refers vaguely to a continuing legal system that changed incrementally over time." He argues further that defining successive legal systems within that tradition allows for the degree of change at particular times that restructured major portions of society and styles of governance (Palmer, n.d.).

Legal tradition is defined as

a set of deeply rooted, historically conditioned attitudes about the nature of law, about the role of law in the society and the polity, about the proper organization and operation of the legal system, and about the way law is or should be made, applied, studied, perfected, and taught (Merryman & Pérez-Perdomo, 2007).

To put it in another sense, legal traditions are understood as the historical underpinnings of modern law. Usually, under comparative law, a fundamental distinction is struck between legal systems and legal traditions. It is posited that a legal system consists of the set of legal institutions, procedures, and rules that govern the operation of the criminal justice system as compared to the definition ascribed to the legal tradition above (Merryman, 1985). A legal system must therefore belong to a legal tradition. This classification is done based on certain criteria such as; sources of law, the historical background and evolution of the system, its mode of pedagogy, and its peculiar institutions, including the roles of judges and lawyers.

The most common legal traditions are the common law legal tradition, the civil law legal tradition, the Islamic legal tradition, the socialist legal tradition and the indigenous legal tradition. However, the traditions are usually limited to the four major ones; Common Law, Civil Law, Socialist Law and Islamic Law in most legal comparative literature (Lerch, 2012).

The common law tradition emerged in England during the Middle Ages and was largely applied within British colonies across continents with Africa as a beneficiary or victim. The common law tradition is generally uncodified. This means that there is no comprehensive compilation of legal rules and statutes. While common law does rely on some scattered statutes, which are legislative decisions, it is largely based on precedent, meaning the judicial decisions that have already been made in similar cases. These precedents are maintained over time through the records of the courts as well as historically documented in collections of case law known as yearbooks and reports. The precedents to be applied in the decision of each new case are determined by the presiding judge. As a result, judges have an enormous role in shaping common law jurisprudence. Common law functions as an adversarial system, a contest between two opposing parties before a judge who moderates. The adversary system is the fundamental characteristic feature of the English civil justice system (Jacob, Ibid). As far back as the thirteenth century, it is trite that the adversarial system is well-rooted as the traditional ground for the conduct of civil procedure in England (Pollock and Maitland, n.d. p. 671). A jury of ordinary people without legal training decides on the facts of the case. The judge then determines the merits of the arguments and pronounces judgments.

By contrast, the civil law tradition developed in continental Europe at the same time as the common law and was applied in the colonies of European imperial powers such as Spain and Portugal. Civil law was also adopted in the nineteenth and twentieth centuries by countries formerly possessing distinctive legal traditions, such as Russia and Japan that sought to reform their legal systems in order to gain economic and political power comparable to that of Western European nation-states. Civil law systems draw a sharp distinction between primary and secondary sources. Primary sources are enacted law, custom, and 'general principles of law.' Of these, the main source is the enacted (statutory) law, which predominates in civil law systems. A code in a civil law system consists of general principles, arranged in order of importance. The basic codes are supplemented in increasing numbers by special statutes or codes of limited coverage with which the legal system reacts to new societal problems. Civil law judges resort to 'general principles of law' as guidelines in the interpretation of statutory norms both for the purpose of defining their interrelation and for their application. This is of particular importance when dealing with statutory norms that are rather abstract in their formulation. It is tempting to consider this process to be not very different from the case law jurisprudence of the common law. There is an important difference, however. The common law judge derives the appropriate rule by reliance on precedent and its interpretation and, only lacking precedent, resorts to general principles or policy considerations. The civil law judge is not so restricted but derives the appropriate rule from the structure of the legal system and from the general principles of law that pervade it; nor will the decision in the present case have a necessary effect on later cases. This is not to say that later cases may not reach the same conclusion. It does when decisions consistently reach the same result (Hay, 2015).

There appears to be an unsettled debate regarding which legal system best serves justice. Most countries, particularly in Africa, are aligned to the common law tradition to the civil law tradition for the simple reason that many African countries inherited their legal systems from colonial administrations. And so far, legislative mechanisms for reforming these antiquated systems to suit the African orientation have been very cumbersome and slow (Durojaye, et al., 2018, p. 54). It is also regarded that the common law tradition guarantees the independence of the judiciary, the legislature and the executive arms of government. Nonetheless, for some legal academics, a legal tradition (in this case, the common law system), which places the strict application and interpretation of the law in the hands of appointed officials cannot serve justice. In essence, such a system is only a tool for perpetuating injustice. Beyond the injustice, there is also concern about how the common law system breeds laziness and kills creativity among judges as they are required to follow precedence.

Socialist legal tradition has its historical origin in the Bolshevik revolution which on 7 November 1917 began a new tradition in Russian history, initiating a new international political and economic order known as socialism or communism. Karl Marx was the political theorist who is credited with the key propositions of communism and for that matter socialism in the nineteenth- century. Unlike the common law and civil law traditions, these communist societies which were based on the principles of Marx and Engels advocated that both the state and the legal system should be extinct. The most distinctive features of the Socialist legal tradition are that, first, it is identified with the political-ideological of communism. I must note that communism and socialism in this context are used interchangeably, even though the two concepts are ideologically not identical. Second, one unique feature is the concept of "comrade court" with the jurisdiction over minor disputes including vandalism, breaking of traffic regulations, the use of vulgar language in public, failure to demonstrate against state officials and misconduct in work places. These courts are established in the farms, factories, villages and Unions (Law and Society, 2018). Socialist judges are selected through parliaments and make their stay, removal or sanctions contingent on abiding by the law that supports their selection or appointments. The roots of pre-1917 Russian law could be traced not only to Roman law but also to other continental European countries. However, for the sake of national security, production and education, the state and law continued after the institutionalization of the socialist state. With the disintegration of the Soviet Union and the former Eastern bloc and the radical political, economic and social reforms, only Albania and Cuba can be said to be in this system.

Islamic law (Koranic law) is unique because it is a religious law that is based entirely on the Islamic religion. As such, unlike the other legal systems where the contents of law can be altered to meet the changing needs of society, Islamic theory takes the view that the law of Allah was given to man once and for all and it is for society to adapt itself to the law. It recognises the important role of Islamic jurists. Islamic law reflects the will of Allah rather than that of a law-maker and thus covers all areas of life not simply those that are of interest to the state or society. Islamic law is a basic set of rules that are based on four primary sources: the Koran, the Sunnah (the model written behavior of the Prophet Muhammad), the consensus (ijima) and the rule by analogy (qiyas) as well as a variety of legal interpretations. Sharia law during the existence of the Prophet Mohammed was seen as reformist and sought to limit the system of "blood revenge" which resulted in endless tragedies of retribution and tribal reprisals. The most controversial feature of Sharia law has to do with the criminal law dimension. It is practiced in Tunisia, Mauritania, Iran and Afghanistan. There are a variety of approaches: some apply Islamic in combination with secular law and some other countries apply strict Islamic legal interpretations in all courts. Islamic law generally recognises a role for victims in the justice system. In present times, Koranic law in most Islamic states exists along with modern laws based on the common law. This is achieved by the medium of treaties designed to be applied to foreigners living in Islamic societies and even by means of colonisation led by the western countries (Law and Society, 2018). According to Lippman (2018, 34-35), in recent times, other Islamic states have accepted Western Commercial law to attract and retain foreign direct investment and trade. Despite these developments, Sharia continues to remain highly significant in these Islamic countries.

Ghana, like most African countries, basically follows the Common law tradition, with its legal system viewed as pluralistic. The legal tradition in Ghana is heavily marked by its history. Beginning from the Bond of 1844 under the auspices of Commander Hill (Yin & Seiwoh, 2021), the chiefs were required to submit serious crimes such as murder and robberies to British jurisdiction. This laid the legal foundation for subsequent colonisation of the coastal area. In time, this system of irregular jurisdiction was formalised with the establishment of a Supreme Court on the Gold Coast, in 1853, as part of the West African Settlements. Ten years earlier, the British Settlements Act of 1843, empowered the British Crown to "establish such laws, institutions and ordinances, and to constitute such courts and offices as may be necessary for the peace, order and good government" of the territories concerned. In 1876, the Gold Coast Supreme Court Ordinance (No. 4 of 1876), was passed. Section 14 of the said Ordinance stipulated that: "The Common law, the doctrines of equity, and the statutes of general application which were in force in England … shall be in force within the jurisdiction of the Court." In conformity with the emerging British colonial policy of indirect rule, section 19 of this Act also provided for the application of customary law. The legal pluralism that was recognized under the 1876 Supreme Court Ordinance still persists today. Therefore, article 11 of the 1992 Ghana Constitution states that the laws of Ghana shall comprise the Constitution, enactments by Parliament, subsidiary legislation, the existing law, and the common law (Constitution of Ghana, 1992).

As discussed earlier, there are at least four major legal traditions underpinning various legal systems across jurisdictions which take root from historical narrations. However, the legal position in Ghana has been identified as pluralistic. This encompasses not just the law inherited from the British colonial power, and supplemented by post-independence legislation, with a system of courts to apply that law, but also a body of tradition or customary law applied mainly in the native or local courts.

CRIMINAL JUSTICE SYSTEM VS. CIVIL JUSTICE SYSTEM

A legal system is distinct from a justice system. I have already made some elaborate notes on a legal system in the previous section so that there will be no ambiguity in understanding the nuances of the justice system as I undertake to discuss in this current section. The Justice system itself can also be divided into criminal and civil dimensions. So, under either a common or civil law legal system, the justice system is either criminal or civil in nature. This will take us to discuss the characteristic features of both justice systems. There are always reasons to make distinctions between the criminal justice system and civil justice system as the primary legal divisions under any jurisprudence in justice administration. It is the reason that offences can be criminal or civil depending on their nature and definition under statutes or case law jurisprudence that the administration of justice in each instance may follow the criminal or civil procedure to adjudicate. Under common law jurisdictions, offences are thus classified as criminal or civil within defined descriptive elements.

In the criminal justice system, the onus lies with the victim of the crime to report the violation or abuse to the law enforcement agency, usually the police in Ghana to investigate and/or arrest the accused if it warrants. If sufficient and chargeable evidence is gathered, the police in this case may prefer criminal charges against the accused in a court of competent jurisdiction and allow the defendant as well to defend himself or herself with or without legal representation, depending on the nature of the offence. In a criminal justice, "the crime" which is the act that caused the harm or damage is seen as committed against the state and therefore requires the accused to contend with the apparatus of the state until he or she is proven guilty or otherwise. The burden of proof in criminal trials is "beyond a reasonable doubt" which is much more difficult to achieve than in civil cases where the court relies on the standard "preponderance of evidence" to pronounce judgment. The state attorney prosecuting the case or any other officer of the state doing so acts on behalf of the state and not for an individual citizen; not even for the victim. This takes away the victim from a position of compromise or intimidation by any such social, cultural, political or religious interferences in order to exert the appropriate punishment as deterrence to potential offenders.

Probable penalties for guilty pleas or conviction upon full trial may include but not limited to fines, and forfeitures, probation, community services, restitution and in the worse scenario imprisonment or incarceration. In Ghana for instance, the district courts, the circuit courts, the regional tribunals and the high courts (which have coordinate jurisdictions) have original jurisdiction in criminal cases. The jurisdiction of every court is determined by law, and if jurisdiction is not expressly conferred on a court by a statute, it cannot entertain any matter brought before it (See the case of *Chief Timitimi vs. Amabebe*, 1953).

Criminal trials under the justice system in Ghana are governed by the Criminal Offences Act, 1960 (Act 29) with amendments Acts: 554(1998) and 646 (2003) and the Criminal and Other Offences (Procedure) Act, 1960 (Act 30). Criminal cases are bench tried, except for certain indictable offenses, which may be tried by a judge or jury. As Adjei (2014) sets it out, criminal cases may be tried in Ghana under different modes, vis a vis: (a) bench trial by a professional judge; (b) bench trial by a nonprofessional judge (referred to as a "career magistrate"); (c) a professional judge sitting with two or four non-professional judges; (d) a professional judge with the aid of assessors; (e) three professional judges, and; (f) a professional judge and a seven-member jury.

Under a civil justice system, on the other hand, prosecution for offences is initiated through civil suits at the traditional courts. It must be noted that a civil suit may be brought against a defendant although the same defendant had not faced criminal charges or had been found guilty or not on the same matter with the same facts. The objective of the civil justice system, unlike the criminal counterpart, is to ascertain whether or not the defendant would be liable for the offence accused of committing against the victim but not to achieve a guilty conviction of the defendant. The remedy for liability in these civil matters are compensation (usually money) or restitution for the victims. In terms of representation for the victim at trial, the victim may elect to hire a lawyer or represent himself in order to control all decisions during the trial. In this sense, it the victim who makes the decision to accept which quantum or form of settlement to compensate him or decides to go for full trial for a determination by the court. Civil offences/harms are those that result in derelicts (tortious acts). The burden of proof required of the victim to win in a civil case is to satisfy the "preponderance of evidence" requirement. This demands persuasiveness along with evidence of harm being complained about. This burden is considered far lower than the burden of proof necessary in criminal matters. Unlike criminal cases which are not time-barred, civil matters in almost all legal systems have what is known as "statutes of limitation" that set time limits on how long you have to file a civil suit following the harm you suffered. Like all other statutes, this may differ from jurisdiction to jurisdiction.

For the civil justice system, the general structure of the court system in Ghana for civil matters is hierarchical. The 1992 Constitution of Ghana classifies the courts into two broad categories, namely, the superior Courts and the lower courts. The Superior Courts consist of the High Court, the Court of Appeal and the Supreme Court, whereas the lower courts consist of the District and Circuit courts. (Constitution of Ghana, 1992, articles 130, 137 and 140). The Judicial Committee of the House of Chiefs is also considered as a lower court to settle chieftaincy disputes (Court Acts, 1993, Section 39). The civil jurisdiction of the courts is determined by the nature and value of the claim. The district court in Ghana has original jurisdiction over monetary claims to the sum of 20,000 Ghanaian cedis. The circuit court on the other hand has original jurisdiction in civil matters with claims not exceeding the sum of 50,000 Ghanaian cedis. The High Court is the most powerful court in Ghana on matters of civil proceedings. In terms of the value of any claim, the High Court has unlimited jurisdiction. The law makes provision for divisions only in respect of the High Court in terms of subject matter that comprise of the Commercial Division, Human Rights Division, and Financial Division. The various legislative instruments that guide civil proceedings in Ghana at the respective courts include the Supreme Court Rules 1996 (C.I. 16) as amended, the Court of Appeal Rules 1997 (C. I. 19) as amended, the High Court (Civil Procedure) Rules 2004 (C.I. 47) as amended and the District Court Rules 2009 (C.I. 59) as amended. Civil cases are tried by the bench in Ghana.

WHAT MAKES A CIVIL JUSTICE SYSTEM EFFECTIVE?

Any judicial system that is efficient has the potential to propel economic development by guaranteeing many civil rights expectations such as property rights and contracts enforcements (OECD, 2013). There is always a considerable expectation of all countries willingly ascribing to the dictates of good governance and rule of law. To assess the functioning of a judicial system, the Organisation for Economic Co-operation and Development (OECD) suggests the measure of trial length, accessibility of justice services and the predictability of decisions as key metrics.[3] In this section I shall be guided by these rooted metrics to assess the perception about the African Civil Justice System as to its effectiveness or otherwise, again using Ghana as my focus.

The reasons for civil justice framework and procedure in any legal system is definitely for the peaceful governance of a civilised society; to resolve disputes, prevent crime and violence and ensure law and order. The more vivid construction is how Bayles (1986) states thus: "The justification of a legal system and procedures must be one of lesser evils, that legal resolution of disputes is preferable to blood feuds, rampant crime and violence." Any nation that desires a restful system and assures its citizens of a fair and predictable justice delivery must as well desire to have a formidable civil justice system (Kourlis, ibid).

In outlining the justification for an effective justice system, Couture (2009) contended that: "The first impulse of a rudimentary soul is to do justice by his own hand. Only at the cost of mighty historical efforts has it been possible to supplant in the human soul the idea of self-obtained justice by the idea of justice entrusted to authorities." Notwithstanding, these justifications cannot be realised if the justice system is affected by factors such as unnecessary trial delay, inaccessibility of justice services and the unpredictability of decisions from the judiciary.

Delays in trial constitute one of the deficiencies in the civil trial procedures most African countries including Ghana face. The expression "justice delayed is justice denied"[4] is a trite legal maxim that is no more a mere cliché. In *Anane v Agyemang and Others* (J4/42/2013) [2014] GHASC 126 (26 February 2014), Wood, CJ (as she then was) rightly emphasised that,

[T]he right to fair trial in a timely manner is neither a courtesy nor a favour, but a fundamental right. Protracted delays in the administration of justice, impact negatively not only on those who access the courts, such as the victims of crime, accused persons who are acquitted at the end of their trial, parties in civil proceedings and their privies, lawyers who practice before the courts but indeed the entire justice system.

This succinct enunciation is a fundamental reason for the justification for seeking an effective justice system in any legal system. Delay in the administration of justice does not support an effective civil justice system. An implicit cause for this challenge may be attributed to the common law practice and attitudes of court officers and litigants towards civil matters. It reinforces the paper's assumption that civil law ligations in Africa are influenced by many other factors based on religion, social and cultural considerations. The longer time spent on civil matters, therefore, becomes a disincentive for even complainants to pursue their cases and also affords the society ample time to talk to victims to accede to pleadings for withdrawal and settlements outside the courts. According to an OECD report (2013), most countries in the OECD jurisdictions take an average length of about 240 days to deal with civil matters and in some cases can last more than 7 years. This is even though the majority of courts in OECD countries have electronic forms, websites and electronic registers that aid higher productivity of judges (OECD, 2013). This is not a challenge of the developed countries alone but more pronounced in most African countries as well. Trial delays can also be attributed to the interplay between demand and supply of judicial services (OECD, 2013; Yin & Seiwoh, 2021). This demand and supply justification hinges on certain factors. On the supply side, one can readily agree with factors such as the quantity and quality of financial and human resources devoted to justice; the efficiency of the production process as influenced, the use of techniques for the efficient management of cases, the spread of information and communication technologies (ICT) among judicial structures; the governance structure of the courts including the structure of incentives for judges and judicial staff that affect trial length. On the supply side for judicial services, factors such as the costs of accessing the service and the rules for allocating them among the parties, lawyers' fee regulation and the structure of the profession, the diffusion of mechanisms of Alternative Dispute Resolution (ADR)[5], and the degree of certainty of the law have been cited (OECD, 2013).

Accessibility to justice services is always a problem for most African communities and citizens. In Ghana, the ratio of legal representation/ lawyer to citizen is estimated at approximately 1: 4000 (Sono, 2017). In a "Global Study on Legal Aid" report by the United Nations Development Programme (UNDP) (2016, p. 125), which detailed account on legal aid challenges in countries across the globe, Ghana's profile, like many African states, is faced with problems such as lack of lawyers, acute shortage of lawyers outside urban areas, low pay of lawyers for legal aid work, people not knowing where to find legal assistance and little support among the population for spending public funds to defend accused criminals. In an effective civil justice system, these are of major concern for national discourse and solutions.

Apart from that, the institution and physical presence of the court is very distant from most communities and people who really need their services. The administration of justice, therefore, becomes accessible to those nearby and can afford to transport themselves to and from court destinations in the course of trial and proceedings. Unlike criminal proceedings where the state prosecutes and represents the victim, the civil justice system requires that the victim or complainant come face to face with the accused or defendant throughout the trial. When these scenarios are not properly anticipated in case of briefings by Attorneys and disseminated timeously to the victims, they present challenging and intervening issues/ reasons to the victims to consider withdrawing or accepting alternative settlements outside the court. The key factors in all the considerations to seek remedies outside the court, or withdraw from official courts interventions, are the time and costs involved in the cases. Access to courts and supporting services in civil trials may be a great factor in building an effective civil justice system. Also, of importance is the urge to avoid a break in social connection and communalism after the settlement of the cases. Often, the latter is the case in most African countries and Ghana is not an exception in this theory.

Though judicial precedent (the doctrine of *stare decisis*) and principles of equity are features of the common law legal system in most African countries (Constitution of Ghana, 1992, article 11(e)), it is also trite to observe that in pluralistic countries such Ghana, it is always uncomfortable for victims of civil offence to be sure of outcomes of suits in order to pursue their cases to the end. This is because, in a pluralistic state, there are also statutes and legal texts that offer the judge in civil proceedings options of reasoning in arriving at his decisions (Constitution of Ghana, 1992, article 11). Against the backdrop of allegations of judicial biases and perceived corruption (AfroBarometer Report, 2019), most victims would rather settle for alternative settlements or abandon their cases in totality.

Africa's civil law jurisprudence is not generally robust due to many factors and is often interfaced with human-centered interventions, and that only criminal offences are given punitive consequences as desired to satisfy the various theories of punishment (Altman, 2021; Ellis, 2018; Meyer, 1969). This is to conclude that the effectiveness of the African civil justice system is often brought into question due to the challenges it has with managing the tripod constraints of delay, accessibility and predictability in civil trials.

TO REFORM OR NOT TO REFORM?

I ask this question to underline my argument that a debate must be set within parameters of viable outcomes. Is there, therefore, any need for the debate on whether or not civil justice jurisprudence in Africa is significantly different from other regions of the globe? If it is, is there any need for reforms?

My answer is not a straight forward one. The first answer will be based on the assumption that the theory and practice of law is patently different as practiced under different forms of governments in Africa. If this assumption is true as I do agree, then there is the natural conclusion that civil justice is efficiently relative in African countries. The second question which is most likely to have a direct response is that, are all African countries under the same legal system? Obviously, no. Like all other countries in other parts of the globe, there is no one single legal tradition or system affecting all jurisdictions. I make the reasonable conclusion that, as long as different legal systems come to play and different governments influence the legal and judicial arrangements differently in Africa, the variation in the form and substance of civil justice lend it to a debatable principle. Debatable because on the parameters of good or bad, efficient or otherwise, well-functioning or not, one can take a position to make alternate proposition for policy and legal consideration.

The demand for reform in the civil justice system has been intensified than any other time in history (Stiefel & Maxeiner, 1994). The current wave for restructuring the civil justice system is well settled and indeed needed more than ever before. For many decades now, the debate to reform the civil justice system has been reasoned on long delays and associated costs borne by parties or litigants (Kakalik et al., 1996). The consequence is therefore the denial of justice to the poor and vulnerable. Many of these affected litigants therefore see the resort to court for case settlement as burdensome and would vie for alternative means for quicker compensation rather than to see their accused punished. The clarion debate on reforms emanates from such reasons and has often received attention from lawmakers, litigators, civil society organisations (CSOs) and the officers of the courts. It rather also serves these judicial and civil actors well to have efficient civil justice administration so much as the litigants in such conditions of civil suits. In many countries, including the US, there have been attacks on the civil justice system to conform to trends and dynamics of societies and the forms of offences permeating and being ranked every day (Stiefel & Maxeiner, 1994). In the US, the view is that the current movement for civil justice reforms has reached an unprecedented level (Stiefel & Maxeiner, ibid). There has also been the argument to focus the debate around three interrelated elements of change which comprises changes in rules at the level of enabling legislations (Quayle, 1992, p. 559), proper case and court management and culture changes with the officers of the bench and the bar (Kourlis, ibid, p. 498). Reforms in the justice system are needed to promote constitutionalism, uphold and strengthen the rule of law.

There has already been literature that identified some challenges with the African legal development; which challenges can be identified with several jurisdictions as mentioned in the discussions before. In the Ghanaian sense, some of the challenges include but are not limited to; poor coordination among the different actors in the legal sector, delays in case management and hearing, unavailability of legal aid services for the vulnerable to access justice and overcrowded prisons (Appiagyei-Atua, 2007).

THE AFRICAN PERSPECTIVE ON CIVIL JUSTICE: THE CASE OF GHANA

In Africa, access to justice is considered a mechanism for the enforcement of the right to development (Durojaye, et al., 2018). In this regard development is considered a justiciable right under the African Charter on Human and Peoples' Rights (African Charter, 1981/1986). In fact, under international law, it is only the African Charter (1981/1986) that explicitly recognises the right to development and provides a mechanism for seeking redress in the courts (Sengupta, 2004). This confirms that African development with respect to civil justice jurisprudence is in tune, especially based on human rights as against the notion of skeptics. To elaborate more on this, the African Charter (1981/1986) envisioned that all African citizens have the right to constant improvement and well-being and anticipated the full achievement of globally recognised human rights in concurrent expectation of sustainable development. Sir Jacobs (ibid) theorised that "civil justice should not be seen as the private preserve of lawyers only, although of course they have the technical and specialized knowledge and expertise of the operation of the civil legal process. Like truth, civil justice has many facets—cultural, historical, moral, social, economic, [and] administrative as well as legal and others besides." The system of civil justice should therefore be the explicit and enduring concern-a concern to make it progressive and improved to provide effectiveness to the system.

The African is thought to be highly religious (Yin, 2018; 2020; 2021), ideologically social and culturally thorough. The remedy to civil offence against an African is naturally to expect a remorseful plea from the accused. If a plea for mercy is done without hesitation, and with reasonably remorseful body language, it is quite certain that the victim will forgive the culprit or the victim's neighbours (relatives and friends) will impress on him to forgive anyway. If the victim insists not to forgive the alleged offender, the victim will either have another opportunity to forgive or would rather be a victim of rejection, rather than being the one to be empathised with. In the worse situation, elders of the community may intervene depending on the case and circumstances. On the side of the victim, he may have the option to seek redress at the Chiefly or Traditional court or make a report to a respectable elder person to reprimand the culprit or in worse situations (especially when the culprit denies the offence) invoke deities and curses on the 'unknown culprit". According to Tweneboah (n. d.), this "duabɔ" (imprecation) is an African mode of resolving disputes and seeking justice. This has lately been influenced by the adulteration of foreign religious norms and western legal system (Tweneboah, n.d.). All these phases and mechanisms are part of the traditional dispute resolution mechanisms prevalent with the African understanding of justice delivery and cherished as such. According to Muigua & Francis (2015), traditional dispute resolution mechanisms comprise all the conflict management procedures that African societies employ from time past and bequeathed from one generation to the other. But according to Karuiki (2014), the African legal system is bifurcated with both formal and informal systems. In essence traditional African practices form important part of the pluralistic nature of the African civil justice system. Its end is towards restorative justice, rather than retributive justice (Karuiki, 2014, p.202). This means its reconciliatory in nature and builds the networks and peace of the communities. This calls for any discussion on the African legal system to be consistent with this peculiar feature in order to bring it under perspective.

The African civil justice practice is largely oral in nature, and lacking codification. This is a socio-cultural practice that has permeated the African customary judicial orientation up till this time. Another perspective also stems from the notion that the African is emphatic and naturally non-litigant. The same attitude that welcomed the alien from the West to invade the African shores, captured its territories and colonised it brutally. It is the "*fa ma Nyame*" (to wit, give it to God) attitude of the African exemplified in the Akan people of Ghana. The new dimension to the African perspective is underpinned by the experiences of how the citizens have perceived and carried out their litigations in the face of the law and custom. I have been a witness to most cases of civil law matters for many years as a civil servant, community leader, teacher, politician and legal academic. I have over these periods witnessed in person and as a mediator, how civil offences were settled or allowed into the law courts. In all cases, the social and cultural considerations were implored to take pre-imminence over the satisfaction of remedies one could get. In most cases, victims or plaintiffs received or are convinced to receive compensations not as restitution but as an evidence of giving up on the matter voluntarily. I understand this rationale underpins the crusade and reasoning behind alternative dispute resolution mechanisms. I argue that, it is therefore not for want of legal precincts that discourages the African from staying away from civil suits or judicial remedies but it is because the socio-cultural and religious tendencies play a defining role for the African in such instances. Because people live in close proximity to each other in villages and towns, the pursuit of social harmony is highly preferred over adversarial (winner-loser) outcomes of cases.

On the other hand, it must be stated unequivocally that the traditional courts are created to dispense justice and justice is always at the bosom of the courts in Ghana. The final judicial decisions in any matter, criminal or civil, lie with the courts at various levels (Constitution, 1992, article 125(3)). In a dispute, a party may opt for a forum appropriate to adjudicate the matter under criminal or civil procedure. When a party to a matter opts for a civil court to sue to attract compensation (in derelict), then the plaintiff is opting for civil justice. The suit for the plaintiff intends to seek compensation and not for the physical incarceration of the culprit. The court therefore with its officers is responsible for ensuring civil justice. The alternative is to go to the police to make a criminal case to seek justice if he wants a criminal penalty against the accused (Centre for Justice Democracy, n. d.). A person seeking civil justice has a direct forum in the court and not the police in the first place. Perhaps part of the complication has to do also with the lack of a clear distinction between civil and criminal courts in Ghana. Judges attend to both civil and criminal cases as assigned.

It has been argued that the civil court's jurisprudence has been in disarray over the last decades mainly because the reason for civil justice itself is being downplayed on the back of many factors (Genn, 2009, p.2). This is despite the fact that civil justice is a beacon for social cohesion and the security of a sustainable economic environment (Genn, ibid). The cost associated with the adversarial common law system in litigations makes civil law alternative a reasonable option to mitigating losses in the conflict. Though the court in civil law matters is practically different from the same court constituted for criminal law matters, the mere association of the court with civil matters even makes it abhorring to the ordinary African citizen. He is not only thinking about the cost, but also the stigma, the break-in social connections and the tag of being litigious. These values set the perspective for the African on civil justice apart from other people of the globe. The African position to civil justice in the current reforms debate must not be pinned to just the doctrinal option imbedded in statutes but I vehemently support the view that it must be based on methods and procedures nurtured on the soil of Africa that align with the practical needs of the people encompassing social, political, cultural and religious values. In this direction, we are assured of a justice system capable of prevailing in any form of political, social and constitutional crises and have the capability to withstand any critical fundamental reforms in the future.

CONCLUSION

From the discussion in this chapter, it is clear that the formalistic Western-system of civil justice jurisprudence under either civil or common law legal system is regarded as cumbersome and unappealing to the African citizen and the marginalised in particular. It is found that the procedure in civil litigations sometimes becomes intimidating to the ordinary African and therefore discourages him from seeking justice as it would be preferred (Stevens, 2000). Delays in civil justice delivery in many African jurisdictions can also be attributed to the antiquated colonial systems that unnecessarily prolong the adjudication of simple civil cases.

The African system of justice delivery is mirrored in the Ghanaian experience in civil jurisprudence. The World Justice Project Rule of Law report (2016) describes civil justice as that which "[M]easures whether ordinary people can resolve their grievances peacefully and effectively through the civil justice system. The delivery of effective civil justice requires that the system be accessible and affordable free of discrimination, free of corruption and without improper influence by public officials. The delivery of effective civil justice also necessitates that court proceedings are conducted in a timely manner and not subject to unreasonable delays, and that orders are enforced. Finally, recognising the value of ADRs, this factor also measures the accessibility, impartiality, and efficiency of mediation and arbitration systems that enable parties to resolve civil disputes." It is to this end that this chapter concludes that, the debate for civil justice reforms must be culturally, socially, and religiously centred, and for Africa, the debate must focus on how to build Africa's jurisprudence around its unique social, cultural and religious values which encourages alternative dispute resolution and improving existing mechanisms. The fundamental merit of ADR is that it allows parties to avoid the time and cost involved in traditional court proceedings (Quayle, ibid). In a nutshell, the effect of every justice system-criminal or civil is to promote constitutionalism and rule of law, and reforms are needed to uphold and strengthen the fundamental principal values that knit society together and not to break it. As opined in my introduction, since this study is a doctrinal exercise, it will be worthwhile for future empirical studies to ascertain the fundamental assumptions put across in this chapter.

REFERENCES

Adjei, D. D. (2014). *Ghana's jury system on trial thesis* (Master's thesis). Duke University, School of law.

African Charter on Human and Peoples' Rights (1981/1986).

AfroBarometer Report. (2019). Ghanaians cite high cost, bias, and long delays as barriers to using formal justice system. In *AD347: Ghanaians cite high cost, bias, and long delays as barriers to using formal justice system*. AfroBarometer.

Altman, M. C. (2021). *A theory of legal punishment deterrence, retribution, and the aims of the state*. Routledge. doi:10.4324/9781003143352

Appiagyei-Atua, K. (2007). Ghana-Justice sector and rule of law. *Open Society Initiative for West Africa*, 3.

Atupare, P. A. (2021). A fundamental law of reason and the constitutional law of elections in Africa. *Journal of Comparative Law in Africa*, *8*(1), 1–41. doi:10.47348/JCLA/v8/i1a1

Bayles, M. (1986). Principles for legal procedure. *Law and Philosophy*, *5*(1), 33–57. doi:10.1007/BF00143011

Callaghan, A. (1992). Utilitarianism and distributive justice: Jeremy Bentham and the civil law. *History of European Ideas*, *14*(5), 739–742. doi:10.1016/0191-6599(92)90011-Z

Centre for Justice Democracy. (n.d.). Retrieved from https://centerjd.org/content/what-does-%E2%80%9Ccivil-justice%E2%80%9D-mean-0 on 14/06/2021

Couture, E. J. (1950). The nature of the judicial process. *Tulane Law Review*, *25*(1), 28.

Crook, R. C. (2012). Alternative dispute resolution and the Magistrate's Courts in Ghana: A case of practical hybridity. *Africa Power and Politics Programme working Paper*, 25.

Diplock, L. (1981). Bremer Vulkan Schiffbau and Maschinenfabrik v South India Shipping Corp, AC 909, HL, 976.

Durojaye, E. (2018). Access to justice as a mechanism for the enforcement of the right to development in Africa. In C. C. Ngang, S. D. Kamga, & V. Gumede (Eds.), *Perspective on the right to development* (pp. 47–69). PULP.

Duve, T. (2018). Legal traditions: A dialogue between comparative law and comparative legal history. *Journal of Comparative Legal History*, *6*(1), 15–3. doi:10.1080/2049677X.2018.1469271

Ellis, A. (2014). Theories of Punishment. In G. Bruinsma & D. Weisburd (Eds.), *Encyclopedia of Criminology and Criminal Justice*. Springer. doi:10.1007/978-1-4614-5690-2_512

Genn, H. (2009). *Judging Civil Justice*. Cambridge University Press. doi:10.1017/CBO9781139192378

Gerdy, K. B. (2000). What is the difference between substantive and procedural law? And how do I research procedure? Perspectives. *Teaching Legal Research and Writing*, 9.

Glendon. (1982). *Comparative legal traditions in a nutshell*. OJP Publications.

Hay, P. (2015). *International encyclopedia of the social & behavioral sciences*. Academic Press.

Introduction to Law. (n.d.). *Substantive law and procedural or adjective law*. Retrieved from https://nios.ac.in/media/documents/SrSec338New/338_Introduction_To_Law_Eng/338_Introduction_To_Law_Eng_L11.pdf on 19/06/2021.

Jacob, J. (1987). *The fabric of English civil justice. The Hamlyn Lectures 38th Series*. Stevens & Sons.

Jolowicz, J. (2000). *Contents on civil procedure: Cambridge studies in international and comparative law*. Cambridge University Press. doi:10.1017/CBO9780511549540

Kakalik, J. S. (1996). *Implementation of the civil justice reform act in pilot and comparison districts*. The Institute for Civil Justice.

Karuiki, F. (2014). Applicability of traditional dispute resolution mechanisms in criminal cases in Kenya; Case study of *Republic v Mohamed Abdow Mohamed. Alternative Dispute Resolution Journal, 2*, 202.

Kourlis, R. L. (2016). Civil Justice Reform: A movement. *Idaho Law Review*, *52*, 497.

Law and Society. (2018). *An introduction to law and society*. SAGE publications, Inc.

Lerch, A. (2012). *Four legal tradition*. Retrieved from https://prezi.com/n6ez55kn9cqo/four-legal on 9/06/2021.traditions/?frame=e3b4ee4f051e99ba112094a9dc693eb7d3ba07f9 on 20/06/2021

Lippman, M. (2018). *Contemporary criminal law: Concepts, cases, and controversies*. SAGE Publications, Inc.

Loggerenberg, D. V. (2016). Civil justice in South Africa. *BRICS Law Journal*, *3*(4).

Merryman, J. H., & Pérez-Perdomo, R. (2007). *The civil law tradition: An introduction to the legal systems of Western Europe and Latin America*. Stanford University Press.

Meyer, J. (1968). Reflections on some theories of punishment. *The Journal of Criminal Law, Criminology, and Police Science*, *59*(4), 595. doi:10.2307/1141839

Muhayu-Deen, I. (2019). *Cutting short the ambition of students who wish to become lawyers in order to preserve the prestige of the legal profession*. Retrieved from https://www.ghanaweb.com/GhanaHomePage/features/Cutting-short-the-ambition-of-students-who-wish-to-become-lawyers-in-order-to-preserve-the-prestige-of-the-legal-profession-787046 on 22/6/2021

Muigua, K. & Francis, K. (2015). Alternative dispute resolution: Access to justice and development in Kenya. *Strathmore Law Journal, 1*(1).

OECD. (2013). *What makes civil justice effective?* OECD Economics Department Policy Notes. No. 18.

Palmer, R. C. (n.d.). *Conceptualization.* Retrieved from http://aalt.law.uh.edu/Conceptualization/Conceptualization.html

Pollock, F., & Maitland, F. W. (2010). The history of English law. Academic Press.

Quayle, D. (1992). Civil justice reform. *The American University Law Review*, 41.

Sengupta, A. (2004). The human right to development. *Oxford Development Studies*, I86.

Sono, A. A. (2017). *A Comparative Study of Legal Aid Institutions in their Pursuit of Social Justice in Ghana* (Thesis). University of Ghana.

Stevens, J. (2000). *Access to justice in sub-Saharan Africa: The role of traditional and informal justice systems*. Academic Press.

Stiefel, E.C., & Maxeiner, J. R. (n.d.). *Civil justice reform in the United States: Opportunity for learning from 'civilized' European procedure instead of continued isolation?* Academic Press.

Tweneboah, E. (n.d.). The Culture of Duabɔ (Imprecation), Legal Dysfunction and the Challenge of Human Rights Development in Ghana. In *The Culture of Duabɔ (Imprecation), Legal Dysfunction and the Challenge of Human Rights Development in Ghana*. Academia.edu.

United Nations. (2016). *Global study on legal aid: Country profiles*. Author.

World Justice Project. (2016). *Civil Justice*. Retrieved from http://worldjusticeproject.org/factors/effective-civil-justice on 16/06/2021

Yin, E. T. (2018). *Religion as an Organising Principle in Ankaful Maximum Security Prison, Ghana* (PhD Thesis). University of Cape Coast.

Yin, E. T. (2020). Religion, rehabilitation and reintegration of inmates into mainstream society. In A. Balloni & R. Sette (Eds.), *Handbook of Research on Trends and Issues in Crime Prevention, Rehabilitation, and Victim Support* (pp. 398–414). IGI Global. doi:10.4018/978-1-7998-1286-9.ch023

Yin, E. T., Atupare, P. A., Kofie, N., Owusu, L. P., & Botchway, T. P. (2021). Rights and belief in maintaining prison social order. UCC Faculty of Law Journal, 1(1), 1-16.

Yin, E. T., & Beamie, M. S. (2021). Costs and delays in accessing justice: A comparative analysis of Ghana and Sierra Leone. In Advancing Civil Justice Reform and Conflict Resolution in Africa and Asia: Comparative Analyses and Case Studies. New York: IGI Global.

Yin, E. T., & Black, J. M. (2014). The legal anthropology of marriage in Ghana: Presenting power dynamics through legal arenas. *International Journal of Current Research*, *6*(12), 10696–10704.

Zuckerman, A. (1999). *Civil justice in crises: comparative perspective of civil procedure*. Oxford University Press. doi:10.1093/acprof:oso/9780198298335.001.0001

ENDNOTES

1 Procedural law consists of the set of rules that govern the proceedings of the court in criminal lawsuits as well as civil and administrative proceedings. The court needs to conform to the standards set up by procedural law, while during the proceedings. These rules ensure fair practice and consistency in the due process. It provides the state with the machinery to enforce substantive laws on the people. Procedural law comprises the rules by which a court hears and determines what happens in civil or criminal proceedings. Thus, it deals with the method and means by which substantive law is made and administered. It has no independent existence.

2 Substantive law is a statutory law that deals with the legal relationship between people or the people and the state. Therefore, substantive law defines the rights and duties of the people, but procedural law lays down the rules with the help of which they are enforced. Sustentative law also defines the types of crimes and the severity depending upon factors such as whether the person is a repeat offender, whether it is a hate crime, whether it was self-defense etc. It also defines the responsibilities and rights of the accused. Substantive law is an independent set of laws that decide the fate of a case. It can actually decide the fate of the under-trial, whether he wins or loses and even the compensation amounts to pay. It tells us how the legal process is to be executed. It has the power to offer legal solutions.

4 coined by the British politician, William Gladstone (1809-1898)

5 ADR in the mode of negotiation, mediation and arbitration, is gaining prominence as a preferable alternative to litigation due to the cost, delay and unpredictability associated with litigation. The Courts Act 1993 (Act 459) and the Alternative Dispute Resolution Act 2010 (Act 798), can offer an amicable settlement of disputes among litigants. See Crook, R. C. (2012). Alternative dispute resolution and the Magistrate's Courts in Ghana: A case of practical hybridity. Africa Power and Politics Programme working Paper 25.

APPENDIX: ADDITIONAL RESOURCES

Legislation

- Alternative Dispute Resolution Act 2010 (Act 798).
- Criminal Offences Act, 1960 (Act 29) as amended.
- Criminal and Other Offences (Procedure) Act, 1960 (Act 30).
- The Constitution of the Republic of Ghana. (1992). Accra. Assembly Press.
- The Courts Act 1993 (Act 459) as amended.
- The Court of Appeal Rules 1997 (C. I. 19) as amended.
- The District Court Rules 2009 (C.I.59) as amended.
- The High Court (Civil Procedure) Rules 2004 (C.I. 47) as amended.
- The Supreme Court Rules 1996 (C.I. 16) as amended.

Case Law

- *Anane v Agyemang and Others* (J4/42/2013) [2014] GHASC 126 (26 February 2014).
- Chief Timitimi vs. Amabebe (1953), 14 (WACA) 374.

Online Sources

- Retrieved from https://www.diffen.com/difference/Procedural_Law_vs_Substantive_Law on 18/06/2021.

Chapter 4
Holding the Police to Account: The Legal Framework for Police Accountability in Zimbabwe

Ishmael Mugari
Bindura University of Science Education, Zimbabwe

ABSTRACT

Whilst there are various mechanisms to curb incidents of police abuse of power, legal control provides one of the most effective ways of enhancing police accountability. Though enforcement of the legal instruments may be a challenge, the mere presence of the legal instruments may provide a fertile ground for other accountability measures. This chapter, which is largely based on literature and documentary survey, explores the legal instruments of accountability in the Republic of Zimbabwe. The chapter specifically focuses on the Constitution and the Criminal Procedure and Evidence Act. The chapter begins by giving an overview of the international and regional legal framework before discussing the national legal framework for police accountability.

INTRODUCTION

Police officers are public servants who represent the executive arm of the government; hence they should also be accountable to the government and the community. Questioning the legitimacy of public institutions is also more pronounced in policing than in other public institutions, mainly because of the nature of police service (Brown, 2012). The police are vested with far-reaching powers and a significant degree of discretion in order to perform their duty to uphold the law and protect citizens. Paradoxically though, the powers that the police possess for the purposes of law enforcement also provide the potential for severe abuse of those powers (Mugari, 2021; Shilston, 2016). This predisposition to abuse of power justifies the need for checks and balances in order to hold the police to account for their actions. The general consensus is that police in a democratic society must operate according to the basic tenets of democratic governance, which include principles of accountability and transparency (Hope, 2020; Mugari, 2021; Shilston, 2016). In this way, accountability may be viewed as a process that binds the

DOI: 10.4018/978-1-7998-7898-8.ch004

police to society, ensuring conformity to social expectations and regulating behaviour (Walker, 2007). Given the complexities of police work, the difficult conditions in which police officers have to work (Payne, 2012), and the huge powers which they wield, it is necessary to have both internal and external accountability systems (Walker, 2007). The accountability of the police to democratic processes has been, and continues to be, one of the central issues confronting the police throughout modern times (Roberg, Novak & Cordner, 2009).

At the heart of police accountability stands the principle that the police are subordinate to the law, just as other citizens are subordinate to the law (Harris, 2013). Much of the parameters of what should be done and not done by the police are determined by the law (Harris, 2013) and this makes legal control a key mechanism for police accountability. In English- speaking democracies, legal control through statutory regulation of police powers, as well as case law pertaining to civil litigation against police abuse has taken centre stage (Jones, 2008). Victims can file civil suits for wrongs done to them by police officers, resulting in monetary damages and injunctive relief. Though civil litigation enables victims to seek recourse for wrongs done against them by the police, such litigation has also been known to expose organizational failures such as failure to follow procedures, inadequate training and inadequate supervision (Ransley, Anderson & Prenzler, 2007). Criminal law, civil and administrative laws are important tools in the control of police (Roberg et al, 2009), and it is the duty of the courts to interpret these laws. The criminal prosecution of an errand police officer provides a direct way to communicate a complaint and to ensure punishment (McDaniel, 2015), especially given the fact that police subjugation to the rule of law is a common trope amongst those who write about police accountability (Mugari, 2021; Shilston, 2016). The bill of rights is one of the major features of the constitution, and any citizen whose constitutional rights have been violated by the police can approach the courts for recourse (Feltoe, 2012).

In light of the above background, this chapter, which is largely based on a documentary survey, explores the legal framework for police accountability in Zimbabwe. The chapter specifically focuses on two statutes that mainly govern police operations in Zimbabwe, namely: The Constitution of Zimbabwe and the Criminal Procedure and Evidence Act [Chapter 9:07]. The chapter also looks at how the Zimbabwean courts have dealt with incidents of violations of constitutional provisions, as well as the provisions of the Criminal Procedure and Evidence Act. Given the previous research finding that the court is the most effective police oversight institution in Zimbabwe (Mugari, 2021), the chapter explores how victims of police abuse of power have sought justice through civil action against the police. There have been concerns that civil justice has attracted relatively little interest from scholars and policy makers as compared to criminal justice (Genn, 2012). Thus, this chapter also explores civil justice issues on victims of police abuse of power in Zimbabwe. The chapter starts by outlining the international and regional legal framework that underpins police accountability. This background is critical because the international and regional legal framework dovetails into the national legal framework. Moreover, it necessitates an evaluation of the national legal framework's adherence to international standards.

THE INTERNATIONAL AND REGIONAL LEGAL FRAMEWORKS

Most of the aspects of police accountability are addressed in various international and regional legal instruments. States are bound by international law in which principles of human rights are enshrined. To this end, Boer & Pyo (2011) highlight that States, which are embedded in an international legal system, are a partner in universal legal frameworks. Also important to highlight is the fact that all international treaties that concern human rights are of direct relevance to policing. States are obliged to protect and promote human rights under the Universal Declaration of Human Rights, which embodies civil, political, economic, social and cultural rights, and it is proclaimed as a common standard to be achieved by all people and all nations (Boer & Pyo: 2011:9). The United Nations framework gives a set of universal norms for good policing, which have to be adopted by all member states.

The International Covenant on Civil and Political Rights

The 1976 International Covenant on Civil and Political Rights (ICCPR) contains some very relevant provisions for police performance. The following are the most notable provisions which have a direct bearing on policing;

Article 9. 1.

Everyone has the right to liberty and security of person. No one shall be subjected to arbitrary arrest or detention. No one shall be deprived of his liberty except on such grounds and in accordance with such procedure as are established by law.

2. Anyone who is arrested shall be informed, at the time of arrest, of the reasons for his arrest and shall be promptly informed of any charges against him.

3. Anyone arrested or detained on a criminal charge shall be brought promptly before a judge or other officer authorized by law to exercise judicial power and shall be entitled to trial within a reasonable time or to release. It shall not be the general rule that persons awaiting trial shall be detained in custody, but release may be subject to guarantees to appear for trial, at any other stage of the judicial proceedings, and, should occasion arise, for execution of the judgement.

Also, Article 9.4 and 9.5 seem to advocate for legal accountability by providing that;

4. Anyone who is deprived of his liberty by arrest or detention shall be entitled to take proceedings before a court, in order that that court may decide without delay on the lawfulness of his detention and order his release if the detention is not lawful.

5. Anyone who has been the victim of unlawful arrest or detention shall have an enforceable right to compensation.

As is clearly expressed in Article 9 of the ICCPR, the right to personal liberty is among the most important individual rights that member states should take steps to protect. Given that police powers of arrest and detention have serious implications on the right to personal liberty, Article 9 of the ICCPR sets the tone for the protection of this fundamental right. In summary, Article 9 outlaws arbitrary arrest and detention; provides for the suspects' right to be informed of the reason for the arrest at the time of arrest; and provides that an arrested person should be brought before a judicial officer promptly or within a reasonable time. It is also important to highlight that Zimbabwe is a signatory to the ICCPR. As shall be seen in this paper, the country has taken the necessary steps to incorporate the provisions of Article

9 in its statutes. Moreover, some court judgements in Zimbabwe have reiterated the importance of the fundamental right to personal liberty and these judgements are discussed in the proceeding sections of the chapter.

The United Nations Convention Against Torture (CAT)

The UN Convention against Torture and Other Cruel or Degrading Treatment (CAT) (1987) also holds considerable relevance for police practices. The following are some of the important provisions for CAT;

Article 2

1. Each State Party shall take effective legislative, administrative, judicial or other measures to prevent acts of torture in any territory under its jurisdiction.

2. No exceptional circumstances whatsoever, whether a state of war or a threat of war, internal political instability or any other public emergency, may be invoked as a justification of torture.

3. An order from a superior officer or a public authority may not be invoked as a justification of torture.

Article 11

Each State Party shall keep under systematic review interrogation rules, instructions, methods and practices as well as arrangements for the custody and treatment of persons subjected to any form of arrest, detention or imprisonment in any territory under its jurisdiction, with a view to preventing any cases of torture.

Article 13

Each State Party shall ensure that any individual who alleges he has been subjected to torture in any territory under its jurisdiction has the right to complain to, and to have his case promptly and impartially examined by, its competent authorities. Steps shall be taken to ensure that the complainant and witnesses are protected against all ill-treatment or intimidation as a consequence of his complaint or any evidence given.

However, as with other international treaties, it is important to highlight that the treaty is only binding upon states that have ratified it. As a member State, Zimbabwe has, however, not yet ratified this important treaty; neither has it shown an interest to do so. Despite reluctance to ratify CAT, the Constitution of Zimbabwe outlaws torture under the Declaration of Rights section. Moreover, several court decisions have been made in which the police had been sued for allegations of torture.

THE AFRICAN CHARTER ON HUMAN AND PEOPLE'S RIGHTS

On the African continent, the most notable instrument that has a direct bearing on policing among member states is the African Charter on Human and People's Rights (ACHPR) (1981). Though not as comprehensive as the UN legal framework, the following are some of the important provisions;

Article 3

1. Every individual shall be equal before the law.

2. Every individual shall be entitled to equal protection of the law.

Article 5

Every individual shall have the right to the respect of the dignity inherent in a human being and to the recognition of his legal status. All forms of exploitation and degradation of man particularly slavery, slave trade, torture, cruel, inhuman or degrading punishment and treatment shall be prohibited.

Article 6

Every individual shall have the right to liberty and to the security of his person. No one may be deprived of his freedom except for reasons and conditions previously laid down by law. In particular, no one may be arbitrarily arrested or detained.

Article 3 of the ACHPR deals with an important aspect of democratic governance, that is, the rule of law. Equal protection of the law imposes a duty upon the police to desist from partisan policing, and from persecuting certain sections of the society. Similarly, Article 5 seems to summarily outlaw torture and inhuman treatment, whereas Article 6 deals with the fundamental right to personal liberty.

The National Legal Framework

While most of the statutes clearly define the roles of the police in the enforcement of the relevant statutes, the Constitution of Zimbabwe and the Criminal Procedure and Evidence Act [Chapter 9:11], are the two key statues that help in constraining police behaviour. The Constitution is the main substantive law that sets the broad parameters within which the police must operate, whilst the Criminal Procedure and Evidence Act provides for other operational aspects of police work. The most important aspect of the Constitution, in as far as policing is concerned, pertains to the declaration of rights in Chapter 4. Perhaps the starting point is to admit that many of the incidents of police abuse of power emanate from the violation of fundamental human rights. Thus, the Bill of Rights sets the confines within which the police have to adhere to as they execute their powers and functions. Importantly, any citizen whose rights have been violated by the police can directly seek recourse through the Court.

Whilst the Constitution, as the supreme law of the land, lays the foundation on issues pertaining to control of police behaviour, other detailed procedures are contained in the Criminal Procedure and Evidence Act [Chapter 9:07] (hereinafter refered to as the CP and E Act). Part V of the CP and E Act deals with arrest- whether arrest without a warrant, or arrest with a warrant. For arrest without a warrant, the CP and E Act emphasises reasonable suspicion to justify the arrest. To this end, any police officer who intends to effect an arrest should have reasonable grounds to suspect that the arrested person has committed an offence. The absence of reasonable suspicion will therefore culminate in arbitrary arrests, for which the arresting officer can be sued for violation of the right to personal liberty.

Part V1 of the CP and E Act provides for issues relating to search and seizure by police officers. Whilst a search warrant would normally be needed before conducting a search, the Act also provides for situations in which the police can search without a warrant, albeit under strict conditions. In a way to prevent arbitrary search and seizure, section 51 of the CP and E Act provides that;

(1) A police officer may, without warrant, search any person or container or premises for the purposes of seizing any article ... and additionally, or alternatively, seize any such article—

(a) if the person concerned consents to the search for and additionally, or alternatively, the seizure of the article in question or if a person who may consent to the search of the container or premises consents to such search and additionally, or alternatively, the seizure of the article in question; or

(b) if he on reasonable grounds believes that—

(i) a warrant would be issued to him if he applied for one; and

(ii) the delay in obtaining a warrant would prevent the seizure or defeat the object of the search, as the case may be.

Whilst it is logical that the police should be allowed to search without a warrant in the interest of justice, the above provisions prescribe limits in carrying out a search without a warrant. Such limits are important to prevent arbitrary searches and seizures by the police. The CP and E Act also provides for the use of force in order to carry out an arrest or to carry out a search. Section 42 provides for the use of reasonably justifiable force to overcome resistance to arrest. To this end, any force that would not be considered reasonable in the given circumstances will amount to excessive force. Also, section 40 authorises police to break open doors after failure to obtain admission for the purpose of arrest and search, though strict conditions are set before embarking on such action.

Another important provisions for curtailing police abuse of power is section 256, which renders inadmissible, any confession which is not made freely, or voluntarily by the accused person. Thus, despite all the hard work that would have been invested in conducting an investigation the court may fail to convict the suspect due to the illegal means of obtaining evidence. Moreover, this will also open floodgates for civil suits against the police, especially if torture is used to obtain confessions.

The Legal Framework and Civil Action Against the Police

Notwithstanding the presence of the two legal instruments that curtail police excesses- The Constitution and the CP and E Act, the Zimbabwean police have had to contend with allegations of abuse of power. Some of the incidents of police abuse of power have resulted in citizens seeking justice through filing civil suits against the police. This section looks at how the courts of law have dealt with incidents of police abuse of power. Importantly, the section looks at constitutional and other statutory provisions that were violated by the police and which gave rise to the civil action.

Civil Action Against Violation of the Right to Personal Liberty

The right to personal liberty is arguably the most notable right which has a direct influence on policing. Section 49 of the Constitution clearly constrains police behaviour through the following provision; *"Every person has a right to personal liberty, which includes the right; a) Not to be detained without trial; and b) Not to be deprived of their liberty arbitrarily without just cause"*. These important provisions literally outlaw unlawful arrests, arbitrary arrests and unlawful detention. The provisions are in congruent with the international and regional legal framework for police accountability, particularly Article 9 of the International Covenant on Civil and Political Rights (ICCPR), and Article 6 of the African Charter on Human and People's Rights (ACHPR). Thus, in this regard, Zimbabwe has embraced international and regional basic standards in dealing with citizens during the execution of their powers.

Several judicial decisions have been made against the violation of personal liberty by the police through unlawful arrest and detention. In the leading case of *Botha v Zvada and Another 1997 (1) ZLR415 (H)*, a 70 year old man was arrested and detained for murder allegations, though there was no strong evidence linking him to the commission of the crime. He was detained under squalid conditions for six days. The Court provided the following reasons of arrest and detention: (1) to stop the suspect from absconding; (2) to prevent the commission of further crimes; and (3) to prevent interference with investigations and witnesses. It was held that, whilst the police officer had reasonable suspicion that the plaintiff had committed an offence, it was unreasonable to believe that the accused person- a 71 year old, would abscond court or commit further crime. It was also held that interference with liberty is a serious matter. In a similar case of *Muskwe v Minister of Home Affairs and Others HH-83-2020*, the plaintiff, a 65 year old man, had been arrested and detained on allegations of unlawful entry and theft. The plaintiff sued the police for unlawful arrest and detention. The court also held that the plaintiff was an aged unsophisticated subsistence farmer, hence the decision to arrest and detain him was not justified, and awarded damages of US$1000 for unlawful arrest and detention, as well as US$500 for *contumelia*. In the case of *Mapuranga v Mungate 1997 (1) ZLR 64 (H)*, it was held that detaining a suspect and subsequently restricting his right to free movement is a serious infraction of liberty, which is far beyond the estimate of mere monetary values. This position was also reiterated in *Minister of Home Affairs v Bangajena 2000(1) ZLR 306 (S)*, in which the Court held that "the deprivation of personal liberty is an odious interference and has always been regarded as serious injury".

There have also been instances in which the police effect an unlawful arrest upon unlawful orders from superior officers. In the case of *Moll v Commissioner of Police and Others 1983 (1) ZLR 238 (H)*, the plaintiff was arrested and charged for contravening a section of the Emergency Powers Regulations after allegations of making derogatory remarks about the Prime Minister. He was detained for over two months by a Detective Inspector, who was acting on the orders of a Senior Assistant Commissioner, despite the fact that an order to release him had been issued by a magistrate. The plaintiff sued for unlawful arrest. The court held;

"...the officer who effects an arrest must himself suspect on reasonable grounds that the person he is arresting has committed an offence...if a senior officer orders a junior to arrest a person without informing him of the grounds on which the arrest is made, the arrest by the junior will be illegal".

In this case justification for the detention lay on the Detective Inspector and not on the Senior Assistant Commissioner. Thus, the police officer who effects an arrest is the one who has to use his instincts on whether he should arrest or not.

Civil Action Against Torture and Inhuman Treatment

Torture is a particularly serious violation of human rights and is strictly prohibited by international law, as well as Zimbabwe's domestic laws. The tort of torture arises when interviewing suspects during police investigations. Article 1 of the CAT defines torture as follows;

"Any act by which severe pain or suffering whether physical or mental, is intentionally inflicted on a person for such purposes as obtaining from him or a third person information or a confession, punishing him for an act he or a third person has committed or is suspected to have committed, or intimidating or coercing him or a third person, or for any reason based on discrimination of any kind, when such pain or suffering is inflicted by or at the instigation of a public official or other person acting on an official capacity."

The definition of torture is all-encompassing and includes assault of suspects and several other methods used to unlawfully obtain confessions from suspects. The dignity of the human being is inviolable under any circumstances, and torture is the most severe violation of human dignity (Jessberger, 2005). Malaba, J (as he then was) summed up the need to act against torture in the case of *Mapuranga v Mungate 1997 (1) ZLR 64 (H)* when he said;

"Every person's body is sacred and inviolable. No other man has a right to meddle with it in the slightest manner except in the circumstances prescribed by the law. The person assaulted is entitled to damages even though he suffered no severe pain, or any damage at all other than the insult of having his bodily integrity interfered with".

Several civil suits have been filed against the Zimbabwean police for torture, degrading and inhuman treatment. In the leading case of *Karimazondo and Another V Minister of Home Affairs and Another 2001 (2) ZLR 363 (H)*, the plaintiffs were both arrested on allegations of murder, but the charges were subsequently dropped. The plaintiffs sued the police after they had been subjected to torture whilst in custody, resulting in them suffering long-lasting physical and psychological effects. The learned judge had this to say;

"The actions of the police in this case were in flagrant and disregard of the rights of the plaintiffs...the brutality and callousness with which the assaults were perpetrated on the first plaintiff instils in any right-thinking person, a sense of horror and shock...The unlawful and inhuman treatment to which the first plaintiff was subjected was, in my view totally unnecessary, vindictive and malicious."

In this case the court awarded significant monetary damages to the plaintiffs for pain and suffering. As a matter of irony, the first plaintiff was a member of the police, whilst the second plaintiff was his wife. One would conclude that the torture could have been worse had they not been dealing with one of their own.

In the case of *State v Slatter 1983 ZLR 144*, the accused persons were charged with aiding and abetting sabotage at the Air force Base. No evidence was adduced implicating the accused apart form their own statements which were procured through threats and torture.

Rendering their confessions inadmissible, the Court held that maltreatment during questioning makes statements inadmissible. The Court also held that magistrates are obliged to question accused persons to ascertain whether confessions were made illegally. In this case, the police had violated section 53 of the Constitution (Freedom from torture, inhuman and degrading treatment), as well as section 256 of the CP and E Act, which renders inadmissible, any confession which is not made freely, or voluntarily by the accused person.

In *Nyandoro v Minister of Home Affairs and Another HH-196-2010*, the plaintiff had been arrested for taking part in a peaceful demonstration. The police broke up the demonstration, arresting the plaintiff in the process. He was assaulted by about 10 police officers on the way to the police station and on arrival at the station. The plaintiff filed a civil suit against the police for assault and torture and was awarded damages amounting to US$5 000. Similarly, the Court ruled against the police in the following cases in which the plaintiffs had sued the police for torture, inhuman and degrading treatment: *Mukumba v Minister of Home Affairs and Another HH-84-2009*; *Mugwagwa v Minister of Home Affairs and Commissioner of Police HH-183-2004*; and *Nathanson V Mteliso and Others HB-176-2019.*

Civil Action Against Indiscriminate Use of Excessive Force

The constitutional duty of preserving peace and maintaining law and order sometimes necessitates the use of force. Moreover, the CP and E Act provides for use of reasonable force to overcome resistance to arrest. However, on numerous occasions, the Zimbabwean police have faced allegations of use of excessive force, with several civil suits being filed against the police. The civil suit relating to indiscriminate use of force arises when effecting an arrest and when dealing with public disorder situations. However, any use of force by the police should be underpinned by three principles: necessity, proportionality and legality.

In the case of *Musadzikwa v Minister of Home Affairs and Another 2000 (1) ZLR 405 (H)*, the police used weapons to quell a riot and an innocent passer-by was injured in the process. The court found that it does not conduce to harmonious community relations for the police force to unleash its members onto an urban shopping centre located in a centre of a densely suburban residential area armed with FN rifles. The court also highlighted that whilst police were entitled to use force and firearms to disperse the rioters it was unreasonable to use FN rifles and so they were liable. In another case of *Mugadza v Minister of Home Affairs 2001 (2) ZLR 134 (H)*, the plaintiff sued the police after he had been shot by a stray bullet during food riots. The court also held that the discharge of firearms by the police was wrongful and culpable, and reiterated the unreasonableness of discharging automatic weapons in a densely populated urban area. In a horrifying case involving the use of excessive force during arrest (*Simbanegavi v Officer Jachi HH-40-2013*), the plaintiff was arrested on suspicion that he had stolen a motor vehicle. At the time of arrest, the defendant's police officer fired six bullets at the plaintiff's legs, resulting in the plaintiff's leg being amputated. The plaintiff was awarded a total of US$21 367 for pain and suffering and special damages.

Civil Action Against Violation of the Right to Privacy

The right to privacy directly impacts on the policing function, mainly on issues relating to search and seizure by police officers. Section 57 of the constitution provides that;

"Every person has the right to privacy, which includes the right not to have-

(a) Their home, premises or property entered without their permission;

(b) Their person, home, premises or property searched;

(c) Their possessions seized;

(d) The privacy of their communications infringed."

Thus, any search that does not conform to the dictates of Section 57 of the Constitution, as well as the relevant provisions of the CP and E Act, will be regarded as either arbitrary or unlawful. Moreover, even if the search is sanctioned by law, the search should be conducted in a decent manner. The provision proscribing the infringement of communications (subsection d) is also very critical in this technological era, as it is also susceptible to abuse by the police. Whilst section 57 outlaws unlawful search and seizure, it does not provide for the circumstances in which the police are expected to carry out search and seizure. In the absence of such provisions, there will be reliance on other statutes such as the Criminal Procedure and Evidence Act [Chapter 9:07].

In the case of *Chinjayani V Minister of Home Affairs and Others HH 76- 2010*, a search was conducted on the 8th of April 2010 and a warrant was later issued on the 20th of April 2010. The search was declared illegal and Uchena, J stated that, "...therefore the warrant must pre-exist the seizure for it to require a police officer to seize the article, and authorize such officer to search persons and enter premises where necessary". In *Gwisai v Minister of Home Affairs and Others HH-587-19*, the plaintiff's motor vehicle was unlawfully seized by the police over allegations that the vehicle had been stolen in South Africa. At the time of the seizure of the motor vehicle from the complainant's premises, the police could not provide reasonable explanation pertaining to the alleged theft of a motor vehicle in South Africa. In its final judgement, the Court ordered the release of the plaintiff's motor vehicle.

CONCLUSION

Legal control constitutes an important component of police accountability. In the international arena, groundwork for police accountability has been set through various instruments and protocols, chief among them being the ICCPR. Taking a leaf from the international legal framework, the ACHPR is the most prominent regional legal instrument of police accountability. As a nation, Zimbabwe has largely embraced the international and regional legal instruments by incoporating most of the provisions within the Constitution, as well as the Criminal Procedure and Evidence Act. The most notable provisions relate to the constitutional Bill of Rights, which proscribes: unlawful arrest and detention; torture, degrading and inhuman treatment; and unlawful invasion of privacy. The legal provisions are also essential for limiting excessive use of deadly force, outlining the procedure for effecting arrest and searches, and proscribing use of illegal methods of gathering evidence. However, the researcher needs to point out that the mere presence of a conducive legal framework does not guarantee strict adherence to the dictates of the law. Notwithstanding the presence of these important legal provisions aimed at holding the police to account, the Zimbabwean police has faced numerous law suits for police abuse of power, which manifests through unlawful arrest and detention, excessive use of force, torture, and unlawful invasion of privacy. Thus, the Court has proven to be an invaluable outlet through which citizens seek justice against errand police officers.

REFERENCES

Boer, M., & Pyo, C. (2011). *Good Policing. Instruments Models and Practices*. Asia- Europe Foundation.

Brown, L. P. (2012). *Policing in the 21st Century. Community Policing*. Author House.

Feltoe, G. (2012). *A Guide to Administrative and Local Government law in Zimbabwe*. University of Zimbabwe.

Genn, H. (2012). *Understanding civil justice*. University College of London.

Harris, F. C. (2013). *Holding police accountability theory to account* (Thesis). Institute of Criminal Justice Studies, University of Portsmouth.

Hope, K. R. Sr. (2020). Civilian Oversight for Democratic Policing and its Challenges: Overcoming Obstacles for Improved Police Accountability. *Journal of Applied Security Research*, 1–33. doi:10.1080/19361610.2020.1777807

Jessberger, F. (2005). Bad Torture- Good Torture? *Journal of International Criminal Justice, 3*, 1059-1073. Available from: www.oxfordjournals.org/our_journals/jicjus/ba

Jones, T. (2008). The accountability of policing. In T. Newburn (Ed.), *Handbook of Policing* (pp. 693–723). Willan Publishing.

McDaniel, J. (2015). *Rethinking Police Accountability and Transparency within the EU: Reconciling national and supranational approaches* (Thesis). University of Kent.

Mugari, I. (2021). Evaluations of selected civilian oversight institutions for police accountability in the Republic of Zimbabwe. *Police Practice and Research, 22*(1), 606-622. . doi:10.1080/15614263.2020.1831921

Ransley, J., Anderson, J., & Prenzler, J. (2007). Civil Litigation Against police in Australia: Exploring its Extent, Nature and Implications for Accountability. *Australian and New Zealand Journal of Criminology, 40*(2), 143–160. doi:10.1375/acri.40.2.143

Republic of Zimbabwe. (1980). *The Criminal Procedure and Evidence Act* [Chapter 9:07]. Government Printers.

Republic of Zimbabwe. (2013). The Constitution of Zimbabwe. Amendment (No 20). Harare: Government Printers.

Roberg, R., Novak, K., & Cordner, G. (2009). *Police and Society* (4th ed.). Oxford University Press.

Shilston, T. G. (2016). Six dimensions of police accountability: An aid to needs assessment in international police development missions. *International Journal of Police Science & Management*, *18*(1), 37–46. doi:10.1177/1461355716638115

United Nations. (1976). *International Covenant on Civil and Political Rights*. Author.

United Nations. (1987). *Convention against Torture and Other Cruel, Inhuman or Degrading Treatment or Punishment*. United Nations.

Walker, S. (2007). *Police Accountability: Current issues and Research Needs*. Paper presented at the National Institute of justice (NIJ) Policing Research Workshop: Planning for the Future, Washington, DC. Available from: www.icjia.state.il.us/public/2012_LE_Workshop/pdf_Files/ReadingMaterials/PoliceAccountability_CurrentIssues.pdf

Chapter 5
Judging the Subordinate Judiciary

Rattan Singh
Panjab University, Chandigarh, India

ABSTRACT

The subordinate judiciary of a nation plays an important role in the administration and dispensation of justice. A judicial officer in the subordinate courts performs a "pious duty" in the service of justice. A majority of the members of the society come in contact with the trial court judges rather than with the appellate or higher court judges. No law, court, precedent, or custom can provide guidelines for better administration of justice, because there is no fixed formula to find the solution of the problem. In such situations, personal qualities, experience, training, and worth of a trial judge make themselves manifest. Through the image of subordinate judiciary and its functioning, the true picture of judiciary presents itself to the nation. The mind of the judiciary can be known to the millions only through the actions and working of the subordinate or trial court judges. In this chapter, researcher has pointed out some problems faced by subordinate courts and judges due to the backlog, and the daily increase, in legal cases.

INTRODUCTION

An independent, active and transparent judiciary is the heart and soul of a country. The foundation of democracy, the spirit of secularism and socialism, principles of equity, and the hope for the effective administration of justice lie in an independent judiciary. For independent of judiciary "Judges should be of strun stuff and tough fibre", unbending before power, economic or political and they must uphold the principles of the rule of law which says "Be you ever so high the law is above you". This is the principle of independence of the judiciary which is vital for the establishment of real participatory democracy, maintenance of the rule of law as a dynamic concept and delivery of social justice to the vulnerable sections of the community as espoused in S.P. Gupta v. Union of India. It was held in R.S. Nayak v. A.R. Antulay [1984, 2 SCR 495] that *"Constitution made a Judge totally independent of the control and influence of the executive and legislature"*

DOI: 10.4018/978-1-7998-7898-8.ch005

In the judicial system of any country subordinate judiciary plays an important role in administration and dispensing justice not only between citizens but also between citizens and the State. Many of us may not be aware of the importance and working of the trial courts. A judicial officer in the subordinate courts performs a "pious duty" in the service of justice. The standards of probity, conduct, and integrity of a judicial officer in the discharge of his duties are not the same of a careerist who is only bothered about advancement in his profession. If we evaluate the role of different functionaries who play their part in the administration of justice, the top position would have to be assigned to the trial court or subordinate judges. They are the key force to our judicial system. It is mostly with the trial judges rather than with the appellate judges that the majority of the members of society come in contact, whether as parties or as witnesses. The image of the Judiciary for a common man is protected by the trial court judges (77th Report Law Commission of India, 1978). A misconception that needs to be removed is that the trial courts do not contribute much to the administration and distribution of justice. The personality of the trial judge makes no difference. Most of us who are familiar with the functioning of the trial courts would bear out that the above notion is divorced from realities. A trial judge's ability, efficiency and tact can make all the difference regarding the fate of cases handled by them. It has to be borne in mind that the judicial work in the court of law is not purely mechanical and technical. The cases do not always proceed on set lines and precedents. There are varieties of situations that can arise in human relationships. No court and no precedents can provide guidance, nor can a fixed formula be laid down to find the solution in those situations. In such situations, personal qualities, experience, training and worth of a trial judge make themselves manifest. The myth that trial court decisions are subject to set-aside, correction and modification in appeal or what has been called the 'Upper-Court Myth' ignores the realities of the situation. Despite the right of appeal, there are many cases in which appeals are not filed. Appellate courts having only the written record before them and are normally reluctant to interfere with the appraisement of evidence of witnesses by the trial judges who have had the advantage of looking at the demeanor of the witnesses. The appellate courts operate in the partial vacuum of the printed record. A stenographic transcript fails to reproduce tones of voice and hesitations of speech that often make a sentence mean the reverse of what the mere words signify. The best and the most accurate record of the oral testimony are like a dehydrated peach, it has neither the substance nor the flavor of the peach before it was dried (Commission of India, ibid). On the anthropomorphic view of our subordinate Judiciary Justice P. A. Choudary remarks that;

I choose to liken the subordinate judiciary to the eyes and ears and hands and legs of the Judiciary as a whole while I compare the superior Judiciary to its mind. However, this comparison like most others might appear to be somewhat arbitrary and even crude, the basic truth behind it, I think, is undeniable. The subordinate judiciary occupies a central place in the body of our judicial system. For one thing, the subordinate judiciary is planted on the ground while the superior judiciary soars in the skies. The subordinate judiciary directly hears the parties to a dispute and listens to their pleadings of woes and makes the first attempts at resolution of the conflicting claims of the contesting parties. It is the lawyer in a subordinate court that draws the horoscope and lays the foundation for the future of the case with his imaginative but difficult art of drafting- pleadings. In the matter of sifting truth that is inextricably found mixed with falsehood and perjury the advantages that the subordinate judiciary enjoys are recognizably superior (AIR, 1990).

It is through the image of the subordinate judiciary and its functioning, that the true picture of the Indian Judiciary presents itself to the nation. For most people the higher courts are unknown and for some, they appear and serve rich classes of society. Even some litigants might not have even heard of superior or appellate courts. Most of them would not have seen the inscrutable mind of the superior judiciary. In many a case, it is a formidable task even for the trained intellect to discern the mind of the superior Judiciary from its pronouncements. The mind of the Indian Judiciary can be known to the millions only through the actions and working of the subordinate judiciary. Without a healthy and independent subordinate judiciary, there cannot be a healthy judicial system. Nothing is, therefore, more important for us than to preserve, protect, defend and ensure the independence and integrity of the subordinate judiciary. It is as important a task as protecting the independence, dignity, and impartiality of the higher judiciary. No doubt, under Article 235 of the Constitution, the High Court is assigned a supervisory role, both over the judicial and administrative matters of the subordinate judiciary. However, its purpose is to ensure the long-desired separation of the judiciary from the executive. Nevertheless, we believe that this supervisory jurisdiction of the High Courts is exercised more by way of friendly instructions rather than through a crude display of superiority. If the subordinate judiciary is the eyes and ears and hands and legs of the judicial system, we should take care not to dim its vision, dampen its hearing, or cripple its legs. Otherwise, we will fail in our collective mission of delivering justice as surely as anyone does, where a task is attempted to be performed without the co-operation of those vital organs of the body. The regime of unquestioned obedience is the rule of the tyrants, said Lord Simon. Only an independent subordinate judiciary will prove to be an asset to the nation. It is, therefore, essential for the successful functioning of the judiciary as a whole that the subordinate judiciary is encouraged to think independently, act justly and decide fairly. In a heterogeneous society such as India, where caste loyalties are still strong, where poverty and illiteracy pervade the lives of millions, where political power is feared and bribery is routinized, the threat to an independent judiciary arises not just from the mainstream society, the executive and the legislature, but from within the court itself. Only a well-trained and well-informed subordinate judiciary can be trusted to be independent and equal to its task of rendering justice (AIR, 1990). Support for the subordinate judiciary is not merely greater powers but also greater awareness of the law. It is not enough that its pay scales are raised. It is also necessary that the subordinate Judiciary is made to realise that the great mission of rendering justice cannot be fulfilled unless it is made constantly aware that there is no law that is beyond or different from justice. The courts are not merely skeletal courts of law. They are like living organisms. They have flesh and blood of justice in the form of learned judges. Population plays an important role in the development of every institution. The more the growth rates of the population the more problems of society. Similarly, with the increase in population, the institution rate of cases grows which becomes a problem for the administration of justice. Some studies have pointed out the problems faced by subordinate courts and judges as follows:

Arrears of Cases

The inadequacy in the strength of the subordinate judiciary to deal with the arrears and the fresh institution contributes to the piling up of arrears. Many times it brings a sense of frustration and helplessness among the litigants, which, for no fault of its own, are prevented from getting appropriate and timely redress from the court. This leads to undermine the public confidence of the judiciary and tarnish the image of the courts.

Long Case List

The practice, which prevails in some courts of fixing many cases on a day on which there is no reasonable chance of their being taken up for hearing, should be avoided. It is evident that some courts spend more than an hour every day in calling certain cases, with a view to adjourn them to a future date. The time spent for this purpose can hardly be considered to have been put to any constructive use. Referring to the practice of some courts fixing more work than they could complete on the ground that if sufficient work is fixed for the day, some cases might collapse and the presiding officer might thus be left without full occupation. As the Rankin Committee observed;

The utmost concession that should be made to this view, would be to fix for hearing on one day perhaps one quarter more than could be done on its and to give the undone work precedence on the next day. We have been unable to find the majority of cases that any such practice has been adopted. More work is fixed for the day than can possibly be got through, whatever drops out, and precedence is not given to the undone work on the next day. In any circumstances, the principle is vicious. It appears to be based upon the idea that the courts may safely ignore the convenience of the public, in order to enable them to show a tale of work, which they suppose will be considered satisfactory by the higher authorities. It must be impressed and impressed very clearly that the first consideration should be the convenience of the public and that all other considerations should give way to that (77th Report Law Commission of India, 1978, p.18).

Strikes by Advocates

In recent times lawyers have adopted a very strange and unjustified attitude of boycotting court work, popularly known as 'strike' for an indefinite period irrespective of the seriousness of their grievances. Even for a small grievance, they boycott court work for months together with the result that the purpose of boycott loses its importance and value but it also adds to the arrears of cases and further delay in disposal of cases. The late Mr. M. C. Setalvad, the first Attorney General of India, in his address to the Bar Association of India said:

"No doubt the British system of administration was very good and led to excellent results, but it had its defects which have been accentuated in two ways. We are now a democratic country and we are a much more populous country. These days, therefore, what is required is a radical change in the method of administration of justice. We want courts to which people can go with ease and with as little cost as possible. It is not merely the quickness of justice but it is the easy approach and quick disposal both which are needed and that only can be achieved if the system is completely overhalted." (Agarwal, n.d., p. 194).

In an organised society, it is in the interest of the citizens as well as the state that the disputes which go to the law courts for adjudication should be decided within a reasonable time, so as to give certainty and definiteness to rights and obligations. If the course of a trial is inordinately long, the chances of miscarriage of justice and the expenses of litigation increase alike. Delay results in witnesses being unable to testify correctly to events that might fade in their memory. It also provides opportunities for the witnesses to be won over by the opponent during this prolonged period. Relief granted to an aggrieved party after a lapse of time loses much of its value and sometimes becomes infructuous. Such is the basis of the principle "justice delayed is justice denied" (14th Report, Law Commission of India, p. 129). The Sixth Amendment to the Constitution of the United States provides that in all criminal prosecutions, the accused shall enjoy the right to a speedy and public trial. It is thus constitutionally guaranteed right in the United States. Article 3 of the European Convention of Human Rights provides that "every one arrested or detained shall be entitled to trial within a reasonable time or a release pending trial". Though, the right to speedy trial has not been specifically enumerated as a fundamental right in our constitution, the court argued that "it is implicit in the broad sweep and content of Article 21 as interpreted by the court in Maneka Gandhi v Union of India" (AIR 1978 SC 597). The court thus observed:

No procedure which does not ensure a reasonably quick trial can be regarded as reasonable, fair or just and it would fall foul of Article 21. There can, therefore, be no doubt that speedy trial, and by speedy we mean reasonably expeditious trial, is an integral and essential part of the fundamental right to life and liberty enshrined in Article 21 of the Constitution.

The problem has been examined in some detail in the Fourteenth Report of the Law Commission on the Reforms of Administration of Justice. Some states such as Bihar, Utter Pradesh, West Bengal and Andhra Pradesh had appointed their own committees to deal with this problem. Various suggestions have been made by all these committees. Many of these have been implemented but the problem still remains the same. The problem is complex and does not admit a simple solution. The Fourteenth Report contains several recommendations for eliminating delay. The problem has also been examined in the Twenty Seventh Report of the Law Commission. The causes of this problem are multiple and various. No single factor can satisfactorily explain the delay. Except for variations in degree, many causes have been commonly identified by foreign and Indian writers. The inefficient and haphazard functioning of courts and lack of scientific management has been agreed upon as major causes of delay (77th Report Law Commission of India, 1978; Forst, 1977). Attention has also been diverted towards the case loads (Nardulli, 1979). The situation in India is even worse with the mounting arrears of cases but the number of courts remained almost static (Pande & Bagga, 1973). This has created an ever-increasing backlog of cases and presently, it has virtually chocked the existing courts (Singhvi, 1976).

Delaying Tactics

There is a popular belief that the technicalities of legal procedure can be exploited and a case continued almost indefinitely if so desired. There is a fertile field in Civil Procedure Code for a clever lawyer to prolong and protect proceedings to any length of time (Narayan, 1987). It is an unbreakable elastic piece of legislation that enables all piecemeal dealing in litigation. After the service of summons parties are supposed to be present in the court in person or by their respective pleaders and the suit shall be heard unless the hearing is adjourned to a future day fixed by the court (Order IX Rule 1 of Code of Civil Procedure). Where both the parties do not appear for hearing, the court may dismiss the suit (Order IX Rule 2 of Code of Civil Procedure). The dismissed suit can be restored if the parties satisfy the court about the reasons of non-appearance (Order IX Rule 4 of Code of Civil Procedure). Sometimes only ex-parte, decree is passed when the defendant does not appear before the court and later on defendant move an application to set aside the ex-parte decree (Order IX Rule 12 of Code of Civil Procedure). In this way applications start piling that causes delay in the disposal of cases. Granting of temporary injunction in cases where property dispute in a suit is in danger of being wasted, damaged or alienated by any party to the suit, or wrongfully sold in execution of a decree or defendant threatens, or intends to remove or dispose of his property with a view to defrauding his creditors, is also one of the causes of delay in the decision making (Order XXXIX Rule 1 of Code of Civil Procedure). The court can appoint a receiver of any property and on the appointment of a receiver, the case can be adjourned a number of times (Order X L Rule 1 of Code of Civil Procedure).

Provisions Regarding Supply of Copies of Documents to Defendant

There is no provision to make it obligatory upon the plaintiff to produce copies of documents referred to and relied upon in the plaint for being served upon the defendant. As a result, thereof summon is generally served with a copy of plaint but without copies of the document. Therefore, invariably the defendant seeks adjournment for filing his written statement, on the ground that he has to inspect the documents relied upon the plaint (Mathur, n.d.). The experience shows this causes delay.

Delay in Filing Written Statement

Compulsive requirement is on the defendant to submit a written statement before the first hearing or within such time as the court provides (Order VIII Rule 1). But there is no maximum time limit fixed for filing the written statement or to reply after the first date of hearing. It has been experienced that a number of frivolous applications are filed at this stage before filing the written statement and this causes unnecessary delay.

Adjournment and Piecemeal Hearing

One of the most important reasons for the delay in the disposal of cases is the widespread practice of judicial officers to deal with the cases in a piecemeal manner and their readiness to grant adjournment either for their own advantage, or for the convenience of the parties, or more frequently in the lawyer's interest [(Bhawan Dass v/s Kareem Bax, 1990 (1) SCC 395 (Ra)]. Judgments in matters heard piecemeal cannot be delivered expeditiously as the judges are unable to keep the evidence adduced alive in their memory and as such for the purpose of making up their mind at the time of writing out the judgment have to make an elaborate study of the whole record which is sheer wastage of time. Undesirable adjournments can be checked under order 17 Rules (1) and (2) of the Civil Procedure Code. Order XVII Rule 1 provides:

1. When the hearing of the suit has commenced, it shall be continued from day to day until all the witnesses in attendance have been examined, unless the court finds that, for the exceptional reasons to be recorded by it, the adjournment of the hearing beyond the following day is necessary.
2. No adjournment shall be granted at the request of a party, except where the circumstances are beyond the control of the party.
3. The fact that the pleader of a party is engaged in another court, shall not be a ground for adjournment.
4. Where the illness of a pleader or his inability to conduct the case for any reason, other than his being engaged in another court, is put forward as a grant the adjournment unless it is satisfied that the party applying for adjournment could not have engaged another pleader in time.

5. Where a witness is present in court but a party or his pleader is not present or the party or his pleader, though present in court, is not ready to examine or cross-examine the witness, the court may if it thinks fit, record the statement of the witness and pass such order as it thinks fit dispensing with the examination-in-chief or cross-examination of the witness, as the case may, by the party or his pleader not present or not ready as aforesaid.

Order XVII Rule 2 also provides that: "where, on any day to which the hearing of the suit is adjourned, the parties or any of them fail to appear, the court may proceed to dispose of the suit in one of the modes directed in that behalf by Order IX…".

Same Court for Civil and Criminal Cases

There are many instances where the same judicial officers exercise powers over both civil cases and criminal cases. Normally, the judicial officer gives preference to criminal cases. Much of their time is consumed in hearing bail applications and recording evidence of witnesses in criminal cases, and very few hours are available for civil cases (Bhalla, 1988).

Insufficient Officers

In spite of the growing volume of work, the strength of the judiciary has not been increased proportionately. The increase in the strength of the judicial officers has not been commensurate with the increase in the number of pending cases. Complaints are also made that whenever the High Court makes a recommendation for increasing the strength of judicial officers in a district, the matter has to be referred to State Government which takes several months, and in a few instances, more than a year to give its decision on the recommendation. The decision quite often is to turn down the recommendation of the High Court. Even when the recommendation is accepted, the lapse of time between the date of recommendation and its acceptance robs the original recommendation of its effectiveness and further aggravating the problem.

Delay in the Course of Service of Summons

The plaintiff is required to pay the processing fee for service of writ of summons on the defendant. Now, this is a stage where one comes across two important drawbacks-one being delay in serving writ of summons by bailiff which in turn give rise to another malady namely corruption amongst bailiffs (Mathur, n.d.). At present summon is served by the bailiff attached to the court. The bailiff has to go to the village to serve summons very often, it is found that the bailiff shirks his work, and more often summons is returned with endorsement 'party not found' or address not known, etc. Closer scrutiny reveals that some bailiffs abdicate their duty to serve the parties (Bhalla, 1988). Members of the Bar frankly conceded that either the defendant succeeds in avoiding service by greasing palms of the Bailiff, or the plaintiff must of necessity satisfy him to effect early service of summons. The provision of issuing process in civil cases subject to deposit of process fee by the plaintiff or by the defendant as the case may lead to unnecessary delay and corruption among the employees of the judicial department (Bhalla, 1988). According to Order 9 Rule 2 of the Civil Procedure Code, the suit of the plaintiff is dismissed, if the processing fee is not deposited by the plaintiff in time (Order IX Rule 2). The summons of witnesses is not issued unless the necessary process fee is deposited in time and the suit of the plaintiff can be dismissed under Order 17

Rule 3 Civil Procedure Code for non-deposit of process fee (Bhalla, 1988). The dismissal of the suit for non-deposit of process fee for the summoning of the defendant or witness leads to unnecessary delay for the disposal of the suit as parties often apply for restoration of the suit, and thus apply for deposit of process fee. The valuable rights of the parties are defeated for mere non-deposit of minor process fee. To this end, the payment of the processing fee is dispensed (Rao, 1994).

Lengthy Arguments

There is a common complaint of lengthy arguments, being presented before the court. It may not be out of place to refer to the observation made by the Law Commission.

It is true that in many cases arguments are unduly prolix, sometimes, the arguments become lengthy because the court either from inexperience or for other reason is unable to control counsel. Some lawyers are long-winded; others are brief and to the point. Similarly, some judges are unable to control the arguments while some are inclined not to hear any arguments at all and cut them very short. The court which has heard the case from day-to-day should be familiar with the evidence and can if necessary go through the record of the case before the arguments are commenced to refresh its memory. The presiding officer who has followed the evidence will be in a much better position to control arguments (14th Report Law Commission of India, p. 345, 346).

It has been experienced that on many occasions advocates start arguments without preparation and kill the valuable time of the court in their own way and on the next day they come prepared to argue, which directly causes a delay in justice. Another important aspect of the matter is that on many occasions advocate advances some arguments for the judge and some arguments for his client to impress upon him that the advocate possesses high calibre (77th Report Law Commission of India, 1978).

Citation of Authorities

One general tendency is to cite a very large number of authorities and to read lengthy passages from those judgments. Experience tells us that the fate of most cases depends upon facts. The law bearing on the cases is well settled by the statute or the pronouncements of the highest court. Burdening of the judgment by citing too many authorities, mostly with a view to showcase their legal prowess, has the effect of making judgments unduly lengthy. This too, also contributes to the delay of justice.

Examination and Cross-Examination of Witnesses

Examination and cross-examination of witnesses consume a good deal of time of the court without any fruitful results. Since there is no limit on the witnesses, the general tendency is to produce as many witnesses as one can. Although, there are some restrictions to the issuing of summons, for the attendance of the witnesses after a certain stage of hearing has been reached. It is open to the parties to produce at any time witnesses who have not been summoned and the court must hear them, irrespective of the value of their evidence and however unprofitable the work of recording such evidence may be. As regard cross-examination, it is often found that the counsel is not equipped with material for cross-examination. He indulges in cross-examination at random for a long time in the hope that some damaging statement may be extracted from them by accident (Mann, n.d.). There is a tendency to over-prove allegations. This is true not only of essential allegations but also of tangential allegations. In a large number of cases, considerable time of court is consumed in recording of oral evidence even at the point of examination-in-chief. If that be true of examination-in-chief, the position is much worse in cross-examination. Cross-examination of witnesses often tends to be unduly prolix. Some clients are inclined to judge the proficiency of the counsel by the length of his cross-examination of a witness. This attitude reveals a pathetic ignorance of the technique of effective cross-examination. It is not too much to say that cross-examination frequently extends over a period which is more than six times as long as is necessary to produce useful results. The waste of time is most noticeable in cases of large value, especially, in which the dispute relates to valuable landed property. It is difficult to exaggerate the unnecessary labour and the delays caused thereby.

Evidence on Commissions

Persons suffering from sickness or infirmity, and unable to attend the court; or persons about to leave the jurisdiction before the date fixed for examination in court; or an official of the government who cannot attend without detriment to the public service and purdah nasin ladies are exempt from attendance in the court. Accordingly, they have to be examined under commission. Delay occurs in the examination of such commissions. Time spent over the examination and cross-examination of the witnesses before commission is unduly protracted. The delay is very much greater in the case of commissioned issued for the examination of witness' resident beyond the local limits of the court's jurisdiction Law (77th Report Commission of India).

Writing Judgement

Under the law, the judge is required to write down the Judgment, before delivering it. He usually takes at least a fortnight to write the judgment after the argument is over. This causes a delay in the finalisation of judicial proceedings. The main reason for the delay in delivering the judgment is that the judges write too long and exhaustive judgments as they attempt to indulge in making a show of erudition. They arrive at a judgment after a long and involved argument. The result is unnecessary waste of time and energy (77th Report Commission of India).

Delay in Criminal Cases

Delay in criminal cases is not of the same nature. But even here the complainant or the accused person against whom a false charge has been made, has to undergo a great deal of harassment because of long delays occasioned in the trial court. Police cases take a lot of time in investigation, and a lot of time is spent in the pre-trial stage itself. The police go on taking remands and the magistrates readily give time. If the accused cannot find sureties or has not been allowed, he has to remain in jail as an under trial prisoner even though he may, subsequently, be honorably acquitted. In a case when the accused absconds, proceedings are started under sections 37 and 38 of the Criminal Procedure Code, which causes considerable delay. The difficulty of procuring attendance of prosecution witnesses also adds to the delay. Intricacies of warrant case procedure also come in the way of expeditious trials. The system of double cross-examination of witnesses also adds to delay. Both, the magistrates and police adopt rather indifferent attitudes. The magistrates fix a large number of cases for a day and they are usually in the habit of examining one or two witnesses in every case that they want to take up. The police do not care to bring all the prosecution witnesses on one day. The other factors which cause delay are inadequacy of prosecuting staff and improper distribution of work amongst the magistrates. Added to this are the frequent adjournments in session cases on account of witnesses not turning up, because either the magistrate failed to exercise due care in issuing summons, or the police neglect in effecting the service of summons on witnesses.

Practice of Fixing Too Many Cases

The practice of fixing a number of cases on a day on which there is no reasonable chance of their being taken up for hearing is also one of the reasons for the speedy disposal of cases. It is found that some courts spend an hour every day calling certain cases to adjourn them to a future date. The time spent for this purpose can hardly be considered to have been put to any constructive use (77th Report Law commission of India). Referring to the practice of some courts fixing more work than they could complete on the ground that if work just sufficient for the day were fixed, some cases might collapse and the presiding officer might thus be without full occupation. The Rankin Committee observed:

The utmost concession that should be made to this view, would be to fix for hearing on one day perhaps one quarter more than could be done on it and to give the undone work precedence on the next date. We have been unable to find in the majority of cases that any such practice has been adopted. More work is fixed for the day than can possibly be got through, whatever drops out, and precedence is not given to the undone work on the next day.

In any circumstances the principle is vicious. It appears to be based upon the idea that the courts may safely ignore the convenience of the public, in order to enable them to show to tale of work, which they suppose, will be considered satisfactory by the higher authorities. It must be impressed that the first consideration should be the convenience of the public and that all other considerations should give way to that.

Deplorable Working Conditions

It is a pity that the people who are expected to administer justice are housed in shabby and dilapidated court rooms. A visit to any lower court will demonstrate how unhealthy and appalling conditions are in the courts. Ants, flies, broken chairs and tables, torn and soiled table cloths, ceaseless noise and complete lack of order characterize the court room of our judges. During the rainy season, some of the courts look like islands in the water. Judges, advocates and others going here and there with the help of rickshaw pullers. Sometimes, even the court rooms are filled with water and the judges have to close their work. It is found that no space is reserved for litigants waiting for the turn. A huge rush like the fish market can be seen in as well as outside the court room. Sometimes, court staff takes money to offer a chair or table to somebody. A top-heavy obsession with the Supreme Courts and High Courts has led to near-total neglect of the Subordinate Courts, which represent the real face of justice for the common man (The Tribune, Chandigarh, March 27, 1998). The conditions of work in the subordinate courts are simply appalling and it is miracle that they continue to dispense justice. No legal or judicial reform will have more than a cosmetic effect unless it reaches down to the subordinate courts and change their operations in a big way.

"Ever thought of getting justice in a building that is about to collapse? Or would one like to rush from one chamber to another spread over a distance? Last but not the least, when one goes to the court, there is no place to sit and a stinking toilet keeps you away from it: neither is there provision for drinking water where one's thirst can be quenched. (The Tribune, Chandigarh, March 27, 1998)

The problems like these are not the problem of one district of Punjab or another but all the districts and the sub-divisions have the same problem along with some variations. In a number of districts, the conditions of court complexes are like that of a fort and deplorable except in the newly constructed buildings. The courts are located in different locations and lawyers and litigants running from one to other court. The courtrooms leak during the rainy season. Some judges sit in the rooms meant for stenos. Some courts have no dias, no podium and no witness box. It is found that there is no separate entry for judges who have to pass through a crowd of litigants and lawyers to reach their work place. Some courtrooms are so small that Ahlamads and clerks are forced to sit in the verandah. In many districts judicial court complex has become congested and the entire complex is occupied by lawyers, petition writers and stamp vendors. It is difficult to believe that some of the rooms in which the judges sit to hear cases and give judgments do not even match the standard of class IV employee's rooms. With the entry of three or four persons, besides the judge and his assistants, such courtrooms become overcrowded and one has to wait outside for some time to get inside. During the rainy season the situation becomes worse since storm water would flow into the court complex, which paralyses court work. Hordes of stray cattle remain sitting in the open court complexes. Heaps of garbage could be seen strewn all around in absence of sweepers. Court complexes stink and give the impression that there is no one to look after its sanitation. There is a lack of basic amenities like drinking water and toilets. There is no sitting arrangement for litigants. If any waiting hall or waiting room is reserved for litigants, these are occupied by lawyers and typists. The judges are over worked and under staffed. Almost every judge has, on average 1500 to 2500 files as against the High Court norms of 500 files. Approximately, 100 cases are listed for daily hearing but effective hearing is granted in only 10 to 15 cases and the rest are adjourned to future dates (The Tribune, Chandigarh, March 27, 1998).

Faulty Distribution of Work

Judges are assigned mélange of cases within their jurisdictions without regard to their professional specialty. He has to deal with all sorts of cases-civil, criminal, administrative, revenue and matrimonial, etc. He cannot be expected to be a specialist in all the fields of law and the variety of the cases makes him exert more which consequently consumes his time and causes delay. In addition, he has to manage his office, control his clerks and menials, keep accounts and conduct a certain amount of correspondence. He is responsible for the examination of plaint and pleadings and the arrangement of his own cause list. On top of this, most of his time is consumed in writing lengthy and elaborate judgments which he has generally to dictate at his residence in view of the paucity of time in the court. Thus, the judge is not only overworked but is expected to be a jack of all trades. He is expected to be a good administrator, a good accountant, and also have up-to-date knowledge of all fields of law. It is but natural that the over-worked presiding officer having inadequate ministerial staff commits procedural irregularities, particularly in the matter of issuing summons, framing of issues, preparing causes list, etc. which ultimately add to the delays.

Over Burden Investigatory Agency

The investigating agency nowadays is not able to devote as much time as it should do to criminal cases pending in courts. The police, which constitutes the investigating agency is over-burdened with manifold other duties, including those relating to the maintenance of law and order. It is found that political interference in the matters of investigating agency is unrelenting. All these factors contribute to the delay of disposal of cases by lower courts.

Absence of One of the Accused

The disposal of cases in which there is a large number of accused gets delayed because one of the accused absents himself on the date of hearing. The result is that the case cannot proceed, and all the witnesses and the other accused who are present have to go back without any substantive accomplishment in the court (77th Report Law Commission of India).

Shortage of Prosecutors

There are not enough number of prosecutors, and quite often the trial court has to wait for the prosecutor to be free from another court before starting the criminal case. Sometimes one public prosecutor has been assigned to represent the state in more than two courts, which results in the delay of justice.

Inadequate Remuneration

In the matters of scales of pay and remuneration, the judiciary compares unfavorably with the executive branches of the Government. It is true that, generally speaking, the scales of pay of the judicial officers and the corresponding executive officers are identical in many of the states. However, it has to be remembered that the executive officers are, by and large, recruited at a much younger age than the judicial officers (ibid). The entrant to the judicial service is required to be a graduate in law and must have practiced for a certain number of years at the Bar. On the other hand, for recruitment to the executive branches of the government service, a degree in arts or science, generally speaking is sufficient. As a result, a person entering the judicial service does so when he is about twenty-six or twenty-seven years of age and at a time when his contemporaries who have entered the executive service of the government have already acquired certain seniority in the service and have come to draw a higher remuneration. It will thus be seen that a person joining the judicial service starts with lower remuneration than what he would have received if he had entered the executive service a few years earlier. It has also to be noted that owing to the lesser proportion of superior posts in the judicial service promotions come less quickly to the judicial officers, and a person who has entered the service as a civil judge (Junior Division), assuming that he is fit and fully qualified, takes much longer time to become a district judge than would an equally competent deputy collector to reach the position of a collector. Again the judicial officer having started at a later age has a shorter span of service than the executive officer and this affects his pension and other retirement benefits.

Lack of Training

The mere selection of a suitable person by the application of the tests does not obviously complete the process of bringing into the service of a competent judicial officer. The law graduate, notwithstanding his experience of few years at the Bar, will still require a course of training before he can be entrusted with the work of a judicial officer. When the officer lacks knowledge in civil, criminal, revenue and administrative matters generally he takes the help of readers, stenos and sometimes advocates which results in delay in the disposal of cases. In the Punjab Judicial Service there is no proper academy for imparting training to newly appointed Judicial Officers. Training of seven days to one month is given, which is not appropriate and fruitful. Considering the fact that from the first day of his assuming office, the judge has to decide, among others, questions of life, liberty, property and reputation of the litigants. To induct graduates with little experience to occupy seats of such vital powers is neither prudent nor desirable (All India Judges Association v Union of India AIR 1993 SC 2493 p. 2496).

Conflict Between Bar and Bench

It is generally believed that justice is something in the pocket of a judge which can be doled out to a needy litigant. This is wholly an erroneous impression. Administration of justice is teamwork. No doubt, judge is the captain of the team. It may be stated at the very outset that the Bench and the Bar are an integral part of the administration of justice. They are like the two wheels of a motorcycle, you snap the one, the other will automatically lose its efficacy. It is, therefore, essential that healthy and courteous relations exist between the two. Intemperate attacks by the Bar on Bench and by the Bench on the Bar gravely affect the administration of justice and consequently lower public esteem for Judges and Advocates alike. Sometimes advocates go on strike on very minor pretexts e.g. rainy day, sunny day, foggy day, festival, death of an advocate or his relative, no mood, they are tired, etc. It is observed that a number of files are concentrated in the hands of a few lawyers but they do not get the time to appear in all the cases; so either they take adjournments or provoke the other lawyers to go on strike. Sometimes advocates go to the extent of causing physical injuries to judges. For instance, an advocate in Solan (H.P) had hurled his shoe at the judge which hit him on the shoulder. Advocate contended that when he appeared before the said judge regarding a case, the judge remarked: "You rascal, I will set you right." He said that under the extreme heat of the moment and passion, his hand fell on his shoe which he threw towards the dias (AIR 1981 SC 1382). In another recent news, a lawyer practicing in Kaithal (Haryana) attacked a lady judicial Magistrate, with a knife in her courtroom and also threatened the Additional Session Judge (The Tribune, Chandigarh, September 6, 2000). Sometimes they induce the judges by filing false and frivolous complaints against them. In retaliation, the judges intentionally do not rule on the case of complainant minded advocates.

Frequent Transfer of Judges

Although the maximum period of stay of an officer at one station is three years, it is observed that he is transferred even after a period of one month or less than that. Some of the officers are transferred three to four times within three years. This type of attitude of the High Court results in delays in the disposal of cases by courts.

Given these seemingly intractable structural, procedural and malpractices in the subordinate judiciary in justice delivery, what follows are practical recommendations.

SUBORDINATE JUDICIARY AND EARLY DISPOSAL OF CASES: SUGGESTIONS

Some of the suggestions to remove the stress from subordinate judiciary are as following:

1. Efforts should be made to stop the practice of pleadings being drawn by clerks and petition writers.
2. Parties should be required to file with their pleadings a registered address, service of processes and notices at which, will be deemed to be service on the party for the purpose of the suit, appeal, revision or execution proceedings.
3. The form of summons to the defendant should be amended by inserting in it a direction to the defendant to file a written statement by a date, which should be the date fixed for settlement of issues and a note added in the summons to the effect that if the written statement is not filed by that date, the matter may be dealt with ex-parte.
4. Parties should be directed to file with their pleadings printed forms of processes, filled in by them leaving only the relevant dates to be filled in by the court.
5. The court should exercise very strict supervision over the process serving establishment to reduce delays in the service of the process.
6. If practicable, a responsible officer should make regular inspections of the work of the process servers by paying surprise visits.
7. The service conditions of process servers should be improved and provision is made for the payment of traveling and other allowances to them.
8. Substituted service should be ordered after two unsuccessful attempts to effect service in an ordinary manner or by post.
9. Order VI, Rule 15 of the Civil Procedure Code should be amended by providing that the verification of pleadings should be on oath, so that in ex-parte cases, the court may in its discretion give judgment on the plaint without requiring additional evidence and the defendant may not falsely deny obvious facts.
10. Whenever there is concentration of several courts at one place, a special officer of the rank of a civil judge should be appointed to receive, scrutinize, and checking pleadings with power to make peremptory orders for dismissal of the suit or direct amendment or rejection of the pleadings.
11. If necessary, after the settlement of issues, one intermediate date may be fixed before the date of hearing for filing supplementary lists of documents.
12. The production of further documents should not be allowed at the stage of hearing save in exceptional circumstances and for good reasons to be recorded in writing.
13. The court should insist upon the list of documents and their production in court being made in chronological or some other methodical order.
14. Parties should be required to file their lists of witnesses within a time to be fixed by the court not exceeding thirty days from the date of the framing of the issues.
15. Judicial officers should pay personal attention to the posting of cases and the fixation of dates for trial.
16. Adjournment should not be granted merely to suit the convenience of the parties or their advocates.

17. The court should encourage the larger use of affidavit evidence for proof of simple and uncontroversial facts.
18. Arguments should, as far as possible, be heard immediately on the conclusion of the evidence or in complicated cases within a short time thereafter.
19. It is not necessary to read out the full judgment in open court. It is sufficient if the findings on the issues and the final order are read.
20. A commissioner appointed by the court for any purpose should be imperatively required to finish his work within the time fixed and in case of delay, his fees should be reduced.
21. Commissioner for recording the evidence of parties or witnesses should be entrusted to junior lawyers not having much work. A list of suitable junior lawyers willing to work as commissioners should be maintained in each court.
22. A good deal of training and experience, in the field of civil, criminal, revenue and administration is needed for judicial officers.
23. The merits of the subordinate judges should not be assessed on the basis of disposals without taking into consideration the nature of cases and the quality of his work handled by him.
24. In compoundable and compromisable cases, some credit should be given to judicial officers, while evaluating the out turn.
25. In order to maintain the dignity and decorum of the court, he must be punctual and should see that there is complete silence in the court. He should not talk in court about anything except the case in hand and should not permit others to indulge in loose talk.

CONCLUSION

In a modern state, a citizen is expected to use the force of the state through the state machinery to avenge the wrongs done to him and seek redress of his grievances instead of resorting to self-help. One of the most important functions of the state is to ensure proper administration of justice by bringing offenders to book and awarding suitable punishment to them and adequate compensation to the persons aggrieved. No innocent person can suffer if justice is properly administered by the state. The faith of the people in the administration of justice is essential for maintaining peace. Although every effort should be made to weed out the defects and infirmities of the system and to improve it with a view to make it responsive to the people's needs, we must guard against saying anything which might have the effect of undermining the basic and broad confidence of the people in the judiciary. It has to be borne in mind that there is a vast difference between constructive and informed criticism and misleading statements and insults which are sometimes hurled. The stake of the public at large in this matter is tremendous. A respected and independent judiciary and a respected and strong bar are indispensable if we want to maintain our system of freedom under the law. Bearing in mind the limitations of a judge, his criticism on various grounds is usually unjustified. A judge is as much dedicated to the service of the people as anyone else, but he has to act according to law. He cannot take liberty with law, Judiciary is the last resort of an innocent man who is accused of an offence as also of a person whose rights have been infringed. The judge is very keen to give due protection to the innocent and to grant due relief to the person whose rights have been infringed, in accordance with the law. It is for the people to strengthen his hands by rendering him necessary assistance in all matters. It's necessary to inculcate in the people respect for truth as well as for the judges, which is so essential for the administration of justice. No doubt, lower courts are under the control and supervision of the High Court but there is no need to make realize that they are subordinates. The word "subordinate" in the judicial hierarchy sounds incongruous. To be precise, when any matter is before a court of competent jurisdiction even at the grass-root level, it handles the matter un-influenced by any extraneous or irrelevant considerations and wholly free from any outside pressure including pressure from upper layers of service. To illustrate, even the district judge, though an administrative superior of Civil Judge (junior division) cannot interfere when the proceedings are before the Civil Judge except when he hears any appeal or revision. If he interferes, a charge of contempt may be made against him. In an administrative hierarchy, a superior officer can give direction to the inferior officer even with regard to matters which is being dealt with by him. This is the basic difference between a hierarchy of officers in the executive and the hierarchy of officers in the judiciary. Therefore, the word 'subordinate' which implies a sort of subordination of one to the other which may inhere or give rise to an inference of something akin to command obedience relationship has to be avoided as far as possible. Undoubtedly, we are conscious of the fact that even the constitution uses the expression 'subordinate courts'. The court structure being paramedic and hierarchical in character may tolerably be described in relation to a superior as a subordinate court. But, as far as the designation of judicial officer is concerned, every attempt must be made to avoid that word. Therefore, it would be proper to devise a uniform designation for the entry cadre[1] to make the lower judiciary more effective and more efficient. The powerful impact which the system of courts and judicial administration has on a vast number of citizens, needs to be pointed out, so that, it may be appreciated that the reform of the system is a matter of vital importance, not only to the lawyer and the judge but also to be State and the average citizen. The smooth and speedy operation of the courts of law is essential to the progress of the country. So, it is in the interest of the citizens as well as the State that the disputes which go to the law courts for adjudication, should be decided within a reasonable time, so as to give certainty and definiteness to rights and obligations. If the course of a trial is inordinately long, the chances of miscarriage of justice and the expenses of litigation increase alike. Delays result in witnesses being unable to testify correctly to events, which may have faded in their memory, and sometimes in their being won over by the opponent. Relief granted to an aggrieved party after a lapse of years loses much of its value and sometimes becomes totally fructuous. Such is the basis of the ubiquity of the comment "justice delayed is justice denied". But speedy justice does not mean a hasty or even a summary dispensation of justice by persons not qualified to administer it. What has to be ensured is that the determination of facts in controversy and the application to the facts so determined of the appropriate legal principles should not be unduly delayed. Applying these standards, there is a great scope for improvement in the working of our judicial machinery.

REFERENCES

Bhalla, M. M. (1988). Case for Abolition of Process Fee in Civil and Criminal Cases. *AIR Journal, 90.*

Forst, M. L. (1977). Trial courts in the Modern System of Criminal Justice. *Criminal Justice Review, 2*(1), 73–88. doi:10.1177/073401687700200107

Kumar, N. (1997). Constitutional Law of India. Academic Press.

Mann, T. K. (n.d.). Administration of Justice in India: A case study of Punjab. Academic Press.

Mathur, V. K. (n.d.). *Early Disposal of Court Cases*. Academic Press.

Narayan, S. (1987). The Procedural Law in India Requires Through Changes. *AIR Journal, 85.*

Nardulli, P. F. (1979). The case Load controversy and the Study of criminal courts. *J. Crime Law Journal, 70*(1), 89–101. doi:10.2307/1142969

Pande, D. C., & Bagga, V. (1973). *Abridged Trial Procedure in Indian Law*. Indian Law Institute.

Rao, M. V. (1994). Legal Reforms for speedy disposal of cases. *AIR Journal, 89.*

Singhvi, G. C. (1976). Mounting Arrears of cases in Courts, Devolution of powers – A key solution. *CBI Bulletin*.

APPENDIX: ADDITIONAL RESOURCES

Statutes and Case Laws

- Law Commission of India 14th Report on Reforms of Judicial Administration.
- Law Commission of India, 77th Report on, Delay and Arrears in Trial Courts.
- All India Judges Association v Union of India AIR 1993 SC 2493 p. 2496
- T.K. Mann, Administration of Justice in India - a case study of Punjab, p. 159.
- The Tribune. Chandigarh, March 27, 1998
- The Tribune, Chandigarh, August 8, 1996
- R.S. Nayak v. A.R. Antulay [1984, 2 SCR 495]
- Agarwal, B. R (n.d.). Our judiciary.

Chapter 6
Administration of Civil Justice and Its Glorious Uncertainty in the Indian Legal System:
A Long, Expensive Journey to Justice

Soma Dey Sarkar
University of North Bengal, India

Rathin Bandyopadhyay
University of North Bengal, India

Bidisha Bandyopadhyay
KIIT University (Deemed), India

ABSTRACT

"Justice delayed is justice denied" and "justice hurried is justice buried" are oft quoted proverbs in legal studies. While the latter is rarely prevalent in India, the former has maligned the image of the Indian legal system considerably. Delay in disposal of cases, pendency of cases, especially those of civil and commercial nature, and inducing unnecessary procedural complexities in litigation process are hindrances that come in the way of access to justice. Several reports of the Law Commission of India have pointed out that the present situation is very grim with escalating number of pending cases in the courts in India. To add to this compelling situation, the COVID-19 pandemic has further disrupted the court proceedings by increasing burden, moving the hearings from physical to virtual courtrooms. The endeavour of the authors in this chapter has been to search for convincing reasons that have led to inordinate delays in disposal of civil cases and to find out possible solutions to this problem plaguing the Indian legal system.

DOI: 10.4018/978-1-7998-7898-8.ch006

1. INTRODUCTION

The Preamble to the Constitution of India guarantees to secure the quaternity of Justice, Liberty, Equality and Fraternity. In its truest sense, the virtue of 'Justice'- 'social, political and economic', is the essence of the Holy Trinity of "LIBERTY, EQUALITY AND FRATERNITY". Thus, access to justice is fundamental to the protection and preserving of Liberty, Equality and Fraternity of all human beings. The right to access to justice, which is of ancient vintage in India and later on emerged as the Magna Carta on 5 May, 1215, in the words of Justice A.K. Ganguly, emanates from:

1. a basic instinct for survival with dignity; and
2. to evolve a mechanism to redress deprivation of basic rights without which human dignity would be a teasing illusion.

Being inherent in Article 14 of the Constitution of India which guarantees equality of law and equal protection of the law, 'access to justice' is placed on high pedestal of fundamental rights, which gets reflected in other Articles like Article 22, 32, 38, 39A, 142, etc. in the years to come, the Supreme Court of India would read 'access to justice' within the folds of Article 21.

Envisioning this 'access to justice' as fundamental, the Constitution of India lays for the establishment of an illustrious and elaborate hierarchy of court system with the Supreme Court placed at the top of the pyramid, followed by High Courts at the states (presently 25 in number) and the lower courts also called the subordinate courts at the lowest tier. The judiciary, therefore, plays an important role in securing justice by providing fora for the enforcement of the rights of individuals, or remedies against their violation.

In spite of having a structured judicial system, the Indian judicial system has failed to offer speedy remedies to its citizens. As Marc Galanter described, delay is endemic (Kirpal, et. al, 2008, p.59). To quote Professor Galanter (2008), "...Indian courts are desperately congested, even though the number of cases filed is small on a per capita basis. They appear to be heavily used because there are relatively few courts (in comparison to other common law countries). These courts are poorly equipped and inefficient" (ibid). The present chapter emphasises on delay in disposal of cases and huge backlogs in courts as a hurdle in accessing justice. The problem of litigation delays becomes acute especially in civil and commercial laws. The objective of this chapter is to find out reasons for such piling of cases and search for practical and long-term solutions to this chronic problem.

2. THE CIVIL JUDICIAL SYSTEM IN INDIA AND ITS PERENNIAL PROBLEMS

a. The Civil Judicial System in India: A Brief History

The modern Indian Judicial System owes its origin to colonial rule which continued for more than 200 years. Though the seeds of a separate judicial system for civil and criminal judicature were sown by the Mughal rulers, a systematic and segregated arrangement of the civil and criminal judicature was done by the British rulers under various Judicial Plans between 1772 and 1859. One could come across courts like the Moffussil Diwani Adalats (courts of civil jurisdiction established in each district), Sadar Diwani Adalats (civil courts of Appeal) and Diwani Adalats. Subsequently, the Supreme Courts of Calcutta

(1773), Madras (1797) and Bombay (1797) were established which also had appellate jurisdiction in civil matters. The problem, however, that needed to be addressed was that the judicial system was restricted only to the provinces of Bengal, Bihar and Orissa and the regions of Madras and Bombay. There was no uniform system of civil administration until 1859 when the first uniform Code of Civil Procedure was enacted to overcome the chaotic situation that prevailed in the administration of civil litigation. Upon making a few amendments to the original Code and after well thought out efforts and experimentation extending over more than half a century, the Code of Civil Procedure was finally adopted in the present form in 1908, which provides for Subordinate Civil Courts with territorial and pecuniary jurisdiction, Courts of District Judge (at District Level), High Courts and Supreme Court having appellate jurisdiction in civil matters.

b. The Subsisting Issues in the Administration of Civil Justice in India

The system of courts and judicial administration has a powerful impact upon citizens and hence, the smooth and speedy operation of the Courts is essential to the progress of the country and the growth of its economic and industrial stature [14th Law Commission of India Report on Reform of Judicial Administration].

Delay in civil courts and defects in the constitution of the Judiciary and the substantive and procedural laws of the country were identified to be the cause that could inevitably pose hindrances to smooth access to justice, as early as 1923. To that effect, a committee was appointed, mainly through the efforts of Sir Tej Bahadur Sapru, the Law Member of the Viceroy's Executive Council with Mr. Justice Rankin as the Chairman "to enquire into the operation and effects of substantive and adjective law, whether enacted or otherwise, followed by the courts in India in the disposal of civil suits, appeals, applications for revision and other civil litigation (including the execution of decrees and orders), with a view to ascertaining and reporting whether any and what changes and improvements should be made so as to provide for more speedy, economical and satisfactory despatch of the business transacted in the courts and for the more speedy, economical and satisfactory execution of the process issued by the courts." [14th Law Commission of India Report on Reform of Judicial Administration, p. 14]

In 1954, in its 14th Report, the Law Commission of India had expressed their concern over piling of the vast volume of ordinary civil litigation in various courts in the country. To quote the report: "The number of suits instituted in civil courts exceeds ten lacs; and of these, nearly nine lacs of cases involve disputes relating to sums of rupees one thousand and below."

The issues and challenges posed to the Indian Civil justice administration that the Constitution makers and the British administrators have foreseen a hundred years ago, continue to plague the justice delivery system in India.

3. UNDERSTANDING AND ASSESSING DELAY IN DISPOSAL OF CASES AND LONG PENDENCY OF CASES WITH REFERENCE TO CIVIL LITIGATIONS

Ideally, any legal system should strive towards enabling economic choice, promoting ethical and sound business policies and practices, cutting transaction costs and enabling healthy commercial dealings through fair contracts. This is as essential as good infrastructure and sound polity. Thus, quick settlement of disputes especially in economic and commercial transactions becomes a prerequisite for a free economy.

The Indian Legal System has been characterised by and criticised for the gigantic issue of delay. Moreso, delays in litigation become acute in civil and commercial laws. In the words of Mr. Hasit B. Seth, an independent counsel practising in Bombay High Court and arbitrations, businesses run on the concept of "time value of money" and the underlying value of an asset or a claim in dispute effectively becomes of negative value, if the dispute is not resolved within a time frame (Hasit, 2021).

a. Pendency of Civil Litigation

Researches and surveys carried on to understand the reason behind such inordinate delay in disposal of cases, especially those of civil and commercial nature, point towards pendency and a towering backlog of cases lying with the judiciary at all stages, right from the lower courts to the apex court. Since, 1958, as many as fourteen reports of the Law Commission of India have been devoted to the issue of large arrears and excessive delays in the Judicial process and recommended reforms to this end.

A glance at the number of pending civil litigations in the Supreme Court, High Courts and Subordinate Courts, displayed in the Table 1, reveal the deep lesion in our judiciary.

Table 1.

Supreme Court of India	67,898	01-05-2021
High Courts	4,168, 350	23-06-2021
District and Taluka Courts	10,172,245	23-06-2021

Source: https://njdg.ecourts.gov.in/

The alarming number of pending civil litigations with more than 4 million in High Courts and 10 million in the Lower Courts show the sad state of affairs of the Indian judiciary.

Table 2.

Time	District and Taluka Courts	High Courts
0-1 years	2,805,045	697,517
3-5 years	1,675,502	673,847
5-10 years	1,627,335	861,386
10-20 years	550,737	711289
<30 years	37,036	109,284

Source: https://njdg.ecourts.gov.in/

The figures in Table 2 represent the number of pending civil cases in District and Taluka courts and High Courts for a period of 1 year, 3 to 5 years, 5 to 10 years, 10 to 20 years and more than 30 years. It can be seen that it is the lower courts, i.e., the District and Taluka Courts who have the maximum pendency of cases with more than 2 million cases pending with them. On the other hand, it is seen that cases pending for more than 30 years are maximum among the High Courts with more than 1 million cases. A report by the Times of India on 16 February, 2021 suggests that in the last two years backlogs of 30-year-old cases have gone up by 61%. The subordinate and district judiciary in six states of Uttar Pradesh, Maharashtra, West Bengal, Bihar, Gujarat and Odisha accounted for 98% of more than a lakh of these three decades old pending cases [timesofindia.indiatimes.com/india/backlog-of-30-year-old-cases-up-by-61-in-2years/articleshow/80956134.cms??utm_source=contentofinterest&utm-medium-text&utm_campaign=cppse].

A report of the Bloomberg Quint which was submitted as written replies by the Ministry of Law and Justice in Parliament, suggests that between February 1 and August 2020, the Supreme Court of India itself has seen a rise in pending cases by 3.0%. To worsen the situation, the Covid-19 pandemic has disrupted the court proceedings moving physical hearings to virtual courtrooms [bloombergquint.com/law-and-policy/Indias-pending-court-cases-on-the-rise-in-charts].

A Report prepared by Daksh, a Bengaluru based civil society organisation, on Access to Justice during 2015-2016 has revealed disquieting glitches in the civil justice system in India. The survey conducted on 9329 litigants stretching across 25 states has revealed the 'litigants' perception of delay in Courts. A clear majority of civil cases litigants (61% of the respondents) suggested that the judges do not pass orders quickly. It was also felt by the respondents that litigations get delayed due to non-appearance of opposite parties on dates fixed for hearing. The survey has also revealed that "lack of judges in subordinate courts is a primary reason for delay in general in the courts." 49.3% of the respondents opened up on lack of judges in civil courts and 63.7% blamed overcrowding of civil litigations in courts as the reason for delay. When Team Daksh enquired the litigants about their expected time for disposal of cases, 55% of the civil litigants expected their cases to be resolved within a year when they first filed their cases. Interestingly, only 32% expected the same on the date of survey. Also, 35.7% of litigants expected that resolving their cases would require as long as 5 years. [Report on Access to Justice available at www.dakshindia.org]

Upon analysing the data extracted from various sources, the researchers have derived the following as the major reasons for delay and pendency of civil litigations in India:

i. Procedural Delays

Civil cases, like its criminal counterparts, traverse through various stages from the time of its institution till its final disposal. Typically, any civil case is initiated with a plaint and upon satisfaction of the judge with the contentions raised in the plaint, the opposite party is summoned to the court [Sections 26 and 27, Code of Civil Procedure, 1908]. The written statement is expected to be filed by the defendant within 30 days which may be extended to 90 days [now 120 days after the amendment introduced in the Code of Civil Procedure by the Commercial Courts, Commercial Division and Commercial Appellate Division of High Courts Act, 2015] followed by filing of replication or interim applications by the parties. The judges proceed with the framing of the issues where the main points of contentions are identified and concretized. Upon framing of the issues, evidences are presented and examined. In the evidence stage, the plaintiff/petitioners first present their evidence followed by the examination of evidence of the defendant/respondent. The final stage in a civil litigation is the argument stage wherein arguments on behalf of the parties are heard on completion of which final order/judgement is passed. It is pertinent to mention here that all civil litigations do not go through all the above-mentioned stages. For instance, execution cases or civil appeals do not have any evidence stage. Theoretically, these stages seem to be simplistic in nature but practically, a considerable amount of time is spent in the initial stages of filing a civil suit. A **Pilot Project on Zero Pendency Courts Project** undertaken by Daksh at the behest of the Delhi High Court shows that a great deal of time is spent in procedural stages comprising of issues and returns of summons, filing of written statements, etc. [Inefficiency and Judicial Delay: New Insights from Delhi High Court, March 2017 available at www.vidhilegalpolicy.in]

Table 3.

Stages in Litigation	Category of Courts	Days Spent
Misc. cases/purposes [including issues and return of summons, filing of written statements]	District court	74
	Labour court	29
	Motor accident claims	17
	Rent controller	54
Framing of issues	District court	46
	Labour court	16
	Motor accident claims	10
Misc. Arguments	District court	44
	Labour court	35
	Motor accident claims	17
	Rent controller	46
Misc. Orders	District court	21
	Labour court	14
	Motor accident claims	16
	Rent controller	
Plaintiff/petitioner evidence	District court	89
	Labour court	27
	Motor accident claims	30
	Rent controller	57
Defendant/respondent evidence	District court	87
	Labour court	27
	Motor accident claims	19
	Rent controller	40
Final arguments	District court	32
	Labour court	22
	Motor accident claims	19
	Rent controller	40
Final order/judgement	District court	20
	Labour court	11
	Motor accident claims	08
	Rent controller	20

Source: www.vidhilegalpolicy.in

Table 3 provides for the number of days spent at various stages in civil litigations instituted at different categories of court in the Union Territory of New Delhi. The survey was conducted at various subordinate courts in Delhi with the object to prepare a report based on the data collected and recorded on a day-to-day basis between January 2017 and December 2018.

The figures in the table show that the average days taken to complete various stages was higher for District Judges when compared to the other categories of courts. On an average, District Courts required 74 days for Misc. Cases, 46 days to frame issues, 89 days to examine evidence for petitioners/plaintiff, 87 days to examine evidence for defendants/respondents and 20 days to pronounce a final order/judgement.

Data extracted from National Judicial Data Grid (NJDG) in Tables 4 and 5 show the stage-wise pendency of the civil proceedings in District and Taluka Courts and High Courts in India.

Table 4.

Stages of Proceeding	No. of Cases Pending	% of Pendency
Hearing	1,676. 273	40.57
Evidence	1,609,584	38.96
Arguments	374,816	9.07
Orders	345,402	8.36
Pre-trial evidence	75,282	1.82
Judgement	22,248	0.54

Source: https://njdg.ecourts.gov.in/ The data shows the position of pending civil cases in District and Taluka Courts at various stages as on 27-06-2021

Table 5.

Stages of Proceeding	No. of Cases Pending	% of Pendency
Admission	1,066,002	79.63
Order	540,784	40.40
Hearing	339,806	25.38
Final hearing	219,172	16.37
Steps	94,993	7.10
Issues	74,355	5.55
Judgement	4,661	0.35

Source: https://njdg.ecourts.gov.in/The data shows the position of pending civil cases in High Courts at various stages as on 27-06-2021

Whereas 40.57% of civil litigations remain pending at the hearing stage in District Courts, a whopping 79.63% of similar cases remain pending at the early stage of admission in various High Courts in India. However, for both the categories of Courts, a least number of cases are pending at the judgement stage which gives us a positive sign.

Effectively, there are certain bottlenecks before civil courts leading to the colossal delays in court procedure and backlog of cases in India which will be testified in the following discussion:

Delay in Summons and Filing Written Statements

summons is a legal procedure to call upon a person to testify claims of the plaintiff (Section 27, Code of Civil Procedure, 1908). It is generally issued to the defendant as well as to witnesses (Section 31). Order V of the Code of Civil Procedure (CPC), 1908 says that "when a suit has properly been initiated, a summons might be issued to the defendant to show up and answer the claim." It is often witnessed that individuals attempt to avoid the summons leading to delays in trials. Personal service of summons and substituted service of summons are two modes of service of summons. Where the defendant is seen to avoid receiving the summons, by applying Rule 20 of Order V, substituted service of summons is seen to be helpful to deal with delay in service of summons. It is also seen that where defendants, witnesses or any other person avoid summons for answering interrogations or admission of documents, facts or inspection of documents, etc., the Court compels the attendance of that person by (i) issuing a warrant for his arrest; (ii) attach and sell his property; (iii) impose a fine upon him (not exceeding five thousand rupees); order him to furnish security for his appearance and in default commit him to the civil prison (Sections 30 and 32, CPC, 1908). This has led to further complications and delays in the disposal of suits.

Ideally, the defendant should file a written statement within a period of 30 days from the date of service of summons on him (Order VIII, CPC). It is seen that the statutory period of 30 days for filing a written statement is not maintained in the majority of the suits resulting in procedural delays. In order to remedy this situation, by an amendment made in 2002 in the Code it has been provided that "where the defendant fails to file the written statement within the said period of thirty days, he shall be allowed to file the written statement on such other day, as may be specified by the Court, for reason to be recorded in writing and on payment of such costs as the court deems fit, but which shall not be later than ninety days from the date of service of summons, the defendant shall forfeit the right to file the written statement and the Court shall not allow the written statement to be taken on record." [Order VIII, CPC, 1908]

However, to the dismay of the victims of the procedural delays, the Supreme Court of India in 2005 in ***Kailash vs. Nanhku (AIR 2005 SC 2441)*** relaxed this statutorily prescribed deadline by interpreting it as mere directory and not mandatory. The Apex Court further held that courts could use their discretion in unspecified exceptional circumstances to accept delayed written statements. The lawyers have been utilising this case as a *carte blanche* to file written statements beyond the statutory period of 30 days making the exceptional the new normal.

The Commercial Courts Act, 2015 which came into force on 23 October 2015 has, fortunately, become a panacea for this incessant plaguing system of delaying in filing a written statement. As a result of the Commercial Courts Act, 2015, certain amendments had to be inserted in sub-rule (1) of Order V Rule 1 to achieve the objective of expeditious disposal of commercial disputes which provides as below:

"... Provided further that where the defendant fails to file the written statement within the said period of thirty days, he shall be allowed to file the written statement on such other day, as may be specified by the Court, for reason to be recorded in writing and on payment of such costs as the court deems fit, but which shall not be later than one hundred and twenty days from the date of service of summons and on expiry of one hundred and twenty days from the date of service of summons, the defendant shall forfeit the right to file the written statement and the court shall not allow the written statement to be taken on record."

In order to reemphasize the need to do away with this practice of indiscriminate extension of time, Order VIII Rule 10 has been amended by inserting the following proviso:

"...Provided further that no Court shall make an order to extend the time provided under Rule 1 of this Order for filing of the written statement..."

The Hon'ble Supreme Court of India in a recent case in ***M/s SCG Contracts India Pvt. Ltd. vs. M/s KS Chamankar Infrastructure Pvt. Ltd. (C.A. No. 1638/2019)*** has held that it is mandatory to file the written statement in a commercial suit within 120 days from the date of service of summons upon the Defendant(s) and if the Defendants fail to do so, the right to file the same is forfeited, which cannot be saved or extended even by invoking Section 151 of the Code of Civil Procedure.

Frequent Adjournments

The 77th Report of the Law Commission had pointed out that frequent adjournments are an imperative reason for delay. (77th Law Commission of India Report on Delay and Arrears in Trial Courts, November, 1978)

The repeated culture of unwanted and unwarranted adjournments employed by lawyers and advocates has bogged down the Indian Judicial System. The Code of Civil Procedure provides for sufficient safeguards under Order XVII which limits pleading for adjournments to three adjournments only during the course of a suit. Order XVII further provides that adjournments will be granted for a 'sufficient cause' and 'where circumstances are beyond the control of a party'. According to a report published in Deccan Chronicle on 16 February, 2020, the average number of adjournments granted in a day in the district and subordinate courts range from 12 to 32. It has also been reported that for an average period of fifteen months to sixty months litigations get delayed in subordinate judiciary due to adjournment orders. [deccanchronicle.com/nation/current-affairs/16022/malady-of-adjournments-continues.html]

Non-Appearance of Parties on the Day of Hearing

non-appearance of parties on the date of hearing is another reason for procedural delay. According to the Report on Access to Justice by Daksh, it was found that 26.1% of the litigants felt that delays in proceedings take place due to the non-appearance of the opposite party.

Administrative Inaction and Laxity in Discharging Statutory Notice

It is a condition precedent under Section 80 of the CPC that the Government must be served a statutory notice before any civil remedy in a civil court is put into motion. The obvious reason behind this provision is to give an opportunity to the Government to redress the grievances of the person serving the notice. The two months period mentioned in Section 80 has been provided so that the Government can examine the claim put on the notice and has sufficient time to send a suitable reply. The object inherent in it is to avoid litigations. The provisions of Sec. 80 of CPC cast an implied duty on all Government and statutory authorities to send appropriate replies to the said notices. A survey conducted in Uttarakhand, showed that this statutory requirement is fulfilled by neither the people willing to file suits nor the Government receiving notice. (Gyanendra Sharma and Pranav Vashishtha, Bottlenecks in the Civil

Justice Administration before the Courts and the Remedies Thereof: A Research Paper, Uttarakhand Judicial and Legal Review, p. 3)

In ***Salem Advocate Bar Association, Tamil Nadu vs. Union of India [2002 Supp. (3) SCR 353]***, the Hon'ble Supreme Court had mentioned that a judicial notice can be taken of the fact that in majority of the cases, where Section 80 is applicable, no reply is sent. This is a clear case of administrative inaction and laxity resulting in backlog of civil litigations in courts.

Judicial Inaction in ADR Mechanism

Section 89 was inserted in CPC by the Civil Laws Amendment Act, 1999, which provides for adopting certain alternative dispute resolution mechanisms. Not resorting to ADR mechanisms has resulted in piling up of cases and hence Parliament introduced Sec. 89 and Rule 1(A) and 1(C) in Order X in CPC to ensure that ADR processes are resorted to before commencement of trial in Suit.

Appeals/Revisions Against Judgements/Orders in Petty Suits

In ***Haryana Dairy Development Cooperative Federation Ltd. vs Jagadish Labs. [(2016) 3 SCC 156],*** it was held by the Supreme Court of India that:

"If the load of such petty cases is taken out of the regular courts, those courts would have time to deal with more serious crimes rather than have their time consumed by such petty cases."

The remedy for unnecessary filing of appeals and revisions lies in action against the officers who are doing it at the coast of State exchequer. The government and its departments should be wise enough to think that it is not in the interest o the State to pay more on litigations than the stake that is actually involved. If the decision is taken by the department/officers, initially the misuse of money from State exchequer can be stopped and the valuable time of litigants, state and courts can be saved.

In addition to these procedural lacunae, the then Chief Justice of India, Justice P.N. Bhagwati while speaking on "Nature and Causes of Delay" in the First International Seminar-Workshop on Managing Delay in the Courts, cited the following as other internal causes of procedural delay:

"(i) the practice of oral arguments that we have inherited from the British;

(ii) the traditional reliance of courts on oral arguments rather than written briefs;

(iii) the plethora of appeals lasting 10, 15 or even 20years;

(iv) patterns of practice in legal profession which encourage postponements and delays as methods fore charging higher legal fees;

(v) incompetent lawyers and poor quality judges."

ii. Vacancies in Judiciary

The 245th Report of the Law Commission has recommended the need for filling of vacancies of the judiciary. It said that "data obtained from High Courts indicates that judicial system is severely back-logged and is also not being able to keep pace with the current filings, thus exacerbating the problem of backlogs. The system requires a massive influx of judicial resources in order to dispose of the backlog and keep pace with the current filings. The data indicates the need for taking urgent measures for in-

Table 6.

State and Union Territories	Total Sanctioned Strength	Total Working Strength	Vacancy
Andaman & Nicobar	0	13	-13
Andhra Pradesh	591	529	68
Arunachal Pradesh	41	27	14
Assam	441	412	29
Bihar	1847A	1161	686
Chandigarh	30	29	01
Chattisgarh	468	394	74
Daman & Diu	4	3	01
Delhi	799	681	118
Goa	50	43	07
Gujarat	1506	1185	321
Haryana	772	475	297
Himachal Pradesh	175	152	23
Jammu & Kashmir	290	232	58
Jharkhand	677	462	215
Karnataka	1345	1106	239
Kerala	536	461	75
Lakshadweep	03	03	00
Madhya Pradesh	2021	1587	434
Maharashtra	2189	1942	247
Manipur	55	39	16
Meghalaya	97	49	48
Mizoram	64	46	18
Nagaland	33	25	08
Odisha	919	771	148
Puducherry	26	11	15
Punjab	675	579	96
Rajasthan	1428	1121	307
Sikkim	25	19	06
Tamil Nadu	1224	1087	137
Telangana	413	334	79
Tripura	120	96	24
Uttar Pradesh	3416	2012	1404
Uttarakhand	294	228	66
West Bengal	1014	920	94

Source: doj.gov.in

creasing, judge strength in order to ensure timely justice and facilitate access to justice for all sections." [245th Law Commission of India, Report No. 245 on Arrears and Backlog: Creating Additional Judicial (Wo)manpower, July 2014]

Whereas the working strength of the Judiciary presently is 19,215 which is way below the sanctioned strength which stands at 24,358 positions. In May 2021, it has been reported by the Department of Justice (DOJ), Government of India, that the strength of High Court judges is 1080. The DOJ website reveals that as of June 1, 2021, there are 430 vacancies among high court judges (the wire.in/law/india-judge-vacancies-justice-delivery). In the past year, the vacancy positions in various high courts have increased from 388 to 430. (doj.gov.in/appointment-of-judges/vacancy-positions)

The problem of judicial vacancies trickles down to the subordinate courts also. On 22 October 2018, a two-judge Bench comprising of Chief Justice Ranjan Gogoi and Justice S.K. Kaul took suo motu cognizance of vacancies of the increasing number of vacancies in the district and lower courts. Pendency due to vacancy in the lower courts is the major predicament that lies ahead of the judicial system in India. The Annual Report presented by the Department of Justice, Government of India 2019-2020 exposes the crisis that the subordinate judiciary is facing with respect to the vacancy thereto. Table 6 represents the state-wise sanctioned strength, the total working strength and the total vacancy.

The table above shows that except Lakshadweep none of the state high courts or subordinate courts have reached their complete complement of sanctioned posts. The states of Uttar Pradesh, Bihar, Madhya Pradesh and Maharashtra have high levels of judicial vacancies. It is worrying that each of the eighteen large and mid-sized states has High Court judge vacancy of more than 25%, i.e., 1 in 4 sanctioned high courts posts have not been filled. At the level of subordinate courts, six of eighteen large and sized states have more than 25% vacancy.

A glance at the judge to population ratio reiterates how impaired the Indian Judiciary is. Law Minister Ravi Shankar Prasad while responding to a query in Rajya Sabha in this regard, stated that as 2020, judges per million population is 20.91. this figure stood at 19.78, 17.48 and 14.7 in 2018, 20214 and 2002 respectively. There seems to be no reason to cheer with the negligible upward movement of the graph from 2018 to 2020 because the same figure stands at 107 for the USA, 75 in Canada and 41 in Australia [theleaflet.in/what-ddoes-data-on-pendency-of-cases-in-indian-courts-tell-us/].

There is no denying the fact that a health judge to population ratio is a necessary manifestation of the right to access to justice and speedy justice. Twenty years ago this view of the 120th Report of the Law Commission was endorsed by the Supreme Court in ***All India Judges Association & Others. Vs. Union of India & Others, [(2002) 4 SCC 247]***, directing that the judge to population be 50 per million which must be achieved within 5 years and not later than 10 years. Unfortunately, this demographic approach to ascertain the judge's strength does not take into account the workload of the judiciary.

iii. Workload

Vacancies in judiciary have a direct bearing upon the workload on the judges which in turn leads to the accumulation of cases. This is a vicious circle. To assess the issue of delay, the India Justice Report took account of current pendency (amount of time a case remains in the court) and clearance rate (the number of cases disposed of by a court in a given year). At the subordinate court level, in twenty-one states and Union Territories(UT), a case remains pending for 5 years on average or more. At the High

Court level, among the large and mid-sized states, cases in Uttar Pradesh remained pending the longest at 4.3 years, while cases in Uttarakhand remained pending for 1.7 years. Among the small states, while the High Courts of Meghalaya (1.3 years), Sikkim (1.7 years), and Mizoram (2 years) had the lowest average pendency, Tripura (2.1 years), Goa (2.9 years), and Himachal Pradesh (3 years) had the highest. The range, too, varied: cases in Gujarat's subordinate courts remained pending for up to 9.5 years on average, while in Rajasthan's subordinate courts the average wait was 3.7 years. [India Justice Report: Ranking States on Police, Judiciary, Prisons and Legal Aid, October 2019]

In general, the number of cases pending in Indian courts is on the rise. One measure of change in the number of pending cases is the clearance rate. If a state disposes of at least as many cases as it receives in a year, it is not adding to its pending workload. Only five High Courts managed this; in the states of Uttar Pradesh, West Bengal, Odisha, Himachal Pradesh, and Tripura. At the subordinate court level, only eight states and UTs qualified; namely Gujarat, Daman and Diu, Dadra and Nagar Haveli, Tripura, Odisha, Lakshadweep, Tamil Nadu, and Manipur. On a five-year basis, the picture is only slightly better: only seven of the eighteen states have managed to lower the number of pending cases in subordinate courts and six of eighteen in High Courts. Some states were more diligent in clearing cases than others. Amongst the large and mid-sized states, at the subordinate court level, Odisha, Tamil Nadu, and Gujarat cleared as many cases in a year as the number that came in, so the arrears didn't grow larger with each year.

iv. Lack of Sufficient Court Rooms and Infrastructure

Sufficient number of court rooms and infrastructure are basic requirements for a sound justice delivery system. The findings of the India Justice Report, 2019, presented by Daksh and Vidhi, Centre for Legal Policy and supported by Tata Trusts shows that if sanctioned strength of judges is filled, there would be a deficit of 18% of court rooms, which implies that if full complement of sanctioned judge strength were appointed there would be a shortfall of 4071 courthalls. (dakshindia.org/india-justice-report-2019/) The Centre had set a target of completing the construction of 2730 court halls within the financial year 2018-2019. The continuing challenge is of renovating and modernising older structures to new standards.

v. Low Budgetary Allocation

The efficiency of the judiciary is significantly influenced by the infrastructure, budgets and human resources available to it. In budgetary allocations of the Centre as well as of the State, judiciary is not perceived as essential as public services like health, housing or education. However, a well functioning judiciary is vital to the maintenance of rule of law, social cohesion and sustainable development. On average, no state or Union Territory in India apart from Delhi spent even 1% of its budget on judiciary. Nationally, India spends 0.08% on the justice delivery system. [https://cbgaindia.org/wp-content/uploads/2019/01/Memorandum-on-Budgeting-for-Judiciary-in-India.pdf]

All states combined (excluding the central government) spent 0.54% of their total expenditure on the judiciary in 2015-2016. Delhi was the only Union Territory which spent more than 1% with 1.9%. Beyond Delhi, the percentage of budget spent on judiciary ranged from 0.1% (Arunachal Pradesh) to 0.96% (Punjab). There were eighteen states spending between 0.5% and 1% on the judiciary, including 13 from the large and mid-sized states. [https://cag.gov.in/sites/default/files/cfra-account_files/CFRA_Vol._3_2015-16.pdf]

4. SMOOTHENING THE WAY TOWARDS ACCESS TO JUSTICE

With the grim scenario of the Indian Civil Justice System, the Department of Justice has taken a few welcome steps to remedy the problems that have been present in the justice delivery system since independence.

The Annual Report of the Ministry of Law and Justice for the year 2019-2020 provides for a few schemes which could resolve the problem of delay and pendency of civil litigations to a considerable extent.

a. Tele-Law Scheme

The Tele-Law Scheme helps the vulnerable people to have access to justice with the help of Para-Legal Volunteers and Village Level Entrepreneurs. Vulnerable people in rural areas are consulting lawyers not only for resolving legal disputes but also if they face any issues with regard to government programmes or documents. Hence, this scheme has become an important tool for the empowerment of marginal communities even in areas other than legal concerns. Some notable challenges in the effectiveness of the scheme include lack of awareness among citizens regarding the scheme, lack of motivation among PLVs, infrastructural quality concerns in CSCs, and changes in lawyers handling the same case. These can mostly be dealt with through some investment to improve conditions at Common Service Centres and through a closer monitoring of the work of PLVs, VLEs, and panel lawyers. This scheme is likely to assume more importance in the future as it provides a feasible way for reaching the vulnerable sections of society who are seeking access to justice at a much larger scale than ever before. [Annual Report, 2019-2020, Ministry of Law and Justice, Government of India]

b. Nyaya Bandhu (Pro Bono Legal Services)

In addition to the above, Nyaya Bandhu (Pro Bono Legal Services) programme aims to provide free legal assistance and counsel to the persons eligible under section 12 of the Legal Service Authorities Act, 1987. This service is provided by advocates who are registered with Department of Justice to volunteer their time and services to represent the cases of registered applicants/litigants. To ensure seamless connectivity between the registered litigant and registered Pro Bono advocate, a Nyaya Bandhu mobile application has been developed that could be downloaded from Google Play Store. Till 9th December 2019, 1108 lawyers have been registered and 516 cases have been assigned. Measures are being taken towards developing the Nyaya Bandhu mobile application for iOS users along with dedicated web-portal and integrating them to facilitate and strengthen the efforts to institutionalize pro bono legal framework in the country. [Annual Report, 2019-2020, Ministry of Law and Justice, Government of India]

c. Nyaya Mitra Programme

Nyaya Mitra Programme is launched to facilitate judiciary in reduction of more than a decade old pending court cases. The Nyaya Mitra (NM) is a retired judicial officer/ executive officer with having legal degree/background, located at High Courts / District Courts. 4 NMs engaged from January 2019 to June, 2019 in Rajasthan, West Bengal and Tripura have facilitated in disposal of 186 pending cases. They also provided assistance during the Lok Adalat in settling pending cases. Engagement process of 93 NMs in

93 District Courts and 7 NMs in 7 High Courts (100 NMs) started in August 2019. Out of advertised positions of 100 Nyaya Mitras, appointment orders of 18 Nyaya Mitras who were recommended by the respective High Courts, have been issued. [Annual Report, 2019-2020, Ministry of Law and Justice, Government of India]

5. RECOMMENDATIONS FOR SPEEDING UP JUSTICE IN CIVIL JUSTICE ADMINISTRATION

There are no two views to the fact that the delay and pendency in judiciary have immensely affected the justice delivery system. An over-worked judiciary can never be expected to do justice to the "right to access of justice" of the citizens. Expediting civil litigations by taking recourse to Alternative Dispute Resolution Mechanisms which involve settlement of disputes through arbitration, conciliation and mediation need not be over-emphasised. These are alternative methods where psychological skills are more operational than legal expertise. One such institution that is unique to India is the Lok Adalat, a statutory body that came into operation under the Legal Services Authorities Act. Legal aid and Lok Adalat are twin institutions that are intended to promote equal justice and free legal aid as envisaged under Article 39-A of the Constitution of India. Again, the Gram Nyayalayas, which came into force in 2009, 20 years after its recommendation by the Law Commission, could be excellent means to realise the right to access to justice. However, there are only 395 Gram Nyayalayas to date, whereas, the Gram Nyayalaya Act, 2008 provides for one or more such institutions in every gram panchayat at the intermediate level or a group of contiguous panchayats at the intermediate level for every district. Failure to implement the laws at hand is the major issue that has cropped up time and again. The main objective for introducing this unique institution is to reduce the burden of the Courts by preventing petty, trivial cases from reaching the courts and adding to the already existing backlog.

Another way of handling older cases is to identify cases that are older than 10 years and hear them on priority and day-to-day basis. These cases may be first grouped, for example, groups of 50 or 100 cases may be made. When the majority of the cases in a group have been disposed of, the second group of prioritized cases may be taken up.

A massive problem that many researchers faced previously while studying the delay and pendency of litigations in Indian Judiciary was the lack of real time data. However, the problem seems to have been resolved with the introduction of the National Judicial Data Grid (NJDG) maintained by the Department of Justice, Government of India. The NJDG does maintain an excellent and real time data-base of the court cases across the country. The data extracted from the NJDG has been of help to a large number of researchers to get meaningful insight. Having said that, it is recommended to develop query-based look-up which will facilitate customized tabulation of cases using filter variables of user's choice.

The Department of Justice and Constitutional Development in South Africa sets performance goals based on strategic objectives, and annually publishes statistics that measure achievement of the goals. A similar goal setting measurement and open publication are desirable for various measures such as sanctioned positions, actual strength, adjournment per case, average adjournments sought by prosecution, time spent on oral arguments, time taken for cases under a certain act, unheard cases from cause list, days of lost business due to foreseeable/unforeseeable circumstances, days of unavailability of the presiding officer, etc.

Since absenteeism and adjournments are major reasons for the delay and pendency of cases, it is recommended that a practical guideline may be drawn to advise the lower judiciary to counter this problem. This could include imposition of fines for not turning up or adjourning for more than the statutory requirement of three times, hearing in absence, imposing a statute of limitation, etc.

There is an urgent need to fill-up the vacancies in order to remedy the problem of delay and pendency. The need of the hour is to develop a zero vacancy or nearly zero vacancy culture. Building of court rooms also is of utmost necessity. However, it is quite understandable that the task is time consuming and involves enormous expenditure. Therefore, a shift system may be introduced so that more cases can be heard at any given point in time.

It is also necessary that every government official and statutory authority who are entrusted to discharge the statutory notice under Section 80, CPC, should be sensitized in this respect with the help of judicial academies and academia.

Oral arguments may be done away with except where it is of utmost necessity. Presiding officers are of the opinion that oral arguments tend to waste the court's time and written arguments and statements may be introduced wherever feasible.

There is a need to embrace automation in courtrooms wherever possible. Eliminating non-human interface from workplace would minimize accompanying inefficiencies, nepotism, corruption, etc.

Lastly, academia including the professors and the students can contribute their bit by spreading awareness among the common people about the various alternative modes of mitigation. The National Law Schools in India and other traditional law institutions have been pioneers in organizing legal aid camps to sensitize the layman about the importance of alternative dispute resolution mechanisms. Legal institutions in association with the local Bars and the Bench may join hands to come forward and organise legal aid camps in resolving petty cases and counsel people on legal matters. It is high time that a close liaison is developed between the bar, bench and academia.

6. CONCLUSION

The public has lost faith in the judicial institutions and has a very low expectation of the law, lawyers and the courts (Malik and Vajpayi, 1990). People tend to avoid court room proceedings and the lower courts are foregone. The courts and the lawyers have failed to deliver remedy or protection to those who have suffered damages. It is seen that courts tend to facilitate only to those who benefit from delay and non-implementation of legal norms, that is parties who are satisfied with a status quo. For those who are in necessary of prompt implementation of remedies and protections against dominant parties- women from husbands or relatives, labourers from landowners, citizens from the government- the system works only haltingly and partially.

The long delay in disposal of civil litigations has led to escalating expenses and meagre damage awards. Precisely, the present value of most suits for money damages is probably close to zero if not negative. In 2016, it was estimated that judicial delays costs 0.5% of the GDP annually, i.e., Rs. 50,387 crore. Delays still persist. Justice Madan Lokur, former Judge of the Supreme Court of India, observed that there is a crying necessity of thinking out of the box and utilising the existing resources available. The Lok Adalat was established as an alternative to court room proceedings and had been extremely successful institution. However, over the past decade some ethical questions have been raised such as whether the litigants are forced to enter into settlements or they are doing so voluntarily! The institution of Lok Adalat has been celebrated by many, however, it is only an instance of illusion of informal remedies as a realm of independent law. For example, a claimant of motor accident who has been doing the rounds of the courts for ten years for a compensation of fifty thousand rupees would be happy to get half the compensation at half the time. This is a preferable outcome given the legal costs avoided and given the uncertainty that lies chasing the court proceedings. The irony is that the claimant has all rights to recover the full amount of the compensation even if it is after ten years. Doesn't he? Even when establishment of Lok Adalats has been recommended in this chapter as a viable alternative to by-pass the delays in courts, it is telling that "Lok Adalats and other manifestations of banyan tree justice are reflections of failing faith in the efficacy and virtue of the formal legal process – at least in the lower courts" (Resnik, 1986, p. 494).

The effects of a failing justice are too serious to ignore. It is not just that commercial and industrial development may be retarded, or that judiciary may lose "any substantial influence on important aspects of social life. If left untreated, growing queues at the courts may lead to public bitterness and a loss of confidence in them.

REFERENCES

Access to Justice Survey, 2015-16. (n.d.). www.dakshindia.org

Bhatia, G. (2021). *The Past is a Foreign Country. In The Transformative Constitution.* HarperCollins Publishers India.

Falt, J. (1983). Congestion and Delays in Asia's Courts. *Pacific Basin Law Journal*, *4*(90), 107.

Galanter, M. (2008). Fifty Years On. In B. N. Kirpal (Ed.), *Supreme but not Infallible: Essays in Honour of the Supreme Court of India* (pp. 59–61). Oxford University Press.

Gyanendra, K. S., & Pranav, V. (n.d.). *Bottlenecks in Civil Justice Administration before the Courts and the Remedies thereof: A Research.* Uttarakhand Judicial and Legal Review. Retrieved from https://ujala.uk.gov.in/files/Ch1.pdf

Hasit, B. S. (2021). Adhering to Statutory Timelines: A Step towards Better Case Management of Civil Trials. *2021 SCC Online Blog Ex. 6.* https://www.scconline.com/blog/post/2021/01/28/adhering-to-statutory-timelines-a-step-towards-better-case-management-of-civil-trials/

Kumar, V. A. (2012). Judicial Delays in India: Causes and Remedies, *Journal of Law. Policy and Globalization*, *4*, 16.

Madan, B. L. (2021). *What is Stopping Our Justice System from Tackling the Pending before Courts?* https://thewire.in/law/india-judiciary-pending-cases-supreme-court

Pragadeeswaran, U. (2018). A Study on Delay in Civil Proceeding. *International Journal of Pure and Applied Mathematics*, *120*(5), 2571.

Report, I. J. (2019). *Ranking States on Police, Judiciary, Prisons and Legal Aid.* Retrieved from https://www.tatatrusts.org/upload/pdf/overall-report-single.pdf

Reports, A. (2019-2020). *Ministry of Law and Justice, Government of India*. https://lawmin.gov.in/documents/annualreports

Resnik, J. (1986). Failing Faith: Adjudicatory Procedure in Decline. *The University of Chicago Law Review. University of Chicago. Law School*, *53*, 494.

Velacharu, N. R. (1990). Courts and Lawyers in India: Images from Literature and Folklore. In Y. K. Malik & D. K. Vajpeyi (Eds.), *Boeings and Bullock-Carts: Studies in Change and Continuity in Indian Civilization* (p. 196). Chanakya Publications.

APPENDIX: ADDITIONAL RESOURCES

Imran Mohd. Khan, *Alternative Mode of Access to Justice*, https://ujala.uk.gov.in/files/ch10_2.pdf.

India's Pending Court Cases in Rise: In Charts, September 29, 2020, https://www.bloombergquint.com/law-and-policy/indias-pending-court-cases-on-the-rise-in-charts.

14th Law Commission Report on Reform on Judicial Administration, 1958, Vol. 1, Ministry of Law and Justice, Government of India.

27th Law Commission Report on Code of Civil Procedure (1908), 1964, Ministry of Law and Justice, Government of India.

54th Law Commission Report on Code of Civil Procedure (1908), 1973, Ministry of Law and Justice, Government of India.

77th Law Commission Report on Delay and Arrears in Trial Courts, 1978, Ministry of Law and Justice, Government of India.

124th Law Commission Report on High Court Arrears-A Fresh Look, 1988, Ministry of Law and Justice, Government of India.

222nd Law Commission Report on Need for Justice Dispensation through ADR etc, 2009, Ministry of Law and Justice, Government of India.

245th Law Commission Report on Arrears and Backlog: Creating Additional Judicial (Wo)manpower, 2014, Ministry of Law and Justice, Government of India.

Inefficiency and Judicial Delay: New Insights from the Delhi High Court, March 2017, www.vidhi-legalpolicy.org.

https://njdg.ecourts.gov.in/hcnjdgnew/

Chapter 7
Costs and Delays in Accessing Justice:
A Comparative Analysis of Ghana and Sierra Leone

Elijah Tukwariba Yin
University of Cape Coast, Ghana

Beamie Moses Seiwoh
Oxford Brookes University, UK

ABSTRACT

This chapter aims to examine the costs and delays in accessing justice in Ghana and Sierra Leone. It is argued that despite the promising and legal history of Ghana and Sierra Leone, with existing court structures and legal procedures on civil and criminal matters, the legal spaces of both countries are fraught with costs and delays in accessing justice. The authors used secondary data from the World Bank, Afrobarometer Report, statutes, court documents, website articles, etc. to underpin the write-up. It was found that citizens in both countries were confronted with delays and costs in accessing justice. It is recommended that in an era of cell phones and various apps, the justice sector should endeavour to go hi-tech by sending alerts to litigants, lawyers, and witnesses warranting their presence at an appointed date and time.

INTRODUCTION

Ghana and Sierra Leone have travelled a long path in terms of their political and legal history. It is expected that with their relative development strides, the challenges of excessive costs and delays associated with accessing justice in court will be at a minimal level. Unfortunately, this is not the case for both countries. It is for this reason that we want to do a comparative analysis of both countries in terms of costs and delays in accessing the court. This enquiry is premised against the following: a political and legal history of Ghana and Sierra Leone, court structures, as well as civil and criminal procedures.

DOI: 10.4018/978-1-7998-7898-8.ch007

Some scholars and legal professionals have delved into the issues of delays and costs associated with accessing justice in the court of law. These scholars (Osse, 2020; Janofsky, 1983; Zuckerman, 1999; Yin, 2018; Boldwin, 2000; Melcame & Ramello, 2016; Yin, 2020; Boniface & Legg, 2010; Felso & Nooij, 2012, Dale, 2007; Wambua, 2017; Koroma; 2016, etc.) and many others have examined the challenges of cost and delays from unique approaches and perspectives. Despite the importance of these scholarly contributions, very few focused on Ghana and Sierra Leone. Osse's (2020) work represents an Afrobarometer report on Ghana. The World Bank (2010) project on specialized courts in Ghana is an important addition because it tackled the issue of delays into details of which this paper drew much on. However, the World Bank project was silent on costs whilst Osse's Afrobarometer report does not adequately discuss the issues of costs. These studies hardly examined the issues of costs and delays as related concepts with reference to other available secondary data. In the case of Sierra Leone, the literature is quite scanty on costs and delays. The works of Dale (2007), Wambua (2017), and Koroma (2016) represent good reports on barriers to justice in Sierra Leone. However, the focus of their studies suggests that there is a paucity of literature in the area of delays and costs in accessing justice. The various literature on both countries reveals a 'crack' in the area of costs and delays in accessing justice. We settled on Ghana and Sierra Leone because, in part, both countries share a common colonial history.

In this chapter, we argue that despite the promising and legal history of Ghana and Sierra Leone, with existing court structures and legal procedures on civil and criminal matters, the legal spaces of both countries are fraught with costs and delays in accessing justice. In our analysis, we used secondary data from different sources such as the World Bank, the Afrobarometer report, statutes, court documents, etc. to underpin our argument. This chapter is divided into six sections: Introduction, Political and legal history of Ghana and Sierra Leone, Court Structure of Ghana and Sierra Leone, Civil and Criminal Procedures, delays and costs associated with accessing justice, and the way forward. In the conclusion, we will review the lessons learned and the insights gained from the analysis.

POLITICAL AND LEGAL HISTORY

Ghana

Ghana (formerly Gold Coast), officially the Republic of Ghana, is a country in West Africa. It spans the Gulf of Guinea and the Atlantic Ocean to the south, sharing borders with the Ivory Coast in the west, Burkina Faso in the north, and Togo in the east. Ghana covers an area of 238,535 km2 (92,099sq mi), spanning diverse geography and ecology that ranges from coastal savannahs to tropical rain forests. With over 31 million people, Ghana is the second-most populous country in West Africa, after Nigeria. The capital and largest city is Accra; other major cities include Kumasi, Tamale, and Sekondi-Takoradi.

Politically, Gold Coast was part of Sierra Leone and was governed by the Governor of Sierra Leone (Opoku-Agyemang, 2009). The Gold Coast became part of British Crown Colony from 1821 to 1957 (Ahuma, 1972). During the colonial regime, trading activities were carried out at Dixcove, Accra, Anomabu, Cape Coast and Winneba. The economic activities were not properly regulated until it was entrusted in the hands of the Committee of Merchants after passing the West African Act. The purpose of the Act was to annex Gold Coast and the Colony of Sierra Leone as well as their dependencies. On 28th March, 1822 Sir Charles McCarthy arrived in Gold Coast, precisely, Cape Coast to take charge of governing activities (Bennion, 1962). He died in the famous battle of Nsamakwa; a skirmish between the Asantes and the British troops in 1824.

Owing to the series of wars at the time, the British signed a peace treaty with the Asantes. This treaty was signed after the British had failed to defeat the Asantes in a war called the battle of Dodowa. Following this treaty was the appointment of George Maclean in 1830 to take charge of trading activities. Peace and order was not at its peak when George Maclean was appointed to oversee the trading activities at that time. Aside from the trading activities, Maclean worked towards the elimination of human sacrifices, panyarring and its related practices in the Gold Coast (Boahen, 1975).

Despite the role of George Maclean, it was held that the powers he exercised in the course of his duty were illegal and irregular. This triggered the appointment of Commander Hill as Lieutenant-Governor and George Maclean as Judicial Assessor in ensuring justice in the Gold Coast. These arrangements took place in 1843. Subsequently, the Foreign Jurisdiction Act of 1843 was passed to enable the British to extend their territories in settling disputes. The British Parliament Act of 1843 was also passed to enable "*Orders in Council to be made providing for the establishment of laws, institutions and ordinances for the peace, order and good government of Her Majesty's subjects and others within the settlements on the African coast*" (Boahen, 1975).

In 1844, a bond was signed between the British government and the Fante Chiefs. The Bond was in the form of declaration, and it states as follows: i. whereas power and jurisdiction have been exercised for and on behalf of Her Majesty the Queen of Great Britain and Ireland, within divers countries and places adjacent to Her Majesty's forts and settlements on the Gold Coast; we, Chiefs of countries and places so referred to, adjacent to the said forts and settlements, do hereby acknowledge that power and jurisdiction, and declare that the first objects of law are the protection of individuals and of property, ii. human sacrifices, and other barbarous customs, such as panyarring, are abominations, and contrary to law, and iii. murders, robberies, and other crimes and offences, will be tried and inquired of before the Queen's judicial officers and the Chiefs of the district, moulding the customs of the country to the general principles of British law… (Quansah, 2011). Commander Hill ensured that the bond was executed to regularize, normalize and legalize the powers which were formally exercised by George Maclean.

Even though the bond marked a significant history in Ghana, different scholars have shared their views on the bond. Prof. Adu Boahen (1975) argued that the bond was a mere declaration. It was neither a Magna Carta nor a Treaty as some scholars described it. J. B. Danquah (1957) also viewed the bond as a document that did not give liberty to the people of Gold Coast. J. B. Danquah stated as thus "*under the bond of 1844 no special rights or liberties were granted by the British Sovereign to the 'Fantes Chief'. If anything, it could be said that it was rather the 'Fantes Chief' who granted rights or liberties to the British Sovereign*". The bond did not create, enlarge or confirm liberties emanating from British sources to Gold Coast. By the Bond, a free people who were not subjects of the British Sovereign voluntarily place themselves under a binding agreement to the British Crown.

On a continuous struggle and battle, Ghana attained independence on 6th March 1957 and became a Republic on 1st July 1960. The first Republican Constitution was the 1960 Constitution. Dr. Kwame Nkrumah became the first President of Ghana. On 24th February 1966 a coup was made to overthrow the first Republican Government. Busia's government took over and enacted the 1969 Constitution. Busia's regime was overthrown by a coup d'etat led by General I. K. Acheampong. On 5th July 1978, there was another coup led by General Fred Akuffo. Subsequently, another coup was made by the Armed Forces Revolutionary Council (AFRC) led by J. J. Rawlings on 4th June 1979. After three months, Dr. Hilla Limann was elected into office under the 1979 Constitution. On 31st December 1981, the Provisional

National Defence Council (PNDC), led by J. J. Rawlings undertook another coup d'état that overthrew Limann's government. The PNDC ruled Ghana until the 1992 Constitution came into existence (Bimpong-Buta, 2005).

Against this important historical background, Ghana's legal system could be traced back to 1853, a period after the 1844 bond, where the first Supreme Court was established in the Gold Coast (Quansah, 2011). The Supreme Court's jurisdiction which was exercised in the various forts and settlements of the British in Gold Coast was nothing different from the Queen's Bench, Exchequer and Common Pleas (Bennion, 1962). The Supreme Court had both criminal and civil jurisdiction. The Supreme Court Ordinance 1876 was created to strengthen the administration of justice in Gold Coast. The preamble of the Supreme Court Ordinance of 1876 was captioned as;

"Whereas by Letters Patent under the Great Seal of the United Kingdom of Great Britain and Ireland, bearing the date 24th day of July, 1874, Her Majesty's Settlements on the Gold Coast and of Lagos were constituted arid erected into one Colony, under the title of the Gold Coast Colony; And whereas it is expedient to make provision for the administration of justice in the said colony" (Quansah, 2011).

Sir David Chalmer had the sole responsibility to draft the Supreme Court Ordinance of 1876. On 2nd December, 1976 he was appointed as the Chief Justice of the Supreme Court of Gold Coast. His appointment letter was captioned in the following words:

Her Majesty has been pleased to appoint Sir David Chalmers to be Chief Justice of the Supreme Court at a salary of £1800 a year; and Mr. James Marshall to be a Puisne Judge at a salary of £1000 a year, and Mr. Thomas W. Jackson, lately Chief Magistrate of the Gambia to be also a Puisne Judge, but at a salary of £900 per annum. The necessary Warrants for these appointments will be forwarded to you in due course, and you will take care to date the Letters Patent to Mr. Marshall earlier than those to Mr. Jackson, so as to prevent any question arising as to their relative rank (Amissah, 1976).

The Supreme Court of Gold Coast which was established by Supreme Court Ordinance 1876 was composed of Court of Appeal (Full Court) and Divisional court with distinct jurisdiction (Quansah, 2011). The structure of the Supreme Court was described by Amissah (1976) in the following words:

The Supreme Court so established was not only a final appellate tribunal as known in modern times. The system created consisted of two tiers of courts rolled up in one. There was first a trial court equivalent of the High Court of today. This court was presided over by a single judge or, in some cases, two judges. Appeals from the High Court lay to a Full Court consisting of two or more of the judges who ordinarily sat in the trial court. Both levels of the court so established together formed the Supreme Court. The formal establishment of the court was followed by provisions on its constitution which stated that it consisted of the Chief Justice of the Gold Coast Colony and so many Puisne judges not exceeding four in number at any one time as the Governor might from time to time appoint in accordance with instructions received from Her Majesty.

Section 6 of Supreme Court Ordinance 1876 indicated that the Court of Appeal which is also called the "The Full Court" was fully constituted by two or more judges. The Chief Justice was part of these justices or any person being appointed for the time being to discharge the functions of Chief Justice. A unanimous decision was preferable. However, while others disagree, the majority decision takes precedent. There was a caveat that "when the Court shall be constituted by two Judges, the Chief Justice or person for the time being discharging the functions of Chief Justice shall have a casting vote." The nature of this court indicated that judges can sit on a case with even numbers like two or four. One defect of the Supreme Court Ordinance 1876 was that it did not provide for situations where there are equal votes from the justices sitting on a particular case. This defect was unfolded in the case of Bainyi v Dantsi (1903) Ren. 287; 2 G. & G. 11. In that case, the issue which had to be resolved was "whether the kings and chiefs of the land could lawfully exercise the judicial powers and functions vested in them by the native law and custom (subject to the limitations imposed by the Native Prisons Ordinance) within the Colony, or was all jurisdiction of all kinds now vested in the Supreme Court to the exclusion of all other jurisdictions except in those cases to which the Native Jurisdiction Ordinance applied." Out of the four judges who sat on the case, two answered 'YES' and the other two answered 'NO'.

The Supreme Court was clothed with the power to apply statutes of general application, doctrines of equity and common law. Section 14 of Supreme Court Ordinance 1876 provided that;

"The common law, the doctrines of equity, and the statutes of general application which were in force in England at the date when the Colony obtained a local legislature, that is to say, on the 24th day of July, 1874, shall be in force within the jurisdiction of the Court."

The doctrines of equity which are affirmed by section 14 of Supreme Court Ordinance 1876 originally came into existence when the English Parliament enacted the Judicature Act 1873 which allowed the application of common law and the doctrines of equity in the various courts. Section 4 of Supreme Court Ordinance 1876 also allowed customary law to be applied in the various courts to the extent that they were consistent with good conscience and existing law in force and prohibited those customary laws which hindered rule of natural justices (Adjei, 2020). The test for applying customary law was stated by W. B. Harvey in 1964 as thus "the customary law could be applied in any court only in so far as it was not "repugnant to natural justice, equity and good conscience" or incompatible either directly or by necessary implication with any ordinance". Customary law before 1960 was considered to be a question of fact for determination by the court. It was after 1960 that customary law became a question of law to be determined by the court as stated by Adjei (2020).

Drawing on the powers of the 1992 Constitution of Ghana, this position was affirmed by section 55 of the Court Act 1993 (Act 459) as amended by (Act 674) as follow: (1) Any question as to existence or content of a rule of customary law is a question of law for the court and not a question of fact, (2) If there is doubt as to the existence or content of a rule of customary law relevant in any proceedings before a court, the court may adjourn the proceedings to enable an inquiry to be made under subsection 3 of this section after the court has considered submissions made by or; on behalf of the parties and after the court has considered reported cases, textbooks and other sources that may be appropriate to the proceedings, (3) The inquiry shall be held as part of the proceedings in such manner as the court considers expedient, and the provisions of this Act relating to the attendance and testimony of witnesses shall apply with such modifications as may appear to the court to be necessary, (4) The decision as to the persons who are to be heard at the inquiry shall be one for the court, after hearing the submissions on it made by or on behalf of the parties, and (5) The court may request a House of Chiefs, Divisional or Traditional Council or other body with knowledge of the customary law in question to state its opinion which may be laid before the inquiry in written form.

The 1992 constitution spelt out that the structure and power of the judiciary are independent of all other branches of government. The Supreme Court has broad powers of judicial review; it rules on the constitutionality of any legislative or executive action at the request of any aggrieved citizen. The hierarchy of courts derives largely from British juridical forms. The hierarchy, called the Superior Court of Judicature, is composed of the Supreme Court of Ghana, the Court of Appeal (Appellate Court), the High Court of Justice, Regional Tribunals, and such lower courts or tribunals as parliament may establish. The courts have jurisdiction over all civil and criminal matters. The jurisdiction of the courts has subsequently been discussed. The next section examines the political and legal history of Sierra Leone.

Sierra Leone

Sierra Leone is located on the West coast of Africa. It has a total area of 27,699 m^2 and of 71,740 km^2. The country's Portuguese name—Serra Lyoa ("Lion Mountains"), denotes the range of hills surrounding her harbor. Archaeological findings show that Sierra Leone has been inhabited for hundreds of years before the Portuguese explorer—Pedro Da Cintra's discovery of Sierra Leone in 1462. Traditional historiography records the peopling of Sierra Leone by successive waves of invaders, but the diverse language patterns suggest that the coastal peoples such as the Bulloms (Sherbro), Temnes, and Limbas were in continuous settled occupation for a long time, with sporadic invasions from inland Mende-speaking people including Vais, Lokos and Mendes. These people organised themselves in small political units of independent kingdoms or chiefdoms, the powers whose rulers were checked by councils. They were involved in several activities, including subsistence farming, fishing and barter trade system. Secret societies, notably the *Poro* society, also exercised political power.

In the eighteenth century, Sierra Leone became one of the main places for the repatriation of freed black slaves from England, Canada and the United States. These groups of liberated slaves settled in and around the present capital city—Freetown and became known as the Creoles. Their language, Krio later became the lingua franca of Sierra Leone. In addition, there are about 18 ethnic groups that exhibit similar cultural features, such as secret societies, chieftaincy, patrilineal heritage, and farming methods. With a population of about seven million—according to its 2020 national statistics report, two-thirds of which are Muslims and a third Christians, including less than a-tenth of those practising a variety of traditional African religions, the Sierra Leone population is equivalent to 0.1% of the total world population.

Sierra Leone became a British colony in 1808 and did not gain its independence until 1961. On independence, the nation was led by a Prime Minister—Sir Milton Margai until he died in 1964. The country was governed by a one-party system from 1967 until 1991 when it adopted a multiparty democratic constitution, which application was suspended due to a military rule prompted by the outbreak of civil war until 1996 when democracy was restored. Following the end of the civil war in 2002, the Truth and Reconciliation Commission and the Special Court for Sierra Leone were instituted as twin transitional justice mechanisms. Two political parties have led the country since independence - the All People's Congress (APC) and the Sierra Leone People's Party (SLPP) - the latter being the ruling party since 2018 replacing the APC's more than a decade rulership.

Sierra Leone's Legal system is a blend of the English Common Law, Customary law and Statutory law (Section 74 of the Courts Act 1965). A leading civil rights lawyer in Sierra Leone - Augustine Sorie-Sengbe Marrah wrote about Common law as follows:

Most, if not all, domestic legal systems are transplants (direct or indirect derivatives) of some ancient corpus of legal code or an amalgam of two or more foreign legal systems. Universally, one of the most popular legal systems is the English common law. The common law of England itself evolved from series of legal codes and procedures dating back to the Anglo-Saxon era. Later, royal courts were established to codify the rules. Local customs and practices of the circuit courts throughout England and the uniform law which evolved in application became known as the "common law.

By Section 170 (1) of the Constitution of Sierra Leone (Act No. 6 of 1991), the sources of laws in Sierra Leone are as follows: The Constitution; Laws made under the authority of Parliament as established by the Constitution; Any orders, rules, regulations and other statutory instruments made by any person or authority pursuant to a power conferred on that behalf by the Constitution or any other law; The existing law and; The common law.

The British common law has always influenced the legal system of Sierra Leone. Under colonial rule, the Privy Council of England was the highest judicial body in the legal system of Sierra Leone, which made final decisions on appeals lodged to it from the then-Supreme Court (now High Court of Sierra Leone). Because of colonial influence, most of the United Kingdom laws became applicable in the colony of Sierra Leone. Few years after Independence, the nation legislated that all laws in England applicable as of 1st January 1880 would be applicable in Sierra Leone. That such provision is applicable to this day and has entrenched the British influence over the legal system of Sierra Leone.

Customary law is mainly applied in the rural areas of Sierra Leone, which make up more than sixty percent of those who access justice. Customary laws in Sierra Leone differ from one ethnic group to another and are employed in their local courts to settle disputes between and amongst their residents. The Local Courts are recognised in the legal system of Sierra Leone by virtue of the Local Courts Act 1963, which has been repealed and replaced by the Local Courts Act 2019.

Some aspects of Islamic law are part of the corpus of laws in Sierra Leone. For instance, the Mohammedan Marriage Act Chapter 96 of the Laws of Sierra Leone 1960 recognises and governs Muslim marriages in Sierra Leone. However, Islamic law provisions regarding inheritance previously applicable under the Administration of Estate Act Chapter 45 of the Laws of Sierra Leone 1960 have been replaced by the Devolution of Estate Act 2007, Sharia law provisions are not part of the body of laws in Sierra Leone.

In Sierra Leone, judicial power is vested in the Judiciary (Section 120 (1) of the Constitution of Sierra Leone Act no 6 of 1991). The judiciary which is headed by the Chief Justice includes the Supreme Court, the Court of Appeal, the High Court, the Magistrate Courts and the Local Courts.

From the political and legal history of Ghana and Sierra Leone, it seems obvious that the two countries share a common colonial heritage. Both countries were ruled by the British and were also greatly influenced by common law. We have shown how laws have evolved over the years and the current state of constitutional affairs. The ensuing section describes the court structure in Ghana which is followed by that of Sierra Leone.

COURT STRUCTURE

Ghana

Article 126(1) of 1992 Constitution of Ghana provides that the Judiciary shall consist of (a) the Superior Courts of Judicature comprising: the Supreme Court, the Court of Appeal and the High Court and Regional Tribunals, (b) such lower courts or tribunals as Parliament may by law establish. Section 39 of the Court Act 1993 (Act 459) as amended by Act 674 provides that the lower courts include: Circuit Courts; District Court; Juvenile Courts; the National House of Chiefs, Regional Houses of Chiefs and every Traditional Council, in respect of the jurisdiction of any such House or Council to adjudicate over any cause or matter affecting chieftaincy; and such other lower courts as Parliament may by law establish. Each of these courts has special jurisdiction. The structure of the court is discussed as follows: Supreme Court, Court of Appeal, High Court, Circuit Court, and District Court.

The Supreme Court is composed of the Chief Justice and not less than nine of other Justices of the Supreme Court. Thus the Supreme Court should at any time maintain at least a minimum of ten justices (Article 128(1) of 1992 Constitution). For Supreme Court to be duly constituted for its work, there should be not less than five Supreme Court Justices except when the Court is exercising its review jurisdiction (Article 128(2) of 1992 Constitution). Article 128(3) of 1992 Constitution imposes a duty on the Chief Justice to preside at sittings of the Supreme Court, except in his absence that the most senior of the Justices of the Supreme Court, as constituted, shall preside. According to Article 128(4) of 1992 Constitution, a person who wants to be a justice of the Supreme Court should be at least fifteen years' standing as a lawyer with high moral character and proven integrity. The Supreme Court has original jurisdiction, appellate jurisdiction, supervisory, review jurisdiction, general jurisdiction and production of official document. Article 130(1) of 1992 Constitution provides that "Subject to the jurisdiction of the High Court in the enforcement of the Fundamental Human Rights and Freedoms as provided in article 33 of this Constitution, the Supreme Court shall have exclusive original jurisdiction in (a) all matters relating to the enforcement or interpretation of this Constitution, and (b) all matters arising as to whether an enactment was made in excess of the powers conferred on Parliament or any other authority or person by law or under this Constitution."

Per Article 136 of the 1992 Constitution, the Court of Appeal shall consist of the Chief Justice; not less than ten Justices of the Court of Appeal; and such other Justices of the Superior Court of Judicature as the Chief Justice may, for the determination of a particular cause or matter by writing signed by him, request to sit in the Court of Appeal for any specified period. The Court of Appeal shall be duly constituted by any three of the Justices and when so constituted, the most senior of the justices shall preside. A person shall not be qualified for appointment as a Justice of the Court of Appeal unless he is of high moral character and proven integrity and is of not less than twelve years' standing as a lawyer. It has only appellate jurisdiction. It hears appeals on civil matters from circuit court and hears appeals on criminal matters from High Court.

Article 136 of 1992 Constitution provides that the High Court shall consist of the Chief Justice: not less than twenty Justices of the High Court; and such other Justice of the Superior Court of Judicature as the Chief Justice may, by writing signed by him, request to sit as High Court Justice for any period. The High Court shall be constituted by a single Justice of the Court; or by a single Justice of the Court and jury; or by a single Justice of the Court with assessors; or by three Justices of the Court for the trial of the offence of high treason or treason as required by article 19 of the Constitution. A person shall not be qualified for appointment as a Justice of the High Court unless he is a person of high moral character and proven integrity and is of at least ten years' standing as a lawyer. The High Court has original jurisdiction in all matters (both criminal and civil), appellate jurisdiction, supervisory jurisdiction and single justice jurisdiction. It has exclusive jurisdiction to enforce the Fundamental Human Rights and Freedoms guaranteed by the 1992 Constitution, Article 140 (2) of 1992 Constitution.

Per section 40(4) of the Court Act 1993 (Act 459) as amended by Act 674 a person could only be appointed as a justice of Circuit Court if he or she is of high moral character and proven integrity and is of not less than five years standing as a lawyer. Also, the jurisdiction of these judges shall be conferred upon them by Act 459 or any other enactment. Per section 40(6) of the Court Act 1993 (Act 459) as amended by Act 674 a Circuit Court shall hold its sittings at such places and times as the Chief Justice may direct.

Per section 42 of Act 459 the circuit court has original jurisdiction in civil matters-

(i) in personal actions arising under contract or tort or for the recovery of any liquidated sum, where the amount claimed is not more than two million Ghana cedis (LI2429 Court Regulation, 2020)

(ii) in actions between landlord and tenant for the possession of land claimed under lease and refused to be delivered up;

(iii) in causes and matters involving the ownership, possession, occupation of or title to land;

(iv) to appoint guardians of infants and to make orders for the custody of infants;

vii) in applications for the grant of probate or letters of administration in respect of the estate of a deceased person, and in causes and matters relating to succession to property of a deceased person, who had at the time of his death a fixed place of abode within the area of jurisdiction of the Circuit Court and the value of the estate or property in question does not exceed two million Ghana cedis (LI2429 Court Regulation, 2020)

The Courts Act 1993 (Act 459) as amended by Act 674 provides that "a person does not qualify to be appointed a magistrate of a District Court unless the person is of high moral character and proven integrity and is a lawyer, or is a person with such judicial or legal knowledge as the Chief Justice shall on the advice of the Judicial Council determine". Per section 42 of Act 459, a District Court shall within the area of its jurisdiction have civil jurisdiction in the following matters-

(a) in personal actions arising under contract or tort for the recovery of any liquidated sum where the amount claimed does not exceed five hundred thousand Ghana cedis (LI2429 Court Regulation 2020).

(b) to grant in any action instituted in the District Court injunctions or orders to stay waste or alienation or for the detention and preservation of any property the subject matter of that action, or restrain breaches of contracts or the commission of any tort;

(c) in claims for relief by way of interpleader in respect of land or other property attached in execution of a decree made by the District Court

(g) in applications for the grant of probate or letters of administration in respect of the estate of a deceased person, and in causes and matters relating to succession to property of a deceased person, who had at the time of his death a fixed place of abode within the area of jurisdiction of the District Court and the value of the estate or property in question does not exceed five hundred thousand Ghana cedis (LI2429 Court Regulation 2020)

(h) hear and determine charges and dispose of other matters affecting juveniles that is persons under the age of eighteen.

The structure of the court discussed above shows the hierarchy as well as the functions of the courts. Aside from the structure, the civil and criminal procedures are also discussed.

Sierra Leone

There are five (5) different courts in Sierra Leone classified under two branches: the Superior Courts of judicature and the Inferior Courts of judicature. The Superior Courts of judicature include: the Supreme Court, the Court of Appeal and the High Court, whilst the inferior court of judicature consists of the Magistrate Court and the Local Court.

The Supreme Court, headed by the Chief Justice, has a composition of not less than five Justices of the superior court. The Supreme Court is the final Court of Appeal in Sierra Leone, and it has appellate, supervisory and original jurisdiction. In its original jurisdiction, the Supreme Court has exclusive jurisdiction to interpret Sierra Leone's Constitution and enforce fundamental human rights.

The Court of Appeal consists of the Chief Justice and not less than seven (7) justices of the Superior Court of Judicature. The Court of Appeal sits on all appeals from the High Court of Sierra Leone. It is bound by its own previous decisions, and Inferior courts are bound to follow the decisions of the Court of Appeal on all questions of law (See section 128 of the constitution of Sierra Leone Act no 6 of 1991).

The High Court consists of the Chief Justice and not less than nine (9) judges (See section 131 (1) of the constitution of Sierra Leone Act no 6 of 1991). The High Court has supervisory jurisdiction over all inferior and traditional Courts in Sierra Leone. It has a very wide jurisdiction to hear and determine most matters except issues of interpretation of the Constitution and enforcement of human rights.

The Magistrate Court is usually presided over by the Magistrate and Justices of Peace, but a magistrate can preside alone for an ordinary criminal matter. It conducts Preliminary Investigations (PI), Summary Trials, Coroner's Inquest, etc. It has original, appellate and supervisory jurisdiction over local courts.

The Local Court determines criminal and civil matters in their localities based on their local laws and traditions. For this reason, it is limited. Therefore, legal practitioners cannot appear in this court (See section 19 of the Local Court Act).

Comparing the structure of the court in Sierra Leone to Ghana, one could see that there is great similarity in terms of the hierarchical structure, however, the composition of the judges differs. For example, in Ghana, the Supreme Court is composed of the Chief Justice and not less than nine judges whilst in Sierra Leone, the Supreme Court is composed of the Chief Justice and not less than four judges. In respect of the Court of Appeal, Ghana is composed of the Chief Justice and not less than ten justices whilst Sierra Leone is composed of the Chief Justice and not less than seven of the justices. The High Court also shows some differences in terms of composition, in that, for Sierra Leone it is composed of the Chief Justice and not less than nine justices whilst Ghana is composed of the Chief Justice and not less than twenty justices. The next section delves into the civil and criminal procedures of Ghana and Sierra Leone.

CIVIL AND CRIMINAL PROCEDURES

Ghana

Civil procedure in Ghana is regulated by the High Court (Civil Procedure) Rules, 2004 (C.I 47). Per rule 1 order 2 the party who commences civil proceedings shall be described as "plaintiff" and the opposing party shall be described as "defendant". Per rule 2 order 2 all civil proceedings are to be commenced by the filing a writ of summons except otherwise provided. Divorce cases, child custody, among others are commenced with a petition. Sometimes civil proceedings could be initiated by a motion. The following factors are normally considered before commencing a civil action: a) Ascertain whether the supposed plaintiff has a cause of action, b) Ascertain whether the cause of action has accrued, c) Identify the proper plaintiff and proper defendant who are the parties to the suit, d) Ascertain whether the parties have capacity to bring the action as established in Akrong v Bulley [1965] GLR 469, e) Ascertain jurisdiction of the court where the writ will be filed, f) Make a decision on the venue where the action will be brought, and g) Verify various statutory requirements surrounding such suit and complied with accordingly before the action is commenced.

On writ and statement of claim (order 2), Rule 6 order 2 provides that every writ is to be filed together with a statement of claim and no writ shall be issued unless a statement of claim is filed with it. Per rule 7 order 2 provides, the Registrar is to seal the writ before the writ is issued. No writ is to be sealed unless at the time it is filed for sealing, the person filing it leaves with the Registrar a copy signed by the plaintiff. If the plaintiff sues in person or by, or on behalf of the plaintiff's lawyer (Per rule 7 order 2), the officer receiving the copy is to file it and make an entry in the Cause Book. Writs are dated on the day in which it was issued. No writ, notice of which is to be served out of the jurisdiction, shall be issued without leave of the Court.

One or more concurrent writs may be issued at the time when the original writ is issued or at any later time after the original writ is issued and before the original writ ceases to be valid upon the request of the plaintiff (order 2 rule 8). However, a writ for service within the jurisdiction may be issued as a concurrent writ of which notice is to be served out of the jurisdiction and within the jurisdiction. A concurrent writ is a true copy of the original writ with no such difference, if any, as are necessary having regard to the purpose for which the writ is issued. A concurrent writ shall be sealed by being marked "concurrent" with an official stamp, and with the date on which it is issued.

A defendant to an action may, whether or not the defendant is sued in a personal capacity or as a trustee or as a personal representative or in any other representative capacity, file appearance in the action and defend it in person or by a lawyer (Appearance, Order 9). Appearance is filed by completing a notice of appearance in triplicate in compliance with rule 3 of this Order and handing it in at, or sending it by post to, the registry together with two stamped envelopes, one addressed to the plaintiff's lawyer or to the plaintiff, if acting in person, at the plaintiff's address for service, and the other addressed to the defendant filing the appearance. These and many other rules as stipulated by High Court (Civil Procedure) Rules, 2004 (C.I 47) spells out the necessary procedures for civil action. The other procedure to be discussed is the criminal procedure.

The Criminal Act 1960 (Act 29) contains the substantive offences such as rape, defilement, stealing, murder, manslaughter, perjury, treason, high treason, among others. Criminal and other offences (Procedure) Act 1960 (Act 30) provides for the procedure to be followed in criminal and other offences and to provide for related matters. It must be noted that Ghana's criminal procedure is not inquisitorial but rather adversarial. The adversarial system or adversary system is a legal system used in the common law countries where two advocates represent their parties' case or position before an impartial person or group of people, usually a judge or jury, who attempt to determine the truth and pass judgment accordingly (Hale, 2004). It is premised on the statement that a person who is alleged to have committed an offence is deemed innocent unless he is proven guilty.

All criminal matters are of great interest to the public. The Attorney General is clothed with the power to institute action against anyone who commits a criminal offence. Per section 60 of Act 30 criminal proceedings can be initiated in only two ways, namely; "by making a complaint and applying for the issue of a warrant or a summons and by bringing a person arrested without a warrant before the Court on a charge contained in a charge sheet". An offence can be tried either summarily or on indictment. Section 2 of Act 30 provides that "an offence shall be tried summarily if the enactment creating the offence provides that it is punishable on summary conviction, and does not provide for any other mode of trial; or the enactment creating the offence does not make a provision for the mode of trial and the maximum penalty for the offence on first conviction is a term of imprisonment not exceeding six months, whether with or without a fine." However, in the case of indictment an "offence shall be tried on indictment if it is punishable by death or it is an offence declared by an enactment to be a first degree felony; or the enactment creating the offence provides that the mode of trial is on indictment."

The fact that a person has been accused of a crime does not mean that his or her right has been taken away. The 1992 Constitution of Ghana confers certain rights on such a person. Article 19 provides as follow:

2) A person charged with a criminal offence shall be given a fair hearing within a reasonable time by a court.

3) A person charged with a criminal offence shall -

a) be presumed to be innocent until he is proved or has pleaded guilty;

b) be informed immediately in a language that he understands, and in detail; of the nature of the offence charged;

c) be given adequate time and facilities for the preparation of this defense;

d) be permitted to defend himself before the court in person or by a lawyer of his choice;

e) be afforded facilities to examine, in person or by his lawyer, the witnesses called by the prosecution before the court, and to obtain the attendance and carry out the examination of witnesses to testify on the same conditions as those applicable to witnesses called by the prosecution."

Where the above rights are infringed upon, the accused can bring an action at the high court for the enforcement of his or her right per article 33(5) of the 1992 Constitution of Ghana. Article 19(11) provides that no person shall be convicted of a criminal offence unless the offence is defined and the penalty for it is prescribed in a written law whilst Article 19(5) provides that a person shall not be charged with or held to be guilty of a criminal offence which is founded on an act or omission that did not at the time it took place constitute an offence.

Section 96(1) of Act 30 provides that "a Court may grant bail to a person who appears or is brought before it on a process or after being arrested without warrant, and who is prepared at any time or at any stage of the proceedings or after conviction pending an appeal to give bail, and enters into a bond in the prescribed manner with or without sureties, conditioned for that person's appearance before that Court or any other Court at the time and place mentioned in the bond". In certain circumstances, the court may refuse a bail if it is satisfied that the defendant:

"(a) may not appear to stand trial, or (b) may interfere with a witness or the evidence, or in any way hamper police investigations, or (c) may commit a further offence when on bail, or (d) is charged with an offence punishable by imprisonment exceeding six months which is alleged to have been committed while the defendant was on bail."

Per section 199(1& 2) of Act 30, where the accused pleads guilty to a charge, the Court before accepting the plea shall, if the accused is not represented by counsel, explain to the accused the nature of the charge and the procedure which follows the acceptance of a plea of guilty. The accused may then withdraw the plea and plead not guilty. The procedure on plea of not guilty s.172 of Act 30 states as follows:

(1) Where the accused does not plead guilty to the charge, the Court shall proceed to hear the evidence that the prosecutor adduces in support of the charge.

(2) The accused or the counsel of the accused may put questions to each witness produced against the accused.

(3) Where the accused does not employ a counsel, the Court shall, at the close of the examination of each witness for the prosecution, ask the accused whether the accused wishes to put questions to that witness and shall record the answer of the accused.

(4) Where the accused instead of questioning the witness makes a statement regarding the evidence of that witness, the Magistrate shall, if desirable in the interest of the accused, put the substance of the statement to the witness in the form of questions.

These procedures and others as may be stated by the Act presuppose that accessing the court is easier. However, this is not the case in Ghana. The case of Sierra Leone is presented below.

Sierra Leone

Civil actions are between individuals or between individuals and the state for breach of contract or tortious liabilities. Civil actions may be begun in the Magistrate for claims which are below Five Million Leones.

The civil process for instituting an action in the Magistrate Court is called a Plaint Note or summons in cases of ejectment proceedings. The said process must be personally served on Defendant otherwise, the action would not be listed for hearing. Once served, the Defendant can file a defence by himself or through counsel. The Plaintiff would make his/her case by testifying and calling witnesses, and thereafter the Defendant would do the same. Afterward, both parties may address the court by themselves or through their legal representatives and judgement is granted subsequently. Any of the parties aggrieved by the judgment may appeal to the High Court within a month of the judgment.

Civil suits in the superior court are commenced in the High Court except where the action is about the interpretation of the Constitution of Sierra Leone or enforcement of a fundamental right enshrined in the constitution of Sierra Leone. In those two instances, the action would be commenced in the Supreme Court.

In the High Court, civil suits are begun by any of four processes: writ of summons; originating summons; originating notice of motion and petitions. The High Court has broad civil jurisdiction over commercial, probate, divorce, corporate, tort, land disputes, etc. A party who is personally served any of the said processes generally has about 14 days to indicate his appearance or defence. Failure to indicate appearance may lead to judgment being taken by the initiating party or granted by the court in default.

In civil actions in the High Court, the parties make and exchange their cases through pleadings. At the close of pleadings, the Plaintiff party would commence their case by calling a witness who would be cross-examined by the defendant party or their counsel. At the end of the case for the Plaintiff, the Defendant would open their own case. At the end of both cases, the parties may address the court through their legal representatives. After such an address, the judge would deliver a judgment. Any party aggrieved by the judgement may appeal to the Court of Appeal within three months from the date of the judgement.

In Sierra Leone, criminal proceedings are governed by the Criminal Proceedings Act 1965. This law prescribes the procedures in criminal prosecution. However, this legislation is subject to the Constitution of Sierra Leone, which defines certain rights of accused persons such as the presumption of innocence, right to a fair and speedy trial, and protection against double jeopardy (section 23 of the Constitution of Sierra Leone).

Criminal prosecutions are two-fold - public and private. Public prosecutions are done by either the police or law officers in the Office of the Director of Public Prosecutions (DPP). Police prosecutions are usually conducted in the Magistrate Court while prosecutions in the superior courts are conducted by law officers—lawyers attached to the office of the DPP in the Chambers of the Attorney General. Public prosecutions are usually preceded by a police investigation. During police investigation, an individual may or may not be arrested or detained. To effect an arrest on an individual, there must be a warrant for that arrest. This warrant must be signed (See Constitution of Sierra Leone Act No. 6 of 1991) by a Judge, Magistrate or Justice of the Peace. However, there are circumstances where a police officer may effect an arrest on an individual without a warrant, such as where a police officer believes that an individual is about to commit a crime, or the commission of a crime is imminent.

During a police investigation, an individual being investigated may be detained for seventy-two hours in cases of all crimes other than capital offences or economic crimes, for which detention can be up to ten days. In addition, persons detained beyond the constitutional limit may apply to the court for habeas corpus order which is essential to enforce their constitutional right against detention beyond the limit prescribed by the constitution.

After police investigations, the police may charge the matter to court depending on the evidence. In some cases, the police would decline to charge the matter to court for lack of evidence. The process used to prefer a charge in the Magistrate Court is called information. Most criminal trials begin at the Magistrate Court, depending on whether the alleged crime is a summary offence. Summary offences specified in law as minor offences, begin and end in the Magistrate Court except when the outcome is appealed in the High Court. In felonious offences, preliminary investigations are only conducted by the police in the Magistrate Court. At the end of the Preliminary Investigations, the Magistrate may or may not commit the matter to the High Court for trial.

Generally, the power to prosecute crimes in Sierra Leone is vested in the Attorney-General (Section 64(8) of the 1991 Constitution). The commissioner of the Anti-Corruption Commission has also been granted prosecutorial powers but only in respect of crimes of corruption (Section 89 of the Anti-Corruption Act of 2008). The Attorney General has special powers to take over proceedings and end matters even when they are not started in his instance (private criminal prosecutions). He is also authorised to give fiat for the prosecution to legal practitioners who are not within his law office.

In a trial in the High Court, the charge sheet is called an indictment. The accused may be tried by a judge alone or a judge and jury if the punishment of the offence, if convicted, is capital punishment. State counsel does trials in the High Court. The prosecution opens their case by calling their witnesses, and at the end, the defence may make a submission of no case, and if successful, that would be the end of the trial. If the bench rules otherwise, the defence would have to open their case and call their witnesses. At the end of the respective cases, counsel for the prosecution and defence may address the judge in the case of a judge-alone trial or the jury in the case of a trial by jury. In the case of a jury trial, the judge would sum up the evidence, and the jury shall then return a verdict. In the case of a judge-alone trial, judgment would be delivered by the judge. After the verdict by the jury or judgment by a judge, in the case of a conviction, counsel for the defence would address the court on mitigation before sentencing. An accused convicted by the High Court shall exercise his right of appeal to the Court of Appeal within one month of the date of the judgment and sentencing.

Private individuals can prosecute other individuals for certain offences, especially public order offences such as trespass, public insult and provocation etc. In addition, private persons may, by a process called criminal summons, require other persons to answer certain count charges in the Magistrate Court. They may or may not be assisted by counsel if they so choose. The Attorney General or the DPP has powers to take over such prosecutions. The summary trial procedure in private prosecutions is the same as in public prosecutions in the Magistrate Court.

The civil and criminal procedures of Ghana and Sierra Leone are clearly spelt out. However, both legal spaces are fraught with similar challenges. It is against this backdrop that we argue that despite an existing court structure and legal procedures on civil and criminal matters, the legal spaces of Ghana and Sierra Leone are fraught with costs and delays in accessing justice. Just like has been approached above, the next section sequentially examines delays and costs associated with accessing justice in Ghana and Sierra Leone.

DELAYS AND COSTS IN ACCESSING JUSTICE

Ghana

According to the World Bank, in collaboration with the Government of Ghana and the Norwegian Ministry of Foreign Affairs (2010), the judicial service of Ghana aims to complete cases within 6 months of their commencement. Therefore, cases that travel beyond six months constitute a delay.

Both civil and criminal procedures involve a number of steps. However, in the case of Ghana, we will focus on civil procedure. It is useful to note that civil procedure in the High Court includes a number of key steps. The steps are namely: the pre-trial stage; trial and judgment stage; the execution of judgment stage; and the review/appellate stage. The pre-trial stage involves the following steps: The issue of a Writ of Summons and a Statement of Claim by the plaintiff; the service of these on the defendant personally, by substituted service, or by service out of the jurisdiction; the entry of appearance within eight days of service by the defendant either in person or through a solicitor; the filing of a statement of defense, with or without a counterclaim, by the defendant within fourteen days after the eight days for the entry of appearance; the optional filing of a reply to the statement of defence of the defendant and/or a defence to any counterclaim of the defendant; closure of pleadings at the expiration of seven days after service of the reply, or where there is no reply but only a defense to a counterclaim, the pleadings close seven days after service of the defense to the counterclaim, or where there is no reply or a defense to counterclaim served, then pleadings close at the expiration of seven days after service of the defense; within one month after the close of pleadings, the plaintiff files an application for directions. The purpose of this procedure is to enable the Court to consider the preparations for trial, so that all matters which have not already been dealt with may be dealt with and directions may be given as to the future course of the action as appear best to secure the just, expeditious and inexpensive disposal of the case. In practice, the main outcome of this process is an agreement between the parties as to the main issues that will go to trial; and the final step is the hearing and determination of the application for directions, and this concludes the pre-trial stage (World Bank, 2010).

There are several delays during the pre-trial phase. It can take a long time to implement the replacement service. When it is impractical or impossible to serve the parties in person through court proceedings, the court may order alternative services. This requires the parties to be notified of the proceeding, for example by publishing it in the media or posting it on the court notice board. To get an alternative service order, you need to show the court that you have tried three or more unsuccessful attempts to serve the document in person. Any further attempt to deliver the document in person will result in undue delay. Publishing such service in print media requires another process (World Bank, 2010).

Another potential source of delay is when the writ is served outside of the jurisdiction. This necessitates a court order granting permission to serve process outside of the jurisdiction. Following the award of leave, the party must arrange for the court to process and submit the appropriate paperwork to the other country. Working with foreign missions on both sides may be required. This entails observing important protocols to avoid breach of law in the country within which the writ is being served.

Many lawyers and litigants make an initial appearance in a case and then do nothing. This delays the hearing process and the ultimate outcome. When the plaintiff secures a default judgment against them, they come in court with a plethora of justifications, successfully set aside the default judgements, and totally reset the clock of the case. Despite the fact that such tactics are frequently sanctioned by the courts and typically involve the plaintiff paying fees, the practice continues unabated. This is sometimes due to ignorance on the part of litigants or other factors that may cause delay on the part of lawyers or litigants (World Bank, 2010).

The trial and judgment step comes next. This stage primarily entails the presentation of oral, written, or other forms of evidence to the court. Witnesses often offer testimony through cross-examination, re-examination, and examination in chief. This causes a considerable passage of time. First, all testimony provided during examination-in-chief, cross-examination, and re-examination is taken in longhand in unautomated courts, and in automated courts in the event of power failures or equipment malfunction. A case can only move forward if all of the witnesses are present, as well as the attorneys or parties who can question, cross-examine, and re-interrogate them. In many situations, the absence of one of them causes the case to be adjourned. Adjournment of cases has been identified as one of the reasons for delays in court. In the 2010 World Bank study of specialised courts in Ghana, it was found that in the Fast track court, 57.4% of plaintiff requested for adjournment while 55.8% of defendants also requested for adjournment. All these adjournments were granted. In the study, the following reasons were given to explain the need for the adjournment: Absence of parties from court; Absence of lawyers of parties from court; To afford parties the opportunity to comply with Rules of Court; To allow for the transfer of a case to another judge; To join other persons as parties to the case; To allow for a change of lawyers; To attempt settlement out of court; To afford parties the opportunity to procure and furnish the court with evidence; To afford parties the opportunity to satisfy orders made by the court; To complete examination-in-chief, cross-examination, or re-examination of witnesses; To enable parties to amend various processes filed in court; To enable parties procure proceedings of previous court hearings; and To enable the court to consider various interlocutory applications.

After collecting all necessary evidence, all parties to the case summarize the evidence and apply appropriate legislation to the proven facts. The court then determines the date of the ruling in accordance with the rules of the court, which should not exceed six weeks after the case is closed. This six-week deadline sometimes exceeds several months.

Before a decision can be implemented, it must first be submitted to the court (Yin, 2014). The verdict is a notice submitted in court and sent to the losing party, notifying them that a favorable verdict has been made and describing the conditions of the trial. In order for the resolution to be effective, further action may be required. This may include controlling or taking back property, seizing cash, surrendering and/or canceling documents, etc. The execution of the judgment refers to these procedures. The procedure for enforcing sentences can be lengthy. When a party files an objection to the judgment, they can apply to the High Court for a stay of enforcement and, if unsuccessful, they can appeal to the Court of Appeal. Once approved, the sentence must be suspended until the result of the appeal.

The review/appellate step of civil process in the High Court is the ultimate level. A party may petition the High Court for a judicial review of the Court's decision. The judgement of the High Court might potentially be appealed at the Court of Appeal. A further appeal to the Supreme Court is pending from the Court of Appeal. These channels for review/appeal also cause a significant amount of time to pass.

The processing of the appeal record is the main source of delay. This entails an agreement between the parties as to which of the case's documents may be transmitted to the Court of Appeal; the gathering and production of at least five copies of all the documentation agreed to by the parties; the payment of the cost of documentation production; the provision of security against the appellant's trial costs; and the transmission of the pleadings to the Court of Appeal (Zeisel, 1962).

These procedures can take years, especially when parties are unable to acquire the relatively large funds required to pay for the duplication of the records or make advance payment for the cost of the trial.

Delays can also occur when court registry technology is unavailable or malfunctions, or when there are several appeals ongoing and one must wait in line. The paperwork for appeals to the Supreme Court is generally more extensive, and the number of copies required is usually twelve. A party who is unhappy with the Supreme Court's judgment may petition the Court for a review of the decision.

All of the aforementioned applications, and many other applications that may be filed in the course of litigation are a vehicle for the review of the decision of the High Court on the application or for seeking an interim appeal with the Court of Appeal. Each of them can often cause delays.

It is important to note that delays in the court system may cause defendants to wait months or even years to resolve their allegations. These long delays will have a negative impact on the lives of the defendant, his friends and family. In many cases, the rights and freedoms of persons accused of crimes will be severely restricted. While waiting for the results of their accusations, the defendants may face

Table 1. Court of Appeal fees

Item	Amount(GHc)
Filing Notice of Appeal against a final judgment or decision	100
Respondent's Notice of Intention to contend that decision of Court below be varied	100
Filing Notice of Appeal against Interlocutory Order or decision	70
Motion for Special Leave to Appeal	100
Filing Notice of Appeal where special leave is granted	200
Bond to secure cost of appeal	50
Settling record of appeal	50
Filing Motion for extension of time *(a)* where time has not yet expired	50
(b) where time has already expired	50
Filing any Motion accompanied by an affidavit not otherwise provided for	100
Filing amended or additional grounds of appeal	100
Amending or adding to grounds of appeal by leave or direction	100
Filing Motion to restore appeal dismissed under rule 18 (3) of the Court of Appeal Rules, 1997 (C.I. 19) or appeal struck out under rule 20(2) of C.I. 19	300
Filing Motion to set aside and re-hear appeal determined ex parte	300
Filing Motion to set aside taxing officer's decision or Order	100
Every certificate of the Order of the Court made on the final determination of appeals	100
Filing every document or exhibit	10
Office copies of any document *(a)* for the first twenty sheets	10
(b) each sheet after the first twenty sheets	5
Lodging a bill of costs for taxation including for the first twenty folios	20
For every ten folios or part of ten folios after the first twenty folios	10
Filing a search at the Court of Appeal	50
Filing a Statement of Case	100
Affidavit	10

Source: C. I. 84, Rule 4

Table 2. Supreme Court of Ghana fees

Item	Amount (GHc)
Writ to invoke Original Jurisdiction	300
Motion to invoke the Supervisory Jurisdiction, Affidavit and Statement of Case generally	300
Motion for Review, Affidavit and Statement of Case	500
Petition to challenge election of President	5000
Filing of Statement of Case	300
Application for Leave or for Amendment or for Extension of time	200
Application generally	100
Filing of Document (s) as exhibits attached to an Affidavit or Statement of Case	20
Service of Document	50
Motion to Relist an appeal	200
Affidavit	50
A search at the Supreme Court	50

Source: C. I. 84, Rule 5

restrictions on their ability to drive, restrictions on who they can contact and where they can live, and even imprisonment (Yin, 2018; 2020; 2021). These delays will not only aggravate the condition, but also endanger the defendant's case.

Civil litigation is quite expensive as a result of the numerous unofficial expenses that litigants have to pay. The financial jurisdiction of courts in Ghana is such that small claims are mostly dealt with by the District Court. As shown in the structure of courts in Ghana, the District Court is the lowest and has jurisdiction over contracts and tort actions and recovery of liquidated sum not exceeding GH¢20,000/$3400. Civil litigations in a District Magistrate Court may cost a litigant about GH¢3000/$1200. This cost includes unofficial payments to private bailiffs and other court officials as well as the statutory filing fees.

The Circuit Court's jurisdiction over contracts, tort actions, recovery of liquidated sum, actions involving occupation, possession and title to land, landlord, and tenant cases does not exceed GH¢50,000/$8500. The expense of pursuing any of these issues before the circuit court may range from GH¢5,000/$850 to more than GH¢10,000/$1700. On the other hand, the High Court has jurisdiction over "all cases." Pursuing a basic claim in the High Court may cost not less than GH¢10000/$1700. Tables 1 and 2 show the statutory charges associated with civil procedures in both the Court of Appeal and the Supreme Court of Ghana as stipulated by C.I. 86 of Civil Proceedings (Fees and Allowances) (Amendment) RULES 2014.

Apart from these stipulated fees, a person who wants to access the court to seek justice should also be ready to pay huge sums of money for legal representation. These fees include initial consultation fees, lawyers' travel expenses, out-of-pocket expenses, among others. The out-of-pocket expenses include filing fees, stamping of documents, swearing of affidavits, service of processes, telephone, fax, e-mail, photocopying, printing and binding, courier services, transportation and accommodation, preparation of appeal records, execution of judgments and notarization, etc. In 2015, the Ghana Bar Association reviewed its scale of fees for legal services. The portion which deals with the initial consultation fee for the lawyer provides as follows: Senior Counsel (10+years) - GH¢1,000 maximum, Counsel (5-9 years) - GH¢750 maximum, and Junior Counsel (under 5 years) - GH¢500 maximum. This scale of fees is for Ghanaian clients. For foreign clients, the fees are as follows: Senior Counsel (10+years) - US$500

Table 3. Cases and Corresponding fees

Case Type	Amount
Land Litigation	10% - 20% of the value of the land or hourly rates would apply if the work involved exceeds the 20% value of the land.
Labour Litigation	10% - 20% of the total award or hourly rates would apply if the hourly rates exceed 20% of the claim.
Human Rights Litigation	GH¢6,000- GH¢30,000 or hourly rates would apply if the hourly rates involved exceed GH¢30,000.
Matrimonial Causes	Dissolution & Custody onlyGH¢15,000 – GH¢45,000 or hourly rates would apply if the hourly rates involved exceed GH¢45,000.
Adoption	Ghana Cedi equivalent of US$2000 –US$4,000
Debt Recovery Litigation	GH¢30,000 – GH¢60,000 or hourly rates would apply if the hourly rates involved exceed GH¢60,000.
Criminal Trial	
Bail Application	GH¢2,500 – GH¢15,000
Misdemeanor Trials	GH¢15,000 – GH¢30,000
Felony Trials	GH¢30,000 – GH¢60,000
Indictable Trials	GH¢20,000 – GH¢150,000

Source: Ghana Bar Association, 2015

– $1,000 maximum, Counsel (5-9 years) - US$375-$750 maximum, Junior Counsel (under 5 years) - US250-$500 maximum. The fees do not include the amount that the client will have to pay for hiring the service of the attorney. Table 3 shows some cases and the corresponding cost of hiring a lawyer.

Looking at the gross salary levels of Ghanaians as shown in Table 4 compared to the scale of fees established by C.I. 84 rule 4 and 84 rule 5 and that of the Ghana Bar Association, it seems very few Ghanaians can afford such legal costs. It is therefore not surprising that most Ghanaians consider accessing justice to be expensive as documented by the Center for Democratic Development.

In the 2020 Afrobarometer report by the Center for Democratic Development (CDD) – Ghana, it was found that the majority (54%) of Ghanaians share that the justice system was too expensive compared to other responses as shown in Figure 1.

All these suggest that access to justice in Ghana is fraught with delays and costs. Against the challenges associated with costs, the government of Ghana introduced the National Legal Aid scheme to provide assistance for all who seek to defend or enforce the constitution in accordance with Article 294 of the 1992 constitution. The Legal Aid scheme is currently regulated under the legal aid scheme Act 1997 (Act 542). The purpose of the scheme is to ensure that all citizens have equal access to justice and equal treatment before the law. Supported by the Government of Ghana, its goal is to achieve a just and equitable society by providing nationwide quality legal aid in order to promote access to justice. Despite the aim of the legal aid system, in practice it is faced with numerous challenges such as under funding from the state, inadequate personnel, lack of logistics, etc. All these challenges undermine the effectiveness of the legal aid scheme. Below also examines the case of Sierra Leone in respect of costs and delays.

Table 4. Gross Salary levels in Ghana

% per Population	Gross Salary Range (GHc)
7.35	6000 -11999
7.84	12000 - 16999
12.87	17000 - 28999
22.92	29000 - 57999
12.75	58000 - 86999
8.95	87000 – 115999
5.88	116000 – 144999
4.2	145000 – 173999
2.08	174000 – 202999
2.21	203000 – 231999
1.96	232000 – 260999
0.86	261000 – 288999
0.98	289000 – 317999
0.86	318000 – 346999
1.23	347000 – 375000
0.74	376000 – 404999
0.49	405000 – 433999
0.12	434000 – 462999
0.74	463000 – 491999
0.25	463000 - 491999
0.37	512000 – 549999, etc.

Source: https://www.averagesalarysurvey.com/ghana

Figure 1. Reasons Ghanaians do not use the court system
Source: CDD-Ghana, 2020

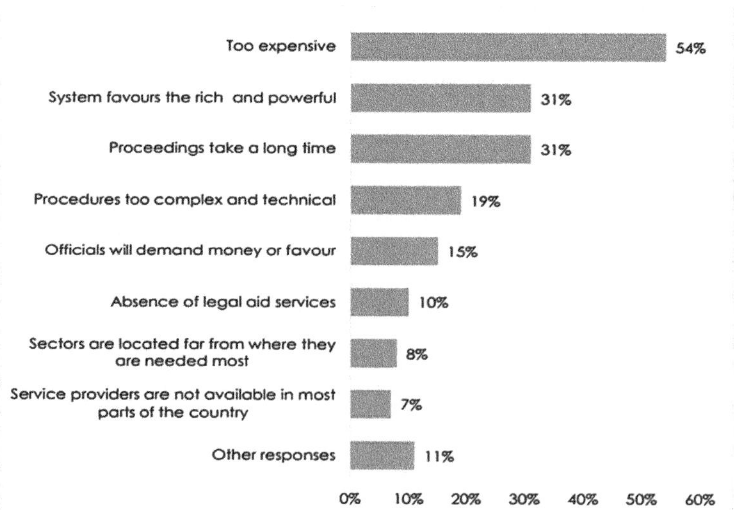

Sierra Leone

The Sierra Leone 1991 Constitution includes entitlement to the right for an accused person to a fair hearing, to be held within a 'reasonable time' and by an appropriate court (Section 23(1), 1991 Constitution). However, for the majority of Sierra Leone's citizens this is a right that is yet to be realised. Delays are one of the crucial issues in the country, especially in the provinces and at magistrate court level. The length of detention for some prisoners without an indictment has been up to a decade. The Constitution mandates time limits in magistrate level courts and above for judgements to be issued, however these are rarely followed. Some courts are yet to issue a judgment, even though the arguments ended three or four years ago. For example, Beamie-Moses Seiwoh vs Station Manager Air France & Air France, a trial before the High Court of Sierra Leone. The trial of this matter concluded on 7th October 2016 and to 30 June 2021 a judgement has not been passed. Meanwhile section 78 of the Constitution requires the High Court and Court of Appeals to issue a judgment within three months of closing a case. A lawyer in Bo Town reported arguing a case of false pretences – a relatively minor offence – which was still without judgment one year after conclusion of the closing arguments.

In recent years, several major reforms have been initiated in the justice sector. However, the critical barriers to a speedy trial remain unresolved. Such barriers include long preliminary investigations, high court fees, detainees' lack of knowledge of their rights, lack of legal representation, poor conditions of service for magistrates and judges, and difficulties in bringing witnesses to court. The average length of a criminal case being heard in a magistrates' court is six months, where all witnesses are available, and all parties are prepared for trial. However, in an interview with magistrates, in Districts x and y, June 2021, it emerged that it was a rare occurrence. For most magistrates, the typical caseload is 15–20 per day, although one reported having to hear up to 40 cases a day.

One of the main reasons for court delays is the preliminary investigations (PI) system, provided for by Section 108 of the Criminal Procedure Act. Though magistrates do not have the jurisdiction to try more serious crimes, such as murder, treason, and sexual assault, Section 108 permits a magistrate to conduct a PI in these cases to ascertain if there is any probable cause to send the case to the High Court. The PI System was introduced to prevent a backlog of frivolous or unsubstantiated cases being sent to higher courts, because if the evidence is too weak to support a trial then the magistrate can drop the charges or indefinitely adjourn the matter until the prosecution can produce sufficient evidence for a trial. However, the PI system has led to serious delays in trials commencing. It has caused proceedings to be duplicated, as witnesses are called to repeat their testimony, with the evidence then presented again during High Court proceedings. During a PI, defendants are also held on remand, further increasing the burden on the prison system. This could violate their constitutional right to a trial within a reasonable time, since the PI process can last for months or years. Although the prosecutor can apply for the case to be heard in the High Court without a PI, the procedure is cumbersome and uncommon.

On April 2020, the Timap for Justice Sierra Leone Focus Group in Bo revealed that most magistrates interviewed for the report were dissatisfied with delays caused by the PI system and have called for its abolition. However, several reforms must be implemented before this can happen. These include increasing the capacity of the police to conduct thorough investigations and gather proper evidence, training police prosecutors to reduce the amount of incorrect or frivolous charges, and increasing the number of High Court judges to handle the increased caseload. Committing cases to the High Court quickly, even after completion of a PI, is rare. For example, Bo, an 11-year-old alleged victim of rape waited over two years for the High Court to resolve her case, only for it to be thrown out because of a lack of corroborating evidence. Other rape victims have waited over three years with no verdict.

Delays in cases being heard are compounded by trying to persuade witnesses to appear in court, especially in the provinces, since witnesses often live some distance from the formal courts. They are consequently reluctant to testify, especially for a second time in the High Court after having already testified in an initial PI. A day in a magistrates' court in Freetown typically produces only one witness for each case, leading to a week-long adjournment until the next witness can appear. In the provinces, judges and civil society activists have attributed the persistence of illegal chiefdom courts to the delays occurring in formal and local courts. Because of ease of accessibility and greater familiarity, the rural population often prefers local courts. However, considerable delays still occur (Legal Aid Board Focus Group in Kambia, April 2021). This often results in the matter being referred to a local chief, who issues a verdict within a couple of days.

Outdated court rules and inadequate systems, amongst other things, have been blamed for undue delays in court proceedings. Thus, in 2007 the judiciary issued Civil Procedure Rules which were aimed at streamlining the processing of civil cases in the High Court. Using this system, after a trial date has been fixed, a pre-trial conference is conducted whereby there is a discussion of all issues relating to the conduct of the trial, including the number of hours to be allocated to the case and the number of witnesses. Under the JSRSIP 2008–2010, the GoSL introduced a small-scale, low-cost Criminal Case Fast Track Project in the High Court. This project allocated funding to resolve any bottlenecks and delays in processing criminal justice cases. A Criminal Case Management Best Practice Handbook was developed in 2006 to deal with criminal matters more rapidly. A fast-track Commercial Court with improved facilities and justice service delivery has also been established. Cases appear to be dispensed more promptly in this court than in other courts.

As a prelude to a wider case-tracking system, the GoSL is working on a database and case-tracking system to be introduced into magistrates' courts. The system aims to keep track of cases and raise the alarm when cases appear to be taking too long. The GoSL emulates the Ugandan Chain Linked Project, which promotes cooperation, coordination and communication between criminal justice sectors. These initiatives must now be implemented and sustained. Although these initiatives are typically welcome, local commentators have complained that the plans may not be able to be implemented without continued financial and technical support from the international community. The APRM recommends the design of an appropriate exit strategy, whereby the government can demonstrate the financial ability and political will to implement these strategies.

The costs for filing a case at the High Court and the Magistrates' Court can be cheaper (see Table 5), but they occasionally present a barrier to indigent citizens. The cost of legal services can be even more difficult to afford, including the main barrier of accessing the formal courts. Order 14(13) of the High Court Rules (Civil Rules of Procedure) 2007 exempts a person from being admitted to sue as a pauper from paying any court fees. However, it requires that they apply to the master and registrar and prove that they have reasonable grounds for proceeding as a pauper (1965 Amended Court Act of Sierra Leone). Most litigants are not aware of this statutory provision; it is therefore rarely used. Local commentators believe that it is even more difficult to access justice in rural communities because of the fluctuating nature of fines imposed in the local or informal courts, coupled with prevalent poverty. In addition, allegations of unreasonably heavy fines are occasionally imposed on people who are considered deviants or political opponents. The statutory minimum wage in Sierra Leone is currently Le 500,000 (approximately USD

Table 5. Schedule of fees payable in the High Court and Magistrate Court Sierra Leone

No.	Description	Fees (SLL)	Fees (USD)
1	Issuing of Claim	30,000.00	2.92
2	Ejectment Notice	5,000.00	0.48
3	Ejectment Summons	10,000.00	0.97
4	Criminal Summons (per court)	10,000.00	0.97
5	Praecipe	5,000.00	0.48
6	Motion	10,000.00	0.97
7	Filing of Defence and Counterclaim	30,000.00	2.92
8	Filing of Defence	30,000.00	2.92
9	Filing of Appeal Notice	25,000.00	2.43
10	Filing of Counterclaim	100,000.00	9.75
11	Entering of Consent judgment	50,000	4.88
12	Addition of Parties	25,000.00	2.43
13	Affidavit of Service	2,000.00	0.19
14	Filing of Affidavits	10,000.00	0.97
15	Court Order	5,000.00	0.48
16	Filing of Court Orders	20,000.00	1.95
17	Issuing of Subpoena	15,000.00	1.46
18	Ejectment Warrant	10,000.00	0.97
19	Execution of Warrant	20,000.00	1.95
20	Filing of Amendment	30,000	2.92
21	Copy per Judgment (per page)	5,000.00	0.48
22	Official copies of Court document 1-10 pages	25,000.00	2.43
23	Official copies of transcript (per page)	2,000.00	0.19
24	Filing of any other court documents not listed above	20,000.00	1.95
25	Search Fee	10,000	0.97

Source: High Court Registry of Sierra Leone

50). As a result of poverty, many litigants required to respond to cases at the High Court should qualify as 'paupers', and thus require legal aid.

No fixed or statutory scale of fees for lawyers currently exists in Sierra Leone. The Legal Practitioners Act of 2000 mandates the General Legal Council to set the scale of fees for legal practitioners for non-contentious matters. Initial consultation fees range from Le 500 000 (approximately USD50) for senior lawyers to Le400 000 (approximately USD40) for junior lawyers. Most litigants cannot afford the financial demands of accessing justice, as provided in section 17(2b) of the Constitution.

A research on the effectiveness of the Family Support Unit, in the Sierra Leone Police in handling and responding to Gender Violence in Sierra Leone noted that "probably more than 40% of the legal needs of the poor people of Sierra Leone go unmet (Seiwoh, 2012), and about 80% of the population living outside the Western Area rely on traditional customary law dispute resolution mechanisms" (Legal Aid Board Annual Report 2019).

The National Legal Aid Act (2012) was introduced by the Parliament of Sierra Leone, increasing the availability of legal aid services nationwide. Prior to this, several local human rights organisations, including Timap for Justice, Lawyers Centre for Legal Assistance and Legal Access through Women Yearning for Equality Rights and Social Justice, with technical and financial support from the United Nations Development Programme, these organisations have provided some legal aid to citizens of Sierra Leone. Though the support is still useful, the challenges of delays and costs still persist.

WAY FORWARD AND CONCLUSION

This chapter examined delays and costs in accessing justice in Ghana and Sierra Leone. Some historical issues, as well as legal procedures related to both countries have been shared. The challenges posed by costs and delays in accessing justice have also been discussed. Based on that, we make the following recommendations to reduce delays and costs. The annual Judicial College should focus on efficiencies and case flows to enable judges, court clerks and administrators to know the reality of their work output. There should be education and consciousness awakening of litigants and their lawyers about the instituted case flow or court procedures, and the punishment for purposeful delaying and disrupting the case flow. In an era of cell phones and various Apps, the justice sector should endeavour to go hi-tech. The Courts should be able to send alerts to litigants and lawyers, and witnesses warranting their presence at an appointed date and time. This should have the effect of decreasing no-shows. Lawyers and clients who know and purposefully engage in tactics to delay trials should be made to pay a steep fine. This will take away the incentive to delay.

The courts should adopt differential case management styles. In that, using the same case management approach across all cases will lead to delay. Some cases require different levels and special judicial arrangements. Also, at the pre-trial stage judges should endeavor to settle the case or refer appropriate cases to Alternative Dispute Resolution programs. There is a need for the courts to monitor and control complex cases to avoid delay. All these recommendations have effects on costs as well. However, the encouragement of cost-effective approaches, and voluntary exchanges can help reduce costs and delays.

Both Ghana and Sierra Leone have made good strides in terms of legal arrangements towards accessing justice. However, these arrangements are fraught with costs and delays. Many cases are not filed, while others settle due to the expense of litigation. Alluding to the above recommendations will be useful in improving the justice situation.

REFERENCES

Adjei, D. D. (2020). Constitutional Law of Ghana: Evolution, Theory and Practice. Accra: Adwinsa Publications (Gm.) Ltd.

Ahuma, A. S. R. B. (1972). One-Man Policy—A Curse to West Africa. *The Gold Coast Nation and National Consciousness*, 54–59.

Baldwin, J. (2000). Access to Justice: The English Experience with Small Claims. PREM Notes; No. 40. World Bank.

Bennion, F. (1962). *The Constitutional Law of Ghana*. Butterworths.

Bimpong-Buta, S. Y. (2005). *The Role of the Supreme Court in the Development of Constitutional Law in Ghana*. University of South Africa.

Boasiako, F. (2017). *Using Technology for Access to Justice in Ghana and Canada: Examining the Digital Divide*. Academic Press.

Boniface, D., & Legg, M. (2010). Cost, Delay and Justice: The High Court of Australia Recognizes the Importance of Case Management in Civil Litigation—Aon Risk Services Australia Limited v Australian National University. *Common Law World Review*, *39*(2), 157–180. doi:10.1350/clwr.2010.39.2.0202

Buahen, A. A. (1975). *Ghana Evolution and Change in Nineteenth and Twentieth Centuries*. Sankofa.

Danquah, J. B. (1957). The Historical Significance of the Bond of 1844. *Transactions of the Historical Society of Ghana*, *3*(1), 3–29.

FelsöF. A.de NooijM. (2012). *When Justice Takes Time: The Social Cost of Legal Delay*. Available at SSRN: doi:10.2139srn.2136897

Government of Sierra Leone. (2019). *Legal Aid Board Annual Report 2019*. Author.

Hale, S. B. (2004). *The Discourse of Court Interpreting: Discourse Practices of the Law, the Witness and the Interpreter*. John Benjamins. doi:10.1075/btl.52

Melcame, A., & Ramello, G. (2016). *Justice delayed, growth denied: Evidence from a comparative perspective*. Retrieved from https://www.siecon.org/sites/siecon.org/files/oldfiles/uploads/2016/09/RAMELLO.pdf on 25/06/2021.

Quansah, E. K. (2011). *Ghana Legal System*. Black Mask Limited.

Seiwoh. (2012). *The Effectiveness of the Family Support in Handling and Responding to Gender Violence in Sierra Leone*. Academic Press.

Sono, A. A. (2017). *A Comparative Study of Legal Aid Institutions in their Pursuit of Social Justice in Ghana*. Retrieved from http://ugspace.ug.edu.gh/bitstream/handle/123456789/32235/A%20Comparative%20Study%20of%20Legal%20Aid%20Institutions%20in%20their%20Pursuit%20of%20Social%20Justice%20in%20Ghana.pdf?sequence=1&isAllowed=y on 17/06/2021

Yin, E. T. (2018). *Religion as an Organising Principle in Ankaful Maximum Security Prison* (PhD Thesis). University of Cape Coast.

Yin, E. T. (2020). Religion, rehabilitation and reintegration of inmates into mainstream society. In A. Balloni & R. Sette (Eds.), *Handbook of Research on Trends and Issues in Crime Prevention, Rehabilitation, and Victim Support* (pp. 398–414). IGI Global. doi:10.4018/978-1-7998-1286-9.ch023

Yin, E. T., Atupare, P. A., Kofie, N., Owusu, L. P., & Botchway, T. P. (2021). Rights and religious belief in maintaining prison social order. *UCC Faculty of Law Journal*, *1*(1), 1–16.

Yin, E. T., & Black, J. M. (2014). The legal anthropology of marriage in Ghana: Presenting power dynamics through legal arenas. *International Journal of Current Research*, *6*(12), 10696–10704.

Zeisel, H. (1962). Delay by the Parties and Delay by the Courts. *Journal of Legal Education*, 27.

APPENDIX: ADDITIONAL RESOURCES

Statutes

- National Legal Aid Act (2012)
- 1992 Constitution of Ghana
- Criminal Act 1960 (Act 29)
- Court Act 1993 (Act 459)
- LI 2429 Court Regulation 2020
- The Legal Aid Scheme Act, 1997 (Act 542)

Chapter 8
Access to Justice and Legal Representation in Nigeria:
Commentaries on the Experiences of Human Rights Lawyers

Oluwaseun Olanrewaju
Academics Stand Against Poverty, Nigeria

Sunday Onuegbu
Renascence (Legal Practitioners and Arbitrators), Nigeria

ABSTRACT

In 2009, the Fundamental Rights Enforcement Procedure (FREP) Rules of 1979 was revised to ease the cumbersome process encountered by applicants/lawyers in advocating for the enforcement of fundamental human rights in court. Despite this, human rights lawyers still encounter several challenges when representing applicants for the enforcement of fundamental human rights in court. This chapter examines these challenges and adopts primary research method. Data were gathered from human rights lawyers via video conferencing platforms: Skype and Zoom. Findings reveal that issues of procedural rules of court and disrespect for court orders are some of the challenges encountered by human rights lawyers. The chapter recommends that judges should avoid placing unnecessary emphasis on the procedural rules of court. In addition, human rights lawyers and non-governmental organizations (NGOs) should maintain continuous advocacy for the enforcement of fundamental human rights towards holding government and its agencies more accountable for disrespect of court orders.

INTRODUCTION

The lack of access to justice has been identified as a major challenge that obstructs the enforcement of fundamental human rights of the citizens. Human rights violations remain proportionately high during the present democratic dispensation in Nigeria (Coker and Obo, 2012). Sadly, many of these sufferers lack access to justice due to poverty, lack of knowledge of human rights as well as procedural rules of

DOI: 10.4018/978-1-7998-7898-8.ch008

court (Ejiogu, 2003; Odeku and Animashaun, 2012; Desmond et al, 2014; Bassey, 2016; Apeh and Onoja; Igwe, Nwocha and Steve, 2019; Olanrewaju, 2020). The pragmatism and efficacy of legal representation promote the principle of human rights and some of the victims of human rights violations who cannot afford the cost of litigation are fortunate to receive legal aid through which they seek justice. Precisely, this study does not seek to discuss the level of human rights abuses or access to justice for the poor in Nigeria. Rather, it focuses on the challenges of enforcing the fundamental human rights guaranteed under the 1999 constitution of the Federal Republic of Nigeria (as amended). In doing this, it examines the experiences of human rights lawyers with respect to the enforcement of fundamental human rights in court. There is no doubt that lawyers are plagued with multifarious challenges when they represent applicants for the enforcement of fundamental human rights. Notwithstanding the Fundamental Rights Enforcement Procedure rules of 2009, the practicality of enforcing fundamental human rights in court by applicants/lawyers remains burdensome. It is apparent that the lapses in the Fundamental Rights Enforcement Procedure rules of 2009 serve as a drawback for its comprehensive effectiveness. Too often, applicants for the enforcement of fundamental human rights are denied justice due to the procedural, institutional and human hurdles encountered during court proceedings. In addressing these challenges, it is imperative to ask what needs to be done and how in order to overcome these impediments. This study seeks to fill this gap in the academic literature on access to justice and human rights jurisprudence. The study examines the challenges encountered by legal practitioners in the enforcement of fundamental human rights proceedings. Section one is the introduction. Section two presents the literature review and research methods. Section three evaluates the research findings. Section four proffers some recommendations and clarifies the issues for further study. Section five contains the author's conclusion.

LITERATURE REVIEW

Access to justice is regarded as a fundamental principle in promoting the rule of law. In the context of human rights, the lack of access to justice creates a barrier against the enforcement of fundamental human rights. To this end, access to justice is essential as an instrument for promoting the principles of fundamental human rights. It is important to underscore that a right without remedy is detrimental to human existence and adversely affects the status of the legal system in a civil society. Shittu (2015) remarks that access to justice is the basic element of any justice system that promotes the human rights of the citizens and serves as a symbol of a civilized society. Access to justice equally entails the processes and procedures of the court and how these determine the final judgments of the court when adjudicating cases between litigants (Muftau, 2016). The lack of access to justice therefore leads to discrimination, inequality, oppression, as well as undue delay in the administration of justice. Conceptually, access to justice is commonly constructed within the scope of the affordability of instituting an action in court as well as having legal representation. In this sense, access to justice is ordinarily viewed from the narrative of indigent members of the society that are vulnerable and lack the financial capabilities to bear the cost of litigation. It is from this perspective that the practice of legal aid and pro bono activism were developed to render legal representation. Access to justice is not comprehensive without an unbiased adjudication process (Omoleye and Eniola, 2018). Crucially, access to justice is an indispensable element in promoting and protecting the human rights of the citizens. In this regard, citizens are able to enforce their rights when they have access to the courts through effective legal representation and a fair hearing anchored on an efficient judicial system. Assuredly, individuals have the leverage to enforce their fundamental rights as guaranteed by the 1999 constitution of Nigeria (as amended) when they have access to justice. Legal representation is aptly provided for in various domestic laws, including the 1999 constitution of the Federal Republic of Nigeria (as amended). Section 35(2) of the constitution states that:

Any person who is arrested or detained shall have the right to remain silent or avoid answering any question until after consultation with a legal practitioner or any other person of their own choice.

Section 36(6) (c-d) state that every person who is charged with a criminal offence shall be entitled to:

(c) Defend himself in person or by legal practitioners of his own choice;

(d) Examine, in person or by his legal practitioners, the witnesses called by the prosecution before any court or tribunal and obtain the attendance and carry out the examination of witnesses to testify on his behalf before the court or tribunal on the same conditions as those applying to the witnesses called by the prosecution.

Section 2 of the preamble to the Fundamental Rights Enforcement (Enforcement Procedure) RULES, 2009 states that:

Parties and their legal representatives shall help the Court to further the overriding objectives of these Rules.

Erugo (2016) argues that the constitution of the Federal Republic of Nigeria and other similar laws are not effective to protect the poor and vulnerable with adequate legal representation. Thus, the efforts of human rights NGOs to promote and protect the human rights of the citizens through advocacy for access to justice are fundamental in sustaining the validity of legal representation and legal aid. The history of human rights in Nigeria is replete with a myriad of human rights abuses from the colonial era to the military regimes. During the colonial era, the political, social and economic policies were formulated and enforced by the British administrators to serve the parochial interests of the colonialist at the detriment of the Nigerian people, thus institutionalizing human rights abuses (Nwachukwu, Aghamelo, & Nwaneri, 2014). The military ruled in Nigeria initially from 1966-1979 and subsequently from 1983-1999. The military regime was replete with various human rights abuses. A larger percentage of the citizens lacked the courage to express their fundamental human rights considering that the military regime was characterized by draconian laws, disrespect for the rule of law and a high level of impunity. Dada (2013, p.84) stated that Military rule was "characterized by arbitrariness, impunity, lengthy detention without trial and other egregious human rights violations". During the military regime, members of the human rights community were harassed, tortured and imprisoned for challenging the legitimacy of military rule. Nigerians had anticipated that the end of military rule and the transition to democratic governance in 1999 would reduce the human rights abuses in the country and improve the enforcement of fundamental human rights of the citizens. On the contrary, there appears to be an upsurge of human rights abuses in Nigeria as witnessed with the increasing level of brutality by state security agencies, kidnapping, banditry, infrastructural challenges as well as Boko haram insurgency. Hence, discussions on the enforcement of fundamental human rights have dominated legal and political discourse from the pre-independence era, to the first, second and third republics, including military regimes and remain relevant even in the present democratic dispensation (Okogbule, 2005). Fundamental human rights are legal rights that are prescribed and protected by the constitution of a country. Justice Oputa distinguished between fundamental human rights and legal rights in RANSOME-KUTI & ORS. V. AG FEDERATION & ORS (1985) JELR 42572 (SC). He elucidated that:

Not every civil or legal right is a fundamental right. The ideal and concept of fundamental rights both derive from the premise of the inalienable rights of man – life, liberty, and the pursuit of happiness. Emergent nations with written constitutions have enshrined in such a constitution some of these basic human rights, each right that is considered fundamental is spelt out.

Although, scholars have addressed the theme of access to justice from diverse analytical views, the importance of legal representation in ensuring access to justice cannot be overemphasized. Law scholars and activists have significantly examined the concept of access to justice from the perspective of the enforcement of fundamental human rights (Aihe, 1973; Okogbule, 2005; Taiwo, 2009; Nwafor, 2009; International Commission of Jurists, 2011; Sanni, 2011; Omidoyin, 2019; Lima & Gomez, 2020). However, no study reflects the experiences of human rights lawyers engaged in legal representation for the enforcement of fundamental human rights. Lawyers are confronted with numerous institutional obstructions in pursuing the enforcement of fundamental human rights in the court of law. This undermines the justice system in promoting access to justice. For this reason, victims of human rights violations are sometimes encumbered from enforcing their constitutionally guaranteed rights when they are violated. This study is relevant considering the importance of effective legal representation and an efficient judicial system in promoting access to justice. It aims to proffer significant recommendations towards effective legal representation by lawyers in the enforcement of fundamental human rights cases in court. This is particularly important to ensure that sufferers of human rights violations have access to justice and are able to enforce their fundamental human rights.

Research Methods

The study adopts the primary research method and gathered qualitative data from open interviews. A total of 25 (23 males and 2 females) lawyers were interviewed over 3 months via video conferencing platforms; Skype and Zoom. The respondents were selected from the researchers' contacts based on their experiences in human rights litigation. The respondents have between 10 – 25 years of experience in human rights litigation. Hence, it was necessary to have contacted them to share their experiences. Their responses were coded in numerical form from 1- 25. Numbers 1 and 2 describe the female lawyers, while numbers 3-25 represent the male lawyers. The interviews lasted for about 45 minutes, and the respondents shared their knowledge and experiences on access to justice, legal representation and enforcement of fundamental human rights.

Although, an open interview may be time-consuming compared to Focused Group Discussions (FGDs), however, it provides a convenient methodological approach to engage with the respondents. The open interview enabled the respondents to freely share their experiences on the subject matter of research. The records of the interviews were reviewed and transcribed to ensure familiarization with the data. In order to identify vital information in the data and describe the contents, codes were assigned to the data. Data were organized into groups bearing in mind the distinct responses. After this, the codes were categorized into themes. Categorization into themes involved collation of the codes into broader themes through active interpretation of the codes and related contents. The themes that were identified during categorization were reviewed to examine if the contents support the themes. Lastly, the themes were described and labeled with different captions. As with any qualitative research, not all the data gathered were used in the analysis as the researchers focused on the responses relevant to the study. However, the totality of the responses provided insights to shape the analysis and inferences drawn.

Discussion

The majority of the respondents identified needless adherence to the procedural rules of court as a challenge to the enforcement of fundamental human rights. While litigation involves defined procedures, some judges strictly focus on court procedures without due consideration for speedy trials. Strict adherence to procedural rules of the court creates delays in the administration of justice. Respondent 4 emphasized that;

In a case at the Court of Appeal, counsel to the Respondents', filed a preliminary objection without serving same on the Applicant. When the court brought this error to the notice of the Respondents' counsel, he pleaded with the Justices that they should allow the Respondents' regularize the error. Although a cost was awarded against the Respondents', the Justices granted their application for regularization and the matter was adjourned at the detriment of the Applicant who was my client. The appeal would have been heard that day but was adjourned.

In most cases, Judges treat such non-compliance as a mere irregularity, and allow for them to be regularized, even when it does not affect the substance and validity of the case. Respondents 7, 11, 12, 15, 18, 20 and 23 added that:

When there is urgency, the court should entertain an *exparte* application as stated in Order 4 Rule 3 of the Fundamental Rights Enforcement Procedure Rules (2009). However, the court has on numerous occasions dismissed their exparte applications based on the principle of fair hearing, despite the fact that the Applicants faced exceptional hardship.

This study supports the work of Brems and Adekoya (2010) that proceedings for the enforcement of fundamental human rights are usually delayed and sometimes hindered due to the cumbersome technicalities and procedures of the court. The decision to blatantly follow procedures and rules by Judges often stalls and delays the administration of justice in the enforcement of fundamental human rights to the detriment of the Applicants. Asuzu (2012) emphasise that the "softening of procedural dogma should feature more in human rights litigation" (p.16). In this regard, Judges are expected to wittingly waive or circumvent any rule that will serve as an impediment to the enforcement of fundamental human rights. Judges should learn to focus on the substance and not the form in order to promote and protect the human rights of the Applicants. Focusing unduly on procedures frustrates the efforts of lawyers and may deny the Applicant access to justice.

The court practice of adjourning cases delays the resolve of Applicants to seek legal redress for the enforcement of fundamental human rights. Reasons for adjourning cases include; strict adherence to court procedures and rules by Judges, absence of respondents and counsel in court, the court not sitting, to mention but a few. Order 4 Rule 2 of the Fundamental Rights (Enforcement Procedure) Rules, 2009 states that:

The hearing of the application may from time to time be adjourned where extremely expedient, depending on the circumstances of each case or upon such terms as the Court may deem fit to make, provided the Court shall always be guided by the urgent nature of applications under these Rules.

However, the respondents stressed that a plethora of cases on the enforcement of fundamental human rights are adjourned on long dates, without the Judges considering the expediency required to determine such cases. In the words of Respondent 10:

Long and unnecessary adjournments are obstacles that hinder access to justice and delay the enforcement of fundamental human rights. I represented an Applicant whose personal liberty was infringed, yet the matter was concluded in 14 months due to unnecessary adjournments. Adjournments should be discouraged in human rights cases to promote access to justice and speedy dispensation of justice.

Respondent 9 voiced that:

I have represented clients who lost their lives while their cases were pending in court due to needless adjournments. Judges should stop encouraging adjournments that are preventable. Justice is for the living and does not make sense to the dead.

Legal Defence and Assistance Project (LEDAP) (2018) asserts that adjournments create obstacles to "the speedy and efficient realization of human rights cases" (p.6). Long and unnecessary adjournments of fundamental human rights cases demonstrate the value placed on the enforcement of fundamental human rights in Nigeria. It further reflects the level of institutional concerns in promoting and protecting the human rights of the citizens. It must be noted that delay in the enforcement of fundamental human rights is a delay to access to justice for Applicants whose human rights have been violated. As often stated, justice delayed is justice denied.

Disobeying court orders by Respondents is a prominent factor that affects the advocacy of lawyers in seeking the enforcement of fundamental human rights. The nonchalant attitude to court orders makes it cumbersome for Applicants to enforce the judgment of the courts. Respondent 1 noted:

There is always a challenge with enforcing the judgment of the court as the government and its agencies flagrantly disrespect court orders. On several occasions, the police have disrespected the orders and judgment of courts delivered in my clients' favour. In a particular case, it took 6 years of struggle and resilience to enforce the judgment of the court.

Respondent 14 stated clearly:

The police seized the property of my client and have yet to release same despite the judgment of the court 6 months ago that the act is illegal and unconstitutional.

Almost 50% of the respondents were of the view that;

It is always difficult to enforce court judgments because it is not within the purview of the court to execute judgments. Worst still, respondents file processes to stop the execution of judgments.

Respondent 21 stated:

On two different occasions, the police disrespected the order of the court to produce the Applicant (my client) who was held in their custody. The Applicant was eventually brought to court when the Judge issued a bench warrant for the arrest of the Investigating Police Officer (IPO). He (my client) had suffered torture and gross abuse of his fundamental human rights.

Dada (2012) admits that disobedience to court orders jeopardizes the enforcement of fundamental human rights. According to him, judgments cannot be enforced by the judiciary and there is little reliance on the executive arm of government to execute judgments considering that the executive is the major violator of human rights in the country. Onwubiko (2019) underlines that disrespect for court orders has become daring and worse under Nigeria's democratic dispensation. The unlawful detention of former National Security Adviser, Sambo Dasuki and the leader of the Islamic Movement of Nigeria (IMN) and his wife by the Buhari administration despite court orders for their release is testamentary of the government's disobedience to court orders. They were eventually released after a national and international outcry by human rights organizations. It is counterintuitive that the ruling regime and its agencies maintain a disposition that portrays them as above the law by denying applicants access to justice, and frustrating their lawyers, thus ridiculing the Nigerian justice system.

The issue of corruption in the judicial system is a challenge that poses a threat to the enforcement of fundamental human rights. Respondents acknowledge that corruption taints the judgment of the courts for economic, political and parochial reasons. Most Applicants for the enforcement of fundamental human rights have had cases decided against them due to corruption. Okogbule (2005) and Brems & Adekoya (2010) explain that corruption in the justice administration system and corrupt judicial officers serve as impediments to the enforcement of fundamental human rights. The level of corruption among Judges as exposed by the Buhari administration lends credence to the burden of judicial corruption and its deeming consequences on the enforcement of fundamental human rights in Nigeria.

Respondents 4, 7, 9, 10, 11, 12, 13, 14, 16 hold the perception that government influences the decision of Judges. In cases where Judges deliver judgment against the government, the government files an application in a concurrent court with similar jurisdiction or at the Court of Appeal to influence the courts to stay enforcement of the judgment or deliver a contrary judgment.

Respondent 25 remarked:

Judges that are corrupt sometimes strike out an application for the enforcement of fundamental human rights on frivolous grounds. In my experience, the Judge said the application lacked merit and was a mere civil claim.

Respondent 3 highlighted:

Judges sometimes deliver false judgments because they are weary of incurring the wrath of the government, which may encumber their careers.

Respondent 22 added:

Lack of independence of the judiciary endorses corruption. Desperate and corruptible Judges are easily threatened by career redundancy, as well as budget cuts.

Corruption in the judiciary has tainted the image of the remedial institution and has equally made justice more expensive and rigorous. It is an irony that the judiciary that should reflect the hope of the common man is enmeshed in various forms of corruption that transcend monetary *quid pro quo*. Corruption blights the institutional function of the judiciary in ensuring justice for the citizens.

In determining an application for the enforcement of fundamental human rights, Judges sometimes restrict the scope of enforcement of fundamental human rights by striking out applications on the basis that they are not principal claims but mere ancillary reliefs. Nwauche (2008) labelled the distinction between principal and ancillary claims as dubious and irrelevant. This is particularly so, considering that the courts in Nigeria will not entertain an application for the enforcement of fundamental human rights unless the principal claim or claims are predicated on the fundamental rights prescribed under Chapter IV of the 1999 Constitution of the Federal Republic of Nigeria (as amended). To this extent, one should consider the justification for creating and determining the distinction between principal and ancillary claims, when fundamentally, the objective of the law is to ensure that victims whose fundamental rights have been infringed are duly recompensed and justice is speedily delivered.

Respondent 8 stated:

My client was detained for 3 weeks and wrongly dismissed from the Police Force for dereliction of duty. The court held that my client's application for unlawful detention brought under chapter IV of the 1999 constitution of Nigeria (as amended) was ancillary to the principal claim, which was wrongful dismissal and the matter was struck out for lack of jurisdiction.

Respondent 2 lamented:

The court struck out an application for the enforcement of fundamental human rights stating that it has no jurisdiction because the violation of my client's fundamental human rights emanated from a matrimonial issue. As such, the principal claim emanated from a matrimonial cause of action and the violation of fundamental rights was ancillary.

Distinguishing between principal and ancillary claims in cases on the enforcement of fundamental human rights is a setback for the enforcement of fundamental rights proceedings in our judicial system. It is apparent that such technicality of court in itself lacks merit and should be discarded. Decisively, what should matter in this regard is whether the claim brought before the court forms part of the provisions of chapter 4 of the 1999 constitution of the Federal Republic of Nigeria (as amended).

In entertaining a suit on the enforcement of fundamental human rights, the courts examine if they have the jurisdiction to hear the matter as mandated by the 1999 constitution of the Federal Republic of Nigeria (as amended). This creates the issue of determining which court has jurisdiction between the Federal and State High Courts to entertain a suit on the enforcement of fundamental human rights.

Respondent 24 suggested:

An application for the enforcement of fundamental human rights should be heard without undue consideration to the circumstance of the original cause of action from which it arose and the constitutional jurisdiction of the court to entertain it ab inito.

Respondent 1 acknowledged:

In some instances the courts have stated that matters that concern state governments should not be entertained at the Federal High Court and such application for the enforcement of fundamental human rights would be struck out.

Respondent 12 stated:

I filed a case against the Nigeria Security and Civil Defense Corps (NSCDC) at the State High Court. The Judge struck out the matter stating that the NSCDC is an agency of the Federal Government and the matter ought to be heard at the Federal High Court.

This study corroborates the work of Felix and Akujobi (2018) that determining which court has the jurisdiction between the Federal High Court and State High Court in matters pertaining to the enforcement of fundamental human rights is a barrier to the enforcement of fundamental human rights in Nigeria.

The court as an adjudicatory body has the responsibility to interpret the laws as enshrined in the constitution and other legislative enactments, however laws should not be interpreted in a manner that appears ambiguous and contradictory to the provisions of the constitution and rules that determine the practice and procedure of courts. Section 46 (1) of the 1999 constitution of the Federal Republic of Nigeria (as amended) states that; "Any person who alleges that any of the provisions of this Chapter has been, is being or likely to be contravened in any State in relation to him may apply to a High Court in that State for redress". Likewise, Under Order 1 Rule 2, (citation and interpretation) of the Fundamental Rights Enforcement Procedure Rules 2009, 'Court' means the Federal High Court or the High Court of a State or the High Court of the Federal Capital Territory, Abuja. Basically, in the enforcement of fundamental human rights cases, what should matter is that a fundamental human right has been breached and an action has been instituted in any of the High Courts stated above regardless of whether the court has original jurisdiction to entertain the cause of action from which the breach of fundamental human rights occurred. The jurisdictional dichotomy by the courts appears to be against the spirit of the law and detrimental to promoting the principle of fundamental human rights.

Section 3(a) of the preamble to the Fundamental Rights (Enforcement Procedure) Rules, 2009 states:

The overriding objectives of these Rules are as follows: (a) The Constitution, especially Chapter IV, as well as the African Charter, shall be expansively and purposely interpreted and applied, with a view to advancing and realizing the rights and freedoms contained in them and affording the protections intended by them.

However, applicants for the enforcement of fundamental human rights cannot enforce their economic, social and cultural rights through the African Charter on Human and Peoples Rights (Ratification and Enforcement) because these rights are not justiciable under Chapter II of the 1999 constitution (Fundamental Objectives and Directive Principle of State Policy). These rights are not included as fundamental human rights under chapter IV of the 1999 constitution (as amended).

Respondent 5 retorted:

Non-justiciability of Chapter II of the 1999 constitution is a suppression of the fundamental human rights of Nigerians. The components of the fundamental objectives and directive principles of state policy in chapter II; include health, education, employment, infrastructure that are fundamental to human existence.

Respondent 8 elaborated further:

Economic and social rights are still not justiciable in our courts. The provisions of sections 6(6)(c) give effect to chapter II of the constitution and serve as a justification for Judges to dismiss cases that seek to enforce social and economic rights through the ratification and enforcement of the African Charter on Human and Peoples Rights.

Section 6(6)(c) of the 1999 constitution of the Federal Republic of Nigeria (as amended) states that:

The judicial powers vested in accordance with the foregoing provisions of this section shall not except as otherwise provided by this Constitution, extend to any issue or question as to whether any act of omission by any authority or person or as to whether any law or any judicial decision is in conformity with the Fundamental Objectives and Directive Principles of State Policy set out in Chapter II of this Constitution.

The disposition of the courts in Nigeria not to recognize the components of chapter II as fundamental human rights have propelled some human rights organizations to seek justice at the Court of Justice of the Economic Community of West African States (ECOWAS). The efforts and victory of the Socio-Economic Rights and Accountability Project (SERAP) in advocating for the environmental protection of the Niger Delta from degradation at the ECOWAS court in 2012 are illustrative in this regard to justify the essence of the justiciability of chapter II of the 1999 constitution of the Federal Republic of Nigeria (as amended). Section 12 of the 1999 constitution empowers the legislative arm of government to domesticate a treaty in order to be enforceable in Nigerian courts. The African Charter on Human and Peoples Rights was domesticated as part of the laws of the Federation of Nigeria on 17 March 1983. The non-justiciability of chapter II on the premise that the components are mere privileges and not fundamental human rights is itself not just and should not be justiciable.

In seeking legal redress, citizens whose fundamental rights have been abused should have easy access to the courts beginning with the process of application. Contrarily, the process for the application for the enforcement of fundamental human rights does not portray the urgency required for the enforcement of fundamental human rights. Sanni (2011) stated that the Fundamental Rights Enforcement Procedure Rules 2009 is not effective in commencing an action for the enforcement of fundamental human rights considering the rigours of preparing the court processes, including a written address for front-loading. The process of commencing an action for the enforcement of fundamental human rights in court and several other factors are challenges against the legal representation of Applicants for the enforcement of fundamental human rights.

RECOMMENDATIONS

In ensuring that human rights lawyers achieve significant impact, it is recommended that Judges avoid placing unnecessary emphasis on the procedural rules of court at the detriment of enforcing the fundamental human rights of Applicants. Furthermore, the judiciary arm of government must be independent and free from government interference in its role to ensure justice and equity for the citizens. From this view, the human rights community should persistently canvass for an independent judiciary, free from government interference in the execution of its primary functions. In addition, human rights NGOs should continuously pressure the government to make the provisions of chapter II of the 1999 constitution on economic, social and cultural rights justiciable and part of the fundamental human rights in chapter IV of the 1999 constitution of the Federal Republic of Nigeria (as amended). Human rights NGOs should continuously educate citizens on their rights to create more awareness of human rights. An application for the enforcement of fundamental human rights should be less cumbersome and not time-consuming with filing and front-loading of numerous court processes. The application should be swift and in most cases should be decided in one sitting. To achieve this, the 2009 rules on the enforcement of fundamental human rights must be revised to ensure that applications are filed and heard without delays. Lastly, human rights lawyers and Non-Governmental Organizations (NGOs) should maintain continuous advocacy for the enforcement of fundamental human rights and enforcement of treaties that have been domesticated towards holding government and its agencies more accountable for disrespect of court orders.

LIMITATION OF STUDY AND ISSUES FOR FURTHER STUDY

The decline to participate in the study by some human rights lawyers is a major limitation of the study. Their participation in the study could have expanded the depth of the study. Secondly, limiting the study to the experience of lawyers, without engaging the Applicants/clients whose rights were violated limits the perspective of the scope of study. Lastly, the study featured 2 female respondents. It is evident that their responses did not holistically capture the experiences of female lawyers that represent clients in proceedings on the enforcement of fundamental human rights. The experiences of the Respondents' lawyers could have created a balanced view of the study. Regardless of these limitations, the data gathered and utilized provided detailed and significant information in analyzing the subject matter of research.

In conducting a further study on the subject, it is necessary to expand the scope to cover the perception and experiences of victims of human rights violations/Applicants for the enforcement of fundamental human rights in court. Similarly, further research should be carried out that will examine the experiences and views of Respondent lawyers on the enforcement of fundamental human rights cases. It is equally important for future studies to bring into perspective the dynamics of gender in the legal representation of Applicants in cases on the enforcement of fundamental human rights. In essence, further investigation should engage a substantial number of female human rights lawyers and compare their experiences to that of their male colleagues.

CONCLUSION

The role of human rights lawyers in promoting access to justice through legal representation in cases that affect the fundamental human rights of the citizens is crucial. The study established that the procedure for the enforcement of fundamental human rights has become less cumbersome following the revision of the Fundamental Rights Enforcement Procedure Rules of 1979 in 2009. However, human rights lawyers still experience several institutional and procedural obstacles that affect their legal representation of clients in fundamental human rights cases. These challenges discussed in the study include procedural challenges, long and unnecessary adjournments, the dichotomy between principal and ancillary reliefs and many more. They expose the limitations of the constitution as well as the judiciary in promoting and protecting the principles of fundamental human rights. Surely, this is a drawback for lawyers in their legal representation of clients for the enforcement of fundamental human rights and in promoting access to justice in the country. Notwithstanding these challenges, human rights lawyers remain undaunted to ensure that the human rights of the citizens are protected and access to justice is promoted.

REFERENCES

Aihe, D. O. (1973). Fundamental Human Rights Provisions as Means of Achieving Justice in Society: The Nigerian "Bill Of Rights". *Malaya Law Review*, *15*(1), 39–54.

Apeh, E. I., & Onoja, U. F. (2018). Literacy Promotion for Human Rights Awareness and Protection-The Case of Nigeria. *Journal of Good Governance and Sustainable Development in Africa*, *4*(1), 14–22.

AsuzuC. (2012). Fundamental Rights Enforcement- The Role of the Office of Public Defender of Lagos State of Nigeria. doi:10.2139srn.2086358

Bassey, R. I. (2016). Natural law theory and its implications for human rights in Nigeria. Sophia: *An African. The Journal of Philosophy*, *17*(1), 208–218.

Brems, E., & Adekoya, C. O. (2010). Human rights enforcement by people living in poverty: Access to justice in Nigeria. *Journal of African Law*, *54*(02), 258–282. doi:10.1017/S0021855310000070

Coker, M. A., & Obo, U. B. (2012). Crisis of governance and the violations of human rights: The Nigerian experience, 1999 to 2007. *African Journal of Political Science and International Relations*, *6*(3), 62–73.

Constitution of the Federal Republic of Nigeria (1999)

Dada, J. A. (2012). Impediments to Human Rights Protection in Nigeria. *Annual Survey of International & Comparative Law*, *18*(1), 67–92.

Dada, J. A. (2013). The Significance and Limits of NGOs in Human Rights Protection in Nigeria. Journal of Law. *Policy and Globalization*, *19*, 82–91.

Desmond, D.E., Cecil, C. and Frederick, M. (2014). Poverty, human rights and access to equity: Reflections from Nigeria. *International Journal of Law and Legal Studies, 1*(2), 40-49.

Ejiogu, A. (2003). Aquinas Conception of Human Dignity: A lesson Against Abuse of Human Rights in Africa. *Amamihe Journal of Applied Philosophy*, *1*(1), 1–17.

Erugo, S. (2016). Legal Assistance by Clinical Law Students: A Nigerian Experience in Increasing Access to Justice for the Unrepresented. *Asian Journal of Legal Education*, *3*(2), 160–173. doi:10.1177/2322005816640335

Felix, O., & Akujobi, A. (2018). Enforcement of Fundamental Rights in National Constitutions: Resolving the Conflict of Jurisdiction between the Federal High Court and State High Court in Nigeria. *Beijing Law Review*, *9*(01), 53–66. doi:10.4236/blr.2018.91004

Fundamental Rights Enforcement Procedure Rules (2009)

Igwe, I., Nwocha, M., & Steve, A. (2019). Enforcement of Fundamental Rights in Nigeria and the Unsolved Issue of Poverty among the Citizens: An Appraisal. *Beijing Law Review*, *10*(01), 1–9. doi:10.4236/blr.2019.101001

International Commission of Jurists. (2011). *Access to Justice: Human Rights Abuses Involving Corporations.* https://www.business-humanrights.org/sites/default/files/media/documents/icj-report-access-to-justice-nigeria-22-feb-2012.pdf

Legal Defence and Assistance Project. (2018). *Report On The Human Rights Situations In Nigeria.* file:///C:/Users/OLANRE~1/AppData/Local/Temp/LEDAP_UPR31_NGA_E_Main.pdf

Lima, V., & Gomez, M. (2020). Access to Justice: Promoting the Legal System as a Human Right. In UN (Ed.), Encyclopedia of the UN Sustainable Development Goals (pp. 1- 10). Springer Publishing.

Muftau, R. (2016). Access to Judicial Justice in Nigeria: The Need for Some Future Reforms. Journal of Law. *Policy and Globalization*, *47*, 144–158.

Nwachukwu, S. N., Aghamelo, A., & Nwaneri, S. (2014). An Account of Human Right Violations In Nigeria (Pre-British, British And Post-Independence). European Scientific Journal, 2, 230-239.

Nwafor, A. O. (2009). Enforcement of Fundamental Human Rights in Nigerian Courts – Processes and Challenges. *African Journal of Legal Studies*, *4*(1), 1–11. doi:10.1163/221097312X13397499736787

Nwauche, E. S. (2008). The Dubious Distinction between Principal and Accessory Claims in Nigeria Human Rights Jurisprudence. *Journal of African Law*, *52*(1), 66–88. doi:10.1017/S002185530800003X

Odeku, K., & Animashaun, S. (2012). Poverty, human rights and access to justice: Reflections from Nigeria. *African Journal of Business Management*, *6*(23), 6754–6764.

Okogbule, N. S. (2005). Access to justice and human rights protection in Nigeria: Problems and prospects. *Sur. International Journal of Human Rights*, *2*(3), 95–113.

Olanrewaju, O. (2020). An Evaluation of the Knowledge and Perception of the Concept of Human Rights by Residents of Selected Suburban Communities of Lagos, Nigeria. *Journal of Human Rights and Social Work*, *5*, 185–190.

Omidoyin, T. J. (2019). Law Clinic and Access to Justice for Pretrial Detainees in Nigeria. *Nnamdi Azikiwe University Journal of International Law and Jurisprudence*, *10*(1), 101–108.

Omoleye, B. O., & Eniola, B. O. (2018). Administration of Justice in Nigeria: Analysing the dominant legal ideology. *Journal of Law and Conflict Resolution*, *10*(1), 1–8. doi:10.5897/JLCR2016.0242

Onwubiko, E. (2019). *Nigeria: Parlous state of human rights.* https://guardian.ng/opinion/nigeria-parlous-state-of-human-rights/

Ransome-Kuti & ORS. v. AG Federation & ORS (1985) JELR 42572 (SC)

Sanni, A. (2011). Fundamental Rights Enforcement Procedure Rules, 2009 as a tool for the enforcement of the African Charter on Human and Peoples' Rights in Nigeria: The need for far-reaching reform. *African Human Rights Law Journal*, *1*(2), 511–531.

Shittu, W. (2015). *The challenges of access to justice.* https://guardian.ng/opinion/the-challenges-of-access-to-justice/

Taiwo, E. A. (2009). Enforcement of fundamental rights and the standing rules under the Nigerian Constitution: A need for a more liberal provision. *African Human Rights Law Journal*, *9*, 546–575.

ADDITIONAL READING

Adetoro, R. A., & Omiyefa, M. O. (2014). Challenges Of Human Rights Abuses in Nigerian Democratic Governance – Which Way Forward? *Journal of Social Economics Research*, *1*(5), 87–96.

Aurora, S. (2016). *Human Rights and Values in Education*. Education International.

EDET v. Nigerian Army & ORS. (2018) JELR 39077 (CA)

Emina, K. (2015). An Analysis of Poverty as a Violation of Human Right in Nigeria. Journal of Poverty. *Investment and Development*, (10), 88–94.

Frynas, J. G. (2001). Problems of Access to Courts in Nigeria: Results of a Survey of Legal Practitioners. *Social & Legal Studies*, *10*(3), 397–419. doi:10.1177/a018603

Latham and Watkins. (2016). Pro Bono Practices and Opportunities in Nigeria. https://www.lw.com/admin/Upload/Documents/Global%20Pro%20Bono%20Survey/pro-bono-in-nigeria.pdf

Nzarga, F. D. (2014). An Analysis of Human Rights Violation by the Nigerian Security Services. Journal of Law. *Policy and Globalization*, *30*, 1–8.

Odiaka, N. O. (2013). The Concept of Gender Justice and Women's Rights in Nigeria: Addressing the Missing Link. *Journal of Sustainable Development Law and Policy*, *2*(1), 190–205.

Onimisi, T. (2018). Trend of Human Right Abuse in Nigeria: 1996-2013. *International Journal of Advanced Studies in Social Science & Innovation*, *2*(2), 70–79.

Palombella, G. (2007). From Human Rights to Fundamental Rights: Consequences of a conceptual distinction. *Archives for Philosophy of Law and Social Philosophy*, *93*(3), 396–426.

KEY TERMS AND DEFINITIONS

Access to Justice: The legal right to seek redress in the court of law.

Adjournment: The act or practice of postponing an event or proceeding to a future date.

Constitution: The fundamental laws that regulate the affairs of a nation or an organization.

Court Rules: These are rules that regulate the procedures of a court and determine the processes for entertaining and hearing of cases.

Enforcement: The act of compelling people to do what is legally mandated.

Fundamental Rights: These are rights guaranteed by the constitution and enforced by law.

Chapter 9
Alternative Dispute Resolution in Ghana:
A Critical Look at Act 798

Christopher Amoasi
University of Cape Coast, Ghana

ABSTRACT

Adjudication of issues in the Ghanaian jurisdiction can be traced back to the pre-colonial era where powers were vested in chiefs, elders, and representatives of all the major tribes. Chiefs and elders adjudicated on most issues with the family heads serving as lawyers. During the colonial era, judicial powers were vested in the Privy Council, which took away the powers of the chiefs and elders. At times parties to a dispute may want to resolve the dispute in a form other than the normal court system, hence the alternative dispute resolution (ADR). However, ADR lacks stare decisis since it set no precedent to guide similar disputes in the future. Also, there is no right of appeal when parties opt for ADR. The purpose of this chapter is to assess the use of ADR in Ghana, the challenges, and the way forward.

INTRODUCTION

The concepts of ADR have been practised in Ghana before the colonial period. These ideals have been ingrained in Ghanaian cultures and communities' traditional standards and values (Ruffin, 2019). The Colonial Courts, which were founded by the colonial administrators at the time, were able to identify, confirm, and implement these conventional settlement outcomes in the courts because of the methods of traditional dispute resolution ingrained in our ancestors' social fabric. Chiefs, elders, and heads of families and clans in each group were involved in the settlement process (Ruffin, 2019). In today's world, the extended family structure consists of the nuclear family (father, mother, and children) as well as other relatives such as uncles and aunties, grandfathers and mothers, cousins, and so on. The head of each extended family is usually the eldest male, known as the "Ebusua Panyin" (Akan). Furthermore, each extended family in the group belongs to a particular clan. Each clan is typically led by the clan's eldest living male or an elected elder from one branch (Zuure, 2018).

DOI: 10.4018/978-1-7998-7898-8.ch009

The majority of disagreements were previously settled by the extended family system. Parents refer family conflicts to the family's head of household, who attempts to settle the conflict. When this attempt fails, the clan chief is summoned to assist. The Chief is usually the last resort, making a final and binding decision. Due to recent urbanisation and rural-urban migration within the region, the extended family system is continuing to deteriorate. The majority of individuals and families have traditionally relied on the court trial process to resolve disputes (litigation). However, due to the public's unfavourable view of the country's judicial systems, litigation is quickly becoming unpopular. Litigation has also been sluggish, costly, and inconvenient. These and other factors have prompted Ghana's judicial service to launch a comprehensive reform programme aimed at reducing the backlog of cases in the courts, reducing the time spent trying cases, and introducing policies and procedures that make justice more available to the poor and vulnerable.

ADR structures can be a welcome and effective replacement for Ghana's conventional and extended family conflict resolution methods (Price, 2018). Owing to the progressive collapse of the extended family structure, these extended family systems have become is weakening or withering away largely because a) mass mobility—people migrating to cities, b) increasing frequency of inter-ethnic marriages, c) formation of nuclear families away from close relatives. Ghana's people have been characterised as being peaceful, hospitable, and peace-loving despite the fact that there is political unrest, intra-ethnic, and religious conflicts persisting in the country. With the weakening of the extended family system and its dispute resolution, which has affected the informal way of adjudicating issues among individuals, it's more important than ever to find new ways to maintain the peace that has brought much-needed stability and economic growth. To this end, the adoption and implementation effective ADR framework in the country is sorely needed in order to nip potentially open hostilities and conflicts in the bud. Alternative Dispute Resolution (ADR) can be described as any means of resolving a legal issue outside of the courtroom. ADR methods have been around for a while and are quickly gaining traction as a favoured form of conflict resolution. Parties that have participated in ADR processes such as mediation express satisfaction and confidence in the process. Negotiations in various ways, mediation, and arbitration are some of the ADR processes widely used by stakeholders in the country (Mensah-Panford, 2018). This paper evaluates alternative conflict resolution in Ghana: A detailed look at Act 798, the problems, and the way forward in this context.

HISTORICAL OVERVIEW OF ADR IN GHANA

Professor Uwaize, known as the "Father of ADR in Africa," is credited with establishing ADR in Ghana. In 1996, he led a group of 12 legal professionals from Nigeria, Senegal, and Ghana to the United States for ADR training. Former Chief Justice Georgina Theodora Wood, Mr. Nene Amegatcher, who represented the Ghana Bar Association, and Professor Henrietta Mensa- Bonsu [now a Justice of the Supreme Court of Ghana] from the faculty of law were among the Ghanaian representatives chosen. They were given the task of raising ADR awareness in Ghana after they completed their training. After a fruitful training session, the team was to train interested individuals and retain them. Former Chief Justices Kwame Wiredu and George Kingsley Acquah worked hard to put in place policies to help Ghana grow ADR (Uwazie, 2014).

Following that, ten more legal practitioners were qualified to assist in the creation of Ghana's ADR institution. ADR was implemented on a trial basis with the assistance of these qualified practitioners to see if it would be adopted and if it was successful in settling conflicts within the country. The Ghana Judicial Service piloted ADR as part of a broader set of initiatives to resolve some of the institution's problems and facilitate successful justice delivery. The need for judicial reforms to serve the needs of the business sector was established by major administrative stakeholders in the justice delivery system. The court had to overcome significant obstacles, including unfriendly procedural regulations, difficult regulatory procedures, out-dated policies, and unsafe working conditions that led to poor work ethics. The public lost faith in the justice system as a result of this. Furthermore, legal costs and long delays in resolving commercial and land disputes and lawsuits were aggravating. The reforms were intended to enhance the administration of commercial and investment laws while also transforming the judicial system.

The Ghanaian government, with the assistance of the World Bank, commissioned a team to recognise the shortcomings and vulnerabilities in the judicial system that needed to be addressed immediately. The team examined Ghana's Administrative Laws on Arbitration Procedures and Alternative Dispute Resolution Mechanisms and supported the proposal to incorporate ADR into the justice system. In 1998, a task force was formed to assist in the piloting of the ADR programme and to draught a standalone bill for its passage into law. The programme was first put to the test in Accra in 2003 to see whether it was feasible. The procedure resulted in the resolution of 300 pending court cases in just 5 days. According to a survey, 90% of disputants who were satisfied with the procedure after having their cases resolved would recommend it to others. In 2007 and 2008, follow-up programmes were held. In 2007, 100 commercial and family cases were successfully resolved within four days out of 155 cases resolved; in 2008, 50 percent of over 2,500 cases were successfully resolved. This showed the ability to further institute and reinforce the significance of ADR in the public's consciousness (Alhassan, 2015).

As a result of the experience, two critical programmes have been developed within mainstream court systems. The opening of the media week, as well as the implementation of court-connected ADR services in the district, magistrate, and high courts. Judges, attorneys, and ADR practitioners participate in the annual media week, which is listed on the judicial service's calendar (Alhassan, 2015). The media week is an annual program registered on the calendar of the judicial service that is observed by all judges, lawyers and ADR practitioners. The ADR week is set aside for the mass settlement of cases that have been in court for years but come under the ADR umbrella, and hence are resolved using ADR mechanisms. Child custody, matrimonial litigation, debt settlement, and property disputes are the most common types of cases. Finally, in 2010, the ADR Act 798 (2010) was passed and implemented as part of the Ghanaian justice delivery system's dispute resolution mechanisms.

THE PHILOSOPHY OF ADR AND ITS LEGISLATION IN GHANA

The main goal of ADR in Ghana is to improve everyone's access to justice through its processes. Mediation, arbitration, and customary arbitration are some of the settlement procedures used in Ghana, all of which are governed by the ADR Act 798. (2010). ADR's goals include reducing the court system's workload and encouraging a more responsive court system. Promoting productivity entails delivering lower-cost services, ensuring prompt dispute resolution, and increasing disputants' satisfaction by ensuring shared benefits for both parties. The aim of launching reform programmes within the justice delivery system was to resolve the system's problems and restore the confidence of disputants.

The ADR mechanism had previously existed within Ghana's court system prior to the enactment of the ADR Act 798 (2010). The Court Act of 1993 (Act 459 as amended), according to former Chief Justice

Georgina Theodora Wood, acted as the basic legal basis for ADR practise in Ghana. It had clauses in it that promoted out-of-court settlements. Sections 72 and 73 of the Act gave courts the authority to promote reconciliation in cases involving criminal and civil offences. This was accomplished by promoting and facilitating peaceful resolution of conflicts between disputants over whom the court has jurisdiction. In addition, cases that were pending in the courts were encouraged to seek resolution by amicable terms of settlement with the court, which aided in the healing process. ADR procedures, such as court-connected arbitral processes, are used as a last resort in settling conflicts, in accordance with Sections 72 and 73 of the Act. Aside from felony questions, this technique may be used to resolve any other situation. The case must first be filed in court before resorting to this form of action. The disputants may then agree to use ADR to resolve their disagreement. When a lawsuit is settled amicably, it becomes a court order; but, if the parties cannot agree on terms of settlement, the case goes to trial.

The ADR Act 798 (2010) was a significant move forward for Ghana's legislature in formalising and broadening its legal framework. Its passage aligned the governing law on arbitration with international treaties, standards, and procedures in the field. This provided the legal and institutional structure required in Ghana to promote and encourage the use of ADR procedures to resolve disputes. The Act's primary aim is to achieve a negotiated solution that is agreeable to all parties. This is important because ADR's main objective is to settle conflict in a non-adversarial way.

THE STRUCTURE OF ACT 798

The Alternative Dispute Resolution Act of 2010 (Act 798) provides the rules and procedures that control ADR proceedings for its practitioners, as previously mentioned. The act is divided into five parts, each of which is further divided into sections. Part 1 of the Act examines arbitration as an alternative dispute resolution (ADR) mechanism for resolving disputes. The Act begins with clauses on matters that are not subject to arbitration. It expressly excludes the use of arbitration for matters involving the public interest, felony offences, the environment, and constitutional interpretation. The use of arbitration as a means of resolving a dispute is then discussed in the following pages, as well as the situations in which this method may be used. Part 1 is broken down further into 62 parts. These sections provide comprehensive details on arbitration proceedings. It examines topics such as who qualifies to be an arbitrator, the position of an arbitrator, the appointment of an arbitrator, the arbitrator's fees and immunity, the arbitrator's actions, the revocation of an arbitrator's authority, the role of parties in the arbitral process, and the authority of the high court in relation to an arbitral award.

Certain core features outlined in Part 1 of the Act are worth remembering. To begin with, the Act deserves praise for the control it bestows on disputing parties by promoting party autonomy. Disputing persons can nominate an arbitrator of their choosing under Section 5 of the Act, and under Section 16 of the Act, they can seek recourse in a court of appeal if they are unconvinced by the negotiated terms of settlement. Section 31 gives parties the freedom to negotiate on mediation procedures and the type of payment to be given at the end of the day. Furthermore, unlike in court, where the language is almost always English, the chosen language used during settlements is at the discretion of the parties in section 32. The aforementioned rights, as outlined in the Act, are still applicable because they address the goals of incorporating ADR into the justice system. One of its main goals is to settle conflicts in a non-adversarial way. As a result, parties that are granted certain rights under the Act continue to be important because it is a step forward in resolving conflicts because parties play an important role in the decision-making process. Parties feel more involved in the decision-making process when they have the option of selecting an arbitrator of their choice and deciding on the awards to be given. During settlements, this encourages faith and trust, and disputants are more likely to follow the decisions made during settlements.

The Act specifies the form of written agreement that may be used as a basis for initiating arbitration proceedings. As a result, section 2 lists the types of written agreements that count as a request for arbitration as a means of dispute resolution. This includes emails, documents, telexes, and any other means by which both parties have kept track of the said Agreement. To reiterate, section 3 of the Act maintains the primacy of the life of an arbitral clause inserted into an agreement by ensuring that the clause remains intact even though the agreement is declared null. The clause takes precedence over the agreement and allows a person who wants to use arbitration to do so with the approval of the other party. This clause is crucial because it eliminates all doubt on what constitutes a written method of arbitration to be used. This eliminates delays that may otherwise arise in the arbitration process due to incorrect interpretation of other types of written communication. This accomplishes the goal of avoiding delays and frustrations commonly associated with the court system. It is also investor-friendly because it encourages foreign investors' ease of doing business and is cost-effective.

Furthermore, in section 24, the arbitral tribunal is given the power to rule over its jurisdiction without intervention from the court, ensuring that the Act is in line with international standards, traditions, and norms. The aim is to foster ADR's autonomy as a valuable conflict resolution tool. This gives the arbitrator more leverage so they can function without intervention from the judge.

Mediation is discussed in Part 2 of the Act as a means of resolving disputes. It addresses the powers of the mediator, the provision of confidentiality, and the outcome of a negotiated settlement and covers sections 63 to 88. Group autonomy is emphasised once more in section 63. It states that a party can choose mediation as a means of resolving a conflict if the other party agrees. Parties are therefore free to choose the number of mediators they want to use to resolve their dispute, but most opt for a single mediator. Parties then have the option of deciding how the proceedings should proceed and are free to withdraw from the mediation process at any time. Party autonomy is important when selecting mediators because it increases confidence and trust in the mediator's neutrality and ability to resolve issues without being impartial. This guarantees accountability, which is often lacking in the legal system.

The medium by which contact can be developed to begin the mediation process is also highlighted by Party 2. Recorded, verbal, or some other electronic means of communication, such as the use of a telephone, may be used. If verbal contact is made, the parties are required to follow up in writing with their names, addresses, email addresses, phone numbers, and the nature of the dispute. However, failure to state in writing does not render the procedure void. This makes the procedure less onerous and more user-friendly.

As a result, section 78 allows the mediator, with the consent of the parties, to obtain advice or technical assistance from other competent mediators in order to settle disputes if the parties are willing to pay additional costs. This provision is important since certain complicated cases necessitate the assistance of other knowledgeable individuals in resolving the dispute. This function is still important because it ensures that the right choices are made even in difficult circumstances in order to achieve mutual benefit. To ensure that decisions are binding and duly executed, section 82 empowers disputants to insist on proper enforcement of reached decisions by granting the mediator the authority to make a decision that is binding on both parties. This is important because it encourages compliance with the law and puts parties in a position of responsibility if they fail to follow the decision.

Part 3 of the Act, which runs from section 83 to section 113, focuses on customary arbitration. It examines the start and end of a traditional arbitration procedure. It raises questions about who is qualified to serve as a customary arbitrator and the general rules that govern arbitration. During the procedure, parties are given the option to select and the power to revoke the person they entrust to settle their dispute as a customary arbitrator. The Act safeguards parties' rights by ensuring that they are not compelled to participate in the process under any circumstances. A customary award must also be recorded at a district court, circuit court, or high court for the purposes of record-keeping to ensure that incentives or judgments taken are followed. Customary arbitration reaffirms the aim of ADR as an alternative to full-scale court processes since it is better suited to meet the country's cultural demands by giving traditional rulers primacy. Traditional rulers and traditional norms continue to play important roles in Ghanaians' lives, as most people have relied on them to resolve disputes since the dawn of time. Due to the country's many land disputes, it's also relevant in corporate governance. Since most lands are stool lands, businesses often have to compete with traditional families for land. As a result, resorting to traditional arbitration is ideally suited to addressing problems of this nature and is thus commendable.

Part 4 of the Act emphasises the establishment of a Ghanaian ADR Centre. This section of the Act covers sections 114-124 and aims to provide administrative support for the growth and development of ADR in Ghana. The establishment of a governing board with a chairperson is required under the Act. As a result, the chairperson must be a practising lawyer with at least 12 years of experience. Each of the Ghana Chamber of Mines, the Bar Association, the Institute of Surveyors, the Judiciary, the Institute of Charted Accountants, and a woman appointed by the President must be represented on the governing board. Representatives from Organized Labour and the Executive Secretary of the Centre must also be present to ensure the Centre's smooth operation. These clauses eliminate ambiguity and ensure a seamless transition. This facilitates the facilitation of ADR operations and avoids potential disputes.

Sections 125 to 138 of the Act make up Part 5. This examines the creation of an ADR fund for the Centre, which will be used for human resource development, research, and analysis. It also discusses fund management, financial reporting standards, staffing, interpretation, investments, and transitional provisions. This section ensures that continuous provisions are made for the smooth operation of ADR operations without bringing them to a halt.

ADR Methods in Ghana

In Ghana, various ADR processes are currently being used to resolve disputes. They operate under a variety of theories, beliefs, and laws. This segment looks at the various processes in place to aid in the resolution of domestic disputes.

Mediation

Mediation is a non-binding, cooperative mechanism in which a neutral third party (Mediator) skilled in facilitation and negotiation strategies assists disputants in reaching a mutually beneficial settlement (Vuković, 2015). It is the mechanism by which a neutral third party assists disputing parties in reaching mutually beneficial decisions without making any judgement on them. Mediation is a voluntary mechanism in which parties may appoint their mediator who will serve as a neutral third party to assist the parties in reaching mutually agreeable settlement terms. The mediator's position and purpose are to assist the parties in defining problems and informing needs, removing communication barriers, seeking alternatives, and concentrating on the needs and interests of those who are most affected by the conflict (Xavier, 2009). The mediator's goal is to assist the parties in visualising potential solutions while also attempting to direct them to areas of common ground. If the procedure ends with an agreement, the parties will be bound by that agreement.

This is accomplished by allowing participants to focus on their needs and the outcomes they want to achieve at the conclusion of the mediation process. Disputants, on the other hand, have the ability to participate in the process by deciding on the meeting's time, date, location, and agenda with the aid of the mediator. The mediator begins the mediation process after the parties and the mediator have agreed on the principles that must be followed for mediation to take place. In contrast to the negotiation process, mediation takes a more systematic and structured approach. Mediation differs from other types of alternative dispute resolution, such as arbitration and mediation, in that the mediator does not implement a solution but rather works with the parties to develop their own. Relief not available in arbitration or trial is often used in mediated solutions. Furthermore, the parties control the outcome in litigation, while the arbitrator decides the outcome in arbitration.

Mediation is a professional job that needs all of the learned expertise and resources to assist disputants in resolving their disputes. A mediator's professional skills and experience come into play at these times. As a result, he refers to a strategy known as POWER, which is used in mediation to assist disputants in resolving their differences (Fuller, 2018).

The letter "P" stands for paraphrasing. The mediator should always be able to paraphrase disputants' submissions to ensure that all parties' points are understood. This eliminates the possibility of misinterpretation, which can stymie the mediation process and cause unnecessary delays. The letter "O" denotes the use of open-ended queries, which contributes to more thorough explanations. "Madam, could you please explain what you meant by freedom?" for example. This allows for the discovery of more precise secret information. This is crucial because, in many cases, disputants will fail to open up about problems and will instead focus on minor information while avoiding the core of the dispute. The letter "W" stands for "Wait." This is a symbol of patience. The mediator must be patient and listen for secret messages in the submissions so that he can ask pertinent questions that will aid in reaching a conclusion. The letter "E" stands for "Empathy." The mediator places himself in both parties' shoes and expresses sincere concern without taking sides. As a result, it is often stated that a mediator must be compassionate but not sympathetic. Since feelings can be deceiving, sympathy breeds partiality. Empathy, on the other hand, fosters trust and confidence, allowing disputants to put their faith in the mediator's ability to make decisions. Finally, the letter "R" stands for rephrasing statements for parties, which can trigger misunderstandings and hinder the resolution process. When a mediator follows these moves, he is sure to assist disputants in finding good solutions.

Furthermore, mediation as a method of resolving a dispute is important because it saves time, is less costly, and allows disputing parties to repair relationships. When disputing parties speak about their issues, Mr. Fancis Kwabla Nanevi, a mediator at the Ashaiman Inter-Community Mediation Centre, says, it helps them recover emotionally and calms them down so they can see the purpose (Edzii, 2018). It assists disputants in focusing on shared interests rather than solely on the issue. According to Mr. Nanevi, there are no recordings of mediated cases to instil the presumption of confidentiality. Symbolic objects with specific meanings in Ghanaian culture are often used to aid the process. Peace is symbolised by things like water and kola nuts. Disagreants, he claims, can appreciate the use of such things after they have been introduced to them because they are associated with the conventional Ghanaian definition of conflict resolution (Yin, 2014).

Negotiation

Negotiation as a word comes from the Latin expression "negotiatus", which means "to carry on business" (Sarkar, (2010). The process of making a deal between different parties where each with its interests and preferences. Negotiation has often been labelled as the "premium mode of conflict resolution," which is unsurprising given its prevalence in almost every aspect of everyday life at the private, institutional, national, and global levels. Any method of direct or indirect contact used by parties with opposing interests to help them handle and resolve their problem is referred to as negotiation. It is the most widely available ADR process, with everyone able to use it. It can be used to settle current conflicts or to lay the groundwork for potential relationships between parties. It can happen on a personal, corporate, national, or international level. As a result, most disputants' first step in settling a dispute without resorting to a third party is negotiation. Negotiation is a voluntary activity, so no one should be forced to participate. Since it is a cooperative procedure, parties may withdraw from the negotiations at any time and reject any decision reached that is not in their favour. Parties may negotiate directly with each other or be represented by family members, attorneys, or other individuals they find appropriate. During the negotiating process, however, the parties are granted autonomy. They have complete influence over the process by deciding on the meeting's time, location, and agenda. They also lay down the groundwork for the negotiating process's laws and regulations. In ***Switchmen's Union v. National Mediation Board***, it was held that one party cannot determine the participants of a negotiation. They are thus free to take whatever approach is required to reach an optimal decision that benefits both parties. Parties may use a position or interest-based approach because of the fluid nature of negotiation.

On the other hand, the broker, who is often an attorney, must be an experienced individual who facilitates the process by directing parties to resolve disputes based on their mutual interests. He must also brace disputants by urging them to pursue further redress if they are unable to reach peaceful settlement terms. He must not enforce any decisions on the parties, but rather aid the process by assisting disputants in drafting a negotiation agenda, time, and place, as well as establishing process rules.

Negotiation as an alternative dispute resolution procedure has many advantages. It is less expensive, quicker, and eliminates unnecessary delays. Many experts use its versatility to pursue an interest-based approach to resolving disputes, as it ensures a win-win situation for all parties concerned. Furthermore, because only parties involved in the dispute are allowed to participate in the resolution process, they have complete control over the decisions made to meet their needs or interests. Furthermore, negotiation improves relationship building, particularly for commercial entities, because it allows them to talk and reach mutually beneficial outcomes that benefit both parties, thus repairing a broken relationship.

Negotiations are probably the most flexible means of resolving disputes in terms of practice since only certain parties and, if any, their representatives are involved in the result. Parties have complete influence over the negotiations, including preparation, forum selection (public or private), and participant nomination. Negotiations, like any other type of dispute resolution, do not guarantee a party's success. Many observers, however, agree that negotiations would be more effective if parties take an interest-based rather than a position-based approach. This approach is often described as a "win-win" strategy. Negotiation is a voluntary procedure. With the procedure nobody is obliged to enter into talks if they do not want to. Furthermore, there is no need for a neutral third party. This is significant because no one wants third parties to be involved in the process, for example when the subject to be resolved is highly sensitive or conflict to be solved. Contrary to the results of other adjudication procedures, such as arbitration, the outcome of negotiations binds only the parties involved.

In a difficult negotiation, a satisfactory result can be achieved. Parties can, however, be of unequal strength, which disadvantages the weaker party (s). The credibility of the agreement is damaged if a party with an interest in the conflict is left out or under-represented, and it becomes vulnerable to potential opposition. If a party's negotiating authority is in doubt, the party will be unable to fully participate in the negotiations. Without the assistance of a neutral third party, the parties are unable to identify the problems at hand or even make any progress toward a solution.

Without the presence of a neutral third party, one party will feel compelled to exploit the other. Nobody has the authority to force a group to continue negotiating. Regardless of how much time, effort, or money the other party or parties have spent, anybody who wants to end negotiations can do so at any point during the process. Any problems or concerns are inevitable. There is almost no hope of reaching an agreement if the parties are separated by competing philosophies and values and have no intention of making concessions. Negotiation cannot ensure that either party is behaving in good faith or is reliable. Negotiation may be seen as a means of delaying the assertion of another party's interests.

Arbitration

Arbitration is a mechanism in which a neutral third party, known as an arbitrator, assists disputants in reaching a decision. Section 135 of Act 798 defines arbitration as the voluntary submission of a dispute to one or more impartial persons for final and binding determination. Both parties are, however, bound by the decisions. Arbitration is used as an alternative dispute resolution tool, especially in commercial cases. It's used in the oil and gas industry, as well as construction, real estate, and land disputes. Parties may nominate their own arbitrator. An arbitrator is a person who is trusted by all parties and whose decisions are respected. Arbitration is a procedure that is done at the request of the parties. However, unlike mediation, an arbitral process is a consensual process, and one party cannot unilaterally withdraw from it. The decisions reached are legally binding and generally simple to execute. Depending on the nature of the case, a judge can opt to refer an issue to arbitration in court. In such cases, once the dispute has been settled, the agreed-upon terms of settlement must be referred to the Judge at a particular date, so if no compromise is reached, the case goes to trial. Arbitration has gradually gained popularity as a means of resolving disputes, especially among businesses. Because of the privacy policies and the benefits it provides, most businesses have turned to arbitration. In the case of ***Premium NAFTA products v Fili Shipping***, the House of Lords commented that if the parties are in a dispute that can be thought to be resolved by the process of Arbitration then it should apparent that because of its advantages over the official court proceeding.

Mrs. Serwaa Ofori, a lawyer working for one of Ghana's largest oil marketing companies (OMC), backs up this claim by sharing her personal experience. She went into great detail on how the law department was overburdened by numerous court proceedings that had taken too long to settle. "It's a waste of time and money," she said. The processes for filing lawsuits in courts are often time-consuming. Due to the difficulties of going to court, the court advises businesses to use arbitration services to resolve disputes.

Companies may, however, take their case to court if arbitration fails to reach an amicable settlement. Arbitration has been perfect for her because of its confidentiality and regard for privacy. As a result, it has aided in the preservation and restoration of long-term business partnerships. This is important since, in most inter-company disputes, long-term business partners' relationships are likely to be strained. Arbitration further reinforces the concept of equity. Whatever the corporation loses as a result of the dispute, arbitration allows parties to claim partial or complete compensation for the harm they have incurred. This encourages restoration and fairness. Furthermore, arbitration has aided in the improvement of relationships. The approach enables clients to reach agreements throughout the process. As a result, arbitration has the potential to improve economic growth and encourage investment.

Customary Arbitration

When disputants turn to a third party who serves as an arbitrator in the role of a traditional leader such as a Chief, it is known as customary arbitration. The judgments reached are legally binding, and they must be recorded at the nearest district, circuit, or high court, as necessary, in order to keep track of the awards and enforcements. In the case of ***Dzasimatu v Dokosi***, the Amua-Sekyi JSC dismissing appeal, among other things held that;

"a purported arbitration was binding if (a) the submission of the dispute was voluntary; (b) the parties agreed to be bound by the decision whichever way it went; (c) the rules of natural justice were observed, although the arbitrator did not need to [p.465] follow any formal procedures; (d) the arbitrator acted within jurisdiction; and (e) the decision or award was made known. Although there was no right in the parties to resile from arbitration, the parties might subsequently resubmit the whole or part of the dispute to a further arbitration. However, where the proceedings felt short of arbitration but met the requirements of a negotiated settlement, the decision would become binding only if it were accepted by the parties. Thereafter neither party could resile from the compromise."

Nobody can force parties to use this method of arbitration, so it gives them control. They will have the right to revoke a customary arbitrator's authority as they see fit. This form of arbitration is critical in a culturally focused country like Ghana, where property and other culture-related disputes, such as child marriage, persist. Furthermore, chiefs continue to play an important role in various societies across Ghana, with the majority of citizens trusting their decision.

Conciliation

Conciliation is similar to mediation in that the conciliator draughts and suggests his own solution, which he believes is a fair and rational compromise to the conflict. After the conciliator has had consultations with the parties, this is finished (Miall, 2016). Conciliation differs from both negotiation and mediation in that it is a more systematic method. It sometimes necessitates the hiring of legal counsel, making it a more costly procedure than the others. It is more regulated, and its administration is governed by a set of institutional laws. Conciliation is a mechanism in which parties seek the assistance of a neutral third party, known as a conciliator, to help them overcome their differences (Christensen, 2016). He is chosen by the parties themselves, and he is required to assist them in reaching amicable solutions to their problems. His decisions are not legally enforceable, and parties may oppose them if they do not agree with them. The conciliator assists in the resolution of disputes by working with the disputing parties individually to assist them in resolving their disagreements through a process known as caucusing. Conciliators use their technical skills to help parties settle conflicts by reducing tensions. They also interpret problems and consider different options in order to reach a mutually acceptable agreement.

Conciliation is important because it saves time, mends relationships, and is focused on mutual interests. This allows the conciliator to be creative in coming up with different proposals that the disputants should consider in order to reach an amicable settlement. The conciliator is given the ability to issue binding decisions at the request of the parties. Disputants can, however, seek relief in a court of appeals at any time.

Early Case Evaluation

After a case has been filed in court, an early case review is normally conducted. Following the filing of a lawsuit, it is forwarded to experts for analysis based on the evidence provided. The specialist then conducts a critical analysis of the case and provides guidance. He explains his results to the disputants and gives them an estimate of their probability of winning or losing the case if they want to go to court. As a result, after hearing the report, the disputants consider their options, with the majority opting for alternative terms of settlement. This is beneficial because it slows the pace at which lawsuits pile up in courts and assists disputants in finding other substantive ways to settle their disagreements. Due to a lack of confidence, this is a rare mechanism used by disputants. In some cases, the party that is most likely to win the case in court takes advantage of the situation by continuing the case in court to the detriment of the opposing party.

Court-Connected Alternative Dispute Resolution

Order 64 of the High Court Civil Procedure Rules, 2004 (CI 47), provides for arbitration. Parties may request that their dispute be referred to an arbitrator under this order. The Courts Act of 1993 (Act 459) promotes the use of alternative dispute resolution (ADR) to settle conflicts before the courts. The Judicial Service has launched a national ADR programme as a mainstream method of settling cases pending in court-connected mediation as part of an effort to speed up the judicial process. In this programme, qualified mediators are assigned to specific courts to assist disputants in reaching an agreement. After informing the parties of the benefits of ADR and proposing mediation as an option, the magistrate or judge seeks their approval to refer the conflict to mediation. The parties are then aided in selecting a mediator and scheduling a mediation session for a mutually convenient time. According to reports, about 45 percent of cases referred to mediation were successfully resolved between January and September 2008. The majority of these cases were resolved in less than two hours, demonstrating the efficiency of the procedure (Quansah, 2012).

MED-ARB

Med-Arb is a collaborative approach to dispute resolution. It is a means of resolving disputes that combine the use of arbitration and mediation (Pappas, 2015). The essence of certain disputes necessitates the use of such a strategy. Depending on the nature of the interests at stake, extra efforts are often required to mitigate tensions and maintain relationships between parties. During Med-Arb, the parties select a neutral third party who serves first as a mediator and then as an arbitrator if they are unable to reach an agreement. Both parties are bound by his decisions. To prevent the parties from opposing the ruling, the mediator informs them prior to the start of the proceedings that if they do not reach an agreement, he will be forced to act as an arbitrator on their behalf. This is a time-consuming and costly procedure. It does, however, encourage productivity. This is because, if mediation fails to find a solution, arbitration steps in to fill the void. It prevents parties from turning to a different arbitrator since the same impartial mediator will render a rational decision after hearing the case from the beginning (Edzii, 2018).

SUCCESSES OF ADR IN GHANA

Despite the fact that ADR is a relatively new institution in Ghana, it has played an important role in resolving disputes at both the interpersonal and community levels. As a result, this segment looks at the performance and strengths of ADR in Ghana since 2010. The incorporation of alternative dispute resolution (ADR) into the courts has assisted in the court's primary mission of reducing case backlogs, lowering costs, encouraging ease of doing business, and avoiding the delays associated with formal courts. The observation of media week is an important step toward achieving this aim. Mr. Nene Amegatcher, a managing partner at Okudzeto and Associates, was especially pleased with the settlement success rates in an interview (Edzii, 2018). It has improved access to justice for all people, especially those who are less fortunate in society. According to Mr. Nene Amegatcher, it has also increased confidence in the judicial system as a means of providing timely and effective justice, which has aided in the reduction of crime rates in the region.

By incorporating the Customary Arbitration Act, the Act has strengthened the role of traditional leaders as arbitrators in resolving disputes. This is commendable because it affirms the importance of traditional leaders in resolving disputes at both the national and local levels even in an era in Ghana where the rational-legal state remains pervasive. Traditional rulers like Otumfuor Osei Tutu II have been instrumental in resolving cross-cultural disputes like the Dagbon chieftaincy dispute in Ghana's northern region. According to Mr. Nene Amegatcher, since such personalities play such important roles in restoring peace in different societies, it is highly impressive that the Act has taken into account the Ghanaian society's cultural orientation to help provide legal backing to such leaders.

ADR has also increased people's ability to try other methods of settling their disputes. Because of the strict processes that were unfriendly to common citizens, the Anglicized existence of the courts discouraged most people from seeking justice. As a result, ADR has as one of its principles the observation of the principle of informality during case settlement procedures in order to promote the interests of such persons in seeking justice and peace. Parties are granted autonomy in the decision-making process, including the appointment of an arbitrator, the creation of procedural rules, and the determination of awards to be made. This is in contrast to the judicial system, in which a judge presides over cases and makes decisions. Judgment often favours one side over the other, fostering bad feelings and a retaliatory community. As a result, ADR has unquestionably aided everyone's access to justice. The vocabulary used during the processes has also been made more user-friendly. Instead of resorting to the court, which mostly makes use of the English language, clients are advised to use a language that is familiar to them to improve communication. This allows participants to openly express themselves and bring up the conflict's central issues.

ADR has aided in the growth of the country's economy by equipping employees with the required skills to overcome problems both at home and at work through training. This has aided in the strengthening of the employer-employee relationship. This has stopped employees from going on strike on a regular basis, disrupting economic activity in the region. People identified as vulnerable groups under the national laws of the country, such as children and women, are also covered by the country's laws. The Children's Act of 1998, for example, protects children, while the Interstate Succession Act of 1985

(PNDC Law111) protects widows by improving access to their husbands' assets after they die. Despite the fact that the legislation is still in place, ADR has helped to improve their productivity. Mr. Nene Amegatcher clarified that, due to the delicate nature of such cases, judges usually refer them, as well as divorce cases, to ADR. Before going to court, lawyers can make sure that all other options, such as ADR, have been exhausted. This is particularly relevant in situations involving children, such as disputes over child custody rights. Through employing the principles of confidentiality and privacy, ADR has aided in the protection of vulnerable communities such as women and children. As a result, people are free to express their genuine concerns without fear of being registered.

The Business Amendment Act, as well as pre-trial meetings, which are new features of ADR systems such as arbitration, prevents employees from losing their jobs as a result of disputes between top executives within and between firms. Companies cannot go to court until all other options for resolving the dispute have been exhausted, according to the Act. Mrs. Serwaa Ofori said in an interview that these ADR processes have aided in the maintenance of business relations with other large corporations. She assumes the procedure enforces the relationship-building principle. Mrs. Serwaa Ofori believes that pre-trials or case management trials have aided in the avoidance of bad debts connected with court litigation.

The ADR theory of equity has also aided in the prevention of unexpected financial or material difficulties. People suffer not only financial losses but also emotional losses as a result of spending years in court. The theory of justice and restoration contained in ADR processes, on the other hand, guarantees that parties are compensated, if not equally, at least in part, to make up for losses. This aids in the process parties get over it and avoid recurrence of disputes. Furthermore, ADR allows for the resolution of problems to the heart, as opposed to the court, where essential reasons for the dispute can be overlooked, allowing for a culture of retribution even after a judgement has been rendered, according to Mrs. Serwaa Ofori.

THE CHALLENGES OF ADR

Political intervention continues to be the most significant impediment to the implementation of ADR, especially in the context of group conflict resolution. In an interview, Mr. Austin Gamey and Mr. Nene Amegatcher alluded to this reality. They both believed that politicians have been a big source of conflict refuelling at this stage. This is a significant challenge because the aim of ADR is to restore confidence in the justice system by empowering disputants to participate in the resolution process. As a result, disputants are granted the freedom to choose a neutral third party to assist them in resolving their differences. Politicians, on the other hand, actively meddle in the settlement of community disputes, preventing this goal from being realised. Since policymakers have forced their preferred mediators on disputants, the majority of on-going disputes remain unresolved. While the mediators are frequently well-known citizens of the region, they lack the necessary expertise to settle the dispute. They are often insensitive to the needs of the people. Mr. Gamey said that politicians are invested in the dispute because of the benefits that come with it [this was an assertion he gave and it has its reference already]. If they declare that they were successful in resolving the dispute, this is typically the time to buy citizens' sympathy by votes. According to Mr. Austin Gamey, such disputes will remain unresolved until politicians learn to separate themselves from them, posing a danger to the state's peace and stability.

Furthermore, despite the large number of ADR professionals such as the ADR Coalition of Ghana, The Ghana Arbitration Centre, Ghana Association of Chartered Mediators and Arbitrators (GHACMA), Gamey & Gamey Academy of Mediation, and West Africa Dispute Resolution Centre (WADREC) in the region, their abilities have yet to be put to use in resolving conflicts. **The ADR Coalition of Ghana** (Governmental/quasi-governmental) comprises a number of organizations involved in ADR, in a joint effort to advocate and unify the various practices and mechanisms of ADR through appropriate regulations. The Coalition is made up of the Judicial Service of Ghana, Commission for Human Rights and Administrative Justice, The Legal Aid Board, Ghana Association of Chartered Mediators and Arbitrators, the Ghana Arbitration Centre and the Attorney Generals Department. Mr. Nene Amegatcher asserted that, rather than relying on ADR practitioners, governments in Ghana and West Africa as a whole rely on the courts to manage conflicts. Curfews are sometimes used by security in such situations to reduce tensions within communities. The risk is that such conflicts will never go away and will continue to recur unless qualified experts are hired to use their specialised expertise to settle these situations.

While informality is an important aspect of the ADR method, it is also a flaw in the system. Since people take this idea for granted, it frequently undermines the institution. Many citizens still hold the court in high regard because of the harsh penalties imposed on clients who fail to follow the court's orders. If an individual refuses to follow established procedures, he will be charged with contempt. People postpone responding to summons sent to them by mediators because of the versatility of ADR. People are more likely to respect an agency if fines are attached to it; this would encourage compliance.

The institutionalisation of ADR is hampered by a lack of funding, insufficient infrastructure, and inadequate logistics. Wooden structures are also used by mediation centres including the Ashaiman intercommunity mediation centre. This reduces the centre's effectiveness in resolving conflicts and, in the worst-case scenario, jeopardises the centre's survival, as it could close at any time. Furthermore, no arrangements are made for the ADR practitioners who are appointed to the courts. Mediators, for example, are only summoned when absolutely necessary. Mr. Nanevi believes that the USAID's attempts to provide adequate infrastructural facilities for the Centre's smooth operation have proved futile because the government obstructs such efforts through external development donors (Edzii, 2018).

For example, while the initial agreement was to set up an office, the ADR institution within the Legal Aid Scheme programmes shares an office within the building with the lawyers. This has hampered the scheme's otherwise successful narrative. The government's lack of funding and ability to assist in the promotion of such institutions has become concerning. Just 19 of the 216 districts have ADR facilities available via the Legal Aid Scheme. This has hampered the recruiting process, as the organisation is unable to hire more professionals or offer instruction to people who want to help with the institution's operations. Most private and non-profit practitioners face remuneration issues as a result of the fact that the majority of people who could benefit from ADR services are unable to pay. As a result, the majority of mediators are not willing to give it their all. Surprisingly, ADR practitioners continue to face resistance from lawyers and judges, who in safeguarding their sources of income, refuses to advise clients to use ADR services.

CONCLUSION

This paper demonstrates that ADR is a solution to interpersonal and community disputes in Ghana, using different methods of dispute resolution such as arbitration, customary arbitration, and mediation, and that it has helped to minimise caseloads in the courts and facilitate access to justice for everyone by providing cheaper, quicker, and timelier justice. Its values of informality, confidentiality, and equality have made it a common method of finding justice. If the institution's problems, such as a shortage of funding, legal professionals' opposition, and low remuneration for practitioners, are resolved, ADR will be able to achieve its maximum potential as a dispute resolution tool. Act 798 aimed to enhance the practise of various ADR approaches by preserving self-determination, process versatility, the neutral person's neutrality and impartiality, and the sanctity of the ADR process. Mediation in Ghana, for example, is facilitative in the sense that the Mediator is a facilitator of the process rather than a position of authority who gives substantive advice or puts pressure on the parties to agree. Act 798 aims to ensure that the parties themselves come up with a solution to their disagreement. This allows the parties to come up with innovative ideas that are acceptable to both parties.

It can be argued that that in as much as ADR facilitates solving of issues between parties, the outcomes are seen not to be binding to subsequent cases, which is antithetical to the idea of the common law recognized in the 1992 Constitution. As Olive Wendell Holmes stated that "the life of the law has not been logic; it is been experience." This describes the tendency on the part of the ADR methods to follow an earlier decision pointing to the doctrine of stare decisis, where the facts in the instant case are similar to one which has already been decided. ADR methods including the customary arbitration the common law and if the doctrine of stare decisis is ensured, will make it easier and simple for the mediators or arbitrators or negotiators to easily see to the resolution of the problem between the parties.

Again, impartiality and independence are necessary qualities for ensuring trust in an ADR process. As a result, mediators, arbitrators, and negotiators must adhere to the highest ethical standards (Blackaby, Partasides, Redfern, & Hunter, 2009). This paper suggests that a better standard to follow is the English standard, which states that arguments will only be considered by the courts if it can be shown that there is a clear risk of bias. With such a high threshold, parties would be forced to consider their options carefully and will not attempt to use the challenge process as a "back door" to escape an unfavourable award. Consequently, despite the lack of consistency in arbitral institutions', professional bodies', and courts' attitudes toward the issue of impartiality and independence, as well as disclosure requirements, their efforts to ensure that they only entertain the most significant or substantial claims of a lack of independence or impartiality that is likely to materially affect the eventual outcome of a case are commendable. Finally, it is proposed that justice and fairness would be best served if mediators, arbitrators, and negotiators are kept to the same, if not stricter, standards as judges, given the critical role they play in the ADR phase, which, if left unchecked, could jeopardise ADR's enviable place as the most appropriate conflict resolution process.

REFERENCES

Alhassan, A. R. (2015). *The Institution and Challenges of ADR in West Africa -The Case of Ghana* (Diss.). University of Ghana.

Alternative Dispute Resolution Act of 2010 (Act 798)

Blackaby, N., Partasides, C., Redfern, A., & Hunter, M. (2009). *Redfern and Hunter on international arbitration*. Oxford University Press. doi:10.1093/law:iic/9780199557189.001.1

Christensen, D. (2016). Conciliation, Uniqueness and Rational Toxicity1. *Noûs (Detroit, Mich.), 50*(3), 584–603. doi:10.1111/nous.12077

Earney, L. (2011). On the advantages of negotiation. *Serials, 24*(3).

Edzii, J. A. (2018). *Is Alternative Dispute Resolution a Solution to Interpersonal and Group Conflicts in West Africa? The Case of Ghana* (Doctoral dissertation). University of Ghana.

Edzii, J. A. (2018). *Is Alternative Dispute Resolution a Solution to Interpersonal and Group Conflicts in West Africa? The Case of Ghana* (Doctoral dissertation). University of Ghana.

Edzii, J. A. (2018). *Is Alternative Dispute Resolution a Solution to Interpersonal and Group Conflicts in West Africa? The Case of Ghana* (Doctoral dissertation). University of Ghana.

Fuller, L. L. (2018). *Mediation—Its forms and functions*. Routledge. doi:10.4324/9781315204826-1

Mensah-PanfordP. (2018). Mediation in Ghana's Criminal Justice System: A Proposal for an Extension to Cover Severe Offences. *Available at* SSRN 3144524.

Miall, H. (2016). *The peacemakers: Peaceful settlement of disputes since 1945*. Springer.

Pappas, B. A. (2015). Med-Arb and the legalization of alternative dispute resolution. *Harv. Negot. L. Rev., 20*, 157.

Price, C. (2018). Alternative dispute resolution in Africa: Is ADR the bridge between traditional and modern dispute resolution. *Pepp. Disp. Resol. LJ, 18*, 393.

Quansah, E. K. (2012). *The Ghana Legal System*. Black Mask Limited.

Ruffin, F. (2019). Land Governance in the Context of Legal Pluralism: Cases of Ghana and Kenya. In *Trajectory of Land Reform in Post-Colonial African States* (pp. 91–108). Springer. doi:10.1007/978-3-319-78701-5_7

Sarkar, A. N. (2010). Navigating the rough seas of global business negotiation: Reflection on cross-cultural issues and some corporate experiences. *International Journal of Business Insights & Transformation, 3*(2), 23–34.

Stone, K. V. (2004). *From widgets to digits: Employment regulation for the changing workplace*. Cambridge University Press. doi:10.1017/CBO9780511617089

Uwazie, E. (Ed.). (2014). *Alternative dispute resolution and peace-building in Africa*. Cambridge Scholars Publishing.

Vuković, S. (2015). Soft power, Bias and manipulation of international organizations in international mediation. *International Negotiation, 20*(3), 414–443. doi:10.1163/15718069-12341315

Xavier, A. (2009). Mediation is here to stay. *Indian Yearbook of International Law and Policy, 15*, 363–378.

Yin, E. T., & Black, J. M. (2014). The legal anthropology of marriage in Ghana: Presenting power dynamics through legal arenas. *International Journal of Current Research, 6*(12), 10696–10704.

Zuure, D. N. (2018). *Legal pluralism, conflict resolution, and human rights_ an exploration of the traditional conflict resolution approach of the Nabdam of Ghana* (Doctoral dissertation). University of Education, Winneba.

APPENDIX: ADDITIONAL RESOURCES

Case Laws

- Ofori, Serwaa. op.cit. [1993-94] 1 GLR 463.

Chapter 10

Unpacking the Dilemma of Alternative Dispute Resolution and Access to Justice by Women in the Ghanaian Context

John Kwame Boateng
University of Ghana, Ghana

Ernest Darkwa
University of Duisburg-Essen, Germany

ABSTRACT

The chapter explores the dilemma of alternative dispute resolution (ADR) and access to justice for women in Ghana. It argues that introduction and use of ADR has contributed to improving access to justice with regards to reducing delays in formal court procedures, cost reduction, time saving, opening spaces for less-resourced individuals and groups, particularly women, to have access to justice. Above all, ADR does bring access to justice systems close to remote areas, serving the needs of disadvantaged individuals including women and others who are most vulnerable. However, the weaknesses and challenges in the formal legal system, coupled with the historical and cultural dynamics of the Ghanaian society, which is patriarchal in nature, have prevented mostly women from reaping the maximum benefits of ADR. Revisiting the challenges of the justice system and the historical and cultural norms of Ghana would help increase and enhance women's access to justice through ADR.

INTRODUCTION

This chapter examines the dilemma of Alternative Dispute Resolution (ADR) and access to justice by women in Ghana. ADR encompasses dispute and conflict resolution practices that fall within but operates outside the normal court system of resolution (Shonk, 2020; LII, 2017:1; Uwazie, 2011). It therefore comes as an informal or traditional mechanism for resolving conflicts and ensuring justice for people (LII,

DOI: 10.4018/978-1-7998-7898-8.ch010

2017:1). The definition does not only entail mediation as a means of resolving conflicts but considers other practices such as facilitation, arbitration, interest-based negotiations and conciliation (LII, 2017:1).

The introduction of ADR does not come necessarily to take over the formal court system, but as an alternative mechanism to support the formal court process (Akin & Noone, 2017; Department of Justice, 2000). ADR is therefore employed for instance; in cases that have crucial implications for public and social policies; cases that are not directly linked with the constitutional interpretation and as such may reflect and require a precedence for setting up the grounds for interpretation (Department of Justice, 2000; Dieng, 2011; Uwazie, 2011).

ADR has been beneficial for accessing justice by the citizens with regards to eliminating delays in court proceedings and high costs that could characterize the formal legal court systems. ADR therefore comes in with a significance on saving time and helping to bring down cost on deciding on everyday cases and disputes that may require immediate attention. Notwithstanding the advantages that shape the ADR system, the process may be faced with several challenges that could disadvantage individuals and groups within the society especially women in reaching a complete access to justice. As such, the chapter aims to unravel the dynamics that are manifested in the ADR system and how it limits particularly women's access to civil justice in Ghana, considering the merits and shortfalls of the system.

The chapter employs relevant existing literature on ADR in Ghana, as well as literature across the world in examining the dynamics of alternative dispute resolution in Ghana. The chapter is structured into seven main sections. Following the introduction and the background of the chapter, the second part looks at the conceptual underpinning of alternative dispute resolution. The third part explores the ADR mechanism in Ghana, with the fourth part considering the inference of the formal legal implantation and people's access to justice. The fifth part examines access to justice and women in Ghana. The sixth part identifies and analyses the strengths and weaknesses of ADR as a system and means of accessing justice. The final part of the chapter looks at major recommendations and the conclusions of the chapter.

BACKGROUND

Ghana's comprehensive ADR system came into effect in the year 2010 as a means of facilitating access to justice and making steps towards enhancing the justice system and procedures (Nolan-Haley & Annor-Ohene, 2014:1; Alternative Dispute Act-798, 2010). It also had the aim of enhancing foreign direct investment in Ghana (Wood, 2011). The legislation of the ADR system has introduced many important elements in the justice mechanism which includes the operation of the traditional customary process of ADR alongside the formal legal justice system. In view of this, the system of mediation as well as traditional arbitration has significantly become a vital part of the civil justice mechanism. Ghana's Alternative Dispute Resolution Act, 2010, Act 798 is applied to matters other than those which are related to:

1. "The National or Public Interest"
2. "The Environment"
3. "The Enforcement and Interpretation of the Constitution", and
4. "Any Other Matter which by Law cannot be settled by an Alternative Dispute Resolution".

The success of the ADR system and procedures that characterize it may depend on the extent to which individuals, groups and parties within a matter or issues of concern relate to and accept the process.

This could depend on how individuals and groups are treated fairly and trust the process when they are involved in a procedure justice system on a dispute resolution (Wright, 2011). In a situation where individuals and or groups involved in a dispute resolution are convinced and trust the justice system as fair, they may be seen to be satisfied with the procedural justice system of the ADR (Hollander-Blumoff & Tyler, 2011; Wright, 2011). On the other hand, where people feel that they are not treated fairly in terms of their experiences with the processes and outcomes of the procedural justice system that entails the ADR system, they may develop less trust in the system and hence would be unsatisfied with the process at large (Hollander-Blumoff & Tyler, 2011).

The ADR structure of Ghana embraces a system of pluralism where the traditional system of customary law is made to operate alongside the common law framework (Nolan-Haley & Annor-Ohene, 2014: 2; Kirgis, 2014; Constitution of Ghana, 1992). With the practice and use of the customary mediation and arbitration been part of Ghana's justice system since the pre-colonial period, the customary system of procedural justice could be regarded as a long-standing facet of the country's dispute resolution and justice system. Most people who used and engaged the services and systems of the customary ADR are those who occupy less-developed and remote parts of the country with limited access to the formal court system (Nolan-Haley & Annor-Ohene, 2014:2; Wood, 2011). Such people including women in most instances resorts to the channel of ADR in their communities either through mediation and or arbitration in resolving disputes and other conflicting matters of interest that may concern them, their families and immediate neighbors. Within the customary ADR system of arbitration and mediation, the key action and decision makers are mostly traditional chiefs, queen mothers, heads of families and community leaders (Kirgis, 2014; Apiagyei-Atua, 2013; Mueller, 2010).

Considering the customary or traditional form of ADR, it could be emphasized that the practice has existed in Ghana prior to colonial rule and as such has a long stand in the country's justice history (Wood, 2011; Adjabeng, 2007). The system has consisted of the methods of mediation and arbitration as a way of resolving conflicts and disputes among people and groups in communities across the country. In many instances, people who occupy rural settings of the country tend to resort to the customary ADR system of resolving their disputes compared to accessing the formal systems of the court (Wood, 2011; Adjabeng, 2007). Most of these rural settings are limited when it comes to access to the formal systems of courts and therefore consider the customary ADR in their districts and communities as a remedy to accessing justice systems and having their cases and disputes resolved. The challenges have included poor road networks which act as a limit on transportation and low financial resources of the people (Kirgis, 2014; Wood, 2011).

Aside from the customary ADR system, the modern practice of ADR represents an important facet of Ghana's mechanism of ADR. The country has been seen as one of the countries in Africa that has embraced and engaged its formal ADR procedures in resolving conflicts and disputes through the court system (Amegatcher, 2011; CLDP, 2003). With the inaction of Ghana's court Act 1993, ACT 459 that incorporates and embraces the application of ADR systems and procedures in deciding on and resolving disputes and conflicts in the court system (Kotia & Aubyn, 2013; ADR ACT, 1993), several activities and mechanisms of ADR have been included in the country's justice procedures. For instance, in the year 2001 a formal task force made up of law and judicial experts and officials of ADR was inaugurated (Ghana Arbitration Centre 2013; Kotia & Aubyn, 2013; GOG, 2008). The purpose of the task force was to plan strategies and mechanisms for initiating, advancing and implementing judicial ideas and policy recommendations that are essential to implement and use ADR processes in Ghana. Prior to this,

Ghana's arbitration centre had been established in 1996 to see to issues and disputes of commercial interest (Kirgis, 2014; Kotia & Aubyn, 2013).

The various institutions and activities that were established to facilitate the ADR systems brought into functioning the court-connected ADR system as well as the implementation of the Labour Act in the years 2002 and 2003 respectively (Kirgis, 2014; GOG, 2008). The Labour Act was established with the focus of promoting and ensuring the use of ADR mechanisms in resolving conflicts and cases that had to do with labour and the concerns of workers in the public and private sphere. In view of these, and the aim to institutionalise and strengthen the ADR system and its structure of activities, an ADR national directorate service was initiated and implemented under the authority of the Chief Justice with the view of facilitating and consolidating the processes and systems of ADR across the entire judicial framework (Kirgis, 2014; Apiagyei-Atua, 2013). This came as an important step that gradually led to the systems that facilitated the establishment of the ADR Act 798, in the year 2010.

A key feature within the ADR system as noted earlier on is the merger that it brings with regards to incorporating traditional or customary ADR processes and structures within mediation and arbitration and the formal legal systems of the judicial structure (Amegatcher, 2011; Adjabeng, 2007; CLDP, 2003). Customary mediation within Ghana's ADR Act 798, 2010 is more of an unwritten system and does not necessarily employ strict legal procedures and conditions, instead it embraces elements of fairness and the principles of natural justice in its mediation and resolution systems. As such, the customary system of ADR mediation and arbitration entails within the ADR Act 798, 2010, as a submission which is willingly done for the resolution of a dispute or conflict be it in relation to a determination or agreement which is binding to parties; that may be involved in a dispute, or if related to an agreement which is documented in the ADR Act (Nolan-Haley & Annor Ohene, 2014). Mediations of the customary nature in most cases are seen within the ADR Act as providing space for and building concern for negotiations of settlement, which in terms of the customary settlements are usually not binding (Kirgis, 2014; Nolan-Harley & Annor Ohene, 2014; Adjabeng, 2007). The non-binding nature of the traditional or customary ADR system vis-a-vis the traditional norms, culture, the patriarchal dynamics of communities and history could in a way hinder a fair resolution and enforcement of decisions in dispute systems. As such, the settlement agreements and decisions in such a system take a similar and equal binding framework just like an arbitral award (Nolan-Harley & Annor Ohene, 2014).

CONCEPTUAL UNDERPINNING OF ALTERNATIVE DISPUTE RESOLUTION

Alternative Dispute Resolution comprises various methods of dispute resolution that may come out of the normal judicial process of adjudication (Ntrakwah, 2018; Sarkodie, 2011; Love, 2011). This does not suggest that the court or legal system does not have an interest in the ADR system and processes as the courts could even require people, parties and groups involved in a dispute to use a particular kind of ADR method including mediation or arbitration for certain types of dispute or conflicts in question (Saylor Academy, 2012). A particular form of ADR method such as the informal system may give the power for resolving a dispute to the parties that are involved in the dispute; on the other hand, a more formal method of ADR may grant the power to decide on resolving a dispute to a neutral person or body (Fiadjor & Okyir, 2016; Saylor Academy, 2012; NYUCS, n.d.). Saylor Academy (2012) shows a continuum of various resolution methods of ADR that may be used.

The Saylor Academy shows that, the alternative dispute resolution system may be applied in resolving the dispute between parties either through the formal system, which may invest much power in the hands of a neutral person or group who decide on the resolution of the dispute. It could also be employed through the use of the informal system that gives more power to the disputants involved in the conflict that comes under consideration. Additionally, the ADR continuum may involve the use of various methods such as mediation, arbitration and negotiation. Hybrid forms that encompass the use of two methods for instance arbitration and mediation could also be employed in a system of a collaborative process in addressing and resolving disputes among parties. The formal system of ADR can be used in resolving disputes such as involving consumers and businesses, as well as between employees and their employers among others. The informal system of ADR on the other hand can be applied in issues and disputes relating to conflicts of family or domestic interest, including divorce and community disputes.

Nevertheless, the application of the ADR system, especially the informal system may not be the most appropriate for resolving certain issues for example cases relating to civil rights which affects the rights of people particularly the vulnerable and less privileged in society (Kirgis, 2014; Saylor Academy, 2012; Sarkodie, 2011). This could create serious consequences in the situation where an unequal bargaining power exists between the parties concerned. For instance, parties with less bargaining power such as people with limited access to money and resources could be disadvantaged in such a situation, as their rights could be trampled on or abused (Kirgis, 2014).

The employment of ADR requires cooperation with regards to the individuals, groups or parties involved in the conflict or dispute concerned. When cooperation is missing, then it becomes difficult to apply ADR mechanisms. ADR has gained root and particularly in recent times as a potential means of providing space for accessing justice (Noone & Akin, 2020; Kirgis, 2014; Owusu-Mensah, 2014; Sarkodie, 2011). Many international organizations and the developed world have promoted ADR, more especially mediation as a path to ensuring justice. Developing countries in Africa, including Ghana have embraced ADR and employed its strategies as a vehicle for facilitating justice for its citizenry (Kirgis, 2014; Apiagyei-Atua, 2013).

THE ADR MECHANISM WITHIN THE GHANAIAN-CONTEXT

Ghana's ADR practices date back to pre-colonial times where non-formal mediation and adjudication procedures and traditional dispute resolution mechanisms were employed in facilitating justice for the people (Ghana Arbitration Centre, 2016; Sarkodie, 2011). Officially the ADR system in Ghana was established in the year 2010 under the administration of Justice Wiredu, who was the then Chief Justice (Apiagyei-Atua, 2013; GoG, 2012). During the month of August 2005, the ADR mechanism was institutionalized and incorporated within the formal court resolution framework (Ghana Arbitration Centre, 2016).

Under the Alternative Dispute Resolution Act 798, 2010, several measures have been laid down to encompass the following (Ghana Arbitration Centre, 2016). In the first place, it emphasized that a decision of resolution through an ADR process should be considered as enforcing and accepted just like a formal court decision (Ghana Arbitration Centre, 2016). Mechanisms including customary arbitration, mediation and customary arbitral processes are considered under the ADR system in Ghana. In addition, an office of ADR was established with the authority of the ADR Act 2010 within section 115(2) and provides mechanisms and facilities to ensure the process of ADR through systems of mediation, arbitration and forms of traditional and customary dispute resolution procedures and arbitration systems (Ghana Arbitration Centre, 2016; Kirgis, 2014). This includes the provision of a category of mediators and arbitrators to take charge of the dispute settlements with authority provided by the state under the national judicial system (Ghana Arbitration Centre, 2016; Sarkodie, 2011).

Furthermore, the ADR system has been instituted to reach most district and circuit courts across Ghana. Under this, judges with special training as mediators are allocated to handle cases of mediation (Ghana Arbitration Centre, 2016; Sarkodie, 2011; Cofie, 2007). With this, if a mediation case is unable to reach success, then it is taken for a trial. It has been noted that mandatory mediation in Ghana has seen a great amount of success, with bringing down the caseload (Apiagyei-Atua, 2013; Cofie, 2007). For instance, between March 2005 and July 2006, about 403 cases were handled by the "Pre-Trial Conference" in Ghana (GoG 2012; Cofie, 2007). Among this, 86 were successfully resolved amicably representing 1 out of every five cases that were dealt with (Cofie, 2007). Also, the fast-track courts in Ghana employ the ADR mechanism as an aspect of its modus operandi (Ghana Arbitration Centre, 2016). This comes under "order 58" of the national court's Act 1993 (Constitution of Ghana, 1992). This states that the courts should as a matter of fact undertake mandatory conferences of pre-trial within a period of thirty days following a written argument by the court (Ghana Arbitration Centre, 2016; CHRAJ, 2005; Constitution of Ghana, 1992).

A unique aspect of Ghana's ADR is that it encompasses formal as well as informal mechanisms of ADR (Sarkodie, 2011). The non-formal mechanisms deal with the traditional non-court resolution procedures. This includes ADR mechanisms under the chief-based systems (Ghana Arbitration Centre, 2016). With this, traditional leaders including chiefs, community leaders and assembly members as custodians of their communities settle inter-personal disputes relating to marriage, land disputes, petty theft and child custody. In addition to this, there is also the family-based ADR mechanism (GoG, 2012; Cofie, 2007; Constitution of Ghana, 1992). With regards to this, family leaders popularly known as "Abusuapanyin" settle interpersonal family disputes amongst family members. This is done mostly in collaboration with other family elders from the families in question (Apiagyei-Atua, 2000; Cofie, 2007).

The non-formal ADR mechanisms date back to the pre-colonial era where traditional leaders had massive powers in matters of dispute resolution and arbitration in communities. During that period, the chief's palace occupied a strong space of tribunal for settling interpersonal conflicts particularly on land, divorce and childcare (Kirgis, 2014; Cofie, 2007; Apiagyei-Atua, 2000). The formal ADR mechanism on the other hand, comes directly under the courts. This entails the court-annexed mechanisms of ADR (Ghana Arbitration Centre, 2016; Constitution of Ghana, 1992). An example is the ADR process which is undertaken by the High Courts of Ghana with its commercial division (GoG, 2012). It also includes the National and Regional House of Chiefs who undertake mediation to settle disputes, such as chieftaincy disputes and issues on land (Kirgis, 2014; Constitution of Ghana, 1992). Another aspect of the formal ADR mechanism in Ghana is the resolution by institutions, such as the Commission on Human Rights and Administrative Justice (CHRAJ), which act as a quasi-judicial institution with cases relating to human rights abuses and issues of administrative justice in Ghana (GoG, 2012; Constitution of Ghana, 1992). The next section examines the inference and impacts of the formal legal system and people's access to justice.

THE INFERENCE OF THE FORMAL-LEGAL SYSTEM AND PEOPLE'S ACCESS TO JUSTICE

The official system of justice has its roots within the civil and common laws systems (Glenn, 2004; Trakman, 1991). This provides space for safeguarding the fundamental and civil rights of the people as well as lays down the framework for monitoring and regulating the behaviour and conducts of people within its jurisdiction (Glenn, 2004). This in turn reiterates and spells out the political and civil liberties and rights of the people and as such gives room for seeking justice within the formal-legal structure for the citizenry. In a situation where a person or group's rights and liberties are infringed upon, the formal legal system provides the space for seeking redress through the legal process in ensuring justice for the individual or group in question (Glenn, 2004; Trakman, 1991).

In reconsidering the legal structures of the Ghanaian and the African legal system at large, it could be noted that there existed a special legal structure, which imbibed customary norms, value systems and traditions (Kirgis, 2014; Apiagyei-Atua, 2000; Ferynhough, 1993). This structure was known as the customary laws with its unique classification of what rights of the people entailed. Such rights included aspects of what was referred to as individual as well community-based rights (Glenn, 2004; Apiagyei-Atua, 2000; Ferynhough, 1993). The individual and community-based rights systems were safeguarded and addressed through the non-adversarial systems of resolving conflicts and disputes.

Notwithstanding the flexibility and significance of the customary law structure of conflict and dispute resolution, the system was viewed as not up to standard and obsolete during the colonial era by the colonial administration (Apiagyei-Atua, 2013; Gyekye, 1987; Robins, 2009). In view of this, the practice was discarded by the colonial administration as a traditional-legal structure for resolving conflicts and disputes within the country (Apiagyei-Atua, 2000; Gyekye, 1987; Proulx, 2003). The system was only used in smaller personal cases amongst natives in the scope of native courts. The colonial administration therefore replaced the customary law and traditional adjudication system with their justice system. This gave way for the new legal and justice system introduced by the colonial administration to take precedence; with regards to the administration of justice and resolving conflicts and disputes amongst the people (Sarkodie, 2011; Gyekye, 1987; Robins, 2009).

The Bond of 1844 for instance was sealed in Ghana by the British colonial administration and a section of chiefs along with the coastal areas (Gyekye, 1987). With this, crimes including theft, robberies and murders were to be handled and trial by the courts of the colonial administration under the supervision of the judicial officers representing the colonial administration with the support of some of the traditional chiefs (Kirgis, 2014; Adjabeng, 2009; Gyekye, 1987). The new judicial system introduced by the colonial administration therefore annexed the local customary system of adjudication of the people. During Ghana's independence in 1957, for instance, the "Native Jurisdiction Ordinance 1883" was repealed, with the formal-legal judicial system brought by the British colonial administration taken the sole precedence (Kirgis, 2014; Apiagyei-Atua, 2013; Gyekye, 1987).

As noted by Gyekye (1987) the precedence of the justice system initiated by the colonial administration, which is in practice today, provides a little space reserved for the traditional chiefs in taking charge of settlements of conflicts and disputes within their local communities. In Ghana, the British colonial administration at the time initiated the "Native Jurisdiction Ordinance 1883" (Gyekye, 1987; Robins, 2009). This gave some powers to the traditional chiefs to take charge of settling basic conflicts and disputes within their local communities.

The formal-legal procedure of justice despite its significance for ensuring justice shows numerous forms of shortfalls that in turn disadvantages the access to justice by the people (Adjabeng, 2009; Proulx, 2003). Its Eurocentric tendency comes with an idea of universality, rationality and abstract nature (Proulx, 2003). The formal justice process with its win or lose system, in addition distorts the process of social cohesion and as such affects social cooperation within and amongst community members (Atuguba, n.d.; Proulx, 2003).

To add to this, the adversarial system of litigation that is followed by the formal-legal process of justice in a way shows a kind of unfriendliness and rigidness with regards to access to dispute resolution and access to justice by the people (Adjabeng, 2009; Fiadjor, 2004). The high cost of the system also to some extent advantages the well-to-do over the less privileged individuals and groups (Adjabeng, 2009). Further, the high resort to evidence as well as rules of procedure that are encapsulated within the formal-legal procedure limits access to justice and resolution of disputes for the ordinary person to an extent (Adjabeng, 2009).

Another major challenge that comes with the formal-legal justice system within Ghana is the existence of dispute resolution and justice institutions that are under-resourced (Adjabeng, 2009; Fiadjor, 2004). Such institutions include CHRAJ, the Social Welfare Department, the Domestic Violence and Victim Support Unit (DOVVSU) of the Ghana Police service, which faces problems of inadequate institutional capacity, including lack of resources, limited personnel, and infrastructural facilities (Adjabeng, 2009). This facilitates problems of delays in the hearing of litigation cases and delays in the enforcement process.

In addition, there is the problem of inadequate and unavailability of justice institutions within some rural communities in Ghana (Wood, 2011; Adjabeng, 2009). This in turn affects the access to the process of justice by the ordinary people and groups within such communities (Adjabeng, 2009; Menkel Meadow, 2004; UNDP, 2012; Wood, 2011). These individuals and groups must travel all the way to the city centre to lodge complaints and have their cases heard.

The numerous challenges that have characterized the formal-legal justice process in Ghana called for the need to buttress and push forward for a more reaching system of justice for the people. This will in turn help the people particularly those in the deprived rural communities in accessing justice and having access to an alternative system of conflict and dispute resolution within their communities (Ghana Arbitration Centre, 2016; Fiadjor, 2004). To this effect, the ADR system was established to facilitate the process of reaching justice and dispute resolution for individuals and groups, more especially women who are unable to have access to the normal court system to have their dispute resolution and other cases heard (Adjabeng, 2009; UNDP, 2012).

ACCESS TO JUSTICE AND WOMEN IN GHANA

Access to justice encompasses the need to give maximum respect to principles of legal as well as natural justice, people's rights to fair and quality trial (Tilda Hum et al., 2006; UNDP, 2004). In this sense, access to justice should be explained and emphasized in relation to how people especially vulnerable individuals and groups including women can exercise their rights to a fair justice system that takes off all forms of structural, socio-economic, cultural and political barriers that limits and fosters unequal opportunities for achieving justice. Access to justice therefore covers a system of qualitative and transparent provision pertaining to representation for the less-privileged people (UNDP, 2004). Qualitative justice is explained here as ensuring justice for all particularly for marginalized groups including the poor, the disabled, women and children. Both national and international efforts including national agenda and laws and declarations have been made with the hope of bridging the gap in access to justice and equality for marginalized groups such as women.

The United Nations Committee on the Elimination of Discrimination Against Women (CEDAW), as a principle states that "women all over the world need to be provided with equality and access to justice just like men'' (CEDAW, 2006). With this, it declares that '' it is a prerogative for all state parties including national and civil society to provide women with an equal capacity in relation to legal, civil matters and be provided with same opportunities in all procedures of courts and tribunals in accessing justice'' (CEDAW, 2006). The convention was ratified in Ghana on February 2, 1986, and since then the country has made substantial efforts towards promoting gender equality and providing steps in ensuring equal opportunities for women. Within international law the following procedures are described as very essential for facilitating access to justice:

1. "The Right to Procedural Justice"
2. "The Right to a Hearing without Delay"
3. "The Right to Legal Advice and Legal Representation"
4. "Equal Access to the Courts"
5. "Equality before the Courts"
6. "The Right to a Competent, Independent and Impartial Tribunal which has been established under the Law"
7. "The Right to a Public Hearing"
8. "The Right to have the Free Assistance of an Interpreter, if needed". Source: (Tilda Hum et al., 2013).

It also takes into significant consideration the efficiency, effectiveness and responsiveness of the formal legal justice system and the customary system of resolving disputes between parties and groups. Access to justice as a matter of fact should not just give provision for legal representation and ensuring the access the people have to the courts and legal procedures but should have as a major concern the promotion and establishment of equitable outcomes for all judicial processes and decisions (UNDP, 2004).

Several mechanisms are used to promote access to justice for all either through formal legal justice system or through informal strategies with the view of ensuring that under-privileged groups are not denied their civil rights and fair treatment in matters of judicial concern (Alkon, 2011; DFID, 2000). In recent times, ADR mechanisms have been embraced by the judicial authorities in Ghana to bring justice close to the people and ensuring that rights to justice and processes towards resolutions of matters of concern reach the ordinary Ghanaian (Apiagyei-Atua, 2013:37-38). ADR has been welcomed by many in present times just like how it was utilized in the past for reasons including easy and quick access to the ordinary person, less costly and as a process that does not take much time compared to normal court proceedings.

The colonial administration saw the customary method of resolution as inferior and as such introduced the Western form of legal justice to replace it and take responsibilities for resolving a dispute that people have (Apiagyei-Atua, 2013; 39-40). In situations where the customary dispute mechanism could operate alongside the formal legal system, the former was still considered inferior to the latter (Apiagyei-Atua, 2013: 39). Nevertheless, upon identifying key drawbacks with the formal justice system, the reformers of it have come to introduce ADR to the developing world forgetting that the practice has been inherent in the justice system of the countries even before colonialism. The originators of the formal justice system have emphasized that the justice system in developing countries has been characterized by a syndrome of ineffectiveness, inefficiency, corruption and politicization (Linn, 2000), and for that matter have reintroduced ADR which was considered inferior and was part of the justice system of most countries in Africa including, Ghana (Apiagyei-Atua, 2013: 40).

The chapter therefore argues here that with the introduction of the ADR system without giving a necessary concern for its socio-cultural and historical antecedents, and the influences it had from the formal legal system, it will be very difficult to meet the maximum objective of the mechanism, which is it to provide justice for the most vulnerable and ensure a fair, efficient and a more equitable justice system. The ADR mechanism has been described as having a key target that is championed by the developed world on promoting the market democracy agenda (Santos, 2006). This is aimed at sustaining and enhancing the efficiency of democratic governance and structures towards laying firm grounds for foreign investors to operate smoothly without any hindrances to their market activities. Also, this will in turn ensure a restructuring of the judicial system and the entire legal structure with reforms towards bringing down delays in the adjudication period and the time involved and case backlogs as well (Kirgis, 2014; Apiagyei-Atua, 2013: 39-40; Santos, 2006). It could therefore be noted to some extent that the notion towards access to justice and equal rights for women, and the introduction of ADR mechanisms is indifferent or nonchalant to the main target of the agenda of promoting access to justice, which is the market democracy (Apiagyei-Atua, 2013:40).

There is no doubt that the introduction of the ADR mechanisms has improved and contributed to increasing women's access to justice in Ghana and other African countries. This includes bringing access to justice closer to the people through ADR, reduction in cost and time that characterizes the formal legal system of adjudication. However, it can be argued that from a gender lens, there is enough evidence that shows that there are still many challenges for women in accessing justice fully and enjoying the full benefits and significance of the ADR mechanism. The inherent weaknesses that are found in the formal legal system have been embedded in the ADR mechanisms and as a result the challenges have also been recorded in the processes of the ADR and acted as an obstacle for achieving a maximum and equality of rights for women (Kirgis, 2014; Apiagyei-Atua, 2013: 39-41). This point was emphasized by Ghana's former Chief Justice, Her Ladyship Georgina Wood that "at the heart of the common law, the civil justice system is a well-known adversarial system of litigation; the general notion is that despite the obvious advantages, the conventional approach to dispute resolution has been found to be inappropriate for the resolution of a number of disputes including interpersonal disputes that involve women and children" (Wood, 2004).

A major factor behind the inherent challenges is incorporated within the historical dynamics of the society that has labelled women's roles as inferior compared to men (Kirgis, 2014; Barriteau, 2003). This coupled with patriarchal notions of male dominance which gives a low status to the women has tended to perpetuate and subordinated women's access to equal rights and justice. The logical structure and language use in the legal system is characterized with male norms and as such labelled female norms as a deviation from the existing norm of activities (Sarkodie, 2011; Barriteau, 2003; Maschke, 1997; Gilligan, 1993). This as a matter of fact reinforces the notions in the Ghanaian society and other parts of the continent making it difficult to ensure qualitative justice and women's significant access to complete legal and conventional justice.

Issues, Controversies and Problems

ADR comes with numerous strengths as well as weaknesses. In the first place, it could be emphasized that ADR is more flexible compared to the formal process of litigation (Albright, 2012; Sossi, 2010). The process of ADR tries to employ solutions that are more workable in resolving disputes and conflicts. According to Oricho (2010) ADR depicts more confidentiality for the factions in dispute and gives room for nominating or having the choice to decide on the decision-makers. Women in communities become more aligned with the process of ADR compared to the formal process of litigation, which shows more of a rigid procedure and adherence to the rules of procedure system. This to an extent explains why ADR has been embraced in recent times in many developing countries (CLF, 2020), including Ghana.

Furthermore, the ADR process is less expensive for the individuals as well as the groups involved in the dispute. In comparison with the formal process of litigation, it could be realized that ADR brings down the cost of resolving conflicts and disputes (Lorman Education, 2018; Oricho, 2010). This brings down the cost not only for the individuals and groups involved in the dispute, but the state also benefits from the lower cost that comes about as a result of employing the ADR mechanism (Noone & Akin, 2020; Adjabeng, 2009; GoG, 2012).

Apiagyei-Atua (2013) has argued that despite the advantage of the ADR process been less-costly compared to the formal process of litigation, it could be seen that ADR does not favor vulnerable and deprived people, particularly women in deprived communities due to the cultural norms that in most cases places men as more superior to the women and sees the female norms of the country as second fiddle to the dominant male norms. Women in absolute poverty face several challenges with regard to fighting for their rights to justice. The reason is that, with their extreme poverty and deplorable condition they are unable to adequately stand for their legal rights of justice (Adjabeng, 2009; Ghana Arbitration Centre, 2016). As such, despite the promises of ADR to promote justice, it does not express this in all instances for all women, especially those in absolute poverty and deprived conditions.

Also, the ADR mechanism facilitates more of a responsive means of resolving conflicts and disputes compared to the formal process of litigation (TLJ, 2021; Oricho, 2010). The process of ADR therefore becomes more variable in terms of employing ADR mechanisms such as, mediation, arbitration, facilitation and conciliation in resolving disputes. As such, ADR gives room for harmonious conflict and dispute resolution for the factions engaged in the conflict or dispute concern (Sarkodie, 2011; CLF, 2020).

Further to this, the ADR process employs a timeline that is fixed (Lorman Education, 2018). This is seen in relation to receiving complaints and attending to them through its mechanisms of dispute hearing and settlement. It, therefore, allows for a clear time to be drawn in deciding on issues and resolving conflicts and disputes within a scheduled timeframe (Oricho, 2010; Sossi, 2010). This takes away the system whereby many delays are encountered in the litigation process.

Another advantage of ADR is that it provides a framework for ensuring the stability of social relations. This comes as a result of the ADR processes opening-up spaces for facilitating harmony and a variable trend of dispute resolution (Noone & Akin, 2020; Kirgis, 2014). With this, disputes are resolved more harmoniously ensuring that social relations within communities are maintained and not scattered by the process of litigation (Ghana Arbitration Centre, 2016). Notwithstanding this, a weakness that comes with this is that, with the view of promoting harmonious social relations, parties who are deprived of their rights; in this case women who are the disadvantaged group, for example, on issues like domestic violence are not allowed to receive the full sense of justice (Fiadjor & Ochir, 2016; Fiadjor, 2004). This is as a result of the point that the coercive aspect of the law is not allowed to deal drastically with men who abuse such women, as the resolution is done in the name of safeguarding and ensuring harmonious social relations (Apiagyei-Atua, 2000).

The role that ADR plays in dispute resolution; for instance, in the case of domestic violence where the women in most cases are the most affected has been questioned by several scholars. Bernard for example questions the role play by ADR in situations such as domestic violence (Bernard, 1992; Grillo, 1991). With this, the women who are the most affected have less power with regards to defending and fighting for their civic rights of justice. This is mostly due to the imbalances of power that characterize the Ghanaian society and the African community at large (Kirgis, 2014; Apiagyei-Atua, 2013).

In addition, Bryan has also argued against the role that is taken by ADR in issues of domestic violence and the effects it has on women as they have an unequal access in defending their legal rights of justice in comparison with their male counterparts (Bryan, 1985). In view of this, Bryan has called for a recalibration of the system of power existing between men and women in overcoming the imbalances of power (Bryan, 1985). He further calls for representatives or lawyers to assist in representing such women in the situation of vulnerability in accessing and seeking their rights to power and justice (Bryan, 1985). Further, the patriarchal position of men is given space to continue disadvantaging the women who become victims of such abuses and inequalities such as, domestic violence.

Turning specifically to the traditional non-court annexed mode of ADR, it could be realized that it allows for proximity and ownership of the system by the indigenes, particularly for women (Adjabeng, 2009; Fiadjor, 2004). The use of the traditional chief's palace as a tribunal creates space for proximity and a reliance on the cultural norms of the people (Sarkodie, 2011; Osi, 2008). Women in rural communities for instance, are able to save a lot of time for travelling to the city centers for their problems to be heard and adjudicated on. Such time could be used by the rural women in visiting their farms or engage in market activities that will earn them profit (LRC, 2008; Osi, 2008).

The nature and the processes of the traditional ADR mechanism make the system friendlier to the public and allow for public participation (LRC, 2008; Osi, 2008). With the chiefs and the community elders as the adjudicators of such a system, the public is given the space to participate and express their views on an issue at hand which allows for more openness of the system.

Notwithstanding the significance of ADR as a means of ensuring justice and opening-up room for public participation, it tends to disadvantage women particularly (Apiagyei-Atua, 2013; Adjabeng, 2009; Ocen, 2013; Osi, 2008). Women are the most affected victims when it comes to issues such as domestic violence. However, with a situation of power imbalance especially in rural communities, where the women have less power, they experience the disadvantage in terms of not receiving justice equally as their male counterparts who possess the greater part of power (Ocen, 2013; Yin, 2014). Women are afforded limited power when it comes to the application of ADR especially in rural communities (CDG, 2012; Ocen, 2013). As noted by CDG (2012), in such a situation ADR becomes counter-productive and less effective in ensuring justice for the women in question.

Another problem with the traditional ADR mechanism is that within a circumstance where a woman becomes victorious in a resolution of a dispute through the ADR process, the process of enforcement becomes very weak (Apiagyei-Atua, 2013; CDG, 2012). The enforcement basis for the traditional ADR, particularly for women becomes very challenging. For instance, in the case where a woman is to be compensated by a man, it could take a very long time for the compensation to be paid (Adjabeng, 2009; Apiegyei-Atua, 2000). This is mostly due to the weak enforcement system that characterizes the traditional ADR system.

In addition, women are the worse sufferers when it comes to issues involving spiritual matters (Vanderpuye, 2008). Such issues include witchcraft, spiritual diseases (Afrikangoddess, 2012; Vanderpuye, 2008). In such situations, women in rural communities are in most cases accused of causing harm to people. Therefore, in deciding on such issues with a lack of scientific proof, such vulnerable women are mostly blamed and due to this, cases are in most instances pre-determined (Albright, 2012; Martin, 2006; Vanderpuye, 2008). The application of ADR in such a situation leads the woman to no room for defending her rights and as such, is unable to have an equal access to justice especially in the rural communities.

Also, issues of human rights are not given the needed attention when it comes to the traditional ADR mechanism (Martin, 2006). Therefore, such issues have a limited space within the application of the traditional ADR process. For instance, the DOVVSU of the Ghana Police Service has been accused of turning on the law; and not ensuring strict enforcement (Adjabeng, 2009; Martin, 2006; CHRAJ, 2004). With issues of domestic violence, DOVVSU tends to employ mechanisms that are amicable and as such, do not treat such situations, where in many cases the women are the worse sufferers of the abuse as issues of criminality (Martin, 2006). DOVVSU with its principle of promoting peace and cooperation employs counseling as the remedy for resolving such issues of domestic abuse (Ghana Arbitration Centre, 2016; Vanderpuye, 2008).

In view of this, the enforcement mechanism is not much strict and turns to put the women mostly at a disadvantage position (Martin, 2006; Vanderpuye, 2008). The next sections provide some key recommendations and conclusions of the chapter and consider some critical remedies for ensuring effective ADR that promotes the rights of women and their access to justice.

SOLUTIONS AND RECOMMENDATIONS

In recommending solutions that would help in effectively employing ADR in ensuring justice particularly for women, it should be noted that, the historical underpinnings of ADR within the Ghanaian society should be revisited. ADR has been part of Ghanaian society in the past with its patriarchal undertones, and as such, in incorporating ADR into the formal legal system of justice, it becomes important to revisit and understand the historical notions that tend to disfavor women and rather favored men with its patriarchal norms. When this is addressed then a country-specific ADR mechanism could be adopted in applying ADR to give access to justice for women and take out the patriarchal undertone that it poses.

Also, it becomes important to note that not all forms of disputes and violations can be addressed using the ADR mechanism. For instance, abuses such as domestic violence which affects women in most cases, cannot be addressed with the employment of mediation as an ADR mechanism. Therefore, to effectively use ADR in ensuring access to justice particularly for women, context-specific mechanisms that ensure justice in certain violations should be employed; and not just applying ADR especially the non-court annexed ADR (traditional ADR) in settling cases such as domestic violence and other human right abuses.

In addition, gender-sensitive training should be employed by the government, civil society and all relevant stakeholders as an important aspect of the training for arbitrators, mediators and all actors who are involved in the ADR mechanism. International human rights laws and the rights of women as equal citizens should be maintained in all facets of ADR and incorporated into its processes in ensuring equality for women in accessing justice with no unforeseen hindrances.

FUTURE RESEARCH DIRECTIONS

Alternative dispute resolution has undoubtedly helped to improve access to justice for less privileged and vulnerable groups including women in Ghana. However, the challenges that characterize the formal justice system have been embedded in ADR mechanisms and continue to affect the effective functioning of ADR in ensuring maximum justice for women. As such, further research could employ a mixed-method technique in examining the dynamics of social, cultural and historical underpinnings of Ghana and how it hinders women's access to contemporary justice through ADR. This would be significant for government, civil society, and other non-state entities and institutions in addressing the root causes of the challenges in making a more informed system of effective and qualitative justice for women.

CONCLUSION

The chapter has examined ADR and access to justice by women within Ghana. It has been seen that due to the inherent obstacles that characterized the formal system of justice, ADR has been welcomed as a system that provides a form of alternative access to justice particularly for women and less-privileged individuals and groups. ADR is much cheaper with its processes, less time-consuming, friendlier, and above all ensures the maintenance and entrenchment of social relations.

Furthermore, it has been realized that ADR has been part of Ghanaian society dating back to the pre-colonial era. During this period, ADR was the sole means of conflict and dispute resolution within and amongst communities across Ghanaian society. With this, the traditional chief's palace served as the tribunal for resolving disputes amicably between individuals, groups and families. The traditional chief with his group of elders sat on issues related to land, childcare, divorce, family disputes and the like. Notwithstanding this, the introduction of the formal justice system by the colonial administration abolished the traditional dispute resolution mechanism, making the formal justice system the sole means of resolving disputes in Ghana.

The inherent shortfalls that characterize the formal justice system and its failure to ensure justice for all individuals and groups, particularly for women have seen the re-introduction of the ADR mechanism in the developed world, with a gradual expansion into developing countries including Ghana. The re-introduction of ADR with its numerous advantages as stated earlier on, including given a wider access to most part of the population to access justice particularly for women and vulnerable individuals and groups has seen the massive acceptance and admiration for the ADR mechanism.

This has to do with both the court-annexed ADR mechanism as well as the non-court annexed mechanism of ADR (traditional ADR system). Nonetheless, the inherent challenges and shortfalls that characterize the formal mechanism of justice and dispute resolution, have also characterized the ADR mechanism, particularly with regards to access to justice for women and other vulnerable individuals and groups. ADR just like the formal mechanism of justice within Ghana has been patriarchal in nature and as such, has not given women especially the needed access to justice.

ACKNOWLEDGMENT

The initial drafts of this chapter were reviewed and proofread by colleagues at the University of Ghana. The research received no specific grant from any funding agency in the public, commercial, or not-for-profit sectors.

REFERENCES

Adjabeng, M. S. (2007). *Alternative dispute resolution in Ghana.* mediate.com/articles/adjabeng3.cfm

Adjabeng, M. S. (2009). *Gender justice in Ghana through court-connected ADR.* Available online at www.mediate.com/articles/adjabengs4.cfm

Akin, O. L., & Noone, M. (2017). Alternative dispute resolution processes: Connections between purposes, values, ethics and justice. *Law in Context (Bundoora, Vic.), 3*(5), 5–23.

Albright, M. (2012). *The advantages and disadvantages of alternative dispute resolution.* AlbrightStoddard.

Alternative Dispute Resolution Act 798, Ghana (2010). http://mariancrc.org/wp-

Alvarez de la Campa, A. (2009). *The private sector approach to commercial ADR: Commercial ADR approach mechanism in Colombia. Investment Climate Department.* World Bank.

Amarteifio, M., Lartey, Aburam, L., Okudzeto, S. (2021). Arbitration procedures and practice in Ghana: Overview. *Thomas Reuters Practical Law.* uk.practicallaw.thomasreuters.com/66107025?transitionType=Default&contextDaata=

Amegatcher, N. O. (2011, September). *A Daniel comes to judgment: Ghana's ADR Act. A progressive or retrogressive piece of legislation.* Paper presented at the Ghana Bar Association Annual Conference, Accra, Ghana.

Apiagyei-Atua, K. (2000). Contribution of the Akan philosophy to the conceptualization of African notions of rights. *Constitutional and International Law Journal of Southern Africa, 16*(5).

Apiagyei-Atua, K. (2013). Alternative dispute resolution and its implications for women's access to justice in Africa: Case study of Ghana. *Frontiers of Legal Research, 1*(1), 36–57.

Atugaba, R. (n.d.). *Access to justice, formal and informal: definitions, experiences, ideas, convergences and non-convergencies.* Paper presented at the CUSO international seminar under the theme: experiences of improvements in access to justice, inter-legality restorative justice, multicultural societies, legal pluralism, gender and human rights.

Barriteau, E. (2003). *Confronting power, theorizing gender: interdisciplinary perspectives in the Caribbean.* UWI Press.

Bernard, E. P. (2006). Begging for justice? Or adapting jurisprudence? Initial reflections on the mandatory ADR to enforce women's rights in Rwanda. *Cardozo Journal of Conflict Resolution, 32*(5), 326–327.

Bryan, P.E. (1997). The coercion of women in divorce settlement negotiations. *Denv. UL. Rev, 931.*

Caenegem, V. (1998). Birth of the English common law. Academic Press.

Calkins Law Firm. (2020). *The pros and cons of alternative dispute resolution*. Calkins. calkinslawfirm.com/resources/the-pros-and-cons-of-alternative-dispute-resolution-26756

Centre for Democracy and Governance. (1998). *Alternative dispute resolution. Practitioner's Guide 8*. Technical Publication Series.

Cofie, S. (2007). *Ghana establishment of the commercial court-smart lessons*. Available at http//: www.doingbusiness.org/media/FPDCM/Ghanacommercialcourts

Constitution of Ghana. (1992). *Constitution of Ghana*. Government of Ghana.

Crook, C. R. (2011). *Alternative dispute resolution and the magistrates' courts in Ghana. A case of practical hybridity*. African Power and Programme Working Paper No. 25.

De Sousa Santos, B. (2000). Law and community-the capitalist changing nature of state power in late capitalism. In The Politics of International Justice. The American Experience.

Dieng, A. (2011). Alternative dispute resolution in Sub-Saharan African countries. In *ADR in business practice and issues across countries and cultures*. Arnold Ingen-Houz.

Fernyhough, T. (1993). *Human rights in pre-colonial Africa*. University Press of Florida.

Fiadjor, A. (2004). *Alternative dispute resolution: a developing world perspective*. Cavendish.

Fiadjor, A., & Okyir, N.T. (2016). The alternative dispute resolution Act of Ghana deconstructed: providing a more positive sum approach to court resolution. *Transnational Dispute Management, 4*.

Ghana News Agency. (2012). Women slam CHRAJ and the Department of Social Welfare on the handling of abuses. *Online (Bergheim)*.

Gilligan, G. (1993). *In a different voice: psychological theory and women's development*. Harvard University Press.

Glenn, H. P. (2004). *Legal tradition of the world*. Oxford University Press.

Government of Ghana. (2012). *Alternative dispute resolution Act, 798, 2010*. Government of Ghana.

Gropper, A. (2010). *Alternative dispute resolution in tax disputes*. Research Note. Washington DC: World Bank.

Grushetsky, A. (2015). *Highlighting coverage of alternative dispute resolution in Ghana*. Ohio Journal on Dispute Resolution.

Gyekye, K. (1987). *An essay on African philosophical thought: The Akan conceptualization scheme*. Cambridge University Press.

Hum. (2006). *The right to a fair hearing and access to justice-submission of the New South Wales young lawyers human rights committee to the senate legal affairs and constitutional committee: inquiry into access to justice*. www.senate.aph.gov.au/submissions committees/viewdocument.aspx?id

Kirgis, P. (2014). Status and contract in an emerging democracy in the evolution of dispute resolution in Ghana. *Cardozo Journal of Conflict Resolution, 10*(1).

Law Reform Commission. (2008). *Consultative on alternative dispute resolution.* LRC.

Legal Information Institute. (2017). *Alternative dispute resolution. LII.* Cornel Law School.

Linn, A. H. (2007). *Envisioning reform: improving judicial performance in Latin America.* Pennsylvania State University Press.

Lorman Education. (2018). *Advantages and disadvantages of alternative dispute resolution.* LORMAN. https://www.lorman.com/resources/advantages-and-disadvantages-alternativedisputeresolution-16190

Love, I. (2011). *Settling out of court: How effective is alternative dispute resolution? Viewpoint, public policy for the private sector. Note No. 329.* The World Bank.

Martin, V. L. (2006). Domestic violence in Ghana: the open secret. *Georgia Journal of Gender and the Law*, 531-597.

Maschke, K. J. (1997). *Feminist legal theories.* Garland Publishers.

Menkel-Meadow, C. (2004). *Institute of civil justice paper prepared for the Scottish Consumer Council Seminar on Civil Justice.* Institute of Civil Justice.

Mueller, L. (2010). The persistence of Asante chieftaincy under colonial rule- the explanation of an enigma. *Africana Studia, 15*, 61–85.

New York State Unified Court System. (n.d.). *Continuum of different alternative dispute resolution methods.* http://www.nycourts.gov/ip/adr/images/continuum 2.jpg

Noone, M., & Akin, O. L. (2020). Alternative dispute resolution and access to justice in Australia. *International Journal of Law in Context, 16*(2), 108–127.

Ntrakwah, K. (2018). *Arbitration in Ghana.* Lexology. www.lexology.com/library/detail.aspx?g=02eed85-3a65f-4fbc-8ac1-a303f5fffe6e

Ntrakwah, K., & Asiama, A. (2017). *Arbitration Guide.* International Bar Association Arbitration Committee.

Oricho, D. O. (1997). Understanding the benefits of alternative dispute resolution in the workplace mediation. *Journal of Law and Conflict Resolution, 2*, 11-19.

Osi, C. (2008). Understanding indigenous dispute resolution processes and western alternative dispute resolution: Cultivating appropriate methods in lieu of litigation. *Cardozo Journal of Conflict Resolution, 10*, 163–232.

Owen, M. (1984). Against settlement. *Yale L.J., 1073.*

Owusu-Mensah, I. (2014). Politics, chieftaincy and customary law in Ghana's 4th republic. *PAN African Studies*, 261.

Proulx, C. (2003). *Reclaiming aboriginal justice, identity and community.* Purich Publishing.

Robin, S. (2009). A place for justice in an effective criminal justice system. Customary justice in Sierra Leone, Tanzania and Zambia. Institute for Security Studies, Policy Brief No. 17.

Santos, A. (2006). The World Bank's uses of the rule of law: Promise in economic development. In The new law and economic development: A critical appraisal. Cambridge University Press.

Sarkodie, K. (2011). *Arbitration in Ghana: The alternative dispute resolution Act 2010*. The International Construction Law Review.

Saylor Academy. (2012). *Alternative dispute resolution*. Saylor Academy.

Shonk, K. (2020). *What is alternative dispute resolution? Familiarize yourself with mediation, arbitration, and a hybrid approach using alternative dispute resolution. Program on Negotiation*. Harvard Law School.

Singer, B. J. (1992). The privatization of family law. *Wis. L.R., 1443*.

Stipanowich, T. (2004). Alternative dispute resolution and the vanishing trial. The growth and impact of alternative dispute resolution. *Journal of Empirical Legal Studies, 1*(3), 843–912.

The Lawyers and Jurists. (2021). Explain the advantages and disadvantages of alternative dispute resolution. *The Lawyers and Jurists*. lawyersnjurists.com/article/advanatges-disadvantages-alternative-dispute-resolution/

Trakman, L. (1991). *Reasoning with the charter*. Butterworths.

United Nations Committee on the Elimination of Discrimination Against Women. (2005). *Combined third, fourth, and fifth periodic reports of States parties, Ghana*. UN CEDAW.

United Nations Committee on the Elimination of Discrimination Against Women. (2006). *Concluding comments, Ghana*. UN CEDAW.

United Nations Development Programme. (2004). *Access to justice: Practice note*. UNDP.

Uwazie, E. E. (2011). *Alternative dispute resolution in Africa: preventing conflict and enhancing stability*. Africa Security Brief 16.

Vanderpuye, F. (2008). *Traditional beliefs cost women their freedom*. www.secularhumanism.org/library/aah/vanderpuye

Walter, A. W. (2000). *Cultural issues in mediation: Individualist and collectivist paradigms*. www.mediate.com/articles/wright.cfm

WiLDAF-Ghana. (2006). *Shadow report of Ghana's 3rd, 4th, and 5th report on the implementation of the CEDAW in Ghana*. Available online at www.iwraw-ap.org/resources/pdf/Gh-SR.pdf

Wisseler, R. (2004). The effectiveness of court-connected dispute resolution in civil cases. *Conflict Resolution Quarterly, 22*, 55–88.

Wood, G. T. (2004). *Non-adversarial conflict resolution: conference proceedings at the West African regional conference on legal and judicial reform to promote improved women's rights in land and family law within plural legal systems*. Accra, Ghana: Academic Press.

Wood, G. T. (2011). *Keynote address at the Catholic University*. The inauguration of the Marian Conflict Resolution Centre. http://mariancrc.org/wp-content/uploads/2011/09/MCRC_openingkeynote

Wychreschuk, E., & Boland B. (2000). *Making it safe: women's restorative justice and alternative dispute resolution*. Department of Justice, Government of Newfoundland and Labrador.

Yin, E. T., & Black, J. M. (2014). The legal anthropology of marriage in Ghana: Presenting power dynamics through legal arenas. *International Journal of Current Research*, *6*(12), 10696–10704.

KEY TERMS AND DEFINITIONS

Access to Justice: Access to justice entails the need to give maximum respect to principles of legal as well as natural justice, people's rights to fair and quality trial equally to all individuals and groups.

Alternative Dispute Resolution: Encompasses dispute and conflict resolution practices that fall within but operates outside the normal court system of resolution.

Arbitration: It is a process of employing the use of an arbitrator who is neutral in making decision on a dispute or conflict between parties.

Conciliation: This is form of mediation whereby both parties in a dispute are separately met by the conciliator and not together as a way of seeking agreements and concessions from the parties that will assist in resolution of the dispute or conflict at hand. Conciliation is different from arbitration in the sense that, as arbitration may be binding conciliation is not legally binding.

Equality: Equality describes the state of all people being equal in terms of opportunities, rights, liberties, freedoms and equal access to socio-economic and political goods and services. This includes gender equality, racial equality, equality of opportunities etc.

Formal Justice System: Is explained as a system that incorporates civil as well as criminal justice through the formal system of state-based institutions of justice, its procedures and rules including the courts, prosecutors, and the police.

Human Rights: Human rights are described as involving the basic or fundamental rights and freedoms which are based on a shared value system including equality, fairness, dignity, independence, and respect for one another; the values here are defined and protected though the system of law.

Justice: It explains the effective administration and maintenance of law through equitable and fairness for all groups and individuals.

Legal System: The legal system entails the rules and procedures through which public as well as private initiatives and systems are undertaken within legitimate measures and means.

Mediation: A process that takes into concern the use of a neutral mediator that enable parties or groups involved in a dispute to make provisions for discussing and deciding on a solution that is mutually agreed by all the parties.

Chapter 11
Challenges Facing Mediation as a Means of Court-Connected Alternative Dispute Resolution in the Ashanti Region of Ghana

Ebenezer Barnes
University of Saskatchewan, Canada

Alex Somuah Obeng
University of Cape Coast, Ghana

ABSTRACT

In 2012-2016, the number of cases referred to CCADR for mediation was 14,900. And out of these cases, 5,789 were successfully resolved to represent 38%. The total number of mediated cases pending were 9,111, representing 62%. Though there seems to be an improvement in terms of a decrease in pending cases, the number of pending cases leaves much to be desired. Premising on the above statistics, it has been noted that 9,111 ADR cases were pending in CCADR. Meanwhile, mediation under the CCADR program is known to be faster, affordable, and to reduce the overloaded courts' dockets. This has boosted the interest, trust, and confidence people had in mediation, and this has resulted in the increasing number of cases referred to ADR for mediation. However, the system, which was instituted to reduce overloaded courts' dockets, is bedeviled with challenges. The study seeks to explore the challenges confronting mediation as a means of ADR approach.

INTRODUCTION

Conflict is a common phenomenon in social life. Thus, social relations in many settings are prone to interpersonal and intrapersonal conflicts in the normal course of social life. Interactions that are intended to bring social harmony between individuals or groups often turn into differences among them. These conflicts may occur at different levels among individuals, individuals and groups, groups and commu-

DOI: 10.4018/978-1-7998-7898-8.ch011

nities, between community groups and government or within private or civil society organisations and between nations (Grimble & Wellard, 1997).

Dispute, as defined by Burton (1990), is a short-term disagreement that can result in the disputants reaching some sort of resolution; it involves issues that are negotiable. Dispute resolution existed in African societies before the advent of colonialism. Karuiki (2014) argued that the framework for dispute resolution was instituted to either prevent conflict escalation or from threatening the social fabric of society. The core of these traditional approaches in Africa reflected the beliefs, values and customs of the traditional society concerned. To avoid disharmony and establish harmony among individuals or groups, the chiefs and elders meted out sanctions to all actors involved in the disputes. Chiefs, although powerful, did not take sole decisions without consulting their elders. The elders provided counsel and performed advisory roles to the chiefs who passed verdicts among disputants. In Rwanda, Gacaca-justice among the grass was popularized. With this traditional system of dispute resolution, the respective family heads were called together to resolve disputes by sitting on the grass. The aims were to restore social harmony, seek the truth, punish perpetrators and compensate victims through gifts such as sheep, goats and goatskin (Karuiki, 2014; Rankopo & Osei-Hwedie, 2011).

The case of Ghana is not dissimilar. The principles of dispute resolution have been in existence as far back as the pre-colonial days. In pre-colonial Ghana, different ethnic groups had their own methods of dispute resolution. Two disputants in the family simply talked about a problem and endeavoured to reach a solution. In instances of unsuccessfulness, family members referred disputes to family heads who tried to resolve them. When this effort failed, the clan head was called upon to help. The last resort was normally the chief, who gave a final and binding verdict. The chief, with his council of elders, would undertake an investigation that would bring the matter to a closure. Reconciliation was pivotal after the dispute had been resolved. This promoted co-existence among disputants. A dispute between two different members of the community was directly resolved by the chief. This type of dispute resolution appears to be gradually dying out from our society as the country is becoming more urbanized and complex with more attention geared towards the statutory courts (Adjabeng, 2007).

The emergence of colonialism influenced the social, cultural, economic and political lives of Africans most fundamentally and radically. The values, norms and beliefs entrenched within the African contexts which provided a grounded framework for dispute resolution were severely destabilised and undermined (Deng & Zartman, 2011). With the advent of colonialism in Ghana, the modes of settling disputes in Ghana have seen modifications leading to the adopting of an adversarial system of settling cases (Merryman & Pérez-Perdomo, 2007). The Chief Justice indirectly performs the role of the paramount chiefs in the typical traditional African system as stated above. There are multiple courts with different functions under the orthodox system. In descending order are the Supreme Court, Appeal Court, High Court, Circuit Court, and Magistrate or District Court. The functions of these courts are mixed to adjudicate both criminal and civil cases in a fair and transparent manner (Ghana Judicial Service, 2016).

Over time, this conventional method of litigation has become not only too expensive but slow due to piled cases. For instance, a huge number of cases were pending in the respective years: in 2012/13, 96,721 cases were pending, 2013/14 had 102,251 cases pending, 2014/2015 had 98,462 cases pending, while 2015/2016 had 84,786 cases pending in Ghana (Judicial Service Report, 12-16). In the Ashanti Region alone, the years 2012/13 and 2103/14 had a settlement rate of 100 percent and 65 percent respectively. However, 2014/15 and 2015/16 also saw a settlement rate of 30 percent and 24 percent respectively. In sum, there currently 382, 220 cases pending in courts as of 2016. Ojeilo (2001) and Adjabeng (2007) echo that the pending of court cases are the results of regular adjournments of cases without a verdict and the expensive legal fees which have become bottlenecks in accessing justice. These challenges have led to thoughts aimed at relieving this legal system of the overburden cases, as well as facilitating access to justice. Hence, the introduction of the Court-Connected Alternative Dispute Resolution (CCADR) (Ojeilo, 2001; Yin, 2014).

Mediation under the CCADR program has over the years gained ground in the judicial service of Ghana (Adjabeng, 2007). It is, currently, the predominant form of CCADR practised in Ghana (CCADR Practitioner Guide, 2017). It was incorporated into the mainstream justice system with the primary aim of reducing overloaded court dockets, expediting the settlement of cases and making the legal process affordable (Chagadama, 2014; Adjabeng, 2007; Ojielo, 2001). The greatest and most probable argument for CCADR, perhaps, lies in its advantages over the orthodox court system (Ojielo, 2001). The parties, with the assistance of a mediator, are able to resolve their disputes, although not always successful. CCADR focuses on civil claims, for example, monetary claims recovery, minor assault maintenance, offensive conduct, landlord and tenant disagreement and defamation. (Ghana Judicial Service Report, 2016).

According to the Ghana Judicial Service Report (2008), more than 60 district courts in Ghana have initiated mediation since 2003. From 2003-2007, there were 493 settled mediated cases out of 1,452 representing a 34 percent settlement rate (Judicial Service Report 2003-7). Again, data available show a settlement rate of 47 percent of cases mediated in lower courts in Accra in 2008 (Judicial Service's report of Ghana, 2008). In 2016, a total of 1181 cases were referred to ADR for mediation, out of which 391 cases were settled representing 44 percent. All these serve as reference points of how mediation has been predominantly practiced in Ghana.

Mediation is an important component of dispute resolution. Over the years, statistics available suggest that the court system is over-burdened with cases. The Judicial Service Report (2012-16) shows that there are 382,220 cases pending in Ghana courts. This is not to say that mediation as a form of ADR has not made any success. The Table below shows the number of cases pending in Ghana Judicial Service that have been transferred to CCADR for mediation.

Table 1. Summary of ADR Cases from 2012-2016 In Ghana

Year	Total Cases Pending in Courts	Cases Referred to CCADR for Mediation	Cases Mediated	Mediation Cases Pending/ Returned to Court
2012/13	96,721	3,247	1,042 (32%)	2,205 (68%)
2013/14	102,251	5,789	2,355 (41%)	3,434 (59%)
2014/15	98,462	4,683	2, 001 (42%)	2,682 (58%)
2015/16	84,786	1,181	391 (33%)	790 (67%)
Total	382,220	14, 900	5789(38%)	9111 (62%)

Source: Ghana Judicial Service Report from 2012-2016

In Table 1, cases referred to CCADR for mediation from 2012-2016 were 14,900, and out of these cases, 5,789 were successfully resolved to represent 38 percent. The total number of mediated cases pending was 9,111 representing 62 percent. Though there seems to be an improvement in terms of the decrease in pending cases, the number of pending cases leaves much to be desired. Meanwhile, mediation under the CCADR program is known to be faster and affordable in order to reduce the overloaded court dockets (Nolan- Haley, 2014; Welsh, 2004).

The complementary (CCADR) legal system which was instituted primarily to reduce overloaded court dockets has been bedevilled with challenges. It is against this backdrop that this chapter seeks to tease out the challenges confronting mediation as a means of the CCADR approach. This paper will tease out the issues resulting in the backlog of CCADR cases and the challenges that have characterised the service in order to come out with findings and recommendations to inform policy-making.

The objective of this chapter is to examine the extent to which CCADR has been able to achieve the desired result in the Ashanti Region.

LITERATURE REVIEW

Mediation: A Distinction between Process and Content

Many proponents define the mediation system in terms of a process or content distinction. Mediators are known to control the process of mediation, while the parties are responsible for the content and substantive outcome. As Koh (2005) pointed out, the word 'neutral' is used in relation to the outcome, rather than the process of mediation. Mackie, Miles & Marsh (1995) also emphasized that it is the process of mediation that is structured and influenced by the intervention of the mediator. The process intervention is said to be compatible with parties' autonomy to make their own choices and control their disputes rather than having a professional telling them. However, there are many other dispute resolution processes in which the parties can request a professional to intervene in the substantive content of their dispute (Koh, 2005).

Process intervention empowers parties by enforcing their abilities to control matters of content (Mackie, Miles & Marsh, 1995). Decisions are more likely to endure over time if the parties have resumed the responsibility of making them. Process only interventions by mediators also promote quality decisions in that the parties are the best-informed persons to define their real interests and issues (Koh, 2005). Allowing the parties to have control over matters of content and also enables them to develop their sense of 'fairness', which is defined by their satisfaction with the results (Alexander, 2002). The process/content is a useful starting point for understanding and explaining the mediation system.

The Uses of Mediation

Mediation can serve a number of functions, for example, is an educational tool. It can, directly and indirectly, train the parties in a method and style of decision-making that can be used in the future (Susskind & Ozawa, 1984). This role can be very important in an environment where conflict is common and the parties' general dispute resolution skills are limited (Andrew, 2003). Where successful, it can develop the parties' confidence in managing their own affairs. There have also been suggestions that one goal of mediation is the growth of the parties. According to Andrew (2003) this approach sees mediation as a transformation process during which the parties develop empowerment and recognition. Mediation also has the potential managerial tool where management comes to rest increasingly on consent rather than an authority (Kanter, 1979). Some parties use mediation as a filtering mechanism in the litigation process thus evaluating the other side's facts, arguments and witnesses in order to assess how to proceed with the matter (Susskind & Ozawa, 1984).

Mediation can also be used for the sole purpose of defining which issues are to be discussed and which are not to be discussed. Austin and Vancouver (1996) refers to this process as 'scoping' and is an appropriate role for mediation in some planning and environmental dispute in which the problem has adequately been defined, it can be referred to other methods of dispute resolution, such as litigation or a public enquiry (Bacow & Wheeler, 2013). Scoping has the advantage of allowing the parties to define the problem with the knowledge that there will be no pressure at this stage to compromise their interests (Bacow & Wheeler, 2013). The mediation may involve the parties setting the outer boundaries of the outcome, regardless of the decision of an external body such as a court (Woo, 1999). This affirms the idea of initiation as part of the mediation processes in which the parties define the basis and grounds for the dispute (Godongs, 2006). Mediation provides the platform to identify the root of the dispute to help the neutral (mediator) facilitates the mediation process (Susskind & Ozawa, 1984).

According to Treacy (1995), mediation can be used in the process of contract formation. Negotiating parties may use a mediator to assist in establishing a positive climate, identifying interests and priorities, improving communications, managing destructive emotions, brainstorming options, formulating proposals, narrowing options and noting and recording agreements (Treacy, 1995). Here mediation is used not to assist in settling disputes, but to manage procedures during the negotiations; to resolve the terms of a contract and to provide ways of dealing with disputes should they arise during the future contractual relationship between parties. The mediator acts as a facilitator, by assisting all parties, not any one party as Johnsen (2011) referred to as 'transactional mediation'.

Transactional mediation has been used in many negotiations. For instance, transactional mediation was used to formalise a joint venture between General Motors and Toyota to establish a motor vehicle manufacturing plant in California. Albeit the agreement in principle of both parties, there were two main obstacles, being the opposition from the Workers' Union and Toyota requirement that it should have the freedom to run the plant as it saw fit. A former United State Secretary of Labour was appointed as a settlement mediator and achieved a resolution of all obstacles (Crocker, Hampson & Aall, 2005).

Mediation can be used where a public authority is required to determine policy, standards or procedures in rules and regulations. Here, the process serves to allow affected parties specifically, and interested members of the public generally, to participate in and influence the policy-making process (Crocker, Hampson & Aall, 2005). The mediation may produce the final policy, or its decisions may be referred to a government body with the ultimate authority to draft the regulations. In some countries such as Britain and Australia environmental, health and safety standards are developed through the mediation process. Beierle (2010) referred to this process as regulatory negotiations or neg-reg. This can also be referred to as policy-making mediation.

Mediation can be used to manage disputes even where it is known that the dispute will continue (Zartman, 2007). Here, dispute refers to the on-going series of misunderstanding with a severe intensity which has occurred over an extended period. Mediation can serve to contain the dispute by establishing appropriate rules, structures and processes for parties. Bercovitch and Foulkes (2012) argued that to regulate the parties' conduct in the short term, mediation can provide an opportunity for the disputes to be dealt with through other methods in the long term. For instance, an example of such a situation would be parenting between warring former spouses where there are irreconcilable differences in religion and culture. Mediation can assist the parties to manage these differences in practical ways without needing to resolve the value differences between them.

Both transactional mediation and policy-making mediation (Johnson, 2011; Susskind and Ozawa, 1984) involve elements of dispute prevention. More generally, mediation can be used to assist parties to anticipate problems, grievances and difficulties and to plan processes for dealing with them when they arise.

Empirical Studies on Alternative Dispute Resolution

In the empirical writings of Affrifah (2015) on "ADR as a tool for conflict resolution in Africa - Ghana", it was found out that lack of infrastructure, inadequate training and lack of funding impeded the progress of ADR in Ghana. Similarly, Abdul-Rafiu's (2015) studied on "Institution and Challenges of ADR in West Africa", using Ghana as a case study, asserted that lack of legislative instrument, inadequate training, lack of funding and the competing nature of other agencies such as DOVVSU, rent control, etc. undermined the ADR mechanism and these have narrowed the effectiveness of ADR. Karuiki (2014) also discovered that negative attitudes from "modernised" Africans have broken down the close social ties and social capital between family and kinsmen. Again, there are underlying principles that undergird the dispute resolution by elders in that the process was based on socio-cultural values, norms and beliefs that are understood and accepted by the people. Moreover, pre-colonialism and post-colonialism have influenced the typical traditional methods of resolving a dispute and this has disrupted the traditional dispute resolution system.

In Zimbabwe, Chagadama (2014) studied on "A critical examination of the use of mediation as a tool for the realisation of women's access to justice in property cases in the legal aid sector in Zimbabwe" also purported that ADR serves as convenient alternatives for women to access their rights and justice. This has long-run positive effects of empowering and capturing their self-actual needs. The study identified a lack of uniformities (standardized guidelines) that contributed to the failure of mediation and alluded to some sort of discrepancies in conducting mediation sessions. In addition, the study again revealed that some mediators persuaded and influenced the mediation process. They incorporated their cultural beliefs and other social perspectives in conducting the mediation sessions and also how the disputants' backgrounds, beliefs and customs affected the mediation outcome. In the empirical findings of Nolan-Haley and Annor-Ohene (2014), their study on *Procedural Justice Beyond Borders: Mediation in Ghana* revealed how disputants have decided to use the mediation process in reaching an agreement to their disputes. The study considered 54 participants; 31 from Sunyani (Brong-Ahafo Region) and 23 from Accra (Greater Accra Region). In the study, 9 percent of the total participants claimed to have been represented by an attorney during the mediation sessions and 91 percent of them did have an attorney to represent them. This was consistent with the findings of the general civil litigants in the United State (American Bar Association, 2006). The 9 percent of the disputants who were represented by the attorney claimed to be very satisfied with the outcome whereas 58 percent of the 91 percent of the disputants claimed to be satisfied whilst 33 percent also claimed to be unsatisfied with the outcome. When asked about their feelings for favouring mediation, they came out clearly that due to the neutrality of the process especially the mediator, affordability, cost-effectiveness and the ability to talk freely during the process made them opted for the process. However, some participants expressed their displeasure with the process for the reasons being that they were not allowed to invite other people who also knew about the case during the mediation session and again their attorney did not get enough time to speak as they expected.

These empirical findings have revealed and made important contributions to the study of mediation as an ADR approach. However, their findings are not exhaustive. My thesis will provide a fresh insight into the issues of mediation and more importantly, from the standpoint of Max Weber's ideal type bureaucracy theory.

Overview of the ADR Act in Ghana

The permissible authorization for Court-Connected ADR practice in Ghana is found in Sections 72 and 73 of the Courts' Act 1993 (Act 459). The act was modified as an Order 58 Rule 4 of the High Court Civil Procedure Rules 2004 C.1 47 as a legal instrument. The court-connected ADR is provided as a legal instrument under section 73 of the Courts Act 1993 (Act 459). It requires any Ghanaian court exercising criminal authority to promote reconciliation, encourage and facilitate defrayal of disputes in a harmonious manner. The dispute among disputants is required first to be filed at the court, after which the disputing parties, with the aid of the judges, may assent to refer their matter to ADR to attempt a resolution. Where an agreement is reached, the terms of the agreement become an order of the court. However, if a solution is not found, the dispute goes to trial. Besides, the Courts Act, the ADR concept in Ghana was given a further boost by the passage of an ADR Act by Ghana's Parliament in 2010 after more than a decade of deliberations and consultations with the various stakeholders. Uwazie (2011) noted that the ADR Act is the most comprehensive legislative instrument in Africa.

The ADR Act sets out a comprehensive legal framework for ADR practice. The provisions in the Act on arbitration and the other methods of ADR are based on internationally recognized principles such as autonomy of the arbitration agreement and the supremacy of the arbitral agreement. It, however, pushes the boundaries of current standards of international arbitration by granting the appointing authority an enhanced role in the process. Significantly, the Act breaks new grounds by first legislating on customary arbitration and secondly by granting the settlement from mediation proceedings an enhanced status equal to an arbitral award. In her view, the Act is a comprehensive, modern and forward-looking piece of information and it is worthy of emulation within sub-Saharan Africa. Essentially the Act also makes provision for an ADR Fund and a national ADR Centre. Again, the Act empowers the Magistrate's Courts to adjudicate criminal matters covering the following kinds of cases: monetary claims for recovery, minor assault, family maintenance claims, offensive conduct, landlord/tenant disputes, defamation, the threat of harm or damage to property, unlawful entry and minor land disputes. Furthermore, Section 1 of the Act, sets out the applicability of the Act, and states clearly that the Act applies to all matters except for issues relating to the national or public interest; the environment; enforcement and interpretation of the Constitution; and any other matter that by law cannot be settled by an alternative dispute resolution.

THEORETICAL UNDERPINNING

Rational-Legal Framework

Stemming from Weber's rational-legal authority, there are two significant components, thus, the promulgation of law/rules obeyed by citizens as legitimate and the officialdom of bureaucrats enforcing enacted laws/rules to exact compliance. To this end, the ADR is an emergent arm of the state under the ADR Act (2010) to provide access to justice and promote domestic and foreign direct investment. The legal mandate for Court-Connected ADR practice in Ghana is found in Sections 72 and 73 of the Courts' Act 1993 (Act 459) as amended and Order 58 Rule 4 of the High Court Civil Procedure Rules 2004 C.1 47. The court-connected ADR is provided under section 73 of the Courts Act 1993 (Act 459) and requires any Ghanaian courts exercising criminal jurisdiction to promote reconciliation, encourage and facilitate a settlement in an amicable manner but only in civil cases and misdemeanors (ADR Practitioner Guide,

2017). The dispute in question is required first to be filed at the court, after which the disputing parties may consent to refer their matter to ADR to attempt a resolution.

Where an agreement is reached, the terms of the agreement become an order of the court (Sarkodie, 2011). However, if a solution is not found, the dispute goes to trial (Abdul-Rafiu, 2015; Bukari, 2013). Apart from the Courts Act, the ADR concept in Ghana was given a further boost by the passage of an ADR Act by Ghana's Parliament in 2010 after more than a decade of deliberations and consultations with the various stakeholders. Affrifah (2015) asserted that the ADR Act 798 is the most comprehensive ADR legislation of its kind in Africa.' This Act sets out a comprehensive legal framework for ADR practice. The new Act is comprehensive, modern and forward-looking and it is worthy of emulation in Ghana. Essentially the Act also makes provision for an ADR Fund and a national ADR Centre.

Division of Labour

The ideal type of bureaucracy theory posits that every bureaucratic institution must be premised on the division of labour. The CCADR is divided between vertical and horizontal lines for the division of work and functional specialization. Every employee in the institution has a well-defined power and authority, based upon the employee's specialization and expertise. Within the operations of CCADR, there are various roles assigned to the members and the key participants of the organization. The key participants in the court-connected ADR are the national ADR coordinator, the Regional ADR coordinators, ADR officers, the neutrals (mediators) and lawyers. These bureaucrats are appointed by the Chief Justice based on their qualifications and expertise. Their roles are assigned based on their expertise and technical know-how on which they were employed. The roles of the participants are detailed as follows. The responsibility of the national coordinator is to be in charge of the implementation and management of the day-to-day activities of the ADR directorate. He/she is responsible for the general administrative requirements needed to sustain a vibrant CCADR scheme.

The Regional ADR coordinator is the person designated by the judicial service of Ghana to be in charge of the ADR program and activities at the Regional level. The coordinator coordinates activities regarding ADR in the Region and ensures that court registrars submit ADR returns to the National ADR directorate at the end of each month.

The ADR officer is someone appointed by the judicial service to facilitate the ADR processes at the court registry. He/she arranges a meeting with the disputants and chooses venues and times for the mediation process. He is assigned to provide orientation for the disputants prior to the mediation session

The mediator is the neutral third person who assists the disputants to resolve their dispute. He or she serves as an intervener obliged to be impartial about the parties to the dispute. Also, mediators facilitate and promote constructive communication between the parties and responsible to assist the parties in reaching a mutually acceptable settlement and analyses the disputes and designs appropriate interventions. It is required of the neutral to separate interests from positions and to generate options for possible settlement (ADR Practitioner Guide, 2017).

A lawyer is a qualified person employed by the CCADR to guide clients in the mediation process. He/she plays a key role in the presentation and conducts of their client's case and participates in drafting the agreements prepared by the mediator and ensures that the agreements are rigorous and legally binding. The roles assigned to the various compartments are agglomerated in ensuring the smooth operations of the CCADR.

Formal Rules and Regulation

Again, the ideal type bureaucracy theory talks about strict rules and regulations. This organization functions within a framework of fixed rules and regulations. An employee, thus, a bureaucrat, has to function within this framework of rules and regulations. ADR functions with specific procedures laid down by the organization. For instance, the neutral or an employee is not liable for any act or omission in the discharge of duty unless the act or omission complained of is in bad faith or is a criminal act (ADR Act, 2010). The mediator must abide by the rules of natural justice which include giving each party an equal opportunity to present his or her case and abstain from personal bias, peculiar bias and official bias (ADR Practitioner Guide, 2017).

Value Neutrality of Mediators

Another tenet of the theory posits the impersonal approach. The interrelationship between and amongst mediators and disputants should be devoid of biases, conflict of interest and discrimination to ensure fair and transparent agreement to a matter at hand. The value-neutrality of mediators must encompass confidentiality, independence, self-determination and voluntariness. Disputants resort to a mediator because of their professionalism and the trust the CCADR has in them. The principle of neutrality seeks to promote the ideals of justice and fairness of the mediator on all issues brought to the negotiation table. This means that the mediator must carry his or her duties free from any external influence which is likely to affect the outcome of the dispute.

The ideal type bureaucracy theory emphasizes the evaluation of the criterion set for CCADR against the realities of its performances. CCADR was set primarily to expedite the settlement of cases, reduce overloaded court dockets and make the process affordable. These are the ideal types of the mechanism which were set to help facilitate justice. However, the institution that was set to help resolve the challenges embedded in the orthodox system is still faced with the same challenges. If indeed these are the goals ADR is set to achieve, what is, therefore, the reality of its performance? This theory, therefore, provided an insight into the issues and highlighted the nitty-gritty embedded within the frameworks of mediation under the CCADR program in order to tease out the challenges.

METHODOLOGY

Research Design

The study adopted a qualitative research design. Qualitative research design goes hand in hand with the qualitative research approach. In dealing with participants' experiences encountered at the CCADR, their experiences were best narrated only through a qualitative approach by the use of an in-depth interview. The approach detailed a comprehensive capturing of their responses, thereby making it easier for the researcher to understand the responses provided by the participants (Grbich, 2012). Therefore the type of questions asked during the process started with "Why", What and "How" (Grbich, 2012) and by enabling participants to tell their stories.

Sampling Techniques and Number of Participants

The purposive sampling technique was used to select the CCADR practitioners, thus, mediators, lawyers, ADR officers (registrars) and ADR coordinators while accidental sampling was used to select the disputants from the various affiliated courts of the CCADR in the Ashanti Region. The CCADR practitioners were selected because of their experience, technical know-how and specializations working with the CCADR for the past six years. The details and contacts of disputants who had engaged in the mediation process over the years were not provided by the CCADR secretariat since it was a breach of their ethical conduct. This situation called for an accidental sampling technique. Invariably, disputants were engaged right after their last sessions of the mediation process. There were 33 participants for the study. This is in line with the views of some scholars such as Bryman (2012) as well as Guest, Bunce and Johnson (2006) share the view that the participant could be adjusted in the course of data collection bearing in mind the concept of saturation and adequacy in qualitative data collection. Therefore, 33 participants used for the study were based on saturation and adequacy.

The research participants included mediators, ADR coordinators, ADR officers, lawyers and disputants. The mediators were included in the study because they serve as the interveners and handle issues during the mediation process. They are resourceful individuals with a lot of experience that can help inform the objective of the study. The lawyers assist their clients in the process hence their views can be ascertained. The ADR coordinator in this case oversees the overall process of operation of the secretariat. Also, ADR officers are those who assigned cases to their respective mediators. Again, they keep records of information of the parties therefore soliciting their views on mediation. The disputants are those who have had encounters with ADR.

The data for the study were collected from both primary and secondary sources. Primary data was obtained directly from participants by the use of In-depth Interviews (IDI) guide. The aim of collecting data through this means was to obtain first-hand information about the issues under study (Yin, 2018; 2021). The secondary data was collected from publications, websites of the Ghana Judicial Service Report and news reports. The secondary data helped to supplement the primary data.

Data Collection Instrument and Procedure

An in-depth interview guide was used as an instrument to obtain information from the participants. The in-depth interview guide was an appropriate technique since it allowed participants the time and scope to narrate their opinions, views and experiences on mediation for which the questionnaire could not provide such data. This allowed the researcher to get closer to the participants to know their interpretations and meanings of their experiences they had encountered.

The instrument and a copy of the proposal were requested by the judicial board and reviewed for six working days at their outfit. We were called by the board and were introduced to the various staff. Though the guide was written in the English language however, most of the interactions were done in Twi (the widely spoken local language in the area). A voice recorder was used to record conversations and discussions with participants. This helped to recollect the discussion that ensued between the researcher and the participants. The participants' consent was sought before the recordings were done.

The responses from the participants were recorded on tapes with a recorder and transcribed. The relevant qualitative information was drawn from them. This is because qualitative data involves organizing data, breaking them into manageable units, synthesizing them, searching for patterns, discovering what is useful and deciding what to tell to your readers (Tesch, 2013). Thematic analysis was the main tool used for the analysis of the narratives because language and practices thematically reinforce each other in a reciprocal process and one cannot exist without the other (Guest, MacQueen, & Namey, 2011). In view of this, all the interviews conducted were fully transcribed verbatim to English. The data were then coded after trends were identified based on the emerging themes according to the research objectives. Although more data were gathered, the study made use of the relevant and informative transcripts to the study. Whereas the ample data remained helped in shaping our overall analysis. These remaining data would be useful as a springboard for additional research. Colour coding was used assigning Red, Yellow and Green to the themes respectively.

Ethical issues were considered. The participants were assured of their privacy, confidentiality and anonymity. Informed consent was sought before the participants were interviewed.

CHALLENGES CONFRONTING MEDIATION AS A CCADR

The study aimed to examine the extent to which the CCADR has performed since its inception with regard to its objectives. In order to ascertain this, participants were asked about the challenges they faced at the mediation session and the challenges facing the institution.

Financial Constraints

According to Moss, Pettersson, Gelander, and Van de Walle (2006), institutional funding over the years has become pertinent. The CCADR in Ashanti Region faces some financial difficulties. The study found out that CCADR was funded and supported by the benign gesture of the Danish International Development Agency (DANIDA) and some other agencies such as the German International Corporation (GIC) and United Nations Development Program (UNDP) at the beginning of its establishment. The Judicial Service of Ghana does not support the CCADR secretariat with any funding. This makes it difficult for the Secretariat to pay their mediators and train them as well. The essence of funding for the secretariat is required to frequently train their mediators and to run sensitization programs to educate the public on the essence of its existence. Some participants expressed their concerns on the aforementioned matter, as indicated below:

In the case of DANIDA funding, it was a contract that lasted for ten years. Within the contract, I had the opportunity to travel overseas for training and to attend some conferences. And after the end of the contract, financing the program has become a challenge. We find it so hard to reach sponsorships to train our mediators and even after training them, paying for their allowances becomes a headache. (A Participant, 39 years; March 28, 2018)

Delay in payments of allowances does not motivate most of the mediators in settling cases. The delays in salaries render them unproductive. This has caused most delays in settling disputes as the number of cases referred to CCADR for mediation far exceeds the number of mediators available. In the course of the study, it came to light that mediators were paid an amount of Gh20 cedis for transport and Gh10 cedis per sitting on every case. These were set to motivate them to mediate as many cases as they can because it is believed that the more cases you mediate the more allowances you earn. Meanwhile, these allowances were either not paid or even took a long time to pay.

Another mediator lamented:

First of all the allowances are meager and they are not even paid. Can you believe that for about five years now I have not received any allowance but yet I have to incur transport cost and feeding anytime I have to come to the office? I incur much more cost than my expected allowance. Again, there is nothing like a welfare policy for us which means I risk my life and earn nothing. In fact there is no motivation. Something must be done about it if they want this program to function well. (A mediator aged 52; May 9, 2018)

This comment corroborates the works of Affrifah (2015) and Abdul-Rafiu (2015) that assert that inadequate funding impedes the very core progress of ADR programs in Ghana. Dual-Agyeman (2012) also posited that in order for CCADR to function as expected there must be enough funding to ensure the smooth running of the program so that the objectives for setting for ADR could be achieved. Affrifah (2015) further espoused that without the needed funding, the need to expand the program to all magistrate courts would not be materialized. Inadequate funding is a hindrance to the provision of the needed infrastructure for the effective functioning of CCADR in Ghana. In light of this, the CCADR secretariat finds it difficult and challenging to fulfil its mandatory roles as expected. To effectively implement CCADR in all the district courts, mediators and the other paralegal staff would have to be provided with the needed structures in all districts to make them fully functional. Vehemently, the ideal type bureaucracy theory failed to postulate the essence of motivation for bureaucrats. The financial aspect of every bureaucratic organisation is to cater for the needs of bureaucrats in this regard. Financial expenses such as payment of salaries and allowances need to be provided for maximum productivity.

Administrative and Logistic Constraints

For any effective CCADR system, there must be an efficient administrative establishment to oversee the day-to-day activities of the secretariat. The administrative system should be structured in a way that can seem flexible to the satisfying interests of both the staff and the public users. The Ashanti Region CCADR secretariat is headed by the ADR coordinator who ensures that administrative issues are well managed in a perfective manner. In the study, it was brought to light that the secretariat faces some administrative hurdles in its operations. These crises diminish the impetus of successful administrative work since most of the tasks set could not be achieved and these, in turn, renders the secretariat fruitless.

During the data collection process, some participants aggrieved that the secretariat lacks a venue to hold mediation sessions. In the quest of getting a dispute resolved, the mediation session must be organised and a venue must be arranged by both the disputants and the mediator at their convenient time and date as highlighted in the ADR Act (2010). This seems pleasant and feasible on paper but does not reflect the actual reality on the grounds. At the Ashanti Regional ADR secretariat, searching for a venue to mediate cases has been a challenge in getting the work done. In other CCADR affiliated courts in the Ashanti Region, mediation cases compete with other cases at the tribunal courts for a venue. The time and day scheduled for the mediation session conflicts with other cases at the tribunal courts. This leads to regular adjournments of cases and which further leads to the piled up of cases at their outfit as reflected in the ADR *data. Below is a participants' assertion;*

Searching for venues to resolve cases has been a challenge. At a point in time, the disputants and I agreed to mediate a case at a restaurant since the venue I booked was occupied by a magistrate at the same time. The environment was not conducive for such a purpose but that was the only place I could think of because the case had been adjourned for the third time and we needed to settle it within time. (A mediator aged, 45 years; May 11, 2018).

Meanwhile, mediation sessions are to be handled in a room so that the disputants will feel free and be comfortable to discuss their issues (ADR Act, 2010). Mediation outside the required venue contradicts the rules and regulations guiding the CCADR program. In spite of this, a disputant lamented;

We scheduled a day, time and venue with the mediator to resolve our dispute. When we reported at the premise, the mediator told us that there was a court session undergoing so we needed to wait. We waited for hours and still could not get to the venue. The mediator agreed with us to adjourn the case to the following week. We agreed and reported on the scheduled day and yet faced the same problem and the case was adjourned again. We nearly lost trust in CCADR and decided to move the case to the court. (A disputant aged, 31; April 24, 2018)

This commentary hammers on the fact that some affiliated CCADR lack venues for mediation sessions and that some cases are compelled to be sent back to court for litigation. Mediation is believed to be faster and therefore cases brought before CCADR should not delay. The regular adjournment of cases due to lack of venues resulted in the poor performance of the CCADR.

Inadequacy of Personnel and Inefficiency of Some Mediators

The CCADR secretariat in the Ashanti Region is known to be understaffed according to the study. The various departments at the secretariat require people to occupy them. These people must be experts in their field of work to ensure the efficiency of the CCADR secretariat. As the Ideal type theory suggests, for every organization to achieve its efficiency, the organization such as the CCADR secretariat must be divided between vertical and horizontal lines for the division of work and functional specialization. Inadequate staff is likely to pose inefficiency since the workload cannot be carried out successfully by the few staff available. This has become worrisome to the secretariat in pursuance of its mandatory roles. In view of this a participant said;

We have a very good secretariat and we do not seem to have the personnel needed. We do not have a secretary who will be recording the day-to-day activities of the operations in the secretariat. We are only two administrators in this secretariat and this makes it difficult for us here. Again, there is no messenger nor clerk and this shows how unserious we are as a secretariat. All these slow down the progress of our operations. (A participant aged, 39; April 16, 2018)

It is required of the secretariat to employ adequate and competent staff to ensure the productivity of the CCADR program. The absence of an employer may decline the progress of the secretariat. As indicated by Weber (1946), the inefficiencies of some mediators stem to explain the unproductiveness of their role set. As already argued, various portfolios require various functions to perform. In situations where one role is tilted to failure, it declines the entire operations of others. The study found out that there were few mediators to mediate the chunk of cases referred from the court. Mediators are seen to be the pivot in terms of dispute resolution as they control the process of mediation (Boulle & Nesic, 2001). In situations where they fail to carry out their tasks, cases are expected to delay. In the study, it was found out that some participants opined that some mediators are retirees and aged above 60 years and they do not perform their mandatory roles as expected of them. With regards to this, a mediator alluded;

I believe this job is not meant for old men and retirees. They do not perform as expected and their performances delay some cases and exceed the required days (30 days). These retirees complain mostly about their health and spend many working hours at the hospital. These leave chunk cases on us and make it difficult for us to deliver (A participant aged, 52; May 9, 2018).

Another mediator added that;

Government work, as they say, should not be carried but rather dragged. With this mind-set how can we progress? Many mediators (with one in my outfit) behave in a way that confirms this unproductive adage. My son looks, I know of this mediator who comes to work twice a week and barely sits at the office and hardly mediates cases. He behaves as if he was recruited to serve the nation on a part-time basis. I have complained about long about his ill attitude towards work. He comes to work twice a week and lives the office exactly at 12 pm and signs out with the reason that he needs to visit the hospital. (A mediator aged 35 years; May 7, 2018)

Meanwhile, the CCADR is already understaffed due to inadequate funds and the few mediators available are not operational in their status. The above assertions are one of the challenges facing the secretariat. These challenges decline the progress and the aims set for the CCADR.

Absence of ADR Officer

Within the fabrics of the ADR Practitioner Guide, it is expected that ADR officers are to be situated at every center to perform important functions at the CCADR program. He or she is expected to arrange meetings with parties and ensures that the consent form is properly completed and signed by both parties. The ADR officer is also intended to organize an orientation to the parties to help them know the nitty-gritty involved in the mediation process before a mediator is assigned. As posited by the ideal type bureaucracy theory, every bureaucrat has specific roles to perform, so in instances where the ADR officer is absent, the work of the mediator is overburdened. This is because he performs significantly different roles and this sometimes creates chaos among the parties and the mediator. In situations like this, certain agreements are not established and prolong the cases brought before the mediators. The absence of an ADR officer causes unbearable behaviours of some disputants who appear before the mediators since the rules and regulations guiding mediation are not well spelled before the commencement. Some disputants behave awkwardly to the point of insulting their opponents in a disruptive manner.

A mediator narrated;

I was mediating a certain case and at the tail end of it the complainant called the defendant 'jullor' (thief) and that brought to the end of the session. The defendant could not tolerate it and that led to a heating exchange of words. The mediation could not continue and the case was sent back to court for trial. (A mediator aged, 39; May 9, 2018).

However, mediation is noted to preserve healthy relationships between parties and restore peace among them (Ojeilo, 2000). This can be materialized when both parties accept the rationale in settling their disputes. In mediation, the primary focus is to encourage the disputants to communicate with each other concerning the dispute. However, in situations where tensions become high, disputants tend to either act more obstinately towards each other or withdraw altogether from the mediation. The lack of orientation on the part of disputants becomes a problem in the mediation sessions. Due to the negligence of the division of labour entrenched in the fabrics of Max Weber's ideal type theory, institutional operations become dysfunctional. The absence of roles set for the ADR officer makes it difficult to settle disputes. This notion should be prudent and must be effected always.

The Biting Effect of Mediation

For mediation to be successful, the disputants must commit to resolving the dispute. Many complainants perceive that mediation creates the avenue to punish their defendants. Meanwhile, mediation under the CCADR is geared towards amicable resolution and not to punish perpetrators. This misconception stems from the fact that disputants are completely uneducated about mediation. This is as a result of the absence of the ADR officer who is mandated to spell out the operations of mediation and its purpose to the disputants. The lack of orientation has caused disputants' poor orientation and misconception of meditation. This causes challenges before, within and after the mediation process for the mediators. Some disputants still do not understand what mediation seeks to offer and expect a punishable outcome for their opponent. In cases such as minor crimes, some complainants always want to see the defendant severely punished and to see the worst of his/her life.

A mediator hinted;

Some people come for mediation with the perception that he/she is going to teach or punish the other opponent a lesson and when the process does not go the way he/she wanted it, they show some sort of displeasure. It will be clearly shown that the body language of that person depicts a different meaning and appreciation. Many disputants did not sign the consent form because they did not get what they wanted. (A mediator aged, 38; May 7, 2018)

Another mediator also said;

Disputants come for mediation with differing minds, especially among complainants. They come for mediation with a fierce attitude and aggrieved nature. Look, all they seek is punishment for their opponents. But they forget that mediation doesn't work like that. It's a win-win affair for both parties. This attitude of theirs is sometimes irritating and it takes a great zeal to control. Most cases are sent back to court for trials. (A participant aged, 52; May 9, 2018).

The misconception and unforgiving nature of people create difficulties in settling the dispute. In situations where disputants are violent and use abusive words, the mediator is expected to intervene as quickly as possible to soothe tension. The mediator can even postpone further proceedings as he or she considers necessary (Shapiro, Drieghe & Brett, 1985). For most times disputants perceive that once a case is mediated the perpetrator must be punished or the victim must be compensated. However, that is not what mediation seeks to achieve. They mostly do not know that mediation sets to resolve disputes and not to sentence perpetrators. This ill perception people have about mediation denounces the aims and values set for it. In such situations, the mediator must determine whether the disputants truly have no commitment to resolve the dispute, or whether they are merely frustrated or puffing about the case. The mediator is expected to send the case back to court for trial when disputants are not willing to comply with the tenets of mediation.

Lack of Value Recognition Among Some Lawyers

Another major challenge that came up in the study was the fact that some lawyers do not value the essence of ADR and view it as a threatening scheme to collapse their legal profession. This stems from the notion amongst most lawyers that frequent referral of cases to mediation might affect their revenue streams. This belief will definitely not allow the survival and flourishing nature of the ADR activities in Ghana. Some of them feel that mediation has come to take away their powers. It is noted that during the traditional litigation processes, most lawyers deliberately prolong cases to fill their pockets because the prolonging of cases leads to higher income (Ojeilo, 2001). The high cost of legal fees is mostly perpetrated by lawyers in terms of transport fees, processing fees and other allowances. In supporting this assertion, it was confirmed by one participant that;

Some lawyers think that mediation does not give them the power to rule over court proceedings. Imagine if they project the tenets of mediation for public consumption, how could they get money? (smiled with the teeth out) to run themselves. They believe mediation is slowing their pace at which they can enrich their financial stands. (A participant aged, 39; April 17, 2018)

I think the authorities in charge of mediation should restructure the activities and operations of CCADR. What will be my possessions (benefits) when I engage in mediation? Why do we work and report on losses instead of gains? As we serve soup, we lick the ladle, but it is not so in mediation. (A lawyer aged, 34; May 9, 2018)

Meanwhile, according to the ADR Practitioner Guide (2010), lawyers who serve as ADR practitioners are required to encourage clients to settle their differences to avoid cost, delays, and to clear the difficulties of traditional litigation (Yin & Seiwoh, 2021). It is the first and foremost duty of a lawyer to protect and represent client interests at mediation sessions. Whenever the facts or the legal situation are unclear, the information provided to the client on the possibility of mediation may have a conflict-averting effect. Invariably, lawyers play a key role in the presentation and conduct of their clients' cases and participate in the drafting of agreements and ensuring that the agreements are accurate and legally binding (consent form).

Non-Neutrality of Some Mediators

One of the challenging issues that came out of the study was the fact that some mediators influenced the outcome of the mediation. Mediators are supposed to be neutral in all spheres of the mediation processes and they should not by any means place their personal interest on a verdict or outcome (ADR Act, 2010). This infringes the codes and conducts set to rule the CCADR program. Some disputants reported that most of the mediators placed their interest first before options were tabled before them. Disputants further expressed their distrust in the mediation processes and vowed not to settle their disputes at the CCADR and would rather prefer the traditional litigation process. Issues regarding biases on the part of mediators are not suitable for the good course of the CCADR program. Mediators are known to control the process of decision making and the essence of neutrality is used in relation to the outcome (Shapiro, 2008). Any personal intervention made by the mediator within the course of the outcome limits the disputants' autonomy to make an informed choice.

There were two fronts that were analyzed to have influenced the outcome of the process; the imposition of the verdict by some mediators and receiving bribes from the disputants. Bribery is known to be a canker in our society that tends to influence a decision with the act of giving out money or gift to favour an individual at the expense of the other. This notion has been reported to find its way into the mainstream CCADR program. This is evident because, many disputants have lodged complaints on the said behaviour perpetrated by some mediators before the commencement of the mediation session. These excerpts were revealed;

As I speak to you now, I can put to you on record that some members in our noble profession unduly receive money from disputants. I have a case on one record that has been evidenced and we are perusing it now. It's hard to flush the bad ones out but with time they can be seen. I only uphold the services of faithful individuals who can report on evidenced-based against some of us. (A participant aged, 39; May 9, 2018)

I am only alleging, there is no smoke without a fire. The mediation process was faithfully on course until I realized a sudden change in focus. I got offended but I knew the power of bribery was at work. The ground suffered because I lacked the evidence to argue my case out, so I left it to God. (A disputant aged, 51; May 11, 2018)

This egregious violation points to the fact that some staff members fail to uphold the duties and responsibilities as officeholders. Although a minority, the corrupt practices of these officeholders undermine the public trust in the ADR as a whole. This setback reduces the rate at which mediation functions and performs. This finding confirms the work of Abdul-Rafiu (2015), Afriffah (2015) and Adjabeng (2007) who established that there are some corruption and ill practices within the CCADR system in Ghana. The CCADR program is believed to be fair and devoid of any personal biases from the neutral third party. Again, the ideal type bureaucracy posits that every bureaucrat must be impartial and carry his or her duties and be free from any external influence such as bribe and any personal influence which is likely to affect the outcome of the dispute.

CONCLUSION

The study made extensive use of the tenets enshrined in Max Weber's ideal type bureaucracy theory in relation to CCADR. The ideal type set for CCADR differs in practice. In reality, the CCADR as a bureaucratic body is deficient in terms of neutrality on a few mediators. Again, the lack of adequate skilled personnel hampers the success of CCADR. However, this is not only peculiar to CCADR but is also prevalent in other institutions. It was also concluded that mediators found it difficult to resolve disputes on time due to the misconception of disputants during the dispute resolution process. This is because disputants did not understand what mediation was set to achieve. More so, there are still perceived corruption practices among mediators in resolving disputes. Lastly, the CCADR struggles to achieve its aim due to financial, administrative and logistical constraints.

RECOMMENDATION

The study recommends that 'the rule of court committee' should propose to the Judicial Service of Ghana to re-strategize their annual budgetary policies to enhance the operations of the CCADR in the Ashanti Region. Again, the CCADR should factor in the appropriate working conditions such as allowances, motivational packages and quick payments of mediators to boost their working force. Moreover, the legal court system should immediately refer cases suitable for mediation at their outfit to avoid delays and chunks of cases at the judicial service to expedite the settlement of cases. This can be deemed feasible if personnel meet every monthly to select cases suitable for CCADR.

REFERENCES

Abdul-Rafiu, A. (2015). *The institution and challenges of alternative dispute resolution (ADR) in West Africa: The Case of Ghana* (Doctoral dissertation). University of Ghana.

Adjabeng, S. M. (2007). *Challenges facing trade unions in modern times. ADR practice guide*. Accra Printing Press.

ADR Practitioner Guide. (2017). Accra, Ghana: Academic Press.

Affrifah, K. K. K. (2015). *Alternative dispute resolution as a tool for conflict resolution in Africa with Ghana as a case study* (Doctoral dissertation). University of Ghana.

Alexander, D. (2002). From civil defense to civil protection–and back again. *Disaster prevention and management. International Journal (Toronto, Ont.)*, *11*(3), 209–213.

American Bar Association, House of Delegates, & Center for Professional Responsibility (American Bar Association). (2006). *Model rules of professional conduct*. American Bar Association.

Andrew, J. S. (2003). Potential application of mediation to land use conflicts in small-scale mining. *Journal of Cleaner Production*, *11*(2), 117–130. doi:10.1016/S0959-6526(02)00032-X

Bacow, L. S., & Wheeler, M. (2013). *Environmental dispute resolution*. Springer Science & Business Media.

Baxter, P., & Jack, S. (2008). Qualitative case study methodology: Study design and implementation for novice researchers. *Qualitative Report*, *13*(4), 544–559.

Bevington, P. R., Robinson, D. K., Blair, J. M., Mallinckrodt, A. J., & McKay, S. (1993). Data reduction and error analysis for the physical sciences. *Computers in Physics*, *7*(4), 415–416. doi:10.1063/1.4823194

Boulle, L. (2005). A history of alternative dispute resolution. *ADR Bulletin*, *7*(7), 3.

Bryman, A. (2001). The nature of qualitative research. *Social Research Methods*, 365-399.

Burton, J. W. (1990). *Conflict: Resolution and prevention* (Vol. 1990). Macmillan.

Chagadama, F. (2014). *A critical examination of the use of mediation as a tool for the realisation of women's access to justice in property cases in the legal aid sector, Zimbabwe* (Doctoral dissertation).

Deng, F. M., & Zartman, I. W. (Eds.). (2011). *Conflict resolution in Africa*. Brookings Institution Press.

Godongs, S. (2006). *Mediation and the mediation process. In Introduction to peace and conflict studies in West Africa: A Reader*. Spectrum Books.

Grbich, C. (2012). *Qualitative data analysis: An introduction*. Sage.

Grimble, R., & Wellard, K. (1997). Stakeholder methodologies in natural resource management: A review of principles, contexts, experiences and opportunities. *Agricultural Systems*, *55*(2), 173–193. doi:10.1016/S0308-521X(97)00006-1

Guest, G., Bunce, A., & Johnson, L. (2006). How many interviews are enough? An experiment with data saturation and variability. *Field Methods*, *18*(1), 59–82. doi:10.1177/1525822X05279903

Johnsen, J. S. (2011). Alternative deal resolution: The facilitated negotiation of transactions. *Windsor Rev. Legal & Soc*, (30), 193.

Kanter, R. M. (1979). Power failure in management circuits. *Classics of Organization Theory*, 342-351.

Kariuki, F. (2015). Conflict resolution by elders in Africa: Successes, challenges and opportunities. *Alternative Dispute Resolution*, *3*(2), 30–53.

Koh, C. P. (2005). *The causes of construction dispute on client organizations* (Doctoral dissertation). Universiti Teknologi Malaysia.

Mackie, K., Miles, D., Marsh, W., & Marsh, W. (1995). *Commercial dispute resolution: An ADR practice guide*. Butterworths.

Merryman, J. H., & Pérez-Perdomo, R. (2007). *The civil law tradition: An introduction to the legal systems of Europe and Latin America*. Stanford University Press.

Moss, T. J., Pettersson Gelander, G., & Van de Walle, N. (2006). *An aid-institutions paradox? A review essay on aid dependency and state building in sub-Saharan Africa*. Academic Press.

Nolan-Haley, J. (2014). Mediation: The best and worst of times. *Cardozo Journal of Conflict Resolution*, *16*, 731.

Ojielo, O. M. (2001). *Alternative dispute resolution (ADR)*. CPA Books.

Rankopo, M. J., & Osei-Hwedie, K. (2011). Globalization and culturally relevant social work: African perspectives on indigenization. *International Social Work*, *54*(1), 137–147. doi:10.1177/0020872810372367

Susskind, L., & Ozawa, C. (1984). Mediated negotiation in the public sector: The planner as mediator. *Journal of Planning Education and Research*, *4*(1), 5–15. doi:10.1177/0739456X8400400103

Tesch, R. (2013). *Qualitative research: Analysis types and software*. Routledge.

Treacy, T. B. (1995). Use of alternative dispute resolution in the construction industry. *Journal of Management Engineering*, *11*(1), 58–63. doi:10.1061/(ASCE)0742-597X(1995)11:1(58)

Uwazie, E. E. (2011). *Alternative dispute resolution in Africa: Preventing conflict and enhancing stability* (Vol. 16). Africa Center for Strategic Studies.

Weber, M. (1946). From Max Weber: Essays in sociology (H. H. Gerth & C. W. Mills, Eds. & Trans.). Academic Press.

Welsh, N. A. (2004). The place of court-connected mediation in a democratic justice system. *No. 2. Cardozo Journal of Conflict Resolution*, *5*, 117. doi:10.2139srn.1726218

Woo, M. Y. (1999). Law and discretion in the contemporary Chinese courts. *Pacific Rim Law & Policy Journal*, *8*, 581.

Yin, E. T. (2018). *Religion as an Organising Principle in Ankaful Maximum Security Prison* (PhD Thesis). University of Cape Coast.

Yin, E. T., Atupare, P. A., Kofie, N., Owusu, L. P., & Botchway, T. P. (2021). Rights and religious belief in maintaining prison social order. *UCC Faculty of Law Journal*, *1*(1), 1–16.

Yin, E. T., & Beamie, M. S. (2021). Costs and delays in accessing justice: A comparative analysis of Ghana and Sierra Leone. In Handbook of Research on Civil Justice. IGI Global.

Yin, E. T., & Black, J. M. (2014). The legal anthropology of marriage in Ghana: Presenting power dynamics through legal arenas. *International Journal of Current Research*, *6*(12), 10696–10704.

Chapter 12
Shielding Members of Parliament Against Court Summons:
Interrogating the Question of Parliamentary Immunity

Mark Asante
Ghana School of Law, Ghana

Thomas Prehi Botchway
University of Education, Winneba, Ghana

ABSTRACT

Immunities, though part of the law of the land, are to a certain extent an exemption from the general law. Certain rights and immunities such as freedom of speech belong primarily to individual members of parliament and exist because the House cannot perform its functions without unimpeded use of the services of its members. Ostensibly, the degree to which members of parliament are immune from legal inquiry may presumably accord them greater probability to abuse their mandate. In general, a court summons is the beginning of a legal case. It signals the issue that needs to be adjudicated. However, the introduction of immunity invalidates some tenets of modern democracy such as a court summons. The authors seek to examine some of the uncertainties and ambiguities that might have arisen out of the court decision in the case Republic v Mahama Ayariga with much consideration of other cases. The chapter provides a thorough picture of the systems of parliamentary immunity and recommends ways of curbing observed challenges with the practice.

DOI: 10.4018/978-1-7998-7898-8.ch012

INTRODUCTION

It is a constitutional right of every Member of Parliament (hereafter MP) of Ghana to enjoy certain immunities as enshrined in the Constitution (Constitution of Ghana, 1992). People generally tend to see parliamentary immunity as a means whereby state officials can put themselves above the law and escape justice. The vision of immunity as an obstacle to the pursuit of justice has sometimes overshadowed the simple fact that MPs need some measure of protection, if they are to carry out their work (United Nations Development Programme, 2006). Immunity protects, in particular, the freedom of expression they require to speak out and empowers the institution of parliament as such. Clearly, only strong parliaments able to count on the unimpeded service of their members will be able to face the challenges of preventing conflict and of strengthening and supporting transitional processes.

An ever interrogated issue within most democratic countries relates to why parliamentary immunity only serves to protect the interests of elected representatives or Members of Parliament rather than the interests of their constituents. Issues of abuse of parliamentary privileges have raised eyebrows and elicited strict criticisms against the subject of immunity at both the level of legal theory and popular political platforms. For instance, an act of an MP suspected of being corrupt or illegal but that is left unexamined by the courts tends to render the justifiability of parliamentary immunity questionable.

Chapter 10, Article 117 of the 1992 Constitution of Ghana states that:

"Civil or criminal process coming from any court or place out of Parliament shall not be served on, or executed in relation to, the Speaker or a member or the Clerk to Parliament while he is on his way to, attending at or returning from, any proceedings of Parliament" (Constitution of Ghana, 1992).

Also, Article 122 of the Constitution states that:

"an act or omission which obstructs or impedes Parliament in the performance of its functions or which obstructs or impedes a member or officer of Parliament in the discharge of his duties, or affronts the dignity of Parliament or which tends either directly or indirectly to produce that result, is contempt of Parliament" (Constitution of Ghana, 1992).

These articles sought to establish non-liability for opinions expressed and votes cast by Members of Parliament in the performance of their duties as well as inviolability of Members of Parliament in criminal matters and hence spell out the conditions thereof. By extension of these articles court summons could constitute contempt of parliament. This compels critical re-examination of the subject of protection for MPs.

Nonetheless, it is not an exaggeration to affirm that Parliaments perform important functions as democratic institutions. These functions widely cover areas of legislation, representation and the oversight of executive government (Constitution of Ghana, 1992, Article 93(2)). Arguably, in order to achieve these objectives and keep the Executive accountable and transparent, Houses of Parliament as a whole and not simply individual MPs possess some privileges, powers and immunities which they enjoy in the performance of their duties. Quite obviously, these privileges are an exception to ordinary law and are intended to allow parliamentarians to perform their duties without fear of intimidation or punishment, and without constraints.

Ostensibly, the degree to which MPs are immune from court or legal inquiry, may presumably accord them greater probability or chances to either advance or abuse their mandated responsibility or function in representative democracy mostly resulting in seeming conflicts between the legislature and the judiciary owing to the fact that those who exercise power are not happy when their power is challenged. Therefore, the discourse on striking the right balance between protecting elected representatives from outside interference and limiting the possibility that they will neglect their democratic purpose often becomes a significant topic of national concern.

In Ghana, for instance, since the inception of the Fourth Republic few elected representatives have appeared before the court of law and were tried for various offences. Thus, MPs are perceived to be above the laws of the land (Botchway, 2018). Their appearance in court amounts to contempt of Parliament as per Article 122. In a recent case, the office of the Special Prosecutor filed a charge sheet in the financial and economic crime division of the High Court where the accused persons (the first one being an MP) stood for various charges. Notwithstanding, there was a ruling on a motion to strike out the charge sheet filed for and on behalf of the first accused person on the basis that the Special Prosecutor (Martin Amidu) is disqualified to hold office by reason of his age and also that the offences are not within the remit or powers of the Special Prosecutor and same cannot be prosecuted by the office (Asante, 2019; Amidu, 2019).

This is a case of the *Republic v Mahama Ayariga & Kendrick Kwesi Marfo*[1]. The fact of the case was that two persons were accused of five criminal charges spanning from fraudulent evasion of customs duties and taxes contrary to section 121(2) of the Customs Act[2], using public office for private benefit contrary to section 179(a) of the Criminal Code[3] dealing in foreign exchange without license contrary to section 3(1) and 29 (1) (a) of the Foreign Exchange Act[4], and transfer of foreign exchange from Ghana through an unauthorized dealer contrary to section 15(3) and 29 (1) (a) of Foreign exchange Act[5].

THE FOCUS OF THE CHAPTER

While MPs are not criminally responsible for their actions as parliamentarians, they are, however, responsible for their actions as private citizens. This lack of criminal immunity is derived from the key tenet of the British Constitution that all are equal before the law. Whereas it is often argued that the partial immunity accorded to MPs by the Constitution is for good reason and any invitation that would obstruct a sitting MP is not acceptable by the 1992 Constitution, the focus of this chapter is to closely examine whether or not it is a violation of the right of the MP to appear in a criminal suit against him with regard to his actions as private citizen. As far as this study is concerned the charges raised are not of primary concern. Instead our focus is on whether an MP should respond to court summons during parliamentary sitting since the privileges and immunities were never intended to place MPs above the laws; neither were they intended to secure an absolute immunity for members in a way that is reminiscent of the dealings of despots and dictators.

Thus, the main objective of this chapter is to look at the extent of how immunity shields MPs against court summons. Specifically, we examine the question of whether or not an MP should respond to court summons during parliamentary sitting; and also analyze the degree to which parliamentary privileges and immunity can result in constitutional crises in Ghana.

We compare a number of cases with the intension of affirming or disagreeing with the decision in the case of *Republic v Mahama Ayariga*[6]. Among the cases compared are *A. v the UK*[7] and *Wilder v*

Qur'an[8]. The chapter consequently contributes to the extant literature by filling the knowledge gap on immunity of MPs.

Immunity as an institution has been the subject of harsh criticism on the level of legal theory, having been called anachronistic, obsolete and contrary to fundamental principles of modern constitutional law (especially the principle of equality). Several acts committed by MPs as private citizens suspected of being corrupt or illegal but that are left unexamined by the courts in modern democracies have greatly waned down the good reasons which gave rise to the introduction of parliamentary immunity into modern constitutions. Arguably, the introduction of immunity as an institution has created a subtle constitutional crisis and thus invalidates the tenets of modern democracy and the principle of equality resulting in a rhetoric interrogation of public integrity (which is defined as the prioritization of public interest over private interest).

The crises further deepen when the debate on justifiability of parliamentary immunity in modern democracy appears not to be in sight. Questions of why the Constitution being the Supreme law of Ghana[9] advocating equality before the law[10] in the doctrines of equity and customary law[11] would grant non-liability and inviolability to MPs and when Article 19(3) states clearly that the trial of a person charged with a criminal offence shall take place in his presence but would exempt an MP during a Parliamentary sitting call for serious scrutiny of Ghana's public policy system.

It is important to indicate that the chapter acknowledges that relatively young democracies usually have certain peculiar challenges that militate against progress (Botchway, 2018a). That notwithstanding, the authors are of the view that after almost three decades of practicing democracy, and given the several efforts that have been made in consolidating Ghana's democracy, some 'questionable' principles and practices that are supported by the 1992 Constitution must be given another look. These include among other things the need to de-couple the office of the Attorney-General and Minister of Justice, the mode of appointing Justices of the Superior Courts of Judicature, and the Parliamentary Immunity (which is the subject this chapter addresses). Indeed the practice of Parliamentary Immunity offers MPs undue advantage as compared to other institutions of state and even the ordinary citizenry. It is therefore the position of the chapter that the provisions of Part IV (Privileges and Immunities) – Articles 115-121 of Chapter Ten of the 1992 Constitution of Ghana deserve to be re-examined to reflect the tenets of modern democratic practices.

With these concerns in mind, this chapter attempts to bring some clarity to the uncertainties and ambiguity that might have arisen out of the Court decision in the case *Republic v Mahama Ayariga*[12]. Considering the nature of the case whether the position of the accused person being a sitting MP who enjoys parliamentary privileges and immunities could affect delivery of justice as far as inviolability of MPs in criminal matters is concerned.

From a practical viewpoint, the chapter is useful to practitioners and students of law as it exposes them to the policy implications of the justifiability of parliamentary privileges and immunity in a modern democracy with weak state institutions without cementing the principle of separation of powers. From a theoretical perspective, the chapter gives access to a theoretical framework that assists in the reexamination of core pillars of democracy, and more specifically, the constitutional provisions that undermine the incipient democratic gains, and thereby sow the seeds of public distrust in democratic governance.

OPERATIONALISATION OF KEY WORDS

Member of Parliament

Parliaments are the institutions through which governments are held accountable to the electorate. Members of Parliament represent voters to a parliament, and act on the basis of formal rules of behavior, including plenary and committee sessions. They are also representatives of political parties, that themselves present programs, pursue collective goal strategies and aim at diminishing inner competition.

Parliamentary Sitting

Parliamentary sitting is the period during which Parliament sits continuously without adjournment. A sitting is a meeting of the House within a session.

Court Summons

Civil procedure in Ghana's High Court involves a number of key steps. These steps are categorized into four stages beginning with pre-trial stage which involves the issue of a Writ of Summons and a Statement of Claim by the plaintiff. A summons also known as a claim form or a court attendance notice (CAN) is a legal document issued by a court or by an administrative agency of government in which the presence of the person is required as witness. However, requests for the arrest or detention of a parliamentarian are issued by the general prosecutor of the competent Court of Appeal.

Parliamentary Privilege and Immunity

Parliamentary immunity is a system in which members of the legislature are granted partial immunity from prosecution in civil cases for slander and libel whilst they are in the House. Members of Parliament may not be sought, prosecuted, judged or imprisoned for actions that they have accomplished within their duties as parliamentarians.

Tracing the Root of Parliamentary Immunity

The Constitution[13] is the supreme law of the Republic of Ghana and for that matter no individual or institution is above it. This Constitution[14] has established a structure for the governance of the country and spelt out the Directive Principles of State Policy. Chapter five (5) of the Constitution[15] guarantees every citizen in Ghana his Fundamental Human Rights (Yin, 2021). Chapter five (5), Article 17 (1) of the same Constitution also guarantees that all persons shall be equal before the law and clause (2) forbid discrimination of any sort against citizens. The Constitution provides that no person is above the law[16] and does not exclude MPs. Nevertheless, the Constitution gives certain limited immunities to Members of Parliament.[17]

Ghana, by joining the Commonwealth of Nations and adopting constitutional democracy has signed into the European constitutional tradition. Parliamentary immunity has its roots in the confrontation between the legislative power for independence and free activity of the House of Commons and the authoritarian executive power represented by the Crown and the House of Lords. The term has first been used by the English to explain the unequal political and legal relationship between the absolute power of the King and the Parliament (Ramshorn, 1841).

Parliamentary Supremacy and Separation of Powers

Emphasis on the legislative supremacy of Parliament as the basic doctrine of constitutional law may cause principles of constitutionalism to be undervalued. The separation of powers found in many modern constitutions is opposed to the concentration of state power in a single person or group, since that is a clear threat to democratic governance. The need for a separation of powers arises not only in political decision-making but also in the legal system, where an independent judiciary is essential if the rule of law is to have any substance (Allan, 2001).

In the words of Lord Mustill:

"Separation of powers is a feature of the peculiarly British conception that Parliament, the executive and the courts have each their distinct and largely exclusive domain. Parliament has a legally unchangeable right to make whatever laws it thinks right. The executive carries out the administration of the country in accordance with the powers conferred on it by law. The courts interpret the laws, and see that they are obeyed" (R v Heome Secretary [1995] ex parte Fire Brigades Union 2 AC 513,567).

Within a system of government based on law, there are legislative, executive and judicial functions to be performed and the primary organs for discharging these functions are respectively the legislature, the executive and the courts. To Henderson (1964), this threefold division of labour, among a legislature, an administrative official and an independent judge, is a necessary condition for the rule of law in modern society and therefore for democratic government itself (Henderson, 1964). It may be argued that essential values of law, liberty and democracy are best protected if the three primary functions of a law-based government are discharged by distinct institutions.

To John Locke,

"It may be too great a temptation to human frailty apt to grasp at power for the same persons who have the power of making laws, to have also in their hands the power to execute them, whereby they may exempt themselves from obedience to the laws they make, and suit the law, both in its making and execution, to their own private advantage" (Locke, 1689).

For this reason, Locke urged that there should exist a legislature to act in the public good when necessary and a separate executive with a continuing existence.

Montesquieu also stated the essence of the doctrine thus:

"When legislative power is united with executive power in a single person or in a single body of the magistracy there is no liberty....Nor is there liberty if the power of judging is not separate from legislative power and from executive power. If it is joined to legislative power, the power over the life and liberty of the citizens would be arbitrary, for the judge would be the legislator. If it were joined to the executive power, the judge could have the force of an oppressor. All would be lost if the same man or the same body of principal men, either of nobles or of the people, exercised these three powers: that of

making the laws, that of executing public resolutions, and that of judging the crimes or the disputes of individuals" (Montesquieu, 1998).

This statement emphasizes that the judicial function should be exercised by a body separate from legislature and executive. Montesquieu did not mean that legislature and executive ought to have no influence or control over the acts of each other, but only that neither should exercise the whole power of the other (Jenings, 2009).

THE RELATIONSHIP BETWEEN THE JUDICIARY AND THE LEGISLATIVE ORGANS OF GOVERNMENT

In other to determine the relationship between the Judiciary and the Executives arms of government, we briefly explore two interrelated questions. Firstly, we seek to explore whether there is any control by the legislature over the judiciary or by the judiciary over the legislature.

With regards to this question, it is important to note that Article 144 (1)[18] states that, The Chief Justice shall be appointed by the President acting in consultation with the Council of State and with the approval of Parliament. Also, Article 114 (2)[19] states that, The Other Supreme Court Justices shall be appointed by the President acting on the advice of the Judicial Council, in consultation with the Council of State and with the approval of Parliament. This then means that, the Legislature plays a key role in the appointment of Judges in the quest for checks and balances.

By statute, judges of the superior courts may be removed by the Crown on an address from both houses, but only once since the Act of settlement has parliament exercised the power of removal (Bradley, 1997). While the courts may examine acts of the executive to ensure that they conform to the law, the doctrine of legislative supremacy denies the courts the power to review the validity of legislation. The judges are under a duty to apply and interpret the laws enacted by Parliament. In one sense, therefore, the courts are constitutionally subordinate to Parliament, but the courts are bound only by Acts of Parliament and not by resolutions of Parliament which may have no legal force. One essential function of the judiciary is to protect the citizen against unlawful acts of government agencies and officials.

Secondly, we ask whether the legislature and the judiciary exercise each other's functions. On this matter, Article 116 of the 1992 Constitution of Ghana provides that;

(1) Subject to the provisions of this article, but without prejudice to the general effect of article 115 of this Constitution, civil or criminal proceedings shall not be instituted against a Member of Parliament in any court or place out of Parliament for any matter or thing brought by him in or before Parliament by petition, bill, motion or otherwise.

(2) Whenever in the opinion of the person presiding in Parliament a statement made by a member is prima facie defamatory of any person, the person presiding shall refer the matter for inquiry to the Parliamentary committee on privileges which shall report its findings to Parliament not later than thirty days after the matter was referred to it.

Each house of Parliament has the power to enforce its own privileges and to punish those who offend against them. This power might in some circumstances lead to a direct conflict with the courts (Bradley,

1997). Owing to the doctrine of precedent, the judicial function of declaring and applying the law has a quasi-legislative effect. But the ability of the judges to create law by their decisions is narrower than the ability of Parliament to legislate since Parliament may readily change established rules of law. However, there is much scope for judicial law-making in relation to individual liberties and the principles of public law. Judicial decisions are important as a source of law on matters where the government is unwilling to ask Parliament to legislate. The executive is slow to propose new measures exposing itself to more effective judicial control. Some judicial decisions directly affect the formal relationship between the courts and Parliament (Ramshorn, 1841).

Obviously, the classification of the powers of government into legislative, executive and judicial powers involves certain conceptual difficulties, especially within a system of government based on law. Therefore, it remains important to distinguish, in constitutional structure, between the primary functions of law-making, law-executing and law-adjudicating. If these distinctions are abandoned, the concept of law itself can scarcely survive. This is so because the value of an independent judiciary would be reduced if essential judicial functions, for example the conduct of civil and criminal trials, were removed from the courts and entrusted to administrative authorities.

THE RULE OF LAW

For many centuries it has been recognized that the possession by the state of coercive powers that may be used to oppress individuals presents a fundamental problem both for legal and political theory. Since the days of Greek philosophers there has been recourse to the notion of law as a primary means of subjecting governmental power to control. Aristotle argued that government by laws was superior to government by men (D' Entreves, 1967). When renaissance and reformation in the 16th century weakened the idea of a universal law, emphasis shifted to the national legal system as an aspect of the sovereignty of the state (Elton, 2010).

A. V. Dicey gave three meanings to the rule of law;

It means the absolute supremacy or predominance of regular law as opposed to the influence of arbitrary power and excludes the existence of arbitrariness, of prerogative, or even of wide discretionary authority on the part of government....; a man may with us be punished for a breach of law, but he can be punished for nothing else (Dicey, 1897, p. 220).

Thus none could be made to suffer penalties except for a distinct breach of law established before the ordinary courts.

Secondly, the rule of law meant: "equality before the law, or the equal subjection of all classes to the ordinary law of the land administered by the ordinary law courts" (Dicey, 1897, p. 220). By this Dicey implied that no one was above the law; that officials like private citizens were under a duty to obey the same law.

Thirdly, the rule of law meant:

that with us the law of the constitution, the rules which in foreign countries naturally form part of a constitutional code are not the source but the consequence of the right of individuals, as defined and enforced by the courts, that in short, the principles of private law have with us been by the action of the courts and Parliament so extended as to determine the position of the Crown and its servants; thus the constitution is the result of the ordinary law of the land (Dicey, 1897, p. 220).

Therefore the rights of the individual were secured not by guarantees set down in a formal document but by the ordinary remedies of private law available against those who unlawfully interfered with his or her liberty, whether they were private citizens or officials.

THE PRIVILEGES OF PARLIAMENT

Parliamentary privilege consists of the rights and immunities which Parliament and their members and officers possess to enable them to carry out their parliamentary functions effectively. Without this protection members would be handicapped in performing their parliamentary duties, and the authority of Parliament itself in confronting the executive and as a forum for expressing the anxieties of citizens would be correspondingly diminished[20].

Parliament privilege provides the necessary framework by which each House and its members can fulfill their duties. The privileges have both external and internal aspects: they protect against outside interference that would erode freedom to conduct Parliamentary proceedings; and they impose duties on its members restraining them from conduct that would abuse their privileged position. Privilege is an important part of the law and custom of Parliament, but aspects of the law are still obscure. It has been developed over centuries by the response of Parliament to changing circumstances outside Parliament, for example the decisions of the courts.

Freedom from Arrest

Article 117 provides that;

Civil or criminal process coming from any court or place out of Parliament shall not be served on, or executed in relation to, the Speaker or member of the Clerk to Parliament while he is on his way to, attending at or returning from, any proceedings of Parliament (Constitution of Ghana, 1992).

This ancient privilege was developed to enable members to attend meetings of the House. It protects a member from arrest in connection with civil proceedings for the customary period from 40 days before to 40 days after a session of Parliament. But MPs have no privilege from arrest in connection with criminal proceedings (Erskine, 2019). Members have no general immunity from having civil actions brought against them but they retain minor privileges in regard to civil litigation. A subpoena addressed to a member to give evidence in a civil court probably cannot be enforced by the High Court while the House is in session, but the House may grant a member leave of absence to attend as a witness. Members are not protected against bankruptcy proceedings, and are no longer exempt from jury service[21].

Freedom of Speech

Freedom of speech is today the most substantial privilege of the House. Its essence is that no penal or coercive action should be taken against members for what is said or done in Parliament. The main effect of this is that no member may be made liable in the courts for words spoken in the course of parliamentary proceedings. Thus members may speak in the House knowing that they are immune from the law of defamation[22].

The protection of members for words spoken extends to criminal as well as civil liability. Thus, disclosures in Parliament may not be made the subject of prosecution under the Official Secrets Acts although the MP concerned may be liable to the disciplinary jurisdiction of the House[23].

Breaches of Privilege and Contempt of the House

The House has inherent powers to protect and punish those who violate its privileges or commit contempt of the House. The penal powers of the House include powers to order the offender to be reprimanded or admonished by the speaker. Members may be suspended or expelled, officials of the House may be dismissed and non-members who are granted certain facilities may have these facilities withdrawn[24]. While the courts assert jurisdiction to decide the existence and extent of privileges of the House, what constitutes contempt of the House is a matter which only the House can decide. If a contempt issue arises relating to internal proceedings of the House, the courts will decline to interfere.

The Courts and Parliamentary Privilege

Questions of privilege used to be a potential source of conflict between the Parliament and the Courts. The House claimed to be the absolute and sole judge of its own privileges, a claim that conflicted with the right of the courts to determine the nature and limit of parliamentary privilege in adjudicating on the rights of individuals outside the House (Erskine, 2019).

It has been said that, "there may be at any given moment two doctrines of privilege: the one held by the courts, the other by either House, the one to be found in the Law Reports, the other in Hansard" (Kier & Lawson, 1954, p. 255).

Members of Parliament and the Criminal Law of Corruption

The position in law of an MP who improperly provides services in return for payment is uncertain. In 1976, a royal commission chaired by Lord Salmon considered that neither statute law nor the common law on corruption applied where an MP was involved and recommended the criminal law be strengthened. Another view is that the existing law does apply to MPs, except that it is not permissible to rely on what has been said in Parliament to prove commission of an offence (Zellick, 1980). However, there should be no uncertainty in this area of the law nor should the Bill of Rights be a shield against conviction for corrupt conduct.

PARLIAMENTARY IMMUNITY: COMPARING SOME CASES

A lot of significant legal and political issues arise in the context of parliamentary immunity. As noted from the introduction, Members of Parliament represent voters to a parliament, and act on the basis of formal rules of behavior, including plenary and committee sessions. According to Chapter 10, article 94 (1) (a) of the 1992 Constitution of Ghana, an MP is first of all a citizen of Ghana. Also, as an MP, he or she enjoys essential privileges and immunities of the House[25] which enables him or her to carry out legitimate official functions in an uninterrupted manner. Parliamentary immunity may be described as legal instrument which restrains or inhibits legal action, measures of investigation, and law enforcement in civil or criminal matters against members of the legislature and can take many forms and shapes.

There are two main forms of parliamentary immunity: non- accountability and inviolability. 'Non-accountability' basically means freedom of the parliamentary vote and freedom of speech in parliament or in a parliamentary context. This is the most universal form of parliamentary immunity whereby parliamentarians may not be held legally accountable for their utterances and voting behaviour in the assembly to which they belong. Usually, non-accountability is materially and temporally absolute. This means that any kind of legal action is barred and that this bar is perpetual, applicable even after the end of their mandate. Lastly, non-accountability usually cannot be lifted by parliament nor renounced by an individual member (Hardt, 2013, p. 4).

'Inviolability' denotes immunity from legal action, detention or measures of prosecution or investigation outside the immediate scope of a member's activities in parliament. Inviolability applies only while parliament is in session and usually ends with the end of the parliamentary mandate. In addition, inviolability may normally be lifted by parliament upon a request by the prosecuting authorities (Hardt, 2013, p. 5).

Whether or Not a Member of Parliament Should Respond to Court Summons During Parliamentary Sitting

In order to offer an appropriate explanation to the query above, we compare a number of cases from different countries.

A. v the UK[26]

In 1996, the British MP Michael Stern delivered a speech in the House of Commons in which he addressed certain problems with public housing in his constituency. In the course of this speech, he disclosed the full name and address of A., one of his constituents, about whom he went on to make the most injurious statements. Mr. Stern referred to A. and her children as 'neighbours from hell' and accused them of anti-social behaviour, littering, loitering, even prostitution. The parliamentarian had, however, never actually been in personal contact with A.; his allegations, which she strongly denied, were merely based on hearsay.

Several newspapers picked up on this public slur in parliament and reported on the 'neighbours from hell'. As a result, A. and her children became the victims of racial abuse, hate mail and threats which eventually forced them to leave their home and neighbourhood. A. tried to seek legal redress from Mr Stern, but her attempt to sue the parliamentarian for defamation failed, since he was protected by parliamentary privilege. The European Court of Human Rights (ECtHR), to which A. finally complained, found that the absolute protection of statements in parliament, however injurious to the applicant, constituted a limitation to the rights of access to court that was justified as necessary in a democratic society.

The determination of this case left crucial questions begging for answers. The first question is "Was A v. the UK" decided correctly? And if so, to what extent does the immunity protect an MP? How far does the curtailment of the rights of citizens serve as an acceptable price for this protection of parliament?

Wilder v Qur'an[27]

In 2007, the Dutch right-wing parliamentarian Geert Wilders published a newspaper article in which he referred to the Qur'an as a 'fascist book' and compared it to Hitler's *Mein Kampf.* He also released the anti-Islamic film Fitna and made a number of public statements in which he demanded a stop to Muslim immigration to the Netherlands. Since Dutch parliamentary immunity does not protect religious bigotry, it was possible for him to be prosecuted and tried for insultation, incitement to hatred and incitement to discrimination. Wilders was finally acquitted of all charges, but the fact that he, an elected representative of the people, could be prosecuted for his public statements sparked some debate as to whether the limited Dutch immunity system provides adequate protection to parliamentarians speaking outside parliament. Thus, do the Netherlands need a higher level of immunity?

While the first school of thought could rely on Chapter 10, Articles 117, 118 and 122 of the Constitution of Ghana, 1992 to support the grounds on which an MP should not respond to court summons during Parliamentary sitting presenting an unchallenged position of parliamentary immunity, other school of thought argues that the scope of this protection is often perceived as excessive. Thus, parliamentary immunity is criticized as facilitating corruption among parliamentarians and affording undeserved protection to libel and slander coming from the ranks of parliament. It is argued that parliamentary immunity enables representatives to 'pursue their own personal and political interests, over and above that which is made possible simply by their position of influence' (Wigley, 2003, p. 23) – a possibility which is seen as highly undemocratic and often leads to calls for immunity to be curtailed or even abolished.

More so, case law and the parliamentary history of many states reveal that the legal institution of parliamentary immunity gives rise to the fact that any legal immunity by definition creates exceptions to the normal application of the law and thereby limits the rights of citizens, who are prevented from enforcing their rights against members of parliament. This is problematic in the light of the principle of equality before the law.

Even if we accept that the aim of parliamentary immunity is not to create a privileged caste of parliamentarians, but to protect the legislature as an institution, individual members of parliament are nevertheless the immediate beneficiaries of any immunity system. By virtue of immunity, their legal position is inevitably unequal to that of an 'ordinary citizen' hence contravening Chapter five (5), Article 12 clauses (1) and (2) as well as Chapter five (5), Article 17 clause (1) (2) and (3) of the 1992 Constitution of Ghana resulting in potential conflict of rights. Constitutional immunity clause further restrains the court's jurisdiction to hear civil claims against parliamentarians. This results in a procedural bar which prevents the enforcement of the law, but in principle it does not affect the validity of a civil claim.

Republic v Mahama Ayariga[28]

In the case of Republic v Mahama Ayariga, with regard to the motion to strike out the charge sheet filed for and on behalf of the first accused person on the basis provided represented a procedural bar seemingly preventing the enforcement of the law, but which in principle does not rule out the criminal nature of an act.

The Court remarked that:

It is important to observe that ensuring compliance with constitutional provisions engenders in the citizenry, a reciprocal respect for the constitution. On the other hand, when courts do not exercise the authority conferred on them to ensure observance with constitutional provisions, respect for the law, which is a pre-requisite for the rule of law and good governance is eroded.

Therefore, since it is in the nature of immunity to create exceptions to the principle of equality, Chapter five (5), Article 12 clauses (1) and (2) as well as Chapter five (5), Article 17 clause (1) (2) and (3) of the 1992 Constitution of Ghana, in addition to engendering citizens respect for the constitution, ensuring rule of law and good governance, point to why parliamentary sitting should not restrain an MP for responding to court summons.

THE POSSIBILITY OF PARLIAMENTARY IMMUNITY CREATING CONSTITUTIONAL CRISES IN GHANA

A constitutional crisis is a problem or conflict in the function of a government that the political constitution or other fundamental governing law is perceived to be unable to resolve (Contiades & Fotiadou, 2017). There are essentially two categories of cases in the context of parliamentary immunity in which Convention rights are at issue (Kloth, 2010). The first and most important category relates to the right of access to court under Article 6(1) of the Convention[29] and Article 19 (2) (f) of the 1992 Constitution of Ghana.

In the determination of his civil rights and obligations or of any criminal charges against him, everyone is entitled to a fair and public hearing within a reasonable time by an independent and impartial tribunal established by law. However, parliamentary immunity of any form bears much potential for conflict with this right, since immunity protects parliamentarians from legal action and thus bars access to court. This is a possible source of conflict of rights and for that matter a constitutional crisis resulting from the situation where citizens may be denied the possibility of legal action against a parliamentarian. This may happen, for instance, in defamation cases where the statements in question are protected by non-accountability.

More so, parliamentarians themselves may not be able to have their rights or charges against them determined in court. This can be the case where an MP is protected by inviolability without the possibility of an individual waiver and where parliament refuses to lift the member's immunity.

Additionally, category of cases under Article 19 (2)[30] concerns the penal powers of parliament and their potential conflict with the requirement of an independent and impartial tribunal established by law. Along with cases concerning the right of access to court under Article 19 (2) of the 1992 Constitution of Ghana, a second main category of case law in the context of parliamentary immunity concerns Article 21 (1)(a) of the 1992 Constitution of Ghana and Article 10 of the ECHR on freedom of expression.

The main issue here is the question of whether members of parliament, when speaking outside of actual debates in parliament, enjoy a wider freedom of expression than 'ordinary' citizens. We may anticipate at this point that this question is of particular interest in the Netherlands, where the prosecution of a right-wing parliamentarian for extra-parliamentary hate speech and insult[31] has led to debates on whether the special position of politicians in society merits a greater freedom of speech than that which other citizens enjoy.

Article 19 (2) of the 1992 Constitution of Ghana: Access to Court

The issue of access to court was first dealt with by the old European Commission of Human Rights (ECHR) in three admissibility decisions on applications complaining that parliamentary immunity had violated the applicants' rights under Article 6 of the ECHR and Article 19 in the case of Ghana's 1992 Constitution (Kloth, 2010, pp. 187-188; 1992 Ghana Constitution).

The first of these decisions was *X v. Austria*[32] in which the Commission decided in 1969 that the application was manifestly ill-founded, considering that all contracting states regarded parliamentary immunity as an important constitutional principle from which they could not have wished to derogate by ratifying the Convention[33].

Seven years later in 1976, the applicant in *Agee v. UK*[34] was a former Central Intelligence Agency agent who had published a book about his work for the Agency and was planning another book on its activities. He was refused re-entry into the UK on grounds of having had regular contacts harmful to national security. These allegations, which the applicant regarded as defamatory, had also been raised by the Home Secretary in the House of Commons. The applicant complained that his right to access to court was violated, since he was barred by parliamentary privilege from suing the Secretary for defamation. The Commission declared the application inadmissible.

Curiously, in *Agee v. UK,* the Commission did not argue that parliamentary privilege constituted a justified exception to Article 6 of ECHR. Instead it held that, due to parliamentary privilege, the applicant had no 'civil right' under UK law to defend his reputation against statements made in parliament, and that Article 6 of ECHR was therefore not applicable.

In his book about immunities and the right of access to court, Matthias Kloth correctly argues that this line of reasoning is flawed, since, had it not been for parliamentary privilege, the applicant would certainly have had the right to sue. Accordingly, the Commission should have based its decision on the justification of privilege, rather than on the non-existence of a civil right to sue for defamation (Kloth, 2010, pp. 160-161).

Inviolability Under Article 6 ECHR and Article 19 of the 1992 Ghanaian Constitution

Even though case law with regard to inviolability is relatively scarce, it is recognizable that the Court is reluctant to accept a limitation of the right of access to court in cases where the object of legal proceedings against the parliamentarian concerned is not, or is insufficient, connected with his parliamentary functions.

In the case Tsalkitzis v. Greece[35], a construction developer wished to bring corruption charges against an MP. The latter had previously been the mayor of Kifissia, a suburb of Athens. In this capacity, in 1997, he had allegedly caused the building permit for one of the applicant's projects to be revoked and construction works to be halted. According to the applicant, the mayor had then demanded a substantial bribe for allowing construction works to resume. The applicant had refused to pay and instead successfully challenged the decision to revoke the building permit in court.

In November 2001, the applicant finally filed a complaint of blackmail and abuse of office and joined the action as a civil party, claiming damages. Meanwhile, however, the former mayor had been elected to parliament in the general elections of 2000 and was now protected by inviolability. The trial court requested parliament to lift the inviolability of the member in question but the request was denied in March 2002.

Kart v. Turkey[36] was the only case till date in which a parliamentarian, thus the beneficiary of parliamentary immunity himself, complained that his rights under Article 6 of the ECHR had been violated as a result of immunity. Before he was elected a deputy of the Turkish Grand National Assembly, the applicant in this case had worked as a lawyer. In this capacity, criminal charges had been brought against him for insulting another lawyer and a public official. However, after his election, proceedings were stayed in accordance with Turkish inviolability rules.

In order to be able to defend his reputation in court, the applicant requested his inviolability to be lifted, but the request was denied by the competent committee of the Grand National Assembly. The applicant appealed the committee's decision, arguing among others that the aim of inviolability was not to render members of parliament unaccountable but only to secure the independent and dispassionate discharge of their functions. In the view of the applicant, "the scope of the immunity, the procedure for lifting it and the shortcomings in its implementation had undermined due respect for the National Assembly".

Article 19 (2) of 1992 Constitution of Ghana and the Penal Powers of Parliament

Apart from the dilemma in respect of the issue of access to court in the context of the possibility of filing lawsuits against members of parliament, legal problems with regard to parliamentary penal powers are very unlikely to arise for parliaments because their jurisdiction is usually limited to the maintenance of order in the plenary hall where parliamentary privilege is largely based on the idea of parliament as a court of law (the High Court of Parliament).

Westminster-type parliaments have the power to punish both members and non-members for contempt or breach of privilege. This may give rise to problems under Article 6(1) ECHR or Article 19 of Ghana's 1992 Constitution, which confers upon everyone the right to have criminal charges determined in a fair hearing by an independent tribunal.

Where a parliament or parliamentary chamber chooses to exercise its penal powers, does the accusation of a breach of privilege or contempt of parliament constitute a 'criminal charge' within the meaning of Article 6(1) ECHR? This is answered in the affirmative per Article 6(1) of ECHR. Since this is answered in the positive, does parliament constitute 'an independent and impartial tribunal established by law' as Article 6 ECHR requires? Even though this is required, it seems to defeat the principle of separation of powers.

CONCLUSION

This chapter has provided us with a thorough picture of the systems of parliamentary immunity. The approach of the European Court of Human Rights towards immunity in its case law was critically examined. The above juxtaposition of the immunity shows that it is hardly possible to speak comprehensively of the emergence of immunity systems: freedom from arrest and freedom of speech separately. The respective time at which this form of immunity appeared reveals its close connection with the institutional evolution of parliaments, their self-image and the circumstances in which they operated. It is therefore true that free speech is the epitome of parliamentarianism. Today, this is rightfully accepted as an axiomatic justification of non-accountability, even where it constitutes a limitation of the rights of third parties.

As indicated in the discussion, a lot of significant legal and political issues arise in the context of parliamentary immunity. Inviolability relates by definition to acts of parliamentarians that lie in the extra-parliamentary sphere. Nonetheless, the Court has in reality adopted a reverse approach to inviolability by making the repeated statement for some restrictions on access to court to be regarded as inherent in Article 6 (1) of the European Convention on Human Rights (ECRH) and Article 19(2) of the 1992 Constitution of Ghana for that matter. In principle, this approach constitutes a disproportionate limitation of the right of access to court especially on the premise where the court makes the case that a violation of right of access to court is not justified by additional reasons such as a manifest relation between the alleged criminal act and parliamentary activities or a political motivation for criminal charges.

Even though the courts have generally acknowledged that parliamentarians deserve and require a wide freedom of expression even when speaking outside parliament, the somewhat blurred picture of the freedom outlined above hinders the conclusion that parliamentarians enjoy special protection. Whilst the prosecution of parliamentarians (though not necessarily members of the government) for criminal acts committed outside the parliamentary sphere can be suspended at the behest of Parliament where it deems this desirable, no such possibility exists in the Ghana per the case of Mahama Ayariga v The Republic[37].

At the same time, political discourse no longer takes place exclusively in the plenary hall of parliament, but increasingly in the public media, where parliamentarians have to disseminate and defend their views, proposals and political goals vis-à-vis their electorate. In addition, parliamentary debates, now often broadcast live on television or the internet, function as a platform for communication with the wider public, while actual political decisions are still taken in the backrooms of parliament, in the quarters of political parties or behind closed doors by the government. Under such changed circumstances, maintaining the strict separation between what is said in and outside of the parliamentary meeting appears artificial and anachronistic.

With regard to the extent of freedom of expression enjoyed by parliamentarians under the ECHR and Chapter Five (5), Article 21 of the 1992 Constitution of Ghana remains dicey and difficult. Hence limitations on freedom of expression in political discourse require "the closest scrutiny" because being a parliamentarian alone does not confer upon an individual a greater freedom of expression but rather a call to greater duty of care. The inconclusiveness of European Court of Human Rights case law in this matter is problematic. Parliamentarians are caught in a nexus between greater freedom and greater responsibility, between being equal citizens before the law and being slightly 'more equal' than others due to their status.

The medieval fiction that the "king can do no wrong", which the sophist interpreted to mean that if the action was wrong, then it was not that of the king, has no place in a republican setting which prides itself on all citizens being equal under the law and therefore obliged to act in conformity with it (Broom, 1845).

In Ghana, the extent to which an MP is inviolable in a specific case depends on whether the Parliament is in session as seen in the case of *Abodakpi and Another v The Republic*[38]. The Court hearings were held on Mondays and during recess periods of Parliament. Also, just as the European Parliament has a right to waive inviolability on request, pursuant to Article 9(3), Ghanaian Parliament also does same as seen in the case of *Mahama Ayariga*[39], who after agreeing to appear before the court as an accused person and not as witness, was released by the Honourable Speaker of Parliament to be tried by the court. This observation point to the fact that an MP's right of access to court is guaranteed hence provide good ground for enhancing the principle of separation of powers.

RECOMMENDATIONS

In the course of this research, it was observed that there have been certain gaps, lapses and inadequacies in some areas of the laws in Ghana. With respect to the cases cited in this chapter, it would be good to broaden the scope of parliamentary immunity so as to effect the absolute protection of the spoken word of members of the chambers outside of parliament since in contemporary times artificial separation of parliamentary and extra-parliamentary political debate may create problems in the adjudication of allegedly criminal extra-parliamentary speech without discriminating between contributors to public debate with or without a parliamentary mandate.

More so, in the words of the former Speaker of Parliament, Hon. Aaron Mike Oquaye, "the House does not sit all year round, neither does it undertake its activities all year round". Similarly, Members are not perpetually on "their way to, attending at, or returning from, any proceedings of Parliament." There are periods of recess and there are periods within a week when the House does not sit or work in Committees. A process from a court or a place may be served on that member during those periods, or during times which does not offend Article 117.

Also, the Courts should be minded to schedule court sittings to accommodate the legislative calendar so as to ensure the smooth administration of the judicial or legislative governance of the State. Under the principle of checks and balances, under the 1992 Constitution of Ghana, there is an advocacy for a relationship between the various organs of government based on institutional corporation and collaboration, with the view of ensuring that the organs of government function closely with each other. This is designed to ameliorate the impact of the principle of separation of powers which, if carried to its logical conclusion, will lead to a breakdown of government.

The Law Reform Commission and other auxiliary bodies should therefore put their heads together to deal with all inadequacies in the laws of Ghana in respect of the crises generated between the legislative and the adjudicative organs of government.

REFERENCES

Allan, T. R. (2001). *Constitutional Justice: A Liberal Theory of the Rule of Law*. Oxford University Press.

Amidu, M. A. (2019, August 8). *The Office of the Special Prosecutor has no jurisdiction to investigate financial and economic crimes – The PDS case*. Retrieved June 19, 2021, from GhanaWeb: https://www.ghanaweb.com/GhanaHomePage/features/The-Office-of-the-Special-Prosecutor-has-no-jurisdiction-to-investigate-financial-and-economic-crimes-The-PDS-case-770385

Asante, K. P. (2019). *An Assessment of the Office of the Special Prosecutor, One Year On*. CorruptionWatch.

Botchway, T. P. (2018). Ghana: A Consolidated Democracy? *Asian Research Journal of Arts & Social Sciences*, 1-13.

Botchway, T. P. (2018a). Civil Society and the Consolidation of Democracy in Ghana's Fourth Republic. *Cogent Social Sciences*, *4*(1), 1452840. doi:10.1080/23311886.2018.1452840

Bradley, A. W. (1997). *Constitutional and Administrative Law* (14th ed.). Longman.

Broom, H. (1845). *A Selection of Legal Maxims, Classified and Illustrated*. T. & J. W. Johnson.

Contiades, X., & Fotiadou, A. (2017). *Participatory Constitutional Change: The People as Amenders of the Constitution*. Routledge.

D' Entreves, A. P. (1967). *The Notion of the State*. Oxford University Press.

Dicey, A. V. (1897). *Introduction of the Study of the Law of the Constitution* (6th ed.). Macmillan.

Elton, G. R. (2010). *Studies in Tudor and Stuart Politics and Government*. Cambridge University Press.

Erskine, M. (2019). *Parliamentary Practice* (25th ed.). LexisNexis.

Hardt, S. (2013). *Parliamentary immunity: a comprehensive study of the systems of parliamentary immunity of the United Kingdom, France and the Netherlands in a European context*. Maastricht University.

Henderson, E. G. (1964). *Foundation of English Administrative Law: Certiorari and Mandamus in the Seventeenth Century*. Harvard University Press.

Jenings, I. (2009). *The Law and the Constitution* (2nd ed.). Cambridge University Press.

Kier, D. L., & Lawson, F. H. (1954). *Cases in Constitutional Law*. Oxford University Press.

Kloth, M. (2010). *Immunities and the right of access to court under Article 6 of the European Convention on Human Rights*. Leiden: Martinus Nijhoff Publishers.

Locke, J. (1689). Two Treatises of Government. Laslett.

Montesquieu, B. (1998). The Spirit of the Laws (Book 11). M. a. Cohler.

Ramshorn, L. (1841). *Dictionary of Latin Synonyms*. Charles C. Little Press.

United Nations Development Programme. (2006). *Parliaments, Crisis Prevention and Recovery: Guidelines for the International Community*. UNDP.

Yin, E. T., Atupare, P. A., Kofie, N., Owusu, L. P., & Botchway, T. P. (2021). Rights and religious belief in maintaining prison social order. *UCC Faculty of Law Journal*, *1*(1), 1–16.

Zellick, G. J. (1980). *Human Rights: A Unique Development*. Guardian.

ENDNOTES

1 Suit no. MSFT/23/2019

2 Customs Act, 2015, (Act 891)

3 Criminal and Other Offences Act, 1960, (Act 29)

4 Foreign Exchange Act, 2006, (Act 723)

5 Ibid

6 Ibid

7 A. v The United Kingdom, ECHR 17 December 2002, App. No. 35373/97

8 Hinke, B., *"Wilders op alle punten vrijgesproken"* (NRC Handelsbald 2011)

9 Article 11 of the Constitution of Ghana, 1992

10 Ibid
11 Ibid
12 Suit no. MSFT/23/2019
13 The Constitution of Ghana, 1992
14 Ibid
15 Ibid
16 Article 17 (1) of the 1992 Constitution of Ghana
17 Articles 115-121 of the 1992 Constitution of Ghana
18 1992 Constitution of Ghana
19 Ibid
20 Report of joint committee on parliamentary Privilege (HL 43-1) HC 214-1, 1998-9, paragraph 3.
21 Insolvency Act, 1986, section 427
22 Lake v King (1667)
23 Duncan Sandy's case, HC 101 (1938-9)
24 Article 116 of the 1992 Constitution of Ghana
25 Articles 115-121 of the 1992 Constitution of Ghana
26 A. v The United Kingdom [2002] ECHR 17 December 2002, App. No. 35373/97
27 Hinke, B., *"Wilders op alle punten vrijgesproken"* (NRC Handelsbald 2011)
28 Suit no. MSFT/23/2019
29 ECHR
30 Constitution of Ghana, 1992
31 Hinke, B., *"Wilders op alle punten vrijgesproken"* (NRC Handelsbald 2011)
32 X v Austria [1969] Commission Decision, 1969, App. No. 3374/69
33 ECHR
34 Agee v. the United Kingdom [1976] Commission Decision, 1976, App No. 7729/76
35 Tsalkitzis v. Greece [2006] ECHR 16 November 2006, App. No. 11801/04
36 *Kart v. Turkey* [2005] ECHR 8 July 2008, App. No. 8917/05.
37 Suit no. MSFT/23/2019
38 Abodakpi & Another v The Republic [2001-2002] 1 GLR 450
39 Suit no. MSFT/23/2019

APPENDIX: ADDITIONAL RESOURCES

Table of Cases

- v The United Kingdom [2002] ECHR 17 December 2002, App. No. 35373/97
- Abodakpi & Another v The Republic [2001-2002] 1 GLR 450
- Agee v The United Kingdom [1976] Commission Decision, App No. 7729/76
- Duncan Sandy's case [1938-1939] HC 101 (1938-9)
- *Kart v Turkey* [2008] ECHR, App. No. 8917/05
- Lake v King [1667] 1 Saunders 131
- R v Heome Secretary [1995] ex parte Fire Brigades Union 2 AC 513,567
- Republic v Mahama Ayariga & Kendrick Kwesi Marfo [Suit number MSFT/23/2019]
- Tsalkitzis v Greece [2006] ECHR, App. No. 11801/04
- X v Austria [1969] Commission Decision, App. No. 3374/69

Table of Legislations

- Criminal and Other Offences Act, 1960, (Act 29)
- Customs Act, 2015, (Act 891)
- Foreign Exchange Act, 2006, (Act 723)
- Insolvency Act, 1986, section 427
- The Constitution of the Republic of Ghana, 1992

Chapter 13
Recent Trends and Repercussions in Civil and Criminal Justice Systems:
A Comparative Analysis of England, Singapore, and India

Mitsu Parikh
World of Legal Research, India

V. S. Krishna
World of Legal Research, India

ABSTRACT

The reform of civil and criminal justice systems is a contentious issue and has become the top priority for the international community in re-establishing the rule of law. The justice systems in many common law jurisdictions are perceived to be 'in crisis' deformed by exorbitant delay, cost, and complexity in proceedings. The level of resources engulfed in the judicial system has very little or no impact on judicial performance. Comparative and comprehensive analysis of the law not only leads to a better realization of the foreign laws, but also it aids with law unification. This chapter will attempt to highlight the issues in the civil and criminal justice system and comparatively analyze the scenario in England, Singapore, and India. In furtherance, the authors explore the possible methods to curb the delay in justice systems and canvas the modern trends in civil and criminal justice policy.

INTRODUCTION

Justice systems across the globe are perceived to be in crisis (Blankenburg, 1999). The prime motive of the authors taking a comparative analysis of the said issue is, it not only leads to better recognition of the foreign laws but also it is lucid with commerce universalization and law unification. Most of the reforms that emanate in the present aeon are based on comparative studies (Dodson, 2009). Civil and

DOI: 10.4018/978-1-7998-7898-8.ch013

Criminal cases take ages and cost too much, and dishonest judges torment the systems. There are different organizations engrossed with a variety of activities across the globe aimed at rebuilding the justice systems. Chronic judicial quiescence calls for streamlining the procedures and reinforcing flexibility. The reform of Civil and Criminal justice systems has become an utmost priority for the international community in its efforts to assist transitional and post-conflict societies in re-establishing the rule of law. A comparative analysis of the civil justice reforms unveils the continual efforts to augment access to Justice through adopting the Alternate Dispute Resolution process. The concept of Rule of Law is an animation of natural law and remains as a historical ideal that makes a powerful appeal to date, i.e. to be ruled by law and not by a powerful man.

James M. Buchanan distinguishes between *'law'* and the *'rule of law'* (Buchman, 2001). All primitive and non-democratic societies have *'law',* but all liberal and progressive societies having *'rule of law'* are not necessarily lawless societies. According to him *'generality'* is at the centre of the rule of law, besides fairness, prospectivity and due process.

The United Nations Secretary-General defines the *"rule of law"* as follows:

The rule of law is a concept at the very heart of the United Nations' mission. It refers to a principle of governance in which all persons, institutions and entities, public and private, including the State itself, are accountable to laws that are publicly promulgated, equally enforced and independently adjudicated, and which are consistent with international human rights norms and standards. It requires, as well, measures to ensure adherence to the principles of supremacy of law, equality before the law, accountability to the law, fairness in the application of the law, separation of powers, participation in decision-making, legal certainty, avoidance of arbitrariness and procedural and legal transparency. (UNSC Report, 2004)

Practitioners and policymakers have widely accepted this definition in the rule of law community.

AN OVERVIEW OF THE JUSTICE SYSTEMS

Every civilized system of the government requires that the State should make available to all its citizens a means for the just and peaceful settlement of disputes between them as to their respective legal rights. Criminal Courts, along with other criminal institutions, are facing a hard time providing security and operate under intense scrutiny from politicians and the media. Justice systems across the globe are often under-resourced, have low-capacity, and lack basic infrastructure. Civil and Criminal matters take too long, and it is never cost-effective compared to alternate methods that have been emerging in the present aeon. The structure of the Courts varies depending on the legal system in place. Data from the United States and countries in Latin America and the Caribbean show no correlation between the overall level of resources and the time of disposition of cases (Buscaglia & Ulen, 1997). Judicial and legal institutions in Asia, in general, and Singapore, in particular, have been criticized on the ground that they are not independent of the government. Both Civil and Criminal Justice Systems in many common law jurisdictions was reportedly *'in crisis',* crippled by excessive delay, cost and complexity in proceedings and out of reach of ordinary people (Woolf, 1995). As rightly stated ***'Justice delayed is justice denied'***. Per contra, the term 'Justice' is not just convicting the wrong-doers. It is also the enforcement of individual rights and protection. The judicial systems are afflicted by corrupt and dishonest judges. This paves the way for judicial inefficiency that destabilizes the growth of the economy and wealth of the nation.

THE CONCEPT OF RULE OF LAW

The concept of the rule of law has been universally recognized as a fundamental value, and at present, it is very fashionable (Jacobs, 2007; Bingham, 2010). The principle has no universal agreement about how it can be *'reconciled with other competing values, notably with the requirements of democratic government' (Jowell, 2011).* The Rule of Law is a viable and a dynamic concept, and like many other concepts, there isn't an exact definition for the same. The term 'rule of law' is used in contradistinction to 'rule of man' and 'rule according to law'. Therefore, the rule of law means that the law rules, which is based on the principles of freedom, equality, non-discrimination, fraternity, accountability and non-arbitrariness, and is certain, regular and predictable, using the word *'law'* in the sense of *'jus' and 'lex'* both.

As aforementioned, the basic concept of the rule of law is not a well-defined legal concept. The courts generally would not invalidate any positive law on the ground that it violates the concepts of rule of law. Per contra, in ***ADM, Jabalpur vs Shivakant Shukla (1976) 2 SCC 521; AIR 1976 SC 1207,*** popularly known as ***the Habeas Corpus case,*** an attempt was made to challenge the detention orders during the Emergency on the ground that it violates the principles of the rule of law as the *'obligation to act in accordance with rule of law is a central feature of our constitutional system and is a basic feature of the Constitution'.* Though the contention did not succeed and some justices even went on to suggest that during an emergency, the emergency provision themselves constitute the rule of law, yet if the reasoning of all the five opinions is closely read, it becomes clear that the contention was accepted, no matter it did not reflect in the final order passed by the court (Baxi, 1982).

The term rule of law can be used in two senses: (a) formalistic sense; and (b) ideological sense.

If used in the formalistic sense, it refers to organized power as opposed to a rule by one man; and if used in an ideological sense, it refers to the regulation of the relationship of the citizens and the government, and in this sense, it becomes a concept of varied interest and contents.

The Supreme Court has rightly observed in the case of ***Som Raj vs State of Haryana*** that the absence of arbitrary power is the first postulate of the rule of law upon which whole constitutional edifice is based. If the discretion is exercised without any principle or any rule, it is a situation amounting to the antithesis of the rule of law.

The modern concept of the rule of law is fairly wide and, therefore, sets up an ideal for any government to achieve. This concept was developed by the ***International Commission of Jurists, known as Delhi Declaration, 1959,*** which was later on confirmed at ***Lagos in 1961.*** According to this formulation, the rule of law implies that the functions of the government in a free society should be so exercised as to create conditions in which the dignity of man as an individual is upheld. This dignity requires not only the recognition of certain civil or political rights but also the creation of certain political, social, economical, educational and cultural conditions which are essential to the full development of his personality.

In 1957, the University of Chicago held a conference on the rule of law. 11 countries including two communist countries, attended it. The Secretary of the colloquium described the broad areas of agreement as follows:

1. The rule of law is an expression of an endeavor to give reality to something which is not readily expressible; this difficulty is primarily due to the identification of the rule of law with the concept of rights of man – all countries recognize that the rule of law has a positive content, though that content is different in different countries; it is real and must be secured principally, but not exclusively, by the ordinary courts.

2. The rule of law is based upon the liberty of the individual and has as its object the harmonizing of the opposing notions of individual liberty and public order. The notion of justice maintains a balance between these notions. Justice has variable content and cannot be strictly defined, but at a given time and place, there is an appropriate standard by which the balance between private interest and the common good can be maintained.
3. There is an important difference between the concept of the rule of law as the supremacy of law over the government and the concept of the rule of law as the supremacy of law in society generally. The first concept is the only feature common connoting as it does the protection of the individual against the arbitrary government – different techniques can be adopted to achieve the same end, and the rule of law must not be conceived of as being linked to any particular technique. But it is fundamental that there must exist some technique for forcing the government to submit to the law; if such a technique does not exist, the government itself becomes the means whereby the law is achieved. This is the antithesis of the rule of law.
4. Although much emphasis is placed upon the supremacy of the legislature in some countries, the rule of law does not depend upon contemporary positive law – it may be expressed in positive law, but essentially it consists of values and not an institution; it connotes a climate of legality and legal order in which the nations wish to continue to live (Goodhart, 1958).

Recent aggressive judicial activism can only be seen as a part of the efforts of the constitutional courts in India to establish a rule of law society which implies that no matter how high a person may be, the law is always above him. The court is also trying to identify the concept of the rule of law with the human rights of the people. The Court is developing techniques by which it can force the government not only to submit to the law but also to create conditions where people can develop capacities to exercise their rights properly and meaningfully. The public administration is responsible for the effective implementation of the rule of law and constitutional commands which effectuate fairly the objective standards laid down by law (State of Punjab vs G.S. Gill, (1997) 6 SCC 129). Every public servant is a trustee of society and is accountable for the due effectuation of constitutional goals (Superintending Engineer, Public Health vs Kuldeep Singh, (1997) 9 SCC 199). This makes the concept of the rule of law highly relevant to the context. Though the concept of the rule of law has all the merits, the only negative side of the concept is that respect for law degenerates into legalism from which its very rigidly works injury to the nation.

ACCESS TO JUSTICE: AN UNSOLVED AGONY

The impact of judicial inefficiency may be particularly severe in poor societies. A comprehensive analysis of justice reforms in England, Singapore and India manifests the continual efforts to access justice through greater use of Alternative Dispute Resolutions (ADR) and struggles in delineating the expansion of ADR. There are several schools of thought about judicial reform. One views the primary issue of the legal system as one of funding and thus sees the solution to judicial inefficiency as lying in more resources – more training, better computer systems, and more courts, judges and clerks. Another school of thought believes that judicial systems are inefficient because of excessive and indiscriminate access. Far from increasing fairness by allowing more people to assert their rights, the democratization of the legal system has paved its way by opening the floodgates, annihilating courts down with mostly frivolous cases and slowing the meritorious ones. A third school views the problem as one of the incentives. Judges who do not bear the costs of their slowness tend to be slow. Court systems unafraid of losing litigants to alternative venues of dispute resolution, such as arbitration or small-claims courts, will treat their litigants as the captive market they are (World Bank, 2003). Yet another group believes that the main problem is overly rigid and ineffective procedures, particularly in developing economies that inherited their legal systems from their colonizers without the systems' being sufficiently adapted to their needs. Reforms can augment efficiency even within the existing system by streamlining procedures and creating specialized courts.

The social importance of justice system is reflected by its significance in literature. Civil justice texts are replete with quotes from Bentham, Shakespeare, Dickens and Kafka. For example, Jeremy Bentham saw the rules of procedure as being central to the machinery of civil justice. For Bentham, the power of procedure was in the link between evidence and correct decisions (rectitude) and the role of procedure in achieving accuracy in decision making continues to be seen as central today by procedural scholars (Zuckerman, 1999). Sir Jack Jacob manages to convey most of the private functions of civil justice economically as follows:

'Civil Justice plays a role of crucial importance in the life and culture of a civilized community. It constitutes the machinery for obtaining what Lord Brougham called "Justice between man and man". It manifests the political will of the State that civil remedies be provided for civil rights and claims, and the civil wrongs, whether they consist of infringements of private rights in the enjoyment of life, liberty, property or otherwise, be made good so far as practicable, by compensation and satisfaction, or restrained, if necessary, by appropriate relief (Jacob, 1982, p. 1).

Civil Justice is the means by which citizens are able to uphold their substantive civil rights against other citizens. It provides a framework in which business can be done, and investment can be protected, thus supporting economic activity and development. Lord Woolf identified three interrelated problems faced in the civil justice system in England and Wales, i.e., delay, cost and complexity. According to him, the cumulative effect has constituted *'denial of justice'*. The same problem has been prevailing with the justices systems in Australia, the United States, India and many more (Access to Justice Interim Report, 1974). The expense of litigation was identified as a fundamental problem confronting the justice system. Lord Woolf argued that:

'Excessive cost deters people from making or defending claims. A number of businesses have told me that it is often cheaper to pay up, irrespective of the merits than to defend an action. For individual litigants, the unaffordable cost of litigation constitutes a denial of access to justice'.

Lord Woolf argued that civil justice *'safeguards the right of individuals, regulates their dealings with others and enforces the duties of government'* (Woolf, 1995). The permeation of justice and justice system issues throughout literature could be a manifestation of Jacob's 'transcendent' importance of civil justice. The significance of the civil justice system is also reflected in the majesty of court buildings – in the iconography of justice. But the question that arises is that in what way? Does the justice system, in general, have practical significance to the everyday resolution of trouble and disputes? Is it of significance because it offers the ultimate backstop providing a sense of order and security?

The answer is that it is of significance because the law fixes obligations and duties through rules governing social and economic and governmental behavior. It is of significance because it is in the light of those rules that people arrange their affairs and seek to avoid disputes. The significance lies in the individual decisions affecting the lives of private citizens, businesses and public bodies and, more importantly in social terms, in the authoritative rulings of the judiciary together with the articulation of their reasoning and the principles applied.

COMPREHENSIVE ANALYSIS OF JUSTICE REFORMS

The main reasons for a reformation of Justice systems in England, Singapore, India and in many other countries are:-

1. ***Formalistic, inflexible, complex:*** These characteristics can be traced to a number of different sources including the existence of multiple judicial hierarchies; the existence of multiple courts within a particular hierarchy, each with different jurisdiction; the existence of separate procedures and rules for each court; convoluted rules of court; the variety of ways of instituting proceedings (wherein in some jurisdictions, there are as many as four different initiating procedures); procedural distinctions which applied to different types of cases; and a multiplicity of practice directions'.
2. ***Overly dependent on party-control of the 'conduct, pace and extent of litigation':*** Until the trial, litigation was heavily reliant on inter-party regulation. Parties, or more often their lawyers, determined the issues and evidence put before the court, and they had complete control over the pace at which matters proceeded through the litigation process. Such rules of procedure as existed were 'all too often ignored by the parties and not enforced by the court'.
3. ***Designed along the lines of trial by battle:*** A strongly adversarial approach can be encouraged, one which Justice Davies referred to as *'the adversarial imperative'* consisting of twin compulsions that each party has *'to see the other as the enemy who must be defeated'* and *'to leave no stone unturned'.* With 'no effective control of (the parties) worst excesses', adversarialism is unrestrained. Lord Woolf asserted that the 'main procedural tools for conducting litigating efficiently had each become subverted from their proper use'. He singled out for attention: pleadings which failed to state the facts as required and to establish the issues in the case; sham defences; voluminous and unnecessary discovery; the approach to expert evidence which resulted in the involvement of too many, too 'eminent' witnesses subject to partisan pressure; and combative interlocutory disputes.
4. ***A closed system:*** The Judicial system was 'designed to keep much of the information available to each party in watertight compartments' so that parties were required to investigate, prepare and progress the case independently without obligation to assist each other. As a consequence, much of the work of opposing lawyers had to be duplicated.
5. ***Too heavily dependent on an 'all-embracing trail':*** The trial was viewed as the main event. Little time or effort was devoted to pre-trial activities, including case preparation. The consequences of focusing on the trial included inadequate or late investigation of the facts, last-minute settlements, and the danger of surprise at trial.

Based on the abovementioned circumstances, it is clear that the Judicial systems across the globe are becoming inefficient in completing the pending cases. Even though there exist many fast track courts like in India, the traditional courts are chocked with many unsettled cases, because of piled up cases. In order to deal with this situation, the existence of the Alternative Dispute Resolution mechanism (ADR) can resolve the conflict between the parties in a peaceful manner (an effective way). The linkage between litigation and alternative dispute resolution has always been a debatable issue or to be precise, it has been an uneasy one. As ***Briggs LJ*** in the case of ***PGF II SA vs IMFS Co Ltd [2013] EWCA Civ 1288; [2014] 1 W.L.R. 1386*** observed, considering the current constraints affecting the provision of resources for civil litigation 'call for an ever-increasing focus upon means of ensuring that court time, both for trial and case management, is proportionately directed towards disputes which really need it, with an ever-increasing responsibility thrown upon the parties to engage in ADR, wherever that offers a reasonable prospect of producing a just settlement at proportionate cost'. The Courts' encouragement of the use of mediation is meant to enhance access to justice and facilitate the proportionate allocation of court resources for civil litigation. Yet the courts have been divided on the question of when mediation indeed offers a *'reasonable prospect of producing a just settlement'*. The Court of Appeal in ***Thakkar vs Patel [2017] EWCA Civ 117,*** obliged a party who was invited to mediation to seriously consider the offer, regardless of the party's belief in the merits of his case (Masood, 2018). In marked contrast, Patten LP in ***Gore vs Naheed [2017] EWCA Civ 369,*** did not consider it unreasonable for a party to decline mediation when mediation had no realistic prospect of success, and there were complex questions of law to be determined. The contrasting judicial positions demonstrate that the connection between using mediation and enhancing access to justice is not always evident in every case.

The concept of Alternative Dispute Resolution can be traced back to 1960s. Since the political and civil of the 1960s ADR has grown firstly in the United States of America (U.S.A). During that time to settle their disputes, a number of civil suits were filed in order to avoid discrimination and injustice. The U.S. Judicial system became overloaded with lawsuits resulting in delayed justice, and sometimes litigants were also faced with judicial turnover. Therefore, processes like mediation, conciliation and arbitration soon became popular means to deal with the variety of conflicts, because ADR helped them to relieve pressure and the overburdened judicial system. Further, the Civil Rights Act, 1964 declared that discrimination in public employment on the basis of race, sex or national origin was outlawed. It is to be noted that resolution rather than the settlement of dispute outside the courts is not a very new concept. Societies across the world have long used non-judicial indigenous methods to resolve their disputes, although, what is new is a wide promotion of ADR models specifically in the corporate world. ADR is a string tool to achieve a friendly settlement of a dispute.

In the United States, the ADR movement was initiated in the early 1970s, as a social movement to settle community-wise civil rights disputes by means of mediation and as a legal movement to diminish increased delay in expensive litigation from an overloaded judicial system. Since then, the legal ADR movement in the United States has witnessed rampant growth.

During the early 1980s, strong demand for ADR in the corporate world attained momentum, and serious efforts were made to grow and find more efficient and effective alternates to litigation. Thereafter, society had witnessed an explosion in the number of private use of arbitration and mediation as ADR was introduced and adopted in the community.

In U.S.A., administrative rulemaking and federal litigation practices were affected by improvement and acceptance of ADR from experimentation to institutionalization. Now, the law which is time being force authorize and encourage agencies to use negotiation and other forms of ADR in public conduction, administrative dispute resolution and also rulemaking. At the international level, the ADR movement had also taken off in developed and developing countries. ADR models were designed and experimented with in a straight forward manner, and the traditional dispute resolution was managed with the modern ADR models. The system of ADR is being implemented to resolve a wide range of social, legal, commercial and political conflicts. Notably, in the developing world, a number of countries including Bolivia, Colombia, Bangladesh, Ecuador, the Philippines, South Africa, Sri Lanka and Uruguay are engaging in the ADR experiment. The success in ADR models in these countries made this system so popular in the developing countries.

A comparative analysis of the recent civil justice reforms in England and Wales and Singapore reflects the continual efforts to enhance access to justice through greater use of ADR, and the attendant struggles in delineating the limits that should constrain the expanding scope of dispute resolution. The Singapore Courts have embedded the use of ADR within the pre-trial civil justice process. The parties are encouraged by a registrar or judge to consider mediation at pre-trial conferences or other hearings. In 2013, the Supreme Court introduced a process to allow parties to file an *"ADR offer"* indicating their willingness to participate in ADR. The party receiving the ADR Offer is given 14 days to file a "Response to ADR Offer", stating whether he or she agrees to the other party's proposal, and providing detailed reasons for any refusal. The failure by a party to file a Response to ADR Offer within the stipulated time is taken to mean that the party is unwilling to participate in ADR without providing any reasons.

The English civil justice system is currently experiencing another wave of major reforms in a further attempt to enhance access to justice for all, with ADR also being a prominent feature of the changes (Woolf, 1995). The most radical proposal of the current reforms is the introduction of an ***Online Solutions Court (OSC)*** in the resolution of low-value monetary claims. As Briggs LJ, the development of the Online Court is the single most radical and important structural change. Forming part of the mainstream civil justice system, the OSC will allow access to justice for people and small businesses of ordinary financial resources.

The English and Singaporean civil justice reforms reflect continual efforts to arrive at an optimal mechanism to encourage the greater use of consensual ADR for appropriate cases. The current array of mechanisms may be charted along a *'continuum of mandatoriness'*, ranging from requiring attendance at a mediation orientation session and imposing soft sanctions, to the more extreme measures of having an opt-out system and mandating mediation with no exemptions (Quek, 2010). Singapore's current regime resembles an opt-out system because the courts embedded the consideration of ADR within the court process, coupled with the spectre of cost sanctions has probably diminished the effectiveness of the opt-out system, resulting in current proposals for the court to order the use of mediation in suitable cases. On the other hand, the English courts have imposed robust cost sanctions, albeit with inconsistent decisions. Although the future OSC will embed ADR into the court process for low-value claims, there is yet to be an opt-out system allowing the parties to decline the use of ADR based on limited grounds.

In one way, it gives relief to the litigants from mental agony caused by the disputed parties for their court proceedings. The mechanism of ADR System and its techniques are an extra-judicial remedy to resolve disputes outside the legal fora. The scope and application of the ADR system are not only beneficial from a litigation or commercial point of view at the international level but also assuage the sentiments of Constitution makers. The scope of ADR is wider and includes civil, commercial, industrial, family, etc. To deal with the situation of pendency of cases in India, ADR plays a significant role in its diverse techniques.

A Resolution was passed by the Prime Minister and Chief Justice of India on 4th December 1993, for bringing in Alternative Dispute Resolution by establishing facilities for dispute settlement through arbitration, conciliation, mediation and negotiation. With the advancement of the internet as a platform of political, financial and social activities, the ADR has also taken a step ahead in the form of Online Dispute Resolution as ***Section 89 of the Civil Procedure Code*** clearly mentions the terms of it. This concept is certainly evolving in India as in the case of ***Salem Advocates Bar Association, Tamil Nadu vs Union of India AIR [2003] SC 189,*** gave rules for the proper functioning of ADR. Section 89 of CPC was inserted to ensure that not all matters need to be decided by the courts. Since there exist long delays and limited judges, it is essential to have an Alternative Dispute Resolution Mechanism to reduce the traditional court proceedings. Moreover, the Court held that, if the parties agree to arbitration, then the provision of Arbitration and Conciliation Act, 1996 would apply and normal court proceedings would be removed, but when the matter is about conciliation or judicial settlement or mediation would not ipso facto take the case outside the judicial system. Thus, the ADR would try all possible efforts to amicable settle the dispute, and if it fails to do so, the case will ultimately go to trial.

In light of the proliferation of technological amelioration and the advent of fully-fledged ADR schemes and providers, access to justice is being reshaped. Digital technology transforms the landscape of dispute resolution. Alternate Dispute Resolution involved not only new tools and techniques in resolving disputes but also implicated different assumptions, principles and values. On the other, Online Dispute Resolution is a subset of Alternate Dispute Resolution.

EMANATION OF ODR

The concept of ODR was first brought to light in a series of online articles by Virtual Courthouse in 1996. ODR is a traditional concept of alternate dispute resolution mechanism espousing the out-of-court procedures and indeed resolving the disputes online. ODR has become the need of the hour for the disputes pertaining to e-commerce and the digital economy. This phenomenon has been referred to as the ***'e-commerce revolution'*** wherein such online claims may emanate from the B2B (business to business), B2C (business to consumer), and C2C (consumer to consumer) e-contracts (Katsh, 2011). Online arbitration is a concoction of conventional arbitration. To be precise, the said concept requires the aid of the Information Technology Act, 2000.

The emerging field of ODR refers to a compilation of conflict resolution methods that employ online technologies to resolve disputes. The Parties might choose to negotiate a conflict through an exchange of emails or by posting a message to each other in a secret chat room wherein a mediator may work with two disputants in real-time online conversations over the web or use information distributed. ODR plays an institutional method of ADR where an array of guidelines are laid down to guide the parties, arbitrators/mediators and the proceedings. The entire proceedings are made available online, but certain ways need to be followed to resolve the disputes. The procedure is as follows:-

- A claim needs to be filed online. There are particular ways to file a claim on online platforms. Many of them include the process of direct negotiation and provide the form to the parties to resolve the disputes. The role of the mediator arises from the failure of direct negotiation.
- Settlement offers are initiated by the professional, and the same is notified to the opposition via fax, email, etc. The respondent tries to settle the claim, or if his offer is less than or equal to the said claim, then the claim settles.
- The issues are discussed by allowing the parties to create an entire ODR system, handling a case document that is shared between the parties and offering full security. The parties share, discuss, collaborate and even reach agreements online as well.

- The agreement needs to be signed by both the parties, which is an essential part of verifying the document (Krause, n.d.).

The process of ODR has been hailed for its simplicity, speed, convenience and least expensive when compared to the traditional ADR and litigation. Due to its delocalized and non-materialized nature, the validity of online arbitration has been questioned time and again and its process has been criticized as there is a lack of face-to-face meetings and the use of Information and Communication Technology (ICT) has led to a plethora of security and confidentiality issues.

The efficacy of Online Arbitration can be divided into three parts.

1. The agreement entered and signed between the parties is valid and enforceable as the Hon'ble Supreme Court of India upholds the validity of online agreements in the case of ***Shakti Bhog Foods Ltd. vs Kola Shipping Ltd.,*** and ***Trimex International FZE Ltd. vs Vedanta Aluminium Ltd.***
2. All documents including Statement of Claim and defence, etc., can be transmitted in electronic form with the aid of Section 4 and 5 of the Information Technology Act, 2000 read with Section 65B of the Indian Evidence Act, 1872.
3. Lastly, the legal sanctity of the Online Arbitral Award has been backed by Section 31(1) of the Arbitration and Conciliation Act, 1996 which states that the arbitration award shall be in writing and shall be signed by the members of the arbitral tribunal. In furtherance, Section 5 of the Information and Technology Act, 2000 elucidates that the digital signature has the same effect as that of a paper signature.

CONCLUSION

The landscape of justice systems has become more complex and challenging through the identification of cases. The intergovernmental initiatives have promoted new conventions, frameworks, guidelines and legislative actions, although the principle institutions of civil and criminal justice systems remain grounded in nation-states. Pursuing claims before the Courts or out of Court comes under the ambit of the right to access to justice which is protected at an international, European and national level.

As recommended by Lord Woolf, Civil and Criminal Justice reforms require not more rules of court enshrining lawyers' obligations to assist courts to deal justly with cases, but a commitment by profession to evaluate, coordinate and elaborate its practice rules and disciplinary processes and to provide appropriate guidance on the rules in the form of commentary appended to the rules. Such rules and commentary should feature the competing roles and responsibilities of lawyers as advisers, advocates, negotiators, and representatives within ADR processes and as neutrals facilitating such processes (Australian Law Reform Commission, 1999).

As Mahatma Gandhi rightly said,

"I realized that the true function of a lawyer was to unit parties. The lesson was so indelibly burnt into me that a large part of my time during the twenty years of my practice as a lawyer was occupied in bringing about private compromise of hundreds of cases. I lost nothing thereby not even money; certainly not my soul".

The availability of ADR methods rests with national initiatives that support the creation of institutions that provides ADR services. The English experience of promoting mediation for civil disputes has demonstrated its value as a supplement to court procedures, as part of a flexible range of dispute resolution processes. The experience also illustrates the difficulty of changing attitudes overnight, the role of the legal profession in influencing those attitudes, and the limitation of ADR as a "fix" for the problems of civil justice. If ADR is to be encouraged, it should be part of what is on offer in a flexible, appropriate and proportionate dispute resolution landscape.

On the other hand, the scope of using ODR is not unlimited. The concept of ODR in cyberspace is indeed a welcomed innovation, especially for online users and those involved in e-commerce. With the advancement of technology, disputes can be resolved instantly and in the comfort of one's home thus, oblivating the need to travel and/or incur expenses that would ordinarily have been incurred during litigation or traditional ADR. The development of online arbitration paves the way for issues related to data security. Where privacy is concerned, the parties to the agreement must be made aware of how their privacy will be protected, and measures are undertaken to store their personal information. With such an immense development in the digital economy, it is the need of the hour to legislate a bill/law within a reasonable time frame.

REFERENCES

Baxi, U. (1982). Developments in Indian Administrative Law. In A. G. Noorani (Ed.), Public Law in India (Vol. 134). Academic Press.

Bingham, T. (2010). *The Rule of Law*. Allen Lane Penguin.

Blankenburg, E. (1999). *Civil Justice: Access, Cost, and Expedition—The Netherlands*. Academic Press.

Buchman, J. M. (2001). Criteria for a free society: Definition, Diagnosis and Prescription. In *Collected works of Buchman*. Academic Press.

Buscaglia, E., & Ulen, T. (1997). A quantitative assessment of the efficiency of the judicial sector in Latin America. *International Review of Law and Economics*, *17*(2), 275–291. doi:10.1016/S0144-8188(97)00007-0

Davies, G. L. (2002). *The Reality of Civil Justice Reform: Why We Must Abandon the Essential Elements of Our System*. Paper presented at the 20th Australasian Institute of Judicial Administration Annual Conference, Brisbane, Australia.

Dodson, S. (2009). Comparative convergences in pleading standards. Academic Press.

Goodhart, J. (1958). The Rule of Law and Absolute Sovereignty. *Pennsylvania Law Review*, 946-63.

Holovaty, S. (2006). *The Rule Of Law*. Phoenix Publishing House.

Jack, J. (1982). The reform of civil procedural law. In *The Reform of Civil Procedural Law and Other Essays in Civil Procedure*. Sweet & Maxwell.

Jacobs, F. G. (2007). *The Sovereignty of Law: The European Way*. Academic Press.

Jowell, J. (2011). The Rule of Law and Its Underlying Values. In The Changing Constitution. Oxford Univ. Press.

Katsh, E. (2011). Online Dispute Resolution, Some lessons from the E-commerce Revolution. *N Ky. L. Rev, 28*(810, 811).

Krause, J. (n.d.). American Bar Association. *ABA Journal, 93*(10).

Masood, A. (2018). Mediation: The Need for a United, Clear and Consistent Judicial Voice. *CJQ, 1*(369).

Quek, D. (2010). Mandatory Mediation: An Oxymoron? Examining the Feasibility of Implementing a Court-Mandated Mediation Program. *Cardozo Journal of Conflict Resolution, 11*(479).

Tamanaha, B. Z. (2002). The Rule of Law for Everyone? *Current Legal Probs*, 97.

United Nations Security Council (UNSC). (2004). *Report of the Secretary-General on the Rule of Law and Transitional Justice in Conflict and Post-conflict Societies*. UN Doc S/2004/106, para.

Upendra, B. (1982). Developments in Indian Administrative Law. In A. G. Noorani (Ed.), Public Law in India (Vol. 134). Academic Press.

Woolf, L. H. (1995). *Access to Justice: Interim Report to the Lord Chancellor on the Civil Justice System in England and Wales*. Academic Press.

World Bank. (2003). *The World Bank Research Observer, 18*(1), 61–88. doi:10.1093/wbro/lkg005

Zuckerman, A. S. (2012). *Civil Justice in Crisis: Comparative Perspectives of Civil Procedure*. Oxford University Press.

APPENDIX: ADDITIONAL RESOURCES

American Bar Association, Jason Krause, ABA Journal, Vol. 93, No. 10.

Australian Law Reform Commission (ALRC), Review of the Federal Civil Justice System, Discussion Paper 62 (1999) chs 3 and 5 (hereafter referred to by the Commission's reference ALRC DP 62"), quoted in ALRC 89, [5.4].

Gore vs Naheed [2017] EWCA Civ 369

Ome Trimex International FZE Ltd v Vedanta Aluminium Ltd, [2010] 3 SCC 1.

PGF II SA vs IMFS Co Ltd [2013] EWCA Civ 1288; [2014] 1 W.L.R. 1386

Salem Advocates Bar Association, Tamil Nadu v Union of India, AIR [2003] SC 189.

Shakti Bhog Foods Ltd v Kola Shipping Ltd, AIR [2009] SC 12.

State of Punjab vs G.S. Gill, (1997) 6 SCC 129.

Superintending Engineer, Public Health vs Kuldeep Singh, (1997) 9 SCC 199.

Thakkar vs Patel [2017] EWCA Civ 117

The World Bank Research Observer, Spring, 2003, Vol. 18, No. 1 (Spring, 2003), pp. 61-88.

What You Should Know About Online Dispute Resolution Hon. Arthur M. Monty Ahalt (ret.).

Compilation of References

Abdul-Rafiu, A. (2015). *The institution and challenges of alternative dispute resolution (ADR) in West Africa: The Case of Ghana* (Doctoral dissertation). University of Ghana.

Access to Justice Survey, 2015-16. (n.d.). www.dakshindia.org

Acquah, G. (1991). Customary Offences and the Courts. *Review of Ghana Law*, *18*, 36–67.

Adjabeng, M. S. (2007). *Alternative dispute resolution in Ghana*. mediate.com/articles/adjabeng3.cfm

Adjabeng, M. S. (2009). *Gender justice in Ghana through court-connected ADR*. Available online at www.mediate.com/articles/adjabengs4.cfm

Adjabeng, S. M. (2007). *Challenges facing trade unions in modern times. ADR practice guide*. Accra Printing Press.

Adjei, D. D. (2014). *Ghana's jury system on trial thesis* (Master's thesis). Duke University, School of law.

Adjei, D. D. (2020). Constitutional Law of Ghana: Evolution, Theory and Practice. Accra: Adwinsa Publications (Gm.) Ltd.

ADR Practitioner Guide. (2017). Accra, Ghana: Academic Press.

Affrifah, K. K. K. (2015). *Alternative dispute resolution as a tool for conflict resolution in Africa with Ghana as a case study* (Doctoral dissertation). University of Ghana.

African Charter on Human and Peoples' Rights (1981/1986).

AfroBarometer Report. (2019). Ghanaians cite high cost, bias, and long delays as barriers to using formal justice system. In *AD347: Ghanaians cite high cost, bias, and long delays as barriers to using formal justice system*. AfroBarometer.

Agyekum, K. (1999). The Pragmatics of Duabɔ "Grievance Imprecation" Taboo among the Akan. *Pragmatics*, *9*(3), 357–382. doi:10.1075/prag.9.3.03agy

Agyekum, K. (2008). Akan Traditional Arbitration: Its Structure and Language. *Journal of Multilingual and Multicultural Development*, *27*(5), 359–374. doi:10.2167/jmmd428.1

Ahuma, A. S. R. B. (1972). One-Man Policy—A Curse to West Africa. *The Gold Coast Nation and National Consciousness*, 54–59.

Aihe, D. O. (1973). Fundamental Human Rights Provisions as Means of Achieving Justice in Society: The Nigerian "Bill Of Rights". *Malaya Law Review*, *15*(1), 39–54.

Akin, O. L., & Noone, M. (2017). Alternative dispute resolution processes: Connections between purposes, values, ethics and justice. *Law in Context (Bundoora, Vic.)*, *3*(5), 5–23.

Akpabli-Honu, K. (2009). The Legal versus Domestic Treatment of Child Sexual Defilement Cases in Ghana. In S. Tonah (Ed.), Contemporary Social Problems in Ghana (pp. 229-240). Legon: Research and Publication Unit.

Albright, M. (2012). *The advantages and disadvantages of alternative dispute resolution.* AlbrightStoddard.

Alexander, D. (2002). From civil defense to civil protection–and back again. *Disaster prevention and management. International Journal (Toronto, Ont.), 11*(3), 209–213.

Alhassan, A. R. (2015). *The Institution and Challenges of ADR in West Africa -The Case of Ghana* (Diss.). University of Ghana.

Allan, T. R. (2001). *Constitutional Justice: A Liberal Theory of the Rule of Law.* Oxford University Press.

Alternative Dispute Resolution Act 798, Ghana (2010). http://mariancrc.org/wp-

Alternative Dispute Resolution Act of 2010 (Act 798)

Altman, M. C. (2021). *A theory of legal punishment deterrence, retribution, and the aims of the state.* Routledge. doi:10.4324/9781003143352

Alvarez de la Campa, A. (2009). *The private sector approach to commercial ADR: Commercial ADR approach mechanism in Colombia. Investment Climate Department.* World Bank.

Amarteifio, M., Lartey, Aburam, L., Okudzeto, S. (2021). Arbitration procedures and practice in Ghana: Overview. *Thomas Reuters Practical Law.* uk.practicallaw.thomasreuters.com/66107025?transitionType=Default&contextDaata=

Amegatcher, N. O. (2011, September). *A Daniel comes to judgment: Ghana's ADR Act. A progressive or retrogressive piece of legislation.* Paper presented at the Ghana Bar Association Annual Conference, Accra, Ghana.

American Bar Association, House of Delegates, & Center for Professional Responsibility (American Bar Association). (2006). *Model rules of professional conduct.* American Bar Association.

Amidu, M. A. (2019, August 8). *The Office of the Special Prosecutor has no jurisdiction to investigate financial and economic crimes – The PDS case.* Retrieved June 19, 2021, from GhanaWeb: https://www.ghanaweb.com/GhanaHomePage/features/The-Office-of-the-Special-Prosecutor-has-no-jurisdiction-to-investigate-financial-and-economic-crimes-The-PDS-case-770385

Andrew, J. S. (2003). Potential application of mediation to land use conflicts in small-scale mining. *Journal of Cleaner Production, 11*(2), 117–130. doi:10.1016/S0959-6526(02)00032-X

Anirvan. (1970). *Veda Mimamsa* (Vol. 3). Sanskrit College.

Apeh, E. I., & Onoja, U. F. (2018). Literacy Promotion for Human Rights Awareness and Protection- The Case of Nigeria. *Journal of Good Governance and Sustainable Development in Africa, 4*(1), 14–22.

Apiagyei-Atua, K. (2000). Contribution of the Akan philosophy to the conceptualization of African notions of rights. *Constitutional and International Law Journal of Southern Africa, 16*(5).

Apiagyei-Atua, K. (2013). Alternative dispute resolution and its implications for women's access to justice in Africa: Case study of Ghana. *Frontiers of Legal Research, 1*(1), 36–57.

Appiagyei-Atua, K. (2007). Ghana-Justice sector and rule of law. *Open Society Initiative for West Africa*, 3.

Asante, K. P. (2019). *An Assessment of the Office of the Special Prosecutor, One Year On.* CorruptionWatch.

AsuzuC. (2012). Fundamental Rights Enforcement- The Role of the Office of Public Defender of Lagos State of Nigeria. doi:10.2139srn.2086358

Atiemo, A. O. (2012). Punish My Husband but not so Hard: Religion, Customary Values and Conventional Approaches to Human Rights in Ghana. *Religion and Human Rights*, *7*(2), 71–93. doi:10.1163/187103212X650059

Atugaba, R. (n.d.). *Access to justice, formal and informal: definitions, experiences, ideas, convergences and non-convergencies*. Paper presented at the CUSO international seminar under the theme: experiences of improvements in access to justice, inter-legality restorative justice, multicultural societies, legal pluralism, gender and human rights.

Atuguba, R. A., Agyebeng, K., & Dedey, E. (2006). *Access to Justice in Ghana: The Real Issues.* Final Report: Desk Review for Civic Foundation.

Atupare, P. A. (2021). A fundamental law of reason and the constitutional law of elections in Africa. *Journal of Comparative Law in Africa*, *8*(1), 1–41. doi:10.47348/JCLA/v8/i1a1

Bacow, L. S., & Wheeler, M. (2013). *Environmental dispute resolution.* Springer Science & Business Media.

Baldwin, J. (2000). Access to Justice: The English Experience with Small Claims. PREM Notes; No. 40. World Bank.

Barriteau, E. (2003). *Confronting power, theorizing gender: interdisciplinary perspectives in the Caribbean.* UWI Press.

Bassey, R. I. (2016). Natural law theory and its implications for human rights in Nigeria. Sophia: *An African. The Journal of Philosophy*, *17*(1), 208–218.

Basu, B. D. (Ed.). (1923). *The Sacred Books of the Hindus.* Panini Office.

Baxi, U. (1982). Developments in Indian Administrative Law. In A. G. Noorani (Ed.), Public Law in India (Vol. 134). Academic Press.

Baxter, P., & Jack, S. (2008). Qualitative case study methodology: Study design and implementation for novice researchers. *Qualitative Report*, *13*(4), 544–559.

Bayles, M. (1986). Principles for legal procedure. *Law and Philosophy*, *5*(1), 33–57. doi:10.1007/BF00143011

BBC. (2020, July 27). *Nanabaa: Ghana community for Kafaba lynch 90-year-old woman who dem accuse of witchcraft.* Retrieved April 11, 2021, from https://www.bbc.com/pidgin/tori-53554465

Bennett, J. (1984). *A Study of Spinoza's Ethics.* Hackett Publishing.

Bennion, F. (1962). *The Constitutional Law of Ghana.* Butterworths.

Bernard, E. P. (2006). Begging for justice? Or adapting jurisprudence? Initial reflections on the mandatory ADR to enforce women's rights in Rwanda. *Cardozo Journal of Conflict Resolution*, *32*(5), 326–327.

Bevington, P. R., Robinson, D. K., Blair, J. M., Mallinckrodt, A. J., & McKay, S. (1993). Data reduction and error analysis for the physical sciences. *Computers in Physics*, *7*(4), 415–416. doi:10.1063/1.4823194

Bhalla, M. M. (1988). Case for Abolition of Process Fee in Civil and Criminal Cases. *AIR Journal, 90.*

Bhatia, G. (2021). *The Past is a Foreign Country. In The Transformative Constitution.* HarperCollins Publishers India.

Bimpong-Buta, S. Y. (2005). *The Role of the Supreme Court in the Development of Constitutional Law in Ghana.* University of South Africa.

Bingham, T. (2010). *The Rule of Law.* Allen Lane Penguin.

Black, A. (2016). *A World History of Ancient Political Thought*. Oxford University Press. doi:10.1093/acprof:oso/9780198790686.001.0001

Blackaby, N., Partasides, C., Redfern, A., & Hunter, M. (2009). *Redfern and Hunter on international arbitration*. Oxford University Press. doi:10.1093/law:iic/9780199557189.001.1

Blankenburg, E. (1999). *Civil Justice: Access, Cost, and Expedition—The Netherlands*. Academic Press.

Boasiako, F. (2017). *Using Technology for Access to Justice in Ghana and Canada: Examining the Digital Divide*. Academic Press.

Bodenheimer, E. (1974) Power, Law and Society: A Study of the Will to Power and the Will to Law. *WASH. U.L.Q.*, 375.

Boer, M., & Pyo, C. (2011). *Good Policing. Instruments Models and Practices*. Asia- Europe Foundation.

Boniface, D., & Legg, M. (2010). Cost, Delay and Justice: The High Court of Australia Recognizes the Importance of Case Management in Civil Litigation—Aon Risk Services Australia Limited v Australian National University. *Common Law World Review*, *39*(2), 157–180. doi:10.1350/clwr.2010.39.2.0202

Botchway, T. P. (2018). Ghana: A Consolidated Democracy? *Asian Research Journal of Arts & Social Sciences*, 1-13.

Botchway, T. P. (2018a). Civil Society and the Consolidation of Democracy in Ghana's Fourth Republic. *Cogent Social Sciences*, *4*(1), 1452840. doi:10.1080/23311886.2018.1452840

Boulle, L. (2005). A history of alternative dispute resolution. *ADR Bulletin*, *7*(7), 3.

Bradley, A. W. (1997). *Constitutional and Administrative Law* (14th ed.). Longman.

Brems, E., & Adekoya, C. O. (2010). Human rights enforcement by people living in poverty: Access to justice in Nigeria. *Journal of African Law*, *54*(02), 258–282. doi:10.1017/S0021855310000070

Brobbey, S. A. (2008). *The Laws of Chieftaincy in Ghana*. Advanced Legal Publications.

Broom, H. (1845). *A Selection of Legal Maxims, Classified and Illustrated*. T. & J. W. Johnson.

Brown, L. P. (2012). *Policing in the 21st Century. Community Policing*. Author House.

Bryan, P.E. (1997). The coercion of women in divorce settlement negotiations. *Denv. UL. Rev, 931*.

Bryman, A. (2001). The nature of qualitative research. *Social Research Methods*, 365-399.

Buahen, A. A. (1975). *Ghana Evolution and Change in Nineteenth and Twentieth Centuries*. Sankofa.

Buchman, J. M. (2001). Criteria for a free society: Definition, Diagnosis and Prescription. In *Collected works of Buchman*. Academic Press.

Burton, J. W. (1990). *Conflict: Resolution and prevention* (Vol. 1990). Macmillan.

Buscaglia, E., & Ulen, T. (1997). A quantitative assessment of the efficiency of the judicial sector in Latin America. *International Review of Law and Economics*, *17*(2), 275–291. doi:10.1016/S0144-8188(97)00007-0

Busia, K. A. (1968). *The Position of the Chief in the Modern Political System of Ashanti: A Study of the Influence of Contemporary Social Changes of Ashanti Political Institution*. Frank Cass & Co. Ltd.

Caenegem, V. (1998). Birth of the English common law. Academic Press.

Calkins Law Firm. (2020). *The pros and cons of alternative dispute resolution.* Calkins. calkinslawfirm.com/resources/the-pros-and-cons-of-alternative-dispute-resolution-26756

Callaghan, A. (1992). Utilitarianism and distributive justice: Jeremy Bentham and the civil law. *History of European Ideas*, *14*(5), 739–742. doi:10.1016/0191-6599(92)90011-Z

Centre for Democracy and Governance. (1998). *Alternative dispute resolution. Practitioner's Guide 8*. Technical Publication Series.

Centre for Justice Democracy. (n.d.). Retrieved from https://centerjd.org/content/what-does-%E2%80%9Ccivil-justice%E2%80%9D-mean-0 on 14/06/2021

Chagadama, F. (2014). *A critical examination of the use of mediation as a tool for the realisation of women's access to justice in property cases in the legal aid sector, Zimbabwe* (Doctoral dissertation).

Christensen, D. (2016). Conciliation, Uniqueness and Rational Toxicity1. *Noûs (Detroit, Mich.)*, *50*(3), 584–603. doi:10.1111/nous.12077

Cofie, S. (2007). *Ghana establishment of the commercial court-smart lessons*. Available at http//: www.doingbusiness.org/media/FPDCM/Ghanacommercialcourts

Coker, M. A., & Obo, U. B. (2012). Crisis of governance and the violations of human rights: The Nigerian experience, 1999 to 2007. *African Journal of Political Science and International Relations*, *6*(3), 62–73.

Constitution of Ghana. (1992). *Constitution of Ghana*. Government of Ghana.

Constitution of the Federal Republic of Nigeria (1999)

Contiades, X., & Fotiadou, A. (2017). *Participatory Constitutional Change: The People as Amenders of the Constitution*. Routledge.

Court for Use of Mimamsa Principles of Interpretation. (2009, Aug. 21). *The Hindu*.

Couture, E. J. (1950). The nature of the judicial process. *Tulane Law Review*, *25*(1), 28.

Crook, C. R. (2011). *Alternative dispute resolution and the magistrates' courts in Ghana. A case of practical hybridity*. African Power and Programme Working Paper No. 25.

Crook, R. C. (2012). Alternative dispute resolution and the Magistrate's Courts in Ghana: A case of practical hybridity. *Africa Power and Politics Programme working Paper*, 25.

Crook, R. C., Asante, K. P., & Brobbey, V. K. (2011b). Popular Concepts of Justice and Hybrid Judicial Institutions in Ghana. *IDS Bulletin*, *42*(4), 64–75. doi:10.1111/j.1759-5436.2011.00212.x

Crook, R. C., Asante, K., & Brobbey, V. (2011a). Popular Concepts of Justice and Fairness in Ghana: Testing the Legitimacy of New or Hybrid Forms of State Justice. In P. Albrecht, H. M. Kyed, D. Isser, & E. Harper (Eds.), *Perspectives on Involving Non-State and Customary Actors in Justice and Security Reform*. International Development Law Organization.

D' Entreves, A. P. (1967). *The Notion of the State*. Oxford University Press.

Dada, J. A. (2012). Impediments to Human Rights Protection in Nigeria. *Annual Survey of International & Comparative Law*, *18*(1), 67–92.

Dada, J. A. (2013). The Significance and Limits of NGOs in Human Rights Protection in Nigeria. Journal of Law. *Policy and Globalization*, *19*, 82–91.

Daniels, W. E. (1991). The Development of Customary Law. *Review of Ghana Law, 18*, 68–94.

Danquah, J. B. (1957). The Historical Significance of the Bond of 1844. *Transactions of the Historical Society of Ghana, 3*(1), 3–29.

Davies, G. L. (2002). *The Reality of Civil Justice Reform: Why We Must Abandon the Essential Elements of Our System.* Paper presented at the 20th Australasian Institute of Judicial Administration Annual Conference, Brisbane, Australia.

De Sousa Santos, B. (2000). Law and community-the capitalist changing nature of state power in late capitalism. In The Politics of International Justice. The American Experience.

Deng, F. M., & Zartman, I. W. (Eds.). (2011). *Conflict resolution in Africa.* Brookings Institution Press.

Desmond, D.E., Cecil, C. and Frederick, M. (2014). Poverty, human rights and access to equity: Reflections from Nigeria. *International Journal of Law and Legal Studies, 1*(2), 40-49.

Dicey, A. V. (1897). *Introduction of the Study of the Law of the Constitution* (6th ed.). Macmillan.

Dieng, A. (2011). Alternative dispute resolution in Sub-Saharan African countries. In *ADR in business practice and issues across countries and cultures.* Arnold Ingen-Houz.

Diplock, L. (1981). Bremer Vulkan Schiffbau and Maschinenfabrik v South India Shipping Corp, AC 909, HL, 976.

Diwan, M. A. (2004). Conflict between State Legal Norms and Norms underlying Popular Beliefs: Witchcraft in Africa as a Case Study. *Duke Journal of Comparative & International Law, 14*, 351–387.

Dodson, S. (2009). Comparative convergences in pleading standards. Academic Press.

Dovlo, E. (2004). Religion and Politics in Africa: The Ghanaian Case. In S. E. Quainoo (Ed.), *Africa Through Ghanaian Lense.* Vesta International Press.

Duodu, S. (2020, July 24). 90-year-old woman accused of witchcraft lynched at Kafaba near Salaga. *Daily Graphic.* Retrieved from https://www.graphic.com.gh/news/general-news/90-year-old-woman-accused-of-witchcraft-lynched-at-kafaba-near-salaga.html

Durojaye, E. (2018). Access to justice as a mechanism for the enforcement of the right to development in Africa. In C. C. Ngang, S. D. Kamga, & V. Gumede (Eds.), *Perspective on the right to development* (pp. 47–69). PULP.

Duve, T. (2018). Legal traditions: A dialogue between comparative law and comparative legal history. *Journal of Comparative Legal History, 6*(1), 15–3. doi:10.1080/2049677X.2018.1469271

Earney, L. (2011). On the advantages of negotiation. *Serials, 24*(3).

Edzii, J. A. (2018). *Is Alternative Dispute Resolution a Solution to Interpersonal and Group Conflicts in West Africa? The Case of Ghana* (Doctoral dissertation). University of Ghana.

Ejiogu, A. (2003). Aquinas Conception of Human Dignity: A lesson Against Abuse of Human Rights in Africa. *Amamihe Journal of Applied Philosophy, 1*(1), 1–17.

Ellis, A. B. (1887). The Tshi-Speaking Peoples of Gold Coast of West Africa: their Religion, Manners, Customs, Laws, Language, Etc. Anthropological Publications.

Ellis, A. (2014). Theories of Punishment. In G. Bruinsma & D. Weisburd (Eds.), *Encyclopedia of Criminology and Criminal Justice.* Springer. doi:10.1007/978-1-4614-5690-2_512

Elton, G. R. (2010). *Studies in Tudor and Stuart Politics and Government.* Cambridge University Press.

Erskine, M. (2019). *Parliamentary Practice* (25th ed.). LexisNexis.

Erugo, S. (2016). Legal Assistance by Clinical Law Students: A Nigerian Experience in Increasing Access to Justice for the Unrepresented. *Asian Journal of Legal Education, 3*(2), 160–173. doi:10.1177/2322005816640335

Falt, J. (1983). Congestion and Delays in Asia's Courts. *Pacific Basin Law Journal, 4*(90), 107.

Felix, O., & Akujobi, A. (2018). Enforcement of Fundamental Rights in National Constitutions: Resolving the Conflict of Jurisdiction between the Federal High Court and State High Court in Nigeria. *Beijing Law Review, 9*(01), 53–66. doi:10.4236/blr.2018.91004

FelsöF. A.de NooijM. (2012). *When Justice Takes Time: The Social Cost of Legal Delay.* Available at SSRN: doi:10.2139srn.2136897

Feltoe, G. (2012). *A Guide to Administrative and Local Government law in Zimbabwe.* University of Zimbabwe.

Fernyhough, T. (1993). *Human rights in pre-colonial Africa.* University Press of Florida.

Fiadjor, A., & Okyir, N.T. (2016). The alternative dispute resolution Act of Ghana deconstructed: providing a more positive sum approach to court resolution. *Transnational Dispute Management, 4.*

Fiadjor, A. (2004). *Alternative dispute resolution: a developing world perspective.* Cavendish.

Forst, M. L. (1977). Trial courts in the Modern System of Criminal Justice. *Criminal Justice Review, 2*(1), 73–88. doi:10.1177/073401687700200107

Fuller, L. L. (2018). *Mediation—Its forms and functions.* Routledge. doi:10.4324/9781315204826-1

Fundamental Rights Enforcement Procedure Rules (2009)

Galanter, M. (2008). Fifty Years On. In B. N. Kirpal (Ed.), *Supreme but not Infallible: Essays in Honour of the Supreme Court of India* (pp. 59–61). Oxford University Press.

Genn, H. (2009). *Judging Civil Justice.* Cambridge University Press. doi:10.1017/CBO9781139192378

Genn, H. (2012). *Understanding civil justice.* University College of London.

Gerdy, K. B. (2000). What is the difference between substantive and procedural law? And how do I research procedure? Perspectives. *Teaching Legal Research and Writing*, 9.

Ghana News Agency. (2012). Women slam CHRAJ and the Department of Social Welfare on the handling of abuses. *Online (Bergheim).*

Ghanaweb. (2013, September 20). *NPP should have gone to antoa instead of court — Kofi Jumah.* Retrieved April 10, 2021, from https://www.ghanaweb.com/GhanaHomePage/NewsArchive/NPP-should-have-gone-to-antoa-instead-of-court-Kofi-Jumah-286392

Gilligan, G. (1993). *In a different voice: psychological theory and women's development.* Harvard University Press.

Glendon. (1982). *Comparative legal traditions in a nutshell.* OJP Publications.

Glenn, H. P. (2004). *Legal tradition of the world.* Oxford University Press.

Godongs, S. (2006). *Mediation and the mediation process. In Introduction to peace and conflict studies in West Africa: A Reader.* Spectrum Books.

Goodhart, J. (1958). The Rule of Law and Absolute Sovereignty. *Pennsylvania Law Review*, 946-63.

Government of Ghana. (2012). *Alternative dispute resolution Act, 798, 2010*. Government of Ghana.

Government of Sierra Leone. (2019). *Legal Aid Board Annual Report 2019*. Author.

Gray, N. (2000). *The Legal History of Witchcraft in Colonial Ghana: Akyem Abuakwa, 1913-1943* (Unpublished doctoral dissertation). Columbia University.

Gray, N. (2001). Witches, Oracles, and Colonial Law: Evolving Anti-Witchcraft Practices in Ghana, 1927-1932. *The International Journal of African Historical Studies*, *34*(2), 339–363. doi:10.2307/3097485 PMID:18198526

Grbich, C. (2012). *Qualitative data analysis: An introduction*. Sage.

Grimble, R., & Wellard, K. (1997). Stakeholder methodologies in natural resource management: A review of principles, contexts, experiences and opportunities. *Agricultural Systems*, *55*(2), 173–193. doi:10.1016/S0308-521X(97)00006-1

Gropper, A. (2010). *Alternative dispute resolution in tax disputes*. Research Note. Washington DC: World Bank.

Grushetsky, A. (2015). *Highlighting coverage of alternative dispute resolution in Ghana*. Ohio Journal on Dispute Resolution.

Guest, G., Bunce, A., & Johnson, L. (2006). How many interviews are enough? An experiment with data saturation and variability. *Field Methods*, *18*(1), 59–82. doi:10.1177/1525822X05279903

Gyanendra, K. S., & Pranav, V. (n.d.). *Bottlenecks in Civil Justice Administration before the Courts and the Remedies thereof: A Research*. Uttarakhand Judicial and Legal Review. Retrieved from https://ujala.uk.gov.in/files/Ch1.pdf

Gyekye, K. (1987). *An essay on African philosophical thought: The Akan conceptualization scheme*. Cambridge University Press.

Hale, S. B. (2004). *The Discourse of Court Interpreting: Discourse Practices of the Law, the Witness and the Interpreter*. John Benjamins. doi:10.1075/btl.52

Hardt, S. (2013). *Parliamentary immunity: a comprehensive study of the systems of parliamentary immunity of the United Kingdom, France and the Netherlands in a European context*. Maastricht University.

Harris, F. C. (2013). *Holding police accountability theory to account* (Thesis). Institute of Criminal Justice Studies, University of Portsmouth.

Hasit, B. S. (2021). Adhering to Statutory Timelines: A Step towards Better Case Management of Civil Trials. *2021 SCC Online Blog Ex. 6*. https://www.scconline.com/blog/post/2021/01/28/adhering-to-statutory-timelines-a-step-towards-better-case-management-of-civil-trials/

Hawkins, S. (2002). *Writing and Colonialism in Northern Ghana: The Encounter Between the LoDagaa and "The Wold on Paper," 1892-1991*. University of Toronto Press Inc. doi:10.3138/9781442657564

Hay, P. (2015). *International encyclopedia of the social & behavioral sciences*. Academic Press.

Henderson, E. G. (1964). *Foundation of English Administrative Law: Certiorari and Mandamus in the Seventeenth Century*. Harvard University Press.

Holovaty, S. (2006). *The Rule Of Law*. Phoenix Publishing House.

Hope, K. R. Sr. (2020). Civilian Oversight for Democratic Policing and its Challenges: Overcoming Obstacles for Improved Police Accountability. *Journal of Applied Security Research*, 1–33. doi:10.1080/19361610.2020.1777807

Hum. (2006). *The right to a fair hearing and access to justice-submission of the New South Wales young lawyers human rights committee to the senate legal affairs and constitutional committee: inquiry into access to justice*. www.senate.aph.gov.au/submissions committees/viewdocument.aspx?id

Igwe, I., Nwocha, M., & Steve, A. (2019). Enforcement of Fundamental Rights in Nigeria and the Unsolved Issue of Poverty among the Citizens: An Appraisal. *Beijing Law Review*, *10*(01), 1–9. doi:10.4236/blr.2019.101001

Illa, R. (1998). *The foundation of Indian Ethics: A special reference to Manu Smriti, Jaimini Sutras and Bhagavad Gita* [Unpublished doctoral dissertation]. University of Hyderabad. http://hdl.handle. net/10603/25297

International Commission of Jurists. (2011). *Access to Justice: Human Rights Abuses Involving Corporations*. https://www.business-humanrights.org/sites/default/files/media/documents/icj-report-access-to-justice-nigeria-22-feb-2012.pdf

Introduction to Law. (n.d.). *Substantive law and procedural or adjective law*. Retrieved from https://nios.ac.in/media/documents/SrSec338New/338_Introduction_To_Law_Eng/338_Introduction_To_Law_Eng_L11.pdf on 19/06/2021.

Jack, J. (1982). The reform of civil procedural law. In *The Reform of Civil Procedural Law and Other Essays in Civil Procedure*. Sweet & Maxwell.

Jacob, J. (1987). *The fabric of English civil justice. The Hamlyn Lectures 38th Series*. Stevens & Sons.

Jacobs, F. G. (2007). *The Sovereignty of Law: The European Way*. Academic Press.

Jenings, I. (2009). *The Law and the Constitution* (2nd ed.). Cambridge University Press.

Jessberger, F. (2005). Bad Torture- Good Torture? *Journal of International Criminal Justice, 3*, 1059-1073. Available from: www.oxfordjournals.org/our_journals/jicjus/ba

Johnsen, J. S. (2011). Alternative deal resolution: The facilitated negotiation of transactions. *Windsor Rev. Legal & Soc*, (30), 193.

Jois, M. R. (2012). *Legal and Constitutional History of India- Ancient Legal, Judicial and Constitutional System*. Universal Law Publishing Co.

Jois, M. R. (2017). *Uniform Law regulating the Constitution and Organization - Durga Das Basu Memorial Lecture*. WBNUJS.

Jolowicz, J. (2000). *Contents on civil procedure: Cambridge studies in international and comparative law*. Cambridge University Press. doi:10.1017/CBO9780511549540

Jones, T. (2008). The accountability of policing. In T. Newburn (Ed.), *Handbook of Policing* (pp. 693–723). Willan Publishing.

Jowell, J. (2011). The Rule of Law and Its Underlying Values. In The Changing Constitution. Oxford Univ. Press.

Kakalik, J. S. (1996). *Implementation of the civil justice reform act in pilot and comparison districts*. The Institute for Civil Justice.

Kanter, R. M. (1979). Power failure in management circuits. *Classics of Organization Theory*, 342-351.

Kariuki, F. (2015). Conflict resolution by elders in Africa: Successes, challenges and opportunities. *Alternative Dispute Resolution*, *3*(2), 30–53.

Karuiki, F. (2014). Applicability of traditional dispute resolution mechanisms in criminal cases in Kenya; Case study of *Republic v Mohamed Abdow Mohamed. Alternative Dispute Resolution Journal, 2*, 202.

Katju, M. (1993). The Mimamsa Principles of Interpretation. *Supreme Court Cases, 1*(16).

Katsh, E. (2011). Online Dispute Resolution, Some lessons from the E-commerce Revolution. *N Ky. L. Rev, 28*(810, 811).

Keith, A. B. (1921). *The Karma Mimamsa*. Association Press.

Kier, D. L., & Lawson, F. H. (1954). *Cases in Constitutional Law*. Oxford University Press.

Kirgis, P. (2014). Status and contract in an emerging democracy in the evolution of dispute resolution in Ghana. *Cardozo Journal of Conflict Resolution, 10*(1).

Kloth, M. (2010). *Immunities and the right of access to court under Article 6 of the European Convention on Human Rights*. Leiden: Martinus Nijhoff Publishers.

Koh, C. P. (2005). *The causes of construction dispute on client organizations* (Doctoral dissertation). Universiti Teknologi Malaysia.

Kourlis, R. L. (2016). Civil Justice Reform: A movement. *Idaho Law Review, 52*, 497.

Krause, J. (n.d.). American Bar Association. *ABA Journal, 93*(10).

Kumar, N. (1997). Constitutional Law of India. Academic Press.

Kumar, V. A. (2012). Judicial Delays in India: Causes and Remedies, *Journal of Law. Policy and Globalization, 4*, 16.

Law and Society. (2018). *An introduction to law and society*. SAGE publications, Inc.

Law Reform Commission. (2008). *Consultative on alternative dispute resolution*. LRC.

Legal Defence and Assistance Project. (2018). *Report On The Human Rights Situations In Nigeria*. file:///C:/Users/OLANRE~1/AppData/Local/Temp/LEDAP_UPR31_NGA_E_Main.pdf

Legal Information Institute. (2017). *Alternative dispute resolution. LII*. Cornel Law School.

Lerch, A. (2012). *Four legal tradition*. Retrieved from https://prezi.com/n6ez55kn9cqo/four-legal on 9/06/2021.traditions/?frame=e3b4ee4f051e99ba112094a9dc693eb7d3ba07f9 on 20/06/2021

Lima, V., & Gomez, M. (2020). Access to Justice: Promoting the Legal System as a Human Right. In UN (Ed.), Encyclopedia of the UN Sustainable Development Goals (pp. 1- 10). Springer Publishing.

Linn, A. H. (2007). *Envisioning reform: improving judicial performance in Latin America*. Pennsylvania State University Press.

Lippman, M. (2018). *Contemporary criminal law: Concepts, cases, and controversies*. SAGE Publications, Inc.

Locke, J. (1689). Two Treatises of Government. Laslett.

Loggerenberg, D. V. (2016). Civil justice in South Africa. *BRICS Law Journal, 3*(4).

Lorman Education. (2018). *Advantages and disadvantages of alternative dispute resolution*. LORMAN. https://www.lorman.com/resources/advantages-and-disadvantages-alternativedisputeresolution-16190

Love, I. (2011). *Settling out of court: How effective is alternative dispute resolution? Viewpoint, public policy for the private sector. Note No. 329*. The World Bank.

Mackie, K., Miles, D., Marsh, W., & Marsh, W. (1995). *Commercial dispute resolution: An ADR practice guide*. Butterworths.

Madan, B. L. (2021). *What is Stopping Our Justice System from Tackling the Pending before Courts?* https://thewire.in/law/india-judiciary-pending-cases-supreme-court

Maier, D. J. E. (1981). The Dente Oracle, the Bron Confederation, and Asante: Religion and the Politics of Secession. *Journal of African History*, *22*(2), 229–243. doi:10.1017/S0021853700019423

Mann, T. K. (n.d.). Administration of Justice in India: A case study of Punjab. Academic Press.

Martin, V. L. (2006). Domestic violence in Ghana: the open secret. *Georgia Journal of Gender and the Law*, 531-597.

Maschke, K. J. (1997). *Feminist legal theories*. Garland Publishers.

Masood, A. (2018). Mediation: The Need for a United, Clear and Consistent Judicial Voice. *CJQ*, *1*(369).

Mathur, V. K. (n.d.). *Early Disposal of Court Cases*. Academic Press.

Max-Wirth, C. (2016). *Juju and Statecraft: Occult Rumors and Politics in Ghana* (PhD dissertation). Victoria University of Wellington.

Mazrui, A. A. (1986). *The African: A Triple Heritage*. Little, Brown and Company.

McDaniel, J. (2015). *Rethinking Police Accountability and Transparency within the EU: Reconciling national and supranational approaches* (Thesis). University of Kent.

Melcame, A., & Ramello, G. (2016). *Justice delayed, growth denied: Evidence from a comparative perspective*. Retrieved from https://www.siecon.org/sites/siecon.org/files/oldfiles/uploads/2016/09/RAMELLO.pdf on 25/06/2021.

Menkel-Meadow, C. (2004). *Institute of civil justice paper prepared for the Scottish Consumer Council Seminar on Civil Justice*. Institute of Civil Justice.

Mensah-PanfordP. (2018). Mediation in Ghana's Criminal Justice System: A Proposal for an Extension to Cover Severe Offences. *Available at* SSRN 3144524.

Merryman, J. H., & Pérez-Perdomo, R. (2007). *The civil law tradition: An introduction to the legal systems of Europe and Latin America*. Stanford University Press.

Merryman, J. H., & Pérez-Perdomo, R. (2007). *The civil law tradition: An introduction to the legal systems of Western Europe and Latin America*. Stanford University Press.

Meyer, B. (1998). "Make a Complete Break With the Past": Memory and Post-Colonial Modernity in Ghanaian Pentecostalist Discourse. *Journal of Religion in Africa. Religion en Afrique*, *28*(3), 316–348.

Meyer, J. (1968). Reflections on some theories of punishment. *The Journal of Criminal Law, Criminology, and Police Science*, *59*(4), 595. doi:10.2307/1141839

Meyerowitz, E. L. R. (1951). *The Sacred State of the Akan*. Faber and Faber Ltd.

Miall, H. (2016). *The peacemakers: Peaceful settlement of disputes since 1945*. Springer.

ModernGhana. (2020, June 5). *Offinso South NPP Youth Invoke Curses On Any Executive Who Tries To Disqualify Any Of The Two Aspirants From Contesting The MP*. Retrieved from https://www.modernghana.com/news/1007195/offinso-south-npp-youth-invoke-curses-on-any-execu.html

Montesquieu, B. (1998). The Spirit of the Laws (Book 11). M. a. Cohler.

Moss, T. J., Pettersson Gelander, G., & Van de Walle, N. (2006). *An aid-institutions paradox? A review essay on aid dependency and state building in sub-Saharan Africa*. Academic Press.

Mueller, L. (2010). The persistence of Asante chieftaincy under colonial rule- the explanation of an enigma. *Africana Studia*, *15*, 61–85.

Muftau, R. (2016). Access to Judicial Justice in Nigeria: The Need for Some Future Reforms. Journal of Law. *Policy and Globalization*, *47*, 144–158.

Mugari, I. (2021). Evaluations of selected civilian oversight institutions for police accountability in the Republic of Zimbabwe. *Police Practice and Research*, *22*(1), 606-622. . doi:10.1080/15614263.2020.1831921

Muhayu-Deen, I. (2019). *Cutting short the ambition of students who wish to become lawyers in order to preserve the prestige of the legal profession*. Retrieved from https://www.ghanaweb.com/GhanaHomePage/features/Cutting-short-the-ambition-of-students-who-wish-to-become-lawyers-in-order-to-preserve-the-prestige-of-the-legal-profession-787046 on 22/6/2021

Muigua, K. & Francis, K. (2015). Alternative dispute resolution: Access to justice and development in Kenya. *Strathmore Law Journal, 1*(1).

Narayan, S. (1987). The Procedural Law in India Requires Through Changes. *AIR Journal*, *85*.

Nardulli, P. F. (1979). The case Load controversy and the Study of criminal courts. *J. Crime Law Journal*, *70*(1), 89–101. doi:10.2307/1142969

New York State Unified Court System. (n.d.). *Continuum of different alternative dispute resolution methods*. http://www.nycourts.gov/ip/adr/images/continuum 2.jpg

Nolan-Haley, J. (2014). Mediation: The best and worst of times. *Cardozo Journal of Conflict Resolution*, *16*, 731.

Noone, M., & Akin, O. L. (2020). Alternative dispute resolution and access to justice in Australia. *International Journal of Law in Context*, *16*(2), 108–127.

Ntrakwah, K. (2018). *Arbitration in Ghana*. Lexology. www.lexology.com/library/detail.aspx?g=02eed85-3a65f-4fbc-8ac1-a303f5fffe6e

Ntrakwah, K., & Asiama, A. (2017). *Arbitration Guide*. International Bar Association Arbitration Committee.

Nwachukwu, S. N., Aghamelo, A., & Nwaneri, S. (2014). An Account of Human Right Violations In Nigeria (Pre-British, British And Post-Independence). European Scientific Journal, 2, 230-239.

Nwafor, A. O. (2009). Enforcement of Fundamental Human Rights in Nigerian Courts – Processes and Challenges. *African Journal of Legal Studies*, *4*(1), 1–11. doi:10.1163/221097312X13397499736787

Nwauche, E. S. (2008). The Dubious Distinction between Principal and Accessory Claims in Nigeria Human Rights Jurisprudence. *Journal of African Law*, *52*(1), 66–88. doi:10.1017/S002185530800003X

Nzrenzah, G. (2015). *Modernizing Indigenous Priesthood and Revitalizing Old Shrines: Current Developments on Ghanas Religious Landscape* (Unpublished PhD dissertation). University of Bayreuth.

Oba, A. A. (2008). Juju Oaths in Customary Law Arbitration and their Legal Validity in Nigerian Courts. *Journal of African Law*, *52*(1), 139–158. doi:10.1017/S0021855308000065

Obeng, S. G. (1999). Grammatical Pragmatics: Power in Akan Judicial Discourse. *Pragmatics*, *9*(2), 199–229. doi:10.1075/prag.9.2.01obe

Odeku, K., & Animashaun, S. (2012). Poverty, human rights and access to justice: Reflections from Nigeria. *African Journal of Business Management*, *6*(23), 6754–6764.

OECD. (2013). *What makes civil justice effective?* OECD Economics Department Policy Notes. No. 18.

Ojielo, O. M. (2001). *Alternative dispute resolution (ADR)*. CPA Books.

Okogbule, N. S. (2005). Access to justice and human rights protection in Nigeria: Problems and prospects. *Sur. International Journal of Human Rights*, *2*(3), 95–113.

Olanrewaju, O. (2020). An Evaluation of the Knowledge and Perception of the Concept of Human Rights by Residents of Selected Suburban Communities of Lagos, Nigeria. *Journal of Human Rights and Social Work*, *5*, 185–190.

Olivelle, P. (2006). *Manu's Code of Law- A Critical Edition and Translation of the Manava Dharamasastra*. Oxford University Press.

Omidoyin, T. J. (2019). Law Clinic and Access to Justice for Pretrial Detainees in Nigeria. *Nnamdi Azikiwe University Journal of International Law and Jurisprudence*, *10*(1), 101–108.

Omoleye, B. O., & Eniola, B. O. (2018). Administration of Justice in Nigeria: Analysing the dominant legal ideology. *Journal of Law and Conflict Resolution*, *10*(1), 1–8. doi:10.5897/JLCR2016.0242

Onwubiko, E. (2019). *Nigeria: Parlous state of human rights*. https://guardian.ng/opinion/nigeria-parlous-state-of-human-rights/

Oricho, D. O. (1997). Understanding the benefits of alternative dispute resolution in the workplace mediation. *Journal of Law and Conflict Resolution, 2*, 11-19.

Osi, C. (2008). Understanding indigenous dispute resolution processes and western alternative dispute resolution: Cultivating appropriate methods in lieu of litigation. *Cardozo Journal of Conflict Resolution*, *10*, 163–232.

Owen, M. (1984). Against settlement. *Yale L.J., 1073*.

Owusu-Mensah, I. (2014). Politics, chieftaincy and customary law in Ghana's 4th republic. *PAN African Studies*, 261.

Palmer, R. C. (n.d.). *Conceptualization*. Retrieved from http://aalt.law.uh.edu/Conceptualization/Conceptualization.html

Pande, D. C., & Bagga, V. (1973). *Abridged Trial Procedure in Indian Law*. Indian Law Institute.

Pappas, B. A. (2015). Med-Arb and the legalization of alternative dispute resolution. *Harv. Negot. L. Rev.*, *20*, 157.

Patel, R. (2009). Indian Muslim Women, Politics of Muslim Personal Law and Struggle for Life with Dignity and Justice. *Economic and Political Weekly*, 44.

Pollock, F., & Maitland, F. W. (2010). The history of English law. Academic Press.

Pragadeeswaran, U. (2018). A Study on Delay in Civil Proceeding. *International Journal of Pure and Applied Mathematics*, *120*(5), 2571.

Price, C. (2018). Alternative dispute resolution in Africa: Is ADR the bridge between traditional and modern dispute resolution. *Pepp. Disp. Resol. LJ*, *18*, 393.

Proulx, C. (2003). *Reclaiming aboriginal justice, identity and community*. Purich Publishing.

Quansah, E. K. (2011). *Ghana Legal System*. Black Mask Limited.

Quansah, E. K. (2012). *The Ghana Legal System*. Black Mask Limited.

Quashigah, E.K. (1999). Legislating Religious Liberty: The Ghanaian Experience. BYU Law Review, 1999(2), 598-607.

Quayle, D. (1992). Civil justice reform. *The American University Law Review*, 41.

Quek, D. (2010). Mandatory Mediation: An Oxymoron? Examining the Feasibility of Implementing a Court-Mandated Mediation Program. *Cardozo Journal of Conflict Resolution, 11*(479).

Ramshorn, L. (1841). *Dictionary of Latin Synonyms*. Charles C. Little Press.

Rangarajan, L. N. (Ed.). (1987). *KAUTILYA- The Arthashastra*. Penguin Book.

Rankopo, M. J., & Osei-Hwedie, K. (2011). Globalization and culturally relevant social work: African perspectives on indigenization. *International Social Work, 54*(1), 137–147. doi:10.1177/0020872810372367

Ransley, J., Anderson, J., & Prenzler, J. (2007). Civil Litigation Against police in Australia: Exploring its Extent, Nature and Implications for Accountability. *Australian and New Zealand Journal of Criminology, 40*(2), 143–160. doi:10.1375/acri.40.2.143

Ransome-Kuti & ORS. v. AG Federation & ORS (1985) JELR 42572 (SC)

Rao, M. V. (1994). Legal Reforms for speedy disposal of cases. *AIR Journal, 89*.

Rattray, R. S. (1929). *Ashanti Law and Constitution*. Clarendon Press.

Report, I. J. (2019). *Ranking States on Police, Judiciary, Prisons and Legal Aid*. Retrieved from https://www.tatatrusts.org/upload/pdf/overall-report-single.pdf

Reports, A. (2019-2020). *Ministry of Law and Justice, Government of India*. https://lawmin.gov.in/documents/annualreports

Republic of Zimbabwe. (1980). *The Criminal Procedure and Evidence Act* [Chapter 9:07]. Government Printers.

Republic of Zimbabwe. (2013). The Constitution of Zimbabwe. Amendment (No 20). Harare: Government Printers.

Resnik, J. (1986). Failing Faith: Adjudicatory Procedure in Decline. *The University of Chicago Law Review. University of Chicago. Law School, 53*, 494.

Roberg, R., Novak, K., & Cordner, G. (2009). *Police and Society* (4th ed.). Oxford University Press.

Robin, S. (2009). A place for justice in an effective criminal justice system. Customary justice in Sierra Leone, Tanzania and Zambia. Institute for Security Studies, Policy Brief No. 17.

Roy, P. C. (1890). The Mahabarharta of Krishna – Dwaipayana Vyasa, Vol. 2: Translated into English Prose from the Original Sanskrit Text, Sabha Parva and Vana Parva (Part 1). Oriental Publishing Co.

Ruffin, F. (2019). Land Governance in the Context of Legal Pluralism: Cases of Ghana and Kenya. In *Trajectory of Land Reform in Post-Colonial African States* (pp. 91–108). Springer. doi:10.1007/978-3-319-78701-5_7

Sanni, A. (2011). Fundamental Rights Enforcement Procedure Rules, 2009 as a tool for the enforcement of the African Charter on Human and Peoples' Rights in Nigeria: The need for far-reaching reform. *African Human Rights Law Journal, 1*(2), 511–531.

Santos, A. (2006). The World Bank's uses of the rule of law: Promise in economic development. In The new law and economic development: A critical appraisal. Cambridge University Press.

Sarkar, A. N. (2010). Navigating the rough seas of global business negotiation: Reflection on cross-cultural issues and some corporate experiences. *International Journal of Business Insights & Transformation, 3*(2), 23–34.

Sarkar, K. L. (1905). *Mimamsa Principles of Interpretation: Tagore Law lectures* (J. M. Katju, Ed.). Modern Law Publications.

Sarkodie, K. (2011). *Arbitration in Ghana: The alternative dispute resolution Act 2010*. The International Construction Law Review.

Sastri, G. A. (1903). A Collection of Sanskrit Works: Tantarvaritka- A Gloss on Sabara Svami's Commentary on the Mimamsa Sutras by Bhatta Kumarila. Benares Sanskrit Series.

Saylor Academy. (2012). *Alternative dispute resolution*. Saylor Academy.

Seiwoh. (2012). *The Effectiveness of the Family Support in Handling and Responding to Gender Violence in Sierra Leone*. Academic Press.

Sengupta, A. (2004). The human right to development. *Oxford Development Studies*, I86.

Sharma, R. S. (1983). *Ancient India*. NCERT.

Shilston, T. G. (2016). Six dimensions of police accountability: An aid to needs assessment in international police development missions. *International Journal of Police Science & Management*, *18*(1), 37–46. doi:10.1177/1461355716638115

Shittu, W. (2015). *The challenges of access to justice*. https://guardian.ng/opinion/the-challenges-of-access-to-justice/

Shonk, K. (2020). *What is alternative dispute resolution? Familiarize yourself with mediation, arbitration, and a hybrid approach using alternative dispute resolution. Program on Negotiation*. Harvard Law School.

Sidgwick, H. (1907). *The Methods of Ethics*. Macmillan.

Singer, B. J. (1992). The privatization of family law. *Wis. L.R., 1443*.

Singhvi, G. C. (1976). Mounting Arrears of cases in Courts, Devolution of powers – A key solution. *CBI Bulletin*.

Sono, A. A. (2017). *A Comparative Study of Legal Aid Institutions in their Pursuit of Social Justice in Ghana* (Thesis). University of Ghana.

Sono, A. A. (2017). *A Comparative Study of Legal Aid Institutions in their Pursuit of Social Justice in Ghana*. Retrieved from http://ugspace.ug.edu.gh/bitstream/handle/123456789/32235/A%20Comparative%20Study%20of%20Legal%20Aid%20Institutions%20in%20their%20Pursuit%20of%20Social%20Justice%20in%20Ghana.pdf?sequence=1&isAllowed=y on 17/06/2021

Srikrishna, B. N. (2004). Maxwell v. Mimamsa. *Supreme Court Cases*, *6*(49).

Stevens, J. (2000). *Access to justice in sub-Saharan Africa: The role of traditional and informal justice systems*. Academic Press.

Stiefel, E.C., & Maxeiner, J. R. (n.d.). *Civil justice reform in the United States: Opportunity for learning from 'civilized' European procedure instead of continued isolation?* Academic Press.

Stipanowich, T. (2004). Alternative dispute resolution and the vanishing trial. The growth and impact of alternative dispute resolution. *Journal of Empirical Legal Studies*, *1*(3), 843–912.

Stone, K. V. (2004). *From widgets to digits: Employment regulation for the changing workplace*. Cambridge University Press. doi:10.1017/CBO9780511617089

Susskind, L., & Ozawa, C. (1984). Mediated negotiation in the public sector: The planner as mediator. *Journal of Planning Education and Research*, *4*(1), 5–15. doi:10.1177/0739456X8400400103

Taiwo, E. A. (2009). Enforcement of fundamental rights and the standing rules under the Nigerian Constitution: A need for a more liberal provision. *African Human Rights Law Journal*, *9*, 546–575.

Tamanaha, B. Z. (2002). The Rule of Law for Everyone? *Current Legal Probs*, 97.

Tawiah, O. (2020, June 5). *Juaben NPP supporters invoke curses on party executives*. Retrieved from https://www.adomonline.com/juaben-npp-supporters-invoke-curses-on-party-executives-video/

Tesch, R. (2013). *Qualitative research: Analysis types and software*. Routledge.

The Lawyers and Jurists. (2021). Explain the advantages and disadvantages of alternative dispute resolution. *The Lawyers and Jurists*. lawyersnjurists.com/article/advanatges-disadvantages-alternative-dispute-resolution/

Trakman, L. (1991). *Reasoning with the charter*. Butterworths.

Treacy, T. B. (1995). Use of alternative dispute resolution in the construction industry. *Journal of Management Engineering*, *11*(1), 58–63. doi:10.1061/(ASCE)0742-597X(1995)11:1(58)

Tweneboah, E. (n.d.). The Culture of Duabɔ (Imprecation), Legal Dysfunction and the Challenge of Human Rights Development in Ghana. In *The Culture of Duabɔ (Imprecation), Legal Dysfunction and the Challenge of Human Rights Development in Ghana*. Academia.edu.

Tweneboah, S. (2014). The Culture of Duabɔ (imprecation), Legal Dysfunction and the Challenge of Human Rights in Ghana. *Human Rights Research Journal*, *9*, 1–10.

Tweneboah, S. (2020). *Religion, Law, Politics and the State in Africa: Applying Legal Pluralism in Ghana*. Routledge.

Tweneboah, S. (2021). *Religion, Law, and Politics in Ghana: Duabɔ (Imprecation) as Spiritual Justice in the Public Sphere*. African Journal of Legal Studies., doi:10.1163/17087384-12340081

United Nations Committee on the Elimination of Discrimination Against Women. (2005). *Combined third, fourth, and fifth periodic reports of States parties, Ghana*. UN CEDAW.

United Nations Committee on the Elimination of Discrimination Against Women. (2006). *Concluding comments, Ghana*. UN CEDAW.

United Nations Development Programme. (2004). *Access to justice: Practice note*. UNDP.

United Nations Development Programme. (2006). *Parliaments, Crisis Prevention and Recovery: Guidelines for the International Community*. UNDP.

United Nations Security Council (UNSC). (2004). *Report of the Secretary-General on the Rule of Law and Transitional Justice in Conflict and Post-conflict Societies*. UN Doc S/2004/106, para.

United Nations. (1976). *International Covenant on Civil and Political Rights*. Author.

United Nations. (1987). *Convention against Torture and Other Cruel, Inhuman or Degrading Treatment or Punishment*. United Nations.

United Nations. (2016). *Global study on legal aid: Country profiles*. Author.

Upendra, B. (1982). Developments in Indian Administrative Law. In A. G. Noorani (Ed.), Public Law in India (Vol. 134). Academic Press.

Uwazie, E. E. (2011). *Alternative dispute resolution in Africa: preventing conflict and enhancing stability*. Africa Security Brief 16.

Uwazie, E. (Ed.). (2014). *Alternative dispute resolution and peace-building in Africa*. Cambridge Scholars Publishing.

Uwazie, E. E. (2011). *Alternative dispute resolution in Africa: Preventing conflict and enhancing stability* (Vol. 16). Africa Center for Strategic Studies.

Vanderpuye, F. (2008). *Traditional beliefs cost women their freedom*. www.secularhumanism.org/library/aah/vanderpuye

Velacharu, N. R. (1990). Courts and Lawyers in India: Images from Literature and Folklore. In Y. K. Malik & D. K. Vajpeyi (Eds.), *Boeings and Bullock-Carts: Studies in Change and Continuity in Indian Civilization* (p. 196). Chanakya Publications.

Vidyarnava, S. C. (1918). Yajnavalkya Smriti- With The Commentary of Vijanesvara Called THE MITAKSARA and Notes from the Gloss of Balambhata (Book 1). The Panini Office.

Vijayaraghavan, B. (Ed.). (2005). *Taittiriya Samhita*. Sanksritweb.net/ index.html

Vuković, S. (2015). Soft power, Bias and manipulation of international organizations in international mediation. *International Negotiation*, *20*(3), 414–443. doi:10.1163/15718069-12341315

Walker, S. (2007). *Police Accountability: Current issues and Research Needs*. Paper presented at the National Institute of justice (NIJ) Policing Research Workshop: Planning for the Future, Washington, DC. Available from: www.icjia.state.il.us/public/2012_LE_Workshop/pdf_Files/ReadingMaterials/PoliceAccountability_CurrentIssues.pdf

Walter, A. W. (2000). *Cultural issues in mediation: Individualist and collectivist paradigms*. www.mediate.com/articles/wright.cfm

Weber, M. (1946). From Max Weber: Essays in sociology (H. H. Gerth & C. W. Mills, Eds. & Trans.). Academic Press.

Welsh, N. A. (2004). The place of court-connected mediation in a democratic justice system. *No. 2. Cardozo Journal of Conflict Resolution*, *5*, 117. doi:10.2139srn.1726218

WiLDAF-Ghana. (2006). *Shadow report of Ghana's 3rd, 4th, and 5th report on the implementation of the CEDAW in Ghana*. Available online at www.iwraw-ap.org/resources/pdf/Gh-SR.pdf

Wisseler, R. (2004). The effectiveness of court-connected dispute resolution in civil cases. *Conflict Resolution Quarterly*, *22*, 55–88.

Wood, G. T. (2004). *Non-adversarial conflict resolution: conference proceedings at the West African regional conference on legal and judicial reform to promote improved women's rights in land and family law within plural legal systems*. Accra, Ghana: Academic Press.

Wood, G. T. (2011). *Keynote address at the Catholic University*. The inauguration of the Marian Conflict Resolution Centre. http://mariancrc.org/wp-content/uploads/2011/09/MCRC_openingkeynote

Woolf, L. H. (1995). *Access to Justice: Interim Report to the Lord Chancellor on the Civil Justice System in England and Wales*. Academic Press.

Woo, M. Y. (1999). Law and discretion in the contemporary Chinese courts. *Pacific Rim Law & Policy Journal*, *8*, 581.

World Bank. (2003). *The World Bank Research Observer*, *18*(1), 61–88. doi:10.1093/wbro/lkg005

World Justice Project. (2016). *Civil Justice*. Retrieved from http://worldjusticeproject.org/factors/effective-civil-justice on 16/06/2021

Wychreschuk, E., & Boland B. (2000). *Making it safe: women's restorative justice and alternative dispute resolution*. Department of Justice, Government of Newfoundland and Labrador.

Xavier, A. (2009). Mediation is here to stay. *Indian Yearbook of International Law and Policy*, *15*, 363–378.

Yatinder, S. J. (2012). *Farewell speech*. gov.in/artical/FarewellJudgesclubAllahabad.pdf

Yin, E. T. (2018). *Religion as an Organising Principle in Ankaful Maximum Security Prison* (PhD Thesis). University of Cape Coast.

Yin, E. T. (2018). *Religion as an Organising Principle in Ankaful Maximum Security Prison, Ghana* (PhD Thesis). University of Cape Coast.

Yin, E. T., & Beamie, M. S. (2021). Costs and delays in accessing justice: A comparative analysis of Ghana and Sierra Leone. In Advancing Civil Justice Reform and Conflict Resolution in Africa and Asia: Comparative Analyses and Case Studies. New York: IGI Global.

Yin, E. T., & Beamie, M. S. (2021). Costs and delays in accessing justice: A comparative analysis of Ghana and Sierra Leone. In Handbook of Research on Civil Justice. IGI Global.

Yin, E. T., Atupare, P. A., Kofie, N., Owusu, L. P., & Botchway, T. P. (2021). Rights and belief in maintaining prison social order. UCC Faculty of Law Journal, 1(1), 1-16.

Yin, E. T. (2020). Religion, rehabilitation and reintegration of inmates into mainstream society. In A. Balloni & R. Sette (Eds.), *Handbook of Research on Trends and Issues in Crime Prevention, Rehabilitation, and Victim Support* (pp. 398–414). IGI Global. doi:10.4018/978-1-7998-1286-9.ch023

Yin, E. T., Atupare, P. A., Kofie, N., Owusu, L. P., & Botchway, T. P. (2021). Rights and religious belief in maintaining prison social order. *UCC Faculty of Law Journal*, *1*(1), 1–16.

Yin, E. T., & Black, J. M. (2014). The legal anthropology of marriage in Ghana: Presenting power dynamics through legal arenas. *International Journal of Current Research*, *6*(12), 10696–10704.

Zeisel, H. (1962). Delay by the Parties and Delay by the Courts. *Journal of Legal Education*, 27.

Zellick, G. J. (1980). *Human Rights: A Unique Development*. Guardian.

Zuckerman, A. (1999). *Civil justice in crises: comparative perspective of civil procedure*. Oxford University Press. doi:10.1093/acprof:oso/9780198298335.001.0001

Zuckerman, A. S. (2012). *Civil Justice in Crisis: Comparative Perspectives of Civil Procedure*. Oxford University Press.

Zurek, K. (2020, June 8). NPP directs suspension of members who invoked curses on leadership. *Daily Graphic*. Retrieved from https://www.graphic.com.gh/news/politics/npp-directs-suspension-of-members-who-invoked-curses-on-leadership.html

Zuure, D. N. (2018). *Legal pluralism, conflict resolution, and human rights_ an exploration of the traditional conflict resolution approach of the Nabdam of Ghana* (Doctoral dissertation). University of Education, Winneba.

About the Contributors

Tarun Arora is serving as Professor and Dean at School of Law, Central University of Punjab, Bathinda. His areas of interest are Constitutional Law, Environmental Law and Jurisprudence. He has wide range of publications on the themes of Judicial Review, Environmental Law, People with Intellectual Disability etc. He authored two books- Environmental Law and Business Law. His work on Interpretation of Statutes is also in progress.

Mark Asante holds a Diploma of Basic Education from the Presbyterian College of Education, Akropong-Akuapem. He also holds a Bachelor of Education in Psychology and Foundations of Education from the University of Cape Coast, Cape Coast. He also holds a Bachelor of Law from the KAAF University College, and currently a student of the Ghana School of Law, Accra, Ghana. His quest for knowledge and insight in matters of law and governance motivates him in all his research work.

Bidisha Bandyopadhyay is a 9th Semester student pursuing BBA LL.B., from School of Law, KIIT (Deemed to be University), Bhubaneswar, Odisha, India.

Rathin Bandyopadhyay is Professor of Law and Former Head, Department of Law, University of North Bengal and has been presently appointed as the Dean of Faculty of Arts, Commerce and Law, University of North Bengal, Dist.: Darjeeling, West Bengal, India.

John Kwame Boateng is a Senior Lecturer at the School of Continuing and Distance Education, University of Ghana. He holds a PhD from the Pennsylvania State University (PSU), USA. He joined the University of Ghana as Lecturer in 2013. His research interests include adult education, human environment interactions, instructional supervision and management. Dr Boateng has over 20 years' experience in research, teaching and outreach. His research areas also covers learning management systems, ICT and mobile technologies integration into curriculum and pedagogical development. He is the Head of the University of Ghana Learning Centres. He is a material developer and a tutor of online courses. He has successfully led numerous fascinating research projects.

Thomas Prehi Botchway is a Social Scientist. He does research in the interdisciplinary fields of Political Science, International Relations and Law. His research interest covers issues of Civil Society, Elections & Democracy; Foreign Policy, Diplomacy and International Law; Human Rights; Global Environmental Governance & Sustainable Development; Security, Peace & Conflict Studies.

Ernest Darkwa is a graduate student at the University of Duisburg-Essen in Germany. He holds a Bachelors Degree in Political Science and Linguistics from the University of Ghana. He also has a Master of Science Degree in International Development from the University of Birmingham, UK. His research interests include peace building and conflict resolution, conflict transformation, international relations and democratic development.

Soma Dey Sarkar is Assistant Professor, Department of Law, University of North Bengal, Dist.: Darjeeling, West Bengal. India.

V. S. Krishna is a Research Associate in World of Legal Research and B.B.A LLB (Hons.) from Sastra University, India.

Neelu Mehra is serving as Assistant Professor at University School of Law and Legal Studies, Guru Gobind Singh Indraprastha University, Dwarka, New Delhi. Her areas of interest are Constitutional Law and Property Law. She has wide range of publications in the field of gender justice and property law. She has co-authored a book on Women and Law.

Ishmael Mugari holds a Doctorate in Police Science and is the current Head of the Department of Intelligence and Security Studies at Bindura University of Science Education, Zimbabwe. His research focuses on criminology, police accountability, police strategy and national security issues. He has published over twenty articles in international peer reviewed journals. He has also authored a book entitled, "An Introduction to Criminological Theory, Penology and Crime Prevention", which was published in 2021 by NOVA Science Publishers.

Alex Somuah Obeng is a senior lecturer at the Department of Sociology and Anthropology, University of Cape Coast, Cape Coast - Ghana, West Africa. He obtained his B.A. (Hons) degree in Economics and Sociology, MPhil in Sociology and PhD in Development Studies from the University of Cape Coast in 1994, 1999 and 2013 respectively. He has been a lecturer in the department since 2001. His research interests include Conflict Management, Criminology, Development Studies, Rural Sociology, Sociology of Development, Sociology of Education, Environmental Sociology, and Research Methods.

Oluwaseun Olanrewaju is a legal consultant and researcher who holds an L.L.B, B.L from Lagos State University and the Nigerian Law School. He is also a graduate of the University of East London where he obtained an MSc in International Relations. Oluwaseun is a member of the International Sociological Association (ISA) and the Peace and Justice Studies Association. His research focuses on gender, human rights and Peace studies. He coordinates the activities of the West Africa Chapter of the International Non-Governmental Organisation, Academics Stand Against Poverty (ASAP).

Sunday Onuegbu has vast experience in litigation and has handled numerous cases for multinational as well as local companies. He is a graduate of University of Lagos and has appeared in trial and appellate courts in various jurisdictions within Nigeria.

Seth Tweneboah (PhD) is a lecturer at the Centre for Conflict, Human Rights and Peace Studies of the University of Education, Winneba, Ghana. He received his PhD in Religious Studies (with specialization in law and politics) from the Victoria University of Wellington, New Zealand. Seth has an MPhil from the University of Ghana, Legon and an MA from the Florida International University, Miami. His research focuses on the religious human rights and the religion-law interrelationships in Africa. He is the author of *Religion, Law, Politics, and the State in Africa: Applying Legal Pluralism in Ghana.*

Index

H

I

J

K

L

M

N

P

R

S

T

U

V

W

www.ingramcontent.com/pod-product-compliance
Lightning Source LLC
LaVergne TN
LVHW062155300926
849161LV00010B/2671
* 9 7 8 1 7 9 9 8 7 8 9 8 8 *